Memory,
Narrative,
and Identity

Memory, Narrative, and Identity

New Essays in Ethnic American Literatures

EDITED BY *Amritjit Singh, Joseph T. Skerrett, Jr., Robert E. Hogan*

Northeastern University Press · Boston

Northeastern University Press
Copyright 1994 by Northeastern University Press

All rights reserved. Except for the quotation of short passages for the purposes of criticism and review, no part of this book may be reproduced in any form or by any means, electronic or mechanical, including photocopying, recording, or any information storage and retrieval system now known or to be invented, without written permission of the publisher.

Library of Congress Cataloging-in-Publication Data

Memory, narrative, and identity : new essays in ethnic American
 literatures / edited by Amritjit Singh, Joseph T. Skerrett, Jr., and
 Robert E. Hogan.
   p. cm.
   Includes bibliographical references and index.
   ISBN 1-55553-203-9
   1. American literature—Minority authors—History and criticism.
 2. Identity (Psychology) in literature.   3. Ethnic groups in
 literature.   4. Memory in literature.   5. Narration (Rhetoric)
 I. Singh, Amritjit.   II. Skerrett, Joseph T.   III. Hogan, Robert E.
 PS153.M56M46   1994
 813.009'353—dc20   94-13779

Designed by David Ford
Composed in Stone Serif by Coghill Composition Company in Richmond, Virginia. Printed and bound by Thomson-Shore, Inc., in Dexter, Michigan. The paper is Glatfelter, an acid-free sheet.

MANUFACTURED IN THE UNITED STATES OF AMERICA
98   97   96   95   94   5   4   3   2   1

Contents

Preface   vii

Acknowledgments   ix

Introduction   3

Narrating Memory
    Terry DeHay   26

Rereading Photographs and Narratives in Ethnic Autobiography: Memory and Subjectivity in Mary Antin's *The Promised Land*
    Betty Bergland   45

The New Man and the Mediator: (Non-)Remembrance in Jewish-American Immigrant Narrative
    Gert Buelens   89

Memory and Silences in the Work of Tillie Olsen and Henry Roth
    Jules Chametzky   114

Nostalgia, Amnesia, and Grandmothers: The Uses of Memory in Albert Murray, Sabine Ulibarri, Paula Gunn Allen, and Alice Walker
    Wolfgang Karrer   128

X Rays of Irish America: Edwin O'Connor, Mary Gordon, and William Kennedy
    William Keough   145

Contents

Expanding the Collective Memory: Charles W. Chesnutt's *The Conjure Woman* Tales

    Sandra Molyneaux   164

Reading Carnival as an Archaeological Site for Memory in Paule Marshall's *The Chosen Place, The Timeless People* and *Praisesong for the Widow*

    Angelita Reyes   179

"Tell me your earrings": Time and the Marvelous in Toni Morrison's *Beloved*

    Sharon Jessee   198

Memory and Mother Love: Toni Morrison's Dyad

    Barbara Offutt Mathieson   212

Maxine Hong Kingston's Fake Books

    Debra Shostak   233

Memory and the Ethnic Self: Reading Amy Tan's *The Joy Luck Club*

    Ben Xu   261

Traveling Light: Immigration and Invisible Suitcases in M. G. Vassanji's *The Gunny Sack*

    Rosemary Marangoly George   278

Rediscovering Nineteenth-Century Mexican-American Autobiography

    Genaro M. Padilla   305

Select Bibliography   333

Editors and Contributors   337

Index   341

Preface

This volume on memory, narrative, and identity originated in a 1990 call for papers for a collection of essays, the response to which exceeded all our expectations. It became obvious that academic discussions of American ethnic literatures were ready to go beyond the rationales generally offered for introductory courses on African American and/or other ethnic writing to consider more focused treatments of critical paradigms embedded in all of them. Memory is one such paradigm. The uses of memory in writing by American ethnic writers calls for special attention by literary historians and scholars. A work such as Toni Morrison's *Beloved* or Joy Kogawa's *Obasan*, for example, explores how individual memory is inseparable from collective memory, which is continually subject to change. In life as also in literature, there is a constant tension between the memory of ordinary folk, that of marginalized groups, and the public memory as viewed and shaped by institutions invested in the ideas of nationhood and citizenship. American writing that is race conscious or ethnic-specific mediates among these diverse memories. In the act of reading, readers are enabled to remember things that culture has asked them to forget, to put into historical perspective the ahistoricized and commercialized sites and scenes of American conflict, to see forbidden scenes from behind closed doors and thus from hidden cultural spaces, and to experience a new sense of identity. The ethnic writer's interrogations of public memory are a reminder that all memories—individual, family, ethnic, or racial—are socially constructed and allow for their reconstruction in narratives in quest of change and new meaning. Narrative recollects in its aspiration to a new "story," a new history.

The essays chosen for this volume explore the following topics: the construction and the narration of the past; the politics of remembrance; collective, generational, and mythic memory; oral storytelling and the role of the storyteller; the emergence of new personal and ethnic identities; and photographic art, ethnic autobiography, and memoir as sites of cultural memory and imagination. Our goal is not to provide systematic

Preface

coverage of major ethnic writers or all ethnic literatures, but to demonstrate the range of approaches to ethnic literatures with reference to how memory informs identity and shapes narrative. These essays raise questions about the uses of memory in various ethnic literatures by focusing sometimes on a single text and at other times in multiethnic frameworks. These fourteen essays along with our introduction demonstrate how a thematic concentration on the issues of memory allows for a deeper understanding of the similarities and differences among American multicultural literatures. Our volume represents an invitation to scholars in American ethnic writing to move beyond their special fields to explore relatively unfamiliar territories.

No such project can be completed without the generous support of friends and colleagues. In many ways, our editorial work has been truly collaborative. For excellent suggestions made at various stages of this project, we are grateful to Betty Bergland, J. Birje-Patil, Janet Casey, G. Thomas Couser, Gurleen Grewal, A. Robert Lee, A. LaVonne Brown Ruoff, Joseph Urgo, Helen Whall, James White, and Stan Yogi. Others who have been supportive in big and small ways include Herman Beavers, William Boelhoewer, Michael Gareffa, S. J., Jon Hauss, Yuko Matsukawa, David and Judy Ray, Angelita Reyes, Arlene Robertson, Leslie Sanders, Prem and Reshma Singh, Daniel Walden, and Margaret Wong. We also owe thanks to Barbara Silliman, Kurt Hemmer, and Ann Flaherty, who served as research assistants at various stages of the project, and to the library staff at Rhode Island College and the University of Massachusetts at Amherst.

Acknowledgments

Grateful acknowledgment is made to the following for permission to reprint previously published material:

Arte Público Press, for Genaro Padilla, "Recovering Mexican-American Autobiography," *Recovering the U.S. Hispanic Literary Heritage*, ed. Ramón Gutiérrez and Genaro Padilla, 1993.

differences: A Journal of Feminist Cultural Studies, for Rosemary Marangoly George, "Traveling Light: Of Immigration, Invisible Suitcases, and Gunny Sacks," *differences* 4, 2 (1992).

Alfred A. Knopf, Inc., for excerpts from Maxine Hong Kingston, *Tripmaster Monkey: His Fake Book*. Copyright 1987, 1988, 1989 by Maxine Hong Kingston.

The Johns Hopkins University Press, for Barbara Offutt Mathieson, "Memory and Mother Love in Morrison's *Beloved*," *American Imago* 47, 1 (Spring 1990).

The Society for the Study of the Multi-Ethnic Literature of the United States, for Ben Xu, "Memory and the Ethnic Self: Reading Amy Tan's *The Joy Luck Club*," *MELUS* 19, 1 (Spring 1994). Copyright The Society for the Study of the Multi-Ethnic Literature of the United States.

Memory,
Narrative,
and Identity

Introduction

> Forgetfulness leads to exile, while remembrance is the secret of redemption.
> —Ba'al Shem Tov

A Historical Perspective

The year is 1972. The place, a large hotel in New York City. The occasion, the annual meeting of the Modern Language Association of America (MLA), the largest organization of teachers of language and literature anywhere. In the hallways has gathered a group of teachers who want to offer a discussion of ethnic American writing but have been denied the space to have a formal session. Within the convention, all the American literature sessions deal entirely with what one unhappy scholar called "WMAL," that is, White Male American Literature.

This exclusion of ethnic American writing was complicated by a general lack of participation by persons of color in MLA activities, programs, and policies. For example, until 1972 and even later, most African American teachers of language and literature were likely to have been more active in the College Language Association (CLA) than in the MLA. The CLA had been formed in 1937 because for decades African Americans did not feel welcome in the MLA, especially at the meetings of its southern wing. On the one hand, it seemed natural for African-American academics—often compelled to work in predominantly black institutions in the South—to participate in MLA's southern affiliate; on the other, their interaction at its conventions was limited by the realities of segregation and racism. Since Native Americans, Asian Americans, and Latin Americans were almost invisible in the humanistic disciplines within the American academy at that time, their absence at MLA meetings was hardly noticed.

Following the 1972 convention, scholars interested in ethnic American writing attempted to establish a relationship with the MLA and to find a place in its annual convention, but to no immediate avail. Some of these scholars came together in 1973 to form an organization known today as MELUS, The Society for the Study of the Multi-Ethnic Literature of the United States. While the 1972 meeting of the MLA signified the familiar resistance of authority to changes in the status quo, what happened as a consequence of this meeting symbolized the changing ways in which Americans were learning to look upon themselves—not as a homogeneous community with well-defined parameters, but as a vital world of multiple communities and consciousnesses that have shaped the United States of America from its beginnings to the present day.

These events surrounding the MLA took place against the backdrop of social and political changes that the United States experienced in the late 1960s. While the conditions that had led to its founding no longer exist, the CLA still functions as a vibrant organization with an agenda and an annual convention of its own. Also, people of color contribute considerable energy now to MLA activities and projects. These changes were symbolized most dramatically by the 1992 convention, when Houston A. Baker, Jr., the first American of African descent to be elected head of the MLA, gave his presidential address. Baker's meteoric rise within the academy has been based not on his UCLA dissertation on Victorian literature, but upon his prolific scholarship in African-American literature. Baker's ascendancy may be seen as the culmination of such MLA efforts to achieve greater inclusiveness as the establishment in 1976 of its Commission on Minority Literature, which continues today as the Committee on the Literatures and Languages of America. The commission's 1977 seminars in Native American and African-American literature were cosponsored by the National Endowment for the Humanities, beginning the process of "decentering" the canon, redefining American literature and literary history. Today the MLA has divisions of African-American and American Indian literatures and discussion groups on Asian and Chicano literatures.

For some MLA members and commentators such as Alan Bloom, Linda Chavez, and Dinesh D'Souza, however, the pendulum seems to have swung to the other extreme. They allege that there is excessive concern in the curriculum with issues of race, gender, and ethnicity, to the exclusion of traditional works. While they would attribute these changes to some vague forces of "political correctness," the MLA membership statistics for 1993 suggest significant shifts in interest that have shaped fundamental questions about the theories and approaches in our teaching and scholarship on American literature and culture. The total membership

Introduction

of the organization stands today at 32,000. At least 1250 members are interested in Black American Literature and Culture, almost the same number as those interested in Chaucer or in Middle English Language and Literature Excluding Chaucer. Two thousand members are interested in Twentieth-Century Latin American Literature, more than the number interested in the English Romantic Period. Nearly 1000 members are interested in Gay Studies in Language and Literature, and as many more in African and Asian literatures together. Women's Studies in Language and Literature attracts 6200 members, and over 1200 members are interested in Ethnic Studies. Even allowing for overlap among some of these categories, it would appear that a substantial sector of the MLA membership in American literature and related areas is involved with issues of canon, literary tradition, and pedagogy. Through the combined efforts of such members, we have learned in the past few years how to frame our questions about American literature and culture in ways unanticipated only twenty years ago. Now we show a marked concern about how multiculturalism, a long-standing if often unacknowledged American reality, might influence the ways in which we teach and read and think about our literatures.

Such a shift must not go unrecognized, for until just after the climax of the Civil Rights movement, most white Americans viewed ethnicity as an issue of the past. They began to feel that ethnicity had been attenuated to a symbolic presence in the United States and was no longer a significant part of the politics affecting their lives. Our grandparents were ethnic, not us. It was they who experienced the pains of ghettos and felt nostalgic for their homelands. Immigrants came to the United States in search of new life and opportunities, often leaving behind terrible economic conditions and/or political persecution. The pressure to create out of the great immigrant masses one homogeneous "American" community, however, also led to much ethnic denial and forgetting. Americans repressed their nineteenth-century ethnic past, which was shaped by arrivals from Ireland, France, and Germany in the 1840s, China in the 1850s and 1860s, and Sweden and Norway in the 1880s and 1890s.

This repression of the ethnic past was complicated in the late nineteenth and early twentieth centuries by nativist hostility to new immigrants. Frightened by the social changes portended by vast numbers of immigrants from Italy, Russia, Poland, Japan, and other non-English-speaking nations, the federal government enacted the Johnson-Reed Act in 1924, which established immigration quotas based on the ethnic population of the United States in 1890. The effect of selecting that year was to exclude most Italians, Slavs, and Jews. In addition, most Asians had already been excluded through other measures. If isolationism shaped nativist sentiment in the 1920s, the Great Depression exacerbated xenophobia and hostility to immigrants in the 1930s. The growing nativism, supported by federal legislation adopted between 1914 and 1930, restricted access to America to just a trickle of immigrants, almost all from northern and western Europe. It was not until 1965 that new immigration laws eliminated race, religion, and nationality as criteria for admission to the United States, resulting in the first wave of legal immigration from Africa, Asia, and Latin America. At the same time, existing populations of Native Americans, Latin Americans, African Americans, and Asian Americans were also being affected very profoundly by factors other than voluntary emigration from homelands. Native Americans, for example, experienced great pressure to assimilate into the dominant culture and were not granted citizenship rights until 1924. For Americans of color, ethnic denial and forgetting are complicated by their attempts to resist and reject majority stereotypes rooted in "race."

The convergence of race, ethnicity, immigration, and culture in American life today makes any easy generalization very difficult to sustain. The range of social attitudes and worldviews among Americans of ethnic consciousness tends to be diverse and complex. Mary Antin in 1912 spoke glowingly of her new Americanness as "inheriting all that went before in history. I am the youngest of America's children and into my hands is given all her priceless heritage." Recent versions of this celebratory attitude may be seen in the writings of new immigrants such as Richard Rodriguez and Dinesh D'Souza, who would probably endorse Bharati Mukherjee's call to immigrant writers to embrace their Americanness ("I am one of you now") as an opportunity instead of wallowing in exile and exoticism ("Immigrant Writing: Give Us Your Maximalists!" *New York Times Book Review* 28 Aug. 1988). This cheerful, forward-looking attitude toward the possibilities of assimilation is balanced by, among other things, the sojourner attitude, wherein immigrants see their American existence as possibly long-term but not permanent. Similar "sojourner" attitudes exist among Native Americans who go back and forth between the reservation and the city as well as in the recent phenomenon of African Americans returning to the South. The experience of "first-wave" Chinese and Japanese workers finds an echo today in the continuing attitudes of some Asian and Latin American immigrants, who sometimes see their lives here primarily in terms of their interest in

Introduction

returning home. Another element in this complex reality is the sharply critical attitude toward issues of American identity within the African American community. Powerful oratory and writing by Frederick Douglass, Sojourner Truth, Martin Delany, W. E. B. Du Bois, Marcus Garvey, Malcolm X, and Martin Luther King, Jr., have been inspired by the perceived disparity between American ideals and practice and continue to serve as a reminder of the levels of discomfort and Americanness experienced by Americans of African descent.

Even more remarkable are the fissures in the assumed American consciousness of long-established ethnic groups such as the Irish Americans, Italian Americans, and Americans of Jewish descent. Their Americanness is constantly being tested and challenged—reflected in issues of class and cultural nuance—by their interaction with new immigrants of similar backgrounds. Herbert Gans's 1979 argument about "symbolic ethnicity," that Americans of ethnic background were gradually turning into indistinguishable groups that marked their ethnicity by relatively arbitrary signs such as St. Patrick's Day parades and "Kiss Me, I'm Polish" buttons, is undercut by the ability of an immigrant group to recharge ethnic memory by contacts with new immigrants of shared descent or through frequent homeland visits facilitated by electronic communication and jet airplanes. One thinks also of Kurt Vonnegut's notion that in the contemporary Untied States, community is often not the immediate neighborhood but an electronically connected group of kindred souls. In this redefined sense of community, many recent immigrants—often middle- and upper-class—participate in new and meaningful ways. They also share the growing recognition within the larger American community of significant African-American contributions to American thought, music, and language. In many ways, these new immigrants are much more in sync with the varied patterns of cultural hybridization in American culture today than those who landed around the turn of the century. Instead of embracing ethnic denial and forgetting, most of them struggle quite openly to maintain a "double citizenship" or a kind of "double consciousness" through contact with homelands, home cultures, and families overseas.

Any sense of American homogeneity is further undermined by complex patterns of real but diffused ethnicity by which Americans—those of mixed ancestries and others—choose ethnic identification as a marker of values, tastes, styles, and attitudes. Those with Italian names may, for example, be palpably "Irish." In many instances, a strong attraction to another ethnic culture may have shaped attitudes—as seems to have happened to many young Americans in the 1960s and 1970s with their African-American involvements. (The "wiggers" phenomenon of today is a continuation, in some ways, of certain elements in Norman Mailer's "White Negro," James Baldwin's *Another Country,* and Lois Mark Stalvey's *The Education of a WASP.*) One could grow up, like writers Susan Straight and Joseph Hillerman, on the cusp of an ethnic group of color and learn to express that group's language, values, and cultural organization with authenticity. Millions of young Americans are growing up today in neighborhoods where they experience the richness and depth of immigrant or ethnic cultures other than their own, right next door—without the filters of multicultural curricula. As Peter Marin argues, ethnic values and traditions never disappear; "There remains always, in every ethnic tradition, in the generational legacy of every individual family, a certain residue, a kind of ash, what I would call 'ghost-values': the tag-ends and shreds and echoes of the past calling to us generations after their real force has been spent" (*Harper's* July 1988: 17–18). But as we noted earlier, these values—in their pure or diffused forms—are often more vigorous than just "shreds and echoes" or "ghost-values." In fact, this diversity of response to the changing configurations of immigration, race, ethnicity, and identity is often experienced within one individual consciousness, which becomes a site for the personal and ethnic to come together.

The need for ethnic writers in the early twentieth century to free themselves from mainstream impositions, stereotypical self-images, and other such limitations placed upon their field of creativity continues to be reflected in the ways new immigrants are learning to handle their cultural baggage, "the gunny sack" in M. G. Vassanji's novel. While all writers are subject to the commercial agendas of agents, editors, and publishers, ethnic writers have often also felt obliged to engage or battle stereotypical and exoticized versions of personality and ethnic life. For example, since the early part of this century, Jewish-American writers have written texts that argue with the idea of religion as a defining factor of Jewishness. From Anzia Yezierska, struggling against her religious father to create an independent self, to Ludwig Lewisohn, recounting a life of movement toward rather than away from religion, the subject dominates much Jewish-American fiction and autobiography. Novelists since World War II have found various strategies for refiguring this subject that so identified "the Jew" for the reading audience: Saul Bellow sidesteps the subject, and Bernard Malamud and Philip Roth Christianize or fantasize

Introduction

or moralize it. In revisiting the same territory, Cynthia Ozick, a more recent writer, has reasserted religious identity as a theme.

During the 1920s, black writers and writing were steamrollered to a large extent by the primitivistic views of Blacks and black life, popularized partly through misinterpretations of Freud. In the forties and fifties, many black writers felt compelled to take on the role of social commentators or political spokespersons for their group. The radicalism of the late sixties and early seventies further complicated matters by valorizing machismo and loud protest. While the mainstream culture's projections of black life may change, they have nonetheless seriously affected the African-American writer's creativity and expression. In the seventies and the eighties, African-American writers' exploration of such issues as the middle passage and slavery, skin color and class, has gained a new resonance through a radical shift in attitude and treatment.

For instance, from William Wells Brown's *Clotel* (1853) to Toni Morrison's *The Bluest Eye* (1970), through writers such as Charles W. Chesnutt, James Weldon Johnson, Jessie Fauset, Nella Larsen, Wallace Thurman, and Chester Himes, African-American fiction demonstrates a remarkable shift in its treatment of the recurring trope of skin color. In Brown, skin color is the primary basis of the plea for better treatment. In Chesnutt and Johnson, there is a heightened sensitivity to the psychological dimensions of this theme. In their fiction, the tragic mulatto trope modulates the reader's response in terms of identification and alienation—the male or female protagonist is both "like" the putative white reader because of skin color and "not like" the reader because of his or her "race." In Larsen's *Quicksand* and *Passing*, we begin also to experience a kind of Jamesian subjectivity in their focus on the consciousness of each protagonist. Similarly, Thurman's daring portrayal in *The Blacker the Berry* (1929) of how someone with darker skin is treated within the African-American community and the strong evocation of the pathological obsession with white skin in Fauset's *Comedy American Style* (1933) prefigure the powerful engagement of this theme in Himes's *The Third Generation* (1954). Morrison's *The Bluest Eye* orchestrates this theme of racial identity in broader cultural contexts—the difficulty of young black children in relation to white middle-class values, which valorize blue eyes and blond hair. The referential and narrative frames of the Morrison text—the Dick and Jane reader, multiple narrative points of view, and the presence of several black families with differing attitudes toward conventions of love, beauty, and maturation—allow for a reading that focuses attention on the humanity and Americanness of its characters without diluting the pain and suffering they discover as racial subjects.

Yet, while Morrison sometimes broadens and internalizes the issues of race in American culture, she and writers like Sherley Anne Williams and Charles Johnson have also deepened our sense of African-American history in some of their fiction. Novels such as Williams's *Dessa Rose*, Johnson's *Middle Passage*, and Morrison's *Beloved* may be seen as developing from roots in historical fiction as practiced by earlier black writers such as Arna Bontemps, but they would be unimaginable without the revisionism of recent historical work on the slave trade and slavery. Also, the work of many black women writers such as Alice Walker, Gayl Jones, Toni Morrison, and Gloria Naylor is both informed and sustained by highly provocative and contemporary feminist perspectives.

These perspectives, both ethnic and feminist, were being shaped within the academy by a wide range of literary scholars and historians. For example, the scholars who organized MELUS and others like them began to modulate the academy's institutional response to this diverse ethnic American literature. They argued for inclusiveness in a democratic, pluralistic curriculum. In editing anthologies of African-American and other ethnic writings, Katharine D. Newman, Abraham Chapman, Daniel Walden and Charles T. Davis, Frank Chin, and others argued the need for the acknowledgment of differences. It was important for nonwhite children in our schools and colleges to find an affirmation of what Newman termed "the goodness of the lifestyle and the beauty of the physical appearance of one's own kind." Curricula would have to be revised to develop ethnic pride and give young students "enhanced self-respect and a sense of permanent identity." Chapman repudiated the use of "universalism" by literary scholars and historians to undermine and reject writing by African-American, Irish, and postcolonial writers. The growing recognition in the United States of writing by African and Caribbean writers such as Chinua Achebe, Ngugi wa Thiong'O, George Lamming, and V. S. Naipaul also helped to shape the need for a more inclusive aesthetic. In conjunction with these calls for pluralism and inclusiveness, the Black Arts movement, led by Amiri Baraka, Larry Neal, and others, resulted in the ideas of the Black Aesthetic, best encapsulated in the two anthologies of criticism *Black Expression* (1969) and *Black Aesthetic* (1971), by Addison Gayle, and in the provocative, influential study *Understanding the New Black Poetry* (1973), by Stephen Henderson. These developments together involved attempts to understand the "blackness" of African-American literature and culture by stressing the quotient of

Introduction

vernacular and voice in individual works and through a conscious identification with the working classes. These approaches were intended to challenge the New Critical and other Eurocentric models of literary evaluation and were rooted in the idea of viewing ethnic writing with reference primarily to elements within the "racial"/ethnic boundary. The 1970s also saw the publication of several major scholarly studies of African-American literature, such as Nathan Huggins's *Harlem Renaissance* (1971), Jean Fagan Yellin's *The Intricate Knot: Black Figures in American Literature, 1776–1863* (1972), James O. Young's *Black Writers of the Thirties* (1973), Michel Fabre's *The Unfinished Quest of Richard Wright* (1973), Theodore R. Hudson's *From LeRoi Jones to Amiri Baraka: The Literary Works* (1973), Arnold Rampersad's *The Mind and Imagination of W. E. B. Du Bois* (1976), Kimberly W. Benston's *Baraka: The Renegade and the Mask* (1976), Amritjit Singh's *The Novels of the Harlem Renaissance* (1976), Onwuchekwa Jemie's *Langston Hughes: An Introduction to the Poetry* (1976), Werner Sollors's *Amiri Baraka/LeRoi Jones: The Quest for a "Populist Modernism"* (1978), and several books by Houston Baker, Blyden Jackson, and others. These studies in different ways established new norms and models for literary judgment and extended the mapping of territory provided by earlier scholars such as Sterling Brown, Saunders Redding, Hugh Gloster, Jean Wagner, and Robert Bone.

However, the historical scholarship on African-American literature during this period did not lead to any clear gain in the reformulation of the American literary canon, nor did it create significant new models of theory and approach for American ethnic writing at large. African-American and other ethnic American literature continued to be treated as categories apart from mainstream literature. As Thomas J. Ferraro has noted, in the fifties and early sixties, critics such as Leslie Fiedler and Irving Howe, who might have been expected to be more receptive, either marginalized ethnic writing as "regional" and, by implication, reductive and parochial, or else, as in the case of Daniel Aaron, celebrated the "de-hyphenation" of ethnic writers in expecting them to transcend ethnic particularities in order to universalize their subject matter.

Since the eighties, the debate has both expanded and deepened. While the issues of inclusiveness and pluralism have been reinscribed in the ongoing debates on multiculturalism and political correctness, we already have a considerable tradition of reading ethnic literature with focus on questions of genre, literary form, and influence, away from the arena of sociology and politics. A major trend is the close alliance between the more established African-American criticism and new developments in ethnic literary criticism. If Thomas Ferraro in *Ethnic Passages: Literary Immigrants in Twentieth Century America* (1993) argues that the best of ethnic narratives require close reading and attention to questions of literary form, critics like Houston Baker, Henry Louis Gates, Robert Stepto, and Hortense Spillers had begun to address such needs in the early eighties.

In the late 1980s, the scholarship of Werner Sollors, William Boelhower, and Mary V. Dearborn brought together "the literatures of old stock Anglo-Saxon families, of the immigrant descended, and of nonimmigrant minorities as representations of 'America' " (Ferraro 5). This emphasis on the "generic Americanness of ethnic self-representation" (Ferraro 7) allows such critics to uncover rhetorical and narrative structures that they believe to be shared by canonized American writers. So, in the approach used by Sollors and others, the works of ethnic writers become, both culturally and aesthetically, "more than exercises in group documentation and self-analysis" (Ferraro 6).

While the "ethnicity school" of Sollors and others attempted to subsume ethnic and racial minority literatures under a single generic category, many other scholars have foregrounded racial and cultural difference. African-American critics such as Gates, Baker, and Stepto, for example, brought to sharper focus questions of genre, periodization, tropology, and intertextuality. Houston Baker's search for a methodology uniquely appropriate to African-American literature and culture led him through various structuralist and poststructuralist phases before he produced his magnum opus—*Blues, Ideology, and African American Literature* (1984). In *From Behind the Veil: A Study of Afro-American Narrative* (1979), Robert Stepto claimed that African-American culture revealed a genre-defining mythos that determined the shape of its narratives—tales of escaped slaves, autobiographies, and fiction. In *The Signifying Monkey* (1988), Henry Louis Gates, who had begun as a cautious deconstructionist in the late seventies, redefined African-American linguistic and performative acts as the basic epistemes of African culture and folklore. Feminist scholars like Barbara Christian and Hortense Spillers revised the agenda and the canon of African-American literature by opening questions of female subjectivity and literary tradition. Scholars of oral and written Native American literatures such as A. LaVonne Brown Ruoff, Arnold Krupat, Gretchen Bataille, Louis Owens, Kenneth Lincoln, David Murray, and Paula Gunn Allen have explored the complex tribal particulars of oral and ceremonial performance—the massive, heterogenous legacies of "the spoken" and of creation (or emergence) myths, dream visions, spirituality, and animism. Theorizing about Chicano literature,

Introduction

José Saldívar, Ramón Saldívar, Juan Bruce-Novoa, Cordelia Candelaria, Norma Alarcón, and Cherrie Moraga explored the eclectic consciousness and *mestizaje* of Mexican Americans and other Latino cultures as expressed in *chicanismo* and *hispanidad*. Books such as *Between Worlds: Women Writers of Chinese Ancestry* (1990), by Amy Ling; *Reading the Literature of Asian America* (1992), edited by Amy Ling and Shirley Geok-lin Lim; *Articulate Silences: Hisaye Yamamoto, Maxine Hong Kingston, Joy Kogawa* (1993), by King-Kok Cheung; and *Reading Asian-American Literature: From Necessity to Extravagance* (1993), by Sau-ling Cynthia Wong, while acknowledging the cultural contextualization in the earlier work of Frank Chin and Elaine Kim, incorporate the more recent Western critical theories to offer new cultural and historical readings and otherwise map issues of definition and approach surrounding Asian-American literatures.

If we were to regard Thomas Ferraro's *Ethnic Passages* as an exemplum of recent trends in criticism and scholarship on ethnic American writing, we could see how he synthesizes approaches established by critics such as Baker and Stepto with those of the "ethnicity school." In response to Fiedler, Howe, and Aaron, Ferraro rejects the notion that ethnic literature is a contradiction in terms, a category that exists primarily for reasons of convenient shelving and effective marketing. According to Ferraro, in ethnic texts, "what is most ethnically specific and what is most aesthetically compelling will be found at the same narrative sites, working not in separate registers but in allied, mutually interrogative, and cross-fertilizing ways. Such writing challenges the critic to determine how sociological inquiry and literary inventiveness serve one another; where local understandings face off against national constructions of individuality, family, and community; and which strategies of minority-culture self-representation and majority-culture literary forms undergo reciprocal transformations" (Ferraro 3). Ferraro rejects the claim of Irving Howe, Gunnar Myrdal, Stephen Steinberg, and Herbert Gans that "ethnic distinctiveness is a mask for class antagonisms, a classic instance of false consciousness." Ethnicity in the United States is, for Ferraro, "more than a matter of ritual, rhetoric, and dialogue. . . . *Otherness* does persist, whether one likes it or not—powerfully so among the offspring of immigrants." So, in variance with Sollors's project of focusing on the "generic Americanness of ethnic self-representation," Ferraro wants to "contextualize immigrant writers within social history" in his specific project of studying the "up-from-the-ghetto" theme in American ethnic writing.

Introduction

Additional developments in recent years have included the appearance of new journals and of reference materials published by the Modern Language Association and other authoritative organizations. After much prompting, the MLA began to publish books in the late seventies addressing the need for scholarly and pedagogical help in dealing with various ethnic literatures. Four volumes resulted from the 1977 seminars and programs organized by the MLA Commission on Minority Literature: Dexter Fisher, editor, *Minority Language and Literature* (1977); Dexter Fisher and Robert Stepto, editors, *Afro-American Literature: The Reconstruction of Instruction* (1979); Houston A. Baker, Jr., editor, *Three American Literatures: Essays in Chicano, Native American and Asian American Literature for Teachers of American Literature* (1982); and Paula Gunn Allen, editor, *Studies in American Indian Literature* (1983). Around the same time, MLA also published *Ethnic Perspectives in American Literature* (1983), edited by Robert di Pietro and Edward Ifkovic, which focuses on white immigrant ethnic writing. The MLA Forum on the New American Literary History and its allied workshop began the process that resulted in *Redefining American Literary History* (1990), edited by A. LaVonne Brown Ruoff and Jerry W. Ward. As Ruoff and Ward put it, this process began with the new conviction that "an adequate American literary history requires a model based on a multiethnic and multiracial, rather than a European theory of culture. . . . A redefinition of literary history means expanding canon, forging new critical perspectives, and scrutinizing underlying cultural and ideological assumptions." These and similar goals inspired scholarly volumes such as Dexter Fisher's *The Third Woman: Minority Women Writers of the United States* (1980), Elaine Kim's *Asian American Literature: An Introduction to the Writings and Their Social Context* (1982), and *Reconstructing American Literature* (1983), edited by Paul Lauter.

While these reference materials were coming together, scholars were also acting out the new definition of American literary study through journal commentary. New journals like the *Journal of Ethnic Studies* (1973) and *MELUS* (1975) were developed to publish essays on a range of ethnic literatures. *Negro American Literature Forum* (1967)—which was renamed *Black American Literature Forum* in 1976 and became *African-American Review* in 1992—has published since its inception both creative writing and scholarship in the humanities and social sciences and serves today as the official publication of MLA's Division on Black American Literature and Culture. *Callaloo* (1977) began to publish both original literature and criticism of African, Caribbean, and African-American writers. *Studies in American Jewish Literature* (1975) and *Studies in American*

Introduction

Indian Literature (1977) focused on new scholarly approaches to Jewish-American and Native American literatures, respectively. The *Revista Chicano-Riqueña* (now *The Americas Review*) was begun in 1973 to offer essays on Chicano and Puerto Rican literature and culture. *Amerasia* (1971), while primarily a social-science journal, offered an occasional article on Chinese- and Japanese-American literature. Some of the scholars involved in ethnic literary studies were also called upon in the late 1980s to help create the first multiculturally oriented anthology of American literature, *The Heath Anthology of American Literature* (1990; 2nd ed., 1993), edited by Paul Lauter and others.

Many of these developments in the study of ethnic American literatures are connected to changes in the location of ethnic groups in the general economy of culture. Ethnic Americans demanded—and received—more respect from the media and political forces during the sixties and the seventies. This prepared the ground for the emergence of new and diverse ethnic writers. Another aspect of current critical practice is that scholars now routinely pay more attention to the influence on ethnic writers from works, writers, and traditions outside their own ethnic groups. Earlier criticisms had often disregarded literary and intellectual contact with writers from outside the ethnic group, as though skin color, race, or heritage were the only factors defining an author's subjects, styles, or attitudes.

For example, Native American literatures, once conceived only as collections of oral texts or narratives recorded and edited by white transcribers—usually missionaries or students of anthropology—are now viewed as consisting of both oral literatures and the written works of Native American authors, who have been publishing since 1772. Recognizing that oral literatures are a performed art, contemporary scholars have stressed the importance of the performer(s) and the response of the audience. Until the 1970s, in Native American literary study—as in African-American literary study—traditions had often been stereotypically defined, without much room allowed for the individuality of the author in relation to ethnic experience. At that time, critical studies of Native American literature were much more ethnocentric and assumed that the key to understanding the text lay within the ethnic boundary. Drawing on new models of criticism such as ethnohistory, feminism, linguistics, and speech-act theory, scholars of Native American literatures developed critical contexts that enriched the understanding of oral traditions and written literatures. Like Houston Baker's concept of the "anthropology of art," these ideas helped scholars to create new continuities between the oral and the written, the voiced and the silent, ritual and reading, artist and audience. A major part of this critical project has been the recovery of lost texts and voices, as part of the revisionist critique of the distortion of native American cultures by well-intentioned white collectors and amanuenses. Recent scholarly editions of oral literatures, such as those by Dennis Tedlock, Larry Evers and Felipe Molina, and Julie Cruikshank, acknowledge the contributions of the narrators, retain the narrator's individual style as far as possible, and provide detailed information on ethnohistorical and performance contexts. The nature of Native American representation in John Hollander's two-volume Library of America anthology entitled *American Poetry: The Nineteenth Century* (1993) is a good example of both the progress made and the challenges that still remain.

The new openness to race and ethnicity in academic discourse since the 1980s also means that works and writers formerly marginalized because of their political content or their unfamiliar religious or cultural ideas have the opportunity now to exert a powerful impact on reading audiences. Leslie Silko's novels *Ceremony* and *Almanac of the Dead*, for example, while exploring and reenacting Laguna tribal myth and healing, also offer fierce critiques of relations between Native Americans and Whites and of environmental damage and nuclear power. In many ways, then, Native American and other ethnic writers function today as mediators between ethnic and white audiences. Discussions raised with reference to ethnic writing—for example, issues of authenticity and representation, of inventiveness and experimentation, of narrative and identity—permit new perspectives not only on ethnic American writings but also on larger issues of nation and culture. The new possibilities thus opened—beyond the study of ethnic texts as representations of coming of age or protest and opposition—find expression in the essays in this collection on the uses of memory in ethnic American writing.

The Narrative of Memory

In recent years, there has been a significant shift in academic discourse from models of the self built on psychological paradigms to those built on social ones. We no longer speak so frequently of "finding ourselves" or "coming to ourselves," as if our self (or "consciousness") were a stable psychological entity. In his essay "Ethnicity: Identity and Difference" (1991), Stuart Hall has noted that identity is neither simple nor stable.

Introduction

Instead, it "is always a structure that is split; it always has ambivalence within it." In preferring to see it as a "process of identification" rather than as "one thing, one moment," Hall reconceptualizes identity as "something that happens over time, . . . that is subject to the play of history and the play of difference." Thus identity, instead of being seen as fixed, becomes a dynamic construction that adjusts continually to the changes experienced within and surrounding the self.

These discourses of the self—sexual, racial, historical, regional, ethnic, cultural, national, and familial—intersect in us to create our individuality and form a net of language that we share with the community. This "collective memory," like individual memory, is a function, not an entity. We negotiate within this net of language, which traverses the body and the mind, for discourses intersect in both the body and the mind of the individual. Memory is one of the ways our consciousness connects items and experiences in the net of language, for as scholars such as Maurice Halbwachs (*The Collective Memory*, 1950) have shown, we "remember" not only things that have actually happened to us personally, but also, and perhaps even more importantly, we "remember" events, language, actions, attitudes, and values that are aspects of our membership in groups. What we study are the traces of memory in language and narrative and the ways individual writers challenge it: opposing to memory its dark shadow, forgetting; reconsidering its relation to history and oral tradition; erasing and revising it; preserving or recovering it. In the process, each writer reorients our sense of both cultural identity and literary form.

Stuart Hall further points to what he calls "four great decenterings in intellectual life and in Western thought that have helped to destabilize the question of identity." The first three of these "decenterings" he associates, for the sake of convenience, with Marx, Freud, and Saussure. Marx, writes Hall, "interrupted that notion of the sovereign subject who opens his or her mouth and speaks, for the first time, the truth . . . [and] reminds us that we are always lodged and implicated in the practices and structures of everybody else's life." Freud reminds us that "social, cultural and political life cannot be understood except in relationship to the formations of the unconscious life." Saussurian linguistics shows that "there is no utterance so novel and so creative that it does not already bear on it the traces of how that language has been spoken before we opened our mouths. Thus we are always within language." Hall's fourth destabilizing force is "the great decentering of identity that is a consequence of the relativization of the Western world—of the discovery of other worlds, other peoples, other cultures, and other languages."

Ethnic writers have, over the years, heightened our awareness of these "other worlds" by subverting traditional narratives in a variety of ways. Their fictions gain vitality not only by returning to oral tradition, but also through the strong sense of shared concerns in contemporary communities. Many contemporary novelists, ethnic and otherwise, have recognized the importance of storytelling, thereby countering the partial neglect, in the metafiction, verbal games, and self-reflexivity of the 1960s, of conventional narrative forms. Ethnic writers, however, have often employed their storytelling to redefine history and culture and to legitimize personal and collective memory. Among Native American creators, for example, there is an insistence that, as Leslie Silko writes in *Ceremony*, stories are "all we have" and they "aren't just entertainment." Silko, N. Scott Momaday, Louise Erdrich, James Welch, Paula Gunn Allen, and Linda Hogan have all found their own ways of empowering the characters and situations in their fictions through the use of oral traditions that allow stories to pass from one generation to the next. Memory interrupts linear, conventional narratives in order to make room for multiple voices and perspectives, as, for example, in the "postmodern" effects achieved in the fiction of Gerald Vizenor. This use of multiple voices, although not entirely unknown elsewhere in literature, becomes in American ethnic writing a means of creating community as part of the dialectic between the past and the present in moving toward the future. It allows for a narrative exploration of the past that rejects or circumvents positivistic assumptions about truth and history. This interest in the past is integral to the ways in which alternative cultures oppose and subvert the dominant culture that has historically both repressed and assimilated them.

The use of oral tales is not exclusive to Native American writers, nor is the use of multivoiced narratives the only way in which ethnic writers extend the boundaries of traditional narrative. Jay Clayton has noted in his essay "The Narrative Turn in Recent Minority Fiction" (1990) that the interest in conventional narrative does not necessarily go hand-in-hand with conservative social views or old-fashioned values, even in nonethnic writers. But, as Clayton reminds us, for ethnic writers the act of storytelling is often also an act of empowerment. In considering the use of narrative in ethnic writing "as an oppositional technique because of its association with unauthorized forms of knowledge," Clayton uses Foucault's argument that power is not a hierarchical relationship and

Introduction

that both the mighty and the humble are positioned by networks of power to organize the social realm by shaping the way one thinks about the body, sexuality, kinship, the family, and so forth. Since narrative is, in Foucault's phrase, one of the "naive knowledges, located low down on the hierarchy, beneath the required level of cognition or scientificity," its appeal to the iconoclast in the ethnic writer is quite understandable.

The ethnic writers' repertoire of subversive strategies includes the introduction of flamboyant storyteller figures (as in Maxine Hong Kingston's *Tripmaster Monkey: His Fake Book* and Cyrus Colter's *The Chocolate Soldier*); the use of myths, rituals, dreams, and legends (as in Toni Morrison's *Song of Solomon,* Leslie Silko's *Ceremony,* and N. Scott Momaday's *House Made of Dawn*); the use of historical tales and incidents (as in David Bradley's *The Chaneysville Incident,* James Welch's *Fools Crow,* and Toni Morrison's *Beloved*); or irreverent treatment of ethnic history and attitudes (as in Gerald Vizenor's *The Heirs of Columbus* and Ishmael Reed's *Mumbo Jumbo* and *The Last Days of Louisiana Red*). By means such as these, ethnic writers valorize the subjectivity of narratives and undermine the very nature of hegemonic constructions of history and culture. Memory in this context shapes narrative forms and strategies toward reclaiming a suppressed past and helps the process of re-visioning that is essential to gaining control over one's life and future. The ethnic narrative thus becomes, in Stuart Hall's phrase, "an act of cultural recovery," and the emergent ethnicity embedded therein develops a new relationship to the past, which is to be recovered through both memory and narrative. These strategies of the ethnic writer often deny the validity of the linear progression of the traditional narrative—which implies a unity through a beginning, middle, and end—or at the very least, reorient our experience of it. Ethnic narratives, like Jean-François Lyotard's "micronarratives," create "narrative knowledge . . . which includes not just verifiable statements about reality but also notions of competence, images of how to do things, how to live, how to care for one another, how to be happy."

The Essays Themselves

The contributors to this collection articulate the variety of ways in which writers of ethnic American literatures chart memory's forays into language, narrative, and identity. Some essays focus on a single writer, while others use a comparative approach. Some are multidisciplinary, drawing on insights from anthropology or semiotics, while others engage in textual analysis. Our objectives are served just as well by an essay focusing on a single text as by one that compares several texts from within one ethnic tradition or yet another that places texts from two or more traditions in a cross-cultural context. We assume an audience that is familiar with—or at least interested in—the ground mapped by the numerous resources in ethnic American literatures mentioned in the preceding pages. The apparent discrepancy between the Contents and the order in which the essays are discussed below is a deliberate choice on our part—an indication of the variety of ways in which our essays speak to one another in their exploration of memory, narrative, and identity.

Issues of personal and collective identity emerged in the early years of this century against the backdrop of social, political, and economic uncertainties faced by the United States as a nation. These uncertainties found expression in Van Wyck Brooks's *America's Coming of Age* (1915) and elsewhere. Nathan Huggins sees a compelling need to examine issues of African-American identity with reference to these broader American uncertainties. In *Harlem Renaissance,* he views black and white identities in the United States as symbiotic. As Huggins sees it, World War I encouraged non-Europeans—as well as African Americans—to "esteem their own cultures as being as valid and civilized as Europe's." On the other hand, in a milieu where popular understandings of Freud and the "new psychology" were in vogue, many white Europeans and Americans, disillusioned by the war, sought to discover a new identity for themselves in the spontaneity, naturalness, and indulgence of impulse they perceived in Blacks. However, in recent decades, American identity, hyphenated or otherwise, has not only confronted white ethnocentrism directed at Blacks and other people of color, but has also struggled with a variety of interethnic tensions. Thus, ethnic identities stemming from European, Latino, and Asian immigration continue to be in shifting relationships with both Black and White. The state of mutual disengagement in which African Americans and new immigrants often inhabit our urban spaces suggests the complexities involved. In the years since World War II, when the United States emerged as an international power, all these American identities have also been affected by patterns of nostalgia and conservatism, idealism and isolationism, and by the short-lived rebellion and radicalism of the late 1960s and the early 1970s. And none of these new and old ethnic identities are immune, at the individual or the group level, to the strident market propensities of mainstream American culture or its invidious pressures of conformism

Introduction

and homogenization. Many of the fourteen essays gathered in this volume measure how ethnic memory engages the uncertainties of identity formation, the pressures of conformity and homogenization, and the power of narrative in both fiction and autobiography.

The first group of essays in this collection approaches issues of memory, narrative, and cultural politics in defining the complex realities of American ethnicity. Terry DeHay's "Narrating Memory" argues that multivocal ethnic narratives are part of a strategy of ethnic resistance, upsetting the authority of conventional narrative and allowing for salutary remembrance. In her examination of four novels by women writers—Amy Tan's *The Joy Luck Club,* Sandra Cisneros's *The House on Mango Street,* Alice Walker's *The Temple of My Familiar,* and Louise Erdrich's *Tracks*—DeHay sees their use of multivoiced narration as breaking from traditional narrative, which, coming from a patriarchal culture, inhibits or represses the awareness that is essential to the achievement of cultural and personal identity. Although multivoiced narration may decenter or disorder the narrative, this disruption, according to DeHay, "acts as a mimetic representation of the way in which other voices have inserted themselves into the writer's consciousness and contribute to an understanding of the structure of society." Jules Chametzky, in "Memory and Silences in the Works of Tillie Olsen and Henry Roth," suggests that the pain of memory may be the reason for the lengthy silences of both these writers, especially Roth. He goes on to link autobiography and autobiographical fiction with history and suggests how facts of personal life, when repeated, eventually become social and political. Chametzky sees the strength of both Roth and Olsen in their ability to take a hard, unblinking look at the facts of their lives and at the memory that recalls and shapes them. In "Traveling Light: Immigration and Invisible Suitcases in M. G. Vassanji's *The Gunny Sack,*" Rosemary Marangoly George discusses the strategies around memory and forgetting that are available to characters in what she calls "the immigrant genre." In these fictions of postcolonial dislocation, the migrant characters create a kind of homeless home that centers on family and largely replaces the need for national identity. The metaphor of personal luggage as memory complicates—and at times obliterates—the immigrant struggle for membership in a new society.

Another set of essays focuses on the role played by the concepts of time and orality in validating both historical and narrative experience. Orality is of course central to Native American narratives, as Terry DeHay

21

points out in her analysis of Louise Erdrich's *Tracks:* "Because of the nature of oral storytelling, the subjective role of the narrator is clear, unlike written *histories;* at the same time, in the sense that the individual story teller is a depository for cultural memory, the story takes on the sanctity of a spiritual history." Or, as Paula Gunn Allen puts it: "The two forms basic to Native American literature are the Ceremony and the Myth. The Ceremony is the ritual enactment of a specialized perception of cosmic relationships, while the Myth is a prose record of that relationship." In the African-American tradition, the significance of telling stories, of sharing "lies" on the porch that tell the truth about black lives, is evidenced strongly in texts such as Zora Neale Hurston's *Their Eyes Were Watching God* and *Mules and Men.* The prose record—the narrative—growing out of these oral traditions is often multilayered and multivoiced, and it validates the ethnic memory through asserting the value of orality over writing. Sharon Jessee's " 'Tell me your earrings': Time and the Marvelous in Toni Morrison's *Beloved*" focuses on West African concepts of time in relation to Morrison's novel, which conflates not only time past and time present, but also, as Jessee shows, this world and the spirit world. The "voices" that clamor for recognition at Sethe's house, Jessee argues, are the sounds of "the many thousands gone," whose names were forgotten by their descendants. Jessee sees Morrison's novel as working out, among other things, patterns of religious oral tradition, memory, and forgetting. Sandra L. Molyneaux's essay, "Expanding the Collective Memory: Charles W. Chesnutt's *The Conjure Woman Tales,*" traces Chesnutt's revisions of his short stories and accumulations of texts into a collection that "validates oral testimony within a literary tradition, models dialogue aiding memory, and illustrates how story acts as a civilizing process." In narratives that "remind us to remember," Chesnutt's "conjuring" voice negotiates delicately between clashing cultures and creates a new kinship through its shared experience of storytelling.

    A third group of essays in this collection concerns the ways in which immigrant or racial memory filters through the expanding net of language and consciousness. These three essays focus on how women writers have rewritten a past full of pain and suffering into regenerative texts of bonding and nurturing. Focusing on *Beloved,* Barbara Offutt Mathieson's "Memory and Mother Love: Toni Morrison's Dyad" explores the intricacies of mother-infant love, with its simultaneous nurture and obsession, as well as communal relations, including the entrapment of Blacks in American slave society. Maternal love, argues Mathieson, serves

Introduction

as a metaphor for memory of the past and can range from the extremes of resistance and total preoccupation to a middle position of "reciprocal adult relations." In her essay, "Reading Carnival as an Archaeological Site for Memory in Paule Marshall's *The Chosen Place, The Timeless People* and *Praisesong for the Widow*," Angelita Reyes examines Marshall's use of carnival as setting, metaphor, and site of cultural memory. More specifically, Marshall deals with both revolt and resignation, the humility and pride of a people who still feel the effects of having come from slavery. Reyes shows how Marshall dramatizes and ritualizes cultural memory, for the communal experience of the carnival is an expression of the nexus of individual and collective memories, the past and the present. Ben Xu's essay, "Memory and the Ethnic Self: Reading Amy Tan's *The Joy Luck Club*," examines the operations of memory in producing a sense of self. Xu argues, with many psychologists, that identity is activated by memory. We are the narrative of our own becoming. As Xu puts it, "Our sense of what has happened to us is entailed not in actual happenings but in *meaningful* happenings, and the meanings of our past experience . . . are constructs produced in much the same way as narrative is produced."

A fourth group of essays in this collection fills out our understanding of imagination and cultural memory, as reflected in photographic art, ethnic autobiography, memoir, and fiction by writers who are "rememberers." Betty Bergland, in "Rereading Photographs and Narratives in Ethnic Autobiography: Memory and Subjectivity in Mary Antin's *The Promised Land*," examines the neglect of visual imagery and conventions of visual representation as sites of memory in ethnic autobiography. She shows how the eighteen photographs omitted from later editions of Mary Antin's *The Promised Land* contradict as well as reinforce the argument of the text. Gert Buelens, in "The New Man and the Mediator: (Non-)Remembrance in Jewish-American Immigrant Narrative," examines several largely autobiographical works, such as Mary Antin's *The Promised Land*, Ezra Brudno's *The Fugitive*, Elias Tobenkin's *Witte Arrives*, and Elizabeth Stern's *My Mother and I*. For Buelens, these works are not simply reflections of the immigrant experience; they are also attempts at assimilation with integrity into the dominant society. In order to achieve acculturation, Buelens suggests, these Jewish autobiographers engage in nonremembrance, forgetting, or putting aside aspects of the cultural past. Their narratives present protagonists who either create new identities for themselves by earning a place in American life as new (wo)men or else attempt to stand between the Old World and the New, establishing their own assimilation as they interpret the immigrant to the American. Pure versions of either form are rare, and the most interesting texts display an awareness of their own complexity. Genaro Padilla, in his essay, "Recovering Nineteenth-Century Mexican-American Autobiography," explores the vast archive of documents engendered by the shock of political and social dispossession after the Mexican-American War. Padilla sees nineteenth-century Mexican-American autobiography as proceeding from the reconstructive acts of memory, setting a prior national/cultural life against "an alien political system in an alien culture." Recovering these documents and attending to their long-silent voices is a massive, collective critical project, which also embodies the operation of memory. In his essay, "X Rays of Irish America: Edwin O'Connor, Mary Gordon, and William Kennedy," William Keough examines the clinical and unsentimental portraits of Irish Americans in works by these three novelists. Keough shows how the drive to de-sentimentalize the collective memory of the Irish-American past in these writers often reveals a darker side of Irish descent.

Finally, two of our contributors focus on how literary memories, in going beyond a reproduction of remembered feelings and thoughts, often become "culturally complex readings" of earlier life experiences. As part of this cultural recovery, the narrator can tell the story of what he or she has experienced, of what parents or grandparents had experienced, modulating in the process our and his or her understanding by both inclusion and exclusion. The strategies and the modes of narration are multiple; each has its limitations, each its advantages. In arguing that ethnicity deeply affects the storage and recall of memory, Wolfgang Karrer's "Nostalgia, Amnesia, and Grandmothers: The Uses of Memory in Albert Murray, Sabine Ulibarri, Paula Gunn Allen, and Alice Walker" shows how the relationship between individual memory and collective memory is embedded in verbal rituals of "recall." In her essay, "Maxine Hong Kingston's Fake Books," Debra Shostak examines the transformation of memory in both the individual and the culture as well as in the interweave of memory and imagination. Through Shostak's analysis, we see how Kingston's *Tripmaster Monkey* illustrates the making of cultural memory, in part by redefining "history" to result from the revision, translation, and transmission of documents of the past, especially those normally considered fictional rather than factual. Through the novel's brilliant narrative technique and its rich ironies, the reader witnesses the

Introduction

creation of a story in which at times the author, the narrator in her various guises, and the community merge and shift.

Our contributors demonstrate how issues of cultural memory are complicated by considerations such as historical conditions, hegemonic discourses that shape acceptable forms of memory, questions of gender and class, and regional differences in historical development. The cultural and political realities of race and ethnicity in American life—as filtered through the memories of our literary creators and their fictional characters—give a special meaning to the identity formation of all hyphenated Americans by reminding us that the effects of the past remain always with us even if sometimes muted. A newly emergent American identity must acknowledge and empower difference without breaking under its weight. In rethinking our complex multicultural past, we need to address issues of distortion and erasure, of shared myths and attitudes, even as they are interrogated, separately and together, by race, immigration, and ethnicity. These essays will, we hope, pay a significant role in energizing future debates in and outside the academy about multicultural realities.

Works Cited

Clayton, Jay. "The Narrative Turn in Recent Minority Fiction." *American Literary History* 2 (1990): 375–93.

Ferraro, Thomas J. *Ethnic Passages: Literary Immigrants in Twentieth Century America*. Chicago: U of Chicago P, 1993.

Narrating Memory

TERRY DEHAY

Third World writers in the United States are increasingly confronting the need to construct alternative histories to those of the dominant culture in order to combat the appropriation and oppression of marginalized cultures. They are creating narratives that actively confront the dominant culture's attempt to destroy and/or neutralize these marginalized cultures through the destruction or appropriation of their collective history. As Barbara Harlow writes in her book *Resistance Literature*, "an important consequence of the First World's military, economic, and political intervention in the Third World . . . has been the catastrophic disruption of Third World people's cultural and literary traditions . . ." (33), which would generally be essential in the preservation of authentic history. This assault on history underscores its power, especially in terms of a dialectic of individual and collective remembering, to give a people a common understanding of beginnings and processes in the act of becoming or resisting. Often a dominant culture will negate the importance of a minority group's shared and different past in favor of a more universal reading—We're all Americans—implying that the difference that the minority group *senses* is not real, but rather imagined. This is the myth of assimilation, "the melting pot"; the mainstream history then incorporates, assimilates, these differences. Even more difficult and more destructive, the dominant culture inevitably writes this "official" version of history and presents it as "fact" and unquestionable. Until recently, history has presented itself as an objective science, against which the intuitive challenge of marginalized memory remained virtually powerless.

Harlow convincingly outlines the importance of *not* reading Third World literature with the "European writer's mania for man without history—solitary and free—with unexplainable despair and anguish and death as the ultimate truth about human condition" (17). She also warns that resistance movements "not be confined by the First World imagination to what Gayatri Spivak, in her seminar "Third World under Erasure" at the Summer Institute for Culture and Society, Pittsburgh, in 1986, criticized as mere representative allegories of "correct political practice" (29, cited by Harlow). Many Third World writers are emphatically attempting to affect and even rewrite the historical record through their work and therefore directly address historical and factual incidences. Their work must not be neutralized by removing specifics to the plane of the symbolic or allegorical, but rather should be recognized in its full historical and political context. At the same time, Harlow points out that the personal accounts related in much literature of the resistance point to convergences within the larger context of the struggle against oppression.

Although Harlow's book focuses on resistance to colonial and neocolonial repression in Third World countries, many of her concepts can also be applied to the literature of Third World writers living in the United States, especially women of color. As Fredric Jameson points out in "Modernism and Imperialism": "in the United States itself, we have come to think and to speak of the emergence of an *internal* Third World and of internal Third World voices, as in Black women's literature or Chicano literature, for example" (51). Women of color in the United States live on the margin in at least two important ways: as members of marginalized "minority" groups and as women in a dominant white male culture. As Alice Walker points out in her essay "In Search of Our Mothers' Gardens," black women, as women from a marginalized culture, were effectively excluded from the institutions of the dominant ideology through the inaccessibility of education. Their creativity was limited to those materials that were appropriate to their marginalized space—scraps of cloth, flower seeds—or to modes of expression that cannot easily be denied—singing, dancing, storytelling. At times, the dominant culture has appropriated or reinterpreted even these cultural expressions to reenforce its values rather than reading them as historical records of struggle as Walker does in her essay. The example she gives of the quilt hanging in the Smithsonian Institution in Washington, D.C., is a poignant example of this process of appropriation: "... there hangs a quilt unlike any other in the world.... Though it follows no known pattern of quilt making, though it is made of bits and pieces of worthless rags, it is obviously the work of a powerful imagination and deep spiritual feeling. Below the quilt I saw a note that said it was made by 'an anonymous black woman in Alabama, a hundred years ago'" (239). A product both of a creative force of the woman who patched it together from "worthless rags" and the oppressive forces of the dominant culture, the quilt, isolated and objectified, hanging in a museum, loses much of the meaning of the circumstances of its creation. This creator is anonymous in large part because of her position in this culture. As Walker states, "If we could locate this 'anonymous black woman from Alabama,' she would turn out to be one of our grandmothers" (239). Today, through new acts of creation, Third World women are looking back, locating these lost ancestors, freeing them from the confines of museums, and reclaiming their histories.

The four novels by minority women writers examined in this essay challenge the domination of hegemonic history and memory in the very structure of the narrative, as they directly confront the importance of memory to personal and cultural identity. Amy Tan's *The Joy Luck Club,* Sandra Cisneros's *The House on Mango Street,* Alice Walker's *The Temple of My Familiar,* and Louise Erdrich's *Tracks* have common strategies of interrupting the surface of the traditional linear narrative to allow for the entry of a multiplicity of voices and perspectives. This deconstruction is a response to what Colin MacCabe calls the "classical [nineteenth century] realist novel," in which the narrative creates "a hierarchy amongst the discourses that compose the text": "In the classical realist novel the narrative prose functions as a metalanguage that can state all the truths in the object language—those words held in inverted commas—and can also explain the relation of this object language to the real" (35). In other words, the narrative "metalanguage" mediates between the "text" and the reader, providing a "window of words" to frame the reader's relationship to the "real." The narrative, according to MacCabe, "simply allows reality to appear and denies its own status as articulation" (35). However, although this metalanguage is "transparent," like all language, it is ideological, and therefore the reality, or "truth" to which it points, is also ideologically informed. In the case of the realist novel, the dominant ideology is that of the patriarchal culture of western Europe and later the United States.

Multiethnic American women's literature, like other marginalized literatures, often uses this deconstruction of the traditional realist narrative metalanguage to produce alternative narrative patterns to those of the dominant culture and to destabilize the "hierarchy amongst discourses" within the text. By providing openings for other narratives, other versions of history, these texts lead to a revisioning or "re-membering" (to borrow Mary DeShazer's term) of minority women's identities. Theirs is not a quest for a new metalanguage, but rather the celebration of what MacCabe calls the "multifarious nature of the real" (34). Barbara Christian, in *Black Women Novelists: The Development of a Tradition, 1892–*

1976, identifies this tendency toward perspectives in her analysis of Paule Marshall's novels, *Browngirl, Brownstones* and *The Chosen Place, The Timeless People:*

> ... her emphasis moves from the way the world affects an individual psyche to how our many psyches create a world ... toward a unity of rather than a specialization of, experience. That type of movement is one of the reasons why persistent creative artists are so important to a culture. In graphically depicting their own growth, in analyzing abstract concepts through the concrete experiences of particular human beings, they fuse the personal and social areas that our fragmented world thrusts one against the other. Only when we see the oneness between politics and the individual psyche, oppression and the nature of human history, culture and the individual, their voices sing, will our species move beyond biting its tail to create its mouth. The wholeness of the creative process continually reminds us that we purposely sleep through much of our lives. (135)

By taking apart the traditional narrative, minority women writers are able to identify the artificial nature of accepted patterns and to reveal authentic unities.

Raymond Williams, in *Marxism and Literature,* defines three distinct aspects of culture that create "internal dynamic relations" within any system. The most easily identifiable is the *hegemonic* or *dominant.* But along with the dominant, the *residual* and the *emergent* function as part of the dynamic process that is, in Williams's terms, culture. The 'residual,' according to Williams "has been effectively formed in the past, but it is still active in the cultural process, not only and often not at all as an element of the past, but as an effective element of the present. Thus certain experiences, meanings, and values which cannot be expressed or substantially verified in terms of the dominant culture, are nevertheless lived and practiced on the basis of the residue—cultural as well as social—of some previous social and cultural institution or formation" (122). He also distinguishes between the residual that has been incorporated into the hegemony and that which presents an alternative or opposition to the dominant aspects of culture. The emergent aspects of culture are "new meanings and values, new practices, new relationships and kinds of relationships" that are continually being created (123).

These categories of the dominant, recessive, and emergent help clarify the importance of the past to the reconstruction of repressed cultural identity. To return to the past is not sufficient, nor is it possible in the dynamic process of cultural formation. However, the past does supply powerful and important connections that are essential to the revisioning of minority women's identities. Steven Knapp, in his article "Collective

Memory and the Actual Past," states that, regardless of whether or not remembered events actually happened, "the narratives preserved sometimes play a *normative* role—that is, they may in various ways provide criteria, implicit or explicit, by which contemporary models of action can be shaped or corrected, or even by which practical ethical or political proposals can be authorized or criticized" (123). He refers to this function as "collective *authority*," by which a culture defines itself. Clearly, understanding one's relationship to this "collective authority" is essential to resisting hegemonic control. If marginalized cultures accept the dominant culture's narratives as normative, they will be powerless to resist domination. If, instead, they denaturalize these narratives, at the same time recuperating their own collective (recessive) memories, they can provide alternative "collective authorities," with alternative (emergent) "models of action" to resist domination.

Adrienne Rich, in her essay "When We Dead Awaken," defines this dialectical process as *re-vision:* "the act of looking back, of seeing with fresh eyes, of entering an old text from a new critical direction," asserting that revisioning is an "act of survival": "Until we can understand the assumptions in which we are drenched, we cannot know ourselves" (35). For minority women, this means a positive recuperation of residual cultural alternatives, as well as the recognition of the distortion of their history by the dominant culture. The act of re-visioning creates fresh connections with the past, which can supply an alternative culture or cultures to stand in opposition to the dominant culture, which has historically both absorbed and repressed them. The emergent provides a synthesis: "new meanings and values, new practices, new relationships and kinds of relationships," which are continually created (Williams 123).

This process of synthesis is often recreated in minority women's novels through the relationships between mothers, as repositories of the recessive culture, and daughters, in their attempts to live in the modern white world. *The Joy Luck Club* and *The Temple of My Familiar,* in particular, examine the importance of the relationship between daughters and mothers in establishing cultural identities. The cultures represented by the mothers provide a means of finding power as women of color in a male-dominated white culture. DeShazer, in *Inspiring Women: Reimagining the Muse,* states that women writers "name their muses not by casting off or consuming or appropriating, but by taking on, connecting, inheriting" (6). She extends her reading of the Demeter/Kore, mother/daughter relationship, so prevalent in women's writing, to women writers of color, in terms of a *familial muse,* the muse that comes not from a distant mythology or tradition, but from their own lives. She cites Maya Angelou: "Image making is very important for every human being. It is especially important for black American women in that we are, by being black, a minority in the United States, and by being female the less powerful of the genders. . . . We need to see our mothers, aunts, our sisters, and grandmothers. We need to see Frances Harper, Sojourner Truth, Fannie Lou Hamer, women of our heritage. We need to have these women preserved" (40 [from *Black Women Writers at Work,* ed. Claudia Tate, 1–2]). The minority woman must look to her history, both to preserve it and to find out who she is. She needs to have a clear vision of her past, in order to re-vision her present. This is the process of re-membering. The female muse, then, in these texts, inspires the writer with a sense of the history of her culture, a connection to a past that the dominant culture may be repressing or reinterpreting away from the authentic history.

Their mothers' histories as they run counter to that of the dominant or official history are primarily oral and generally passed through stories and other acts of creation (such as the making of feathered capes by Zedé in *The Temple of My Familiar*). These stories may, in fact, conflict directly with the mother's advice on how to survive in the closed world of the dominant culture. But the mothers' stories, memories, and works of art provide other models and choices, the possibility of alternative and oppositional identities. In Tan's *The Joy Luck Club,* the narrative alternates between the mothers' remembering and the daughters' telling of their stories. The novel is divided into four sections, in which Tan explores the link between language and tradition through the relationships between four immigrant Chinese mothers and their Chinese-American daughters. The mythic nature of the mothers' narratives contrasts with the more prosaic, conventional narratives of the daughters' stories, giving the impression that they are occurring simultaneously but on different levels. The contrast between the two types of narratives creates a dialogue between the two voices, the multiple perspectives on the Chinese and Chinese-American experience of living in the United States. The mothers' voices, the oral storytelling, almost intrude on the written narrative, uncontrolled but supplying meaning and cultural associations that are missing in the other memories. The cultural memory comes almost unconsciously through the mothers' storytelling, a type of recessive cultural resource that the mothers ironically attempt to counter in the messages to the daughters.

The central, but not controlling, narrative voice is that of Jing-Mei

Woo, whose mother, Suyuan Woo, has died before the opening of the narrative. Her absence triggers her daughter's active remembering and confrontation with her mother's and her own Chinese identity. Her quest for understanding, through a return to her mother, ends with a trip to China and to a reunion with sisters she has never known and a virtual re-membering of her mother. In confronting the loss of her mother and the need to tell her half-sisters about her, she realizes that she has never really known her mother: "What will I say? What can I tell them about my mother? I don't know anything. She was my mother" (40). Her words sum up the separation between a mother and a daughter, which is magnified through linguistic and cultural otherness. Her quest to re-member and to understand begins with this recognition and her commitment to "remember everything about her and tell them" (40).

The final section of the book recounts this trip to China, as Jing-Mei's return to her mother and a re-visioning of herself as a result. The narrative weaves immediate impressions of China with memories of the mother, with Jing-Mei's father's story of Suyuan's past, and finally with the meeting of the sisters, into a coherent whole through which Jing-Mei discovers her own Chinese self. In discovering the pieces of her mother's past and in beginning to understand her as a complete person, she also discovers her Chinese nature, which she had attempted to erase as she approached the American culture: "And now I see what part of me is Chinese. It is so obvious. It is my family. It is in our blood. After all these years, it can finally be let go" (288). After denying for so long her own cultural history, she is able to reclaim it and become a whole person.

Jing-Mei's account of her re-membering of her mother and herself gives form to *The Joy Luck Club,* providing a framework for the stories of the other three mothers and daughters. The mothers were all members of the Joy Luck Club, which Jing-Mei's mother had formed on arriving in the United States, and the daughters had grown up together as friends and rivals. This interweaving of multiple individual stories is very common in many minority women's novels as it breaks down the isolation of the individual characteristic of the conventional novel. Jing-Mei's quest for her own intercultural identity through a synthesis of her past and present, her American and Chinese selves, is not separate from that of the other Joy Luck Club mothers and daughters, although their own histories are unique. In completing her own quest at the end of the novel, she in a sense supplies them with an alternative "collective authority," which demands neither the total rejection of one culture nor the absorption by another. Jing-Mei experiences the truth of her mother's observation about being born Chinese in America: " 'Some day you will see,' said my mother. 'It is in your blood waiting to be let go' " (267).

Like Tan's *The Joy Luck Club,* Alice Walker's *The Temple of My Familiar* confronts the alienation of Third World men and women living within the dominant culture of the United States, focusing on the way in which this alienation prevents them from forming bonds with others. In this recent novel, as in many of her earlier novels, each of the characters, male and female, must look backward in order to progress. As Barbara Christian points out in *Black Women Novelists,* Walker's poetry, fiction, and essays focus to some extent "on the major characters' perceptions of their past as crucial to their personal transformation in the present and the possibility of change in the future" (235). In *The Temple of My Familiar,* the narrative jumps continually from past to present, from one perspective to another, from the West Coast to the East Coast, from North to South America to Africa. Two of the major characters, Zedé and Fanny, return to their countries of origin. For Zedé, it is a true return from exile to the Central American country that was her home and to herself as a member of that cultural reality. Her return and remembering of herself also enables her daughter, Carlotta, to incorporate this remembered identity into her own sense of self as a Latina living in the United States.

Fanny, whose mother is African American and who was raised in the United States, returns to Africa to discover her father and to recover her own identity. In the process, she, like Jing-Mei, finds a sister she didn't know she had, who helps give her a better understanding of the African part of her identity. As they have mirror names, Fanny Nzingha and Nzingha Anne, Fanny also feels that, in looking at her half-sister, she is "looking into a mirror as an African-American . . . and the mirror is reflecting only the African" (251). Fanny's discovery of her African self, and also of the truth of the sociopolitical nature of Africa, helps her to integrate the separate parts of herself and to reconstruct the nature of her relationship with the culture in which she lives. Her alienation comes from her anger at the society in the midst of which she lives. She confronts her anger with white society by returning to the African country that represents half of her cultural heritage, where she learns that her anger is real but that in directing it at white people, she is missing the real target: any society that represses is the enemy, regardless of color. This need to explore backgrounds extends to all the main characters in the *new* generation, and the resources the individuals must explore in order to discover themselves are not limited to the modern United

States. Neither their history nor their future recognizes the limitations of geographic or temporal boundaries.

The character in *The Temple of My Familiar* who most embodies this transcendence of boundaries is Lissie. She is like a collective consciousness, memory incarnate, a guide for Suwelo in his quest for understanding. She is the epitome of the storyteller, whose conscious memory spans the entire development of the black culture. The stories that Lissie tells empower Suwelo with the knowledge of both his cultural history and the role of women in that history, so that he can return as a complete human being. Although his physical journey takes him only as far as his uncle's house in New Jersey, his re-membering, guided by Lissie, takes him back to the beginning of time. Suwelo, who has the stereotypical male attitudes, must accept the guidance of an archetypal black female in order to regain his wife, and in a sense, himself and his culture.

The message that Walker emphasizes in each of these separate narratives is that the search for self cannot be limited by the dominant culture's vision of the past, that individuals have unique pasts that will reveal their present and their relationship to the "collective authority" that their remembering recreates. The cultural other, the mother, the father, the sister, sometimes symbolized in art—feather capes, music, storytelling, writing—must be discovered, experienced, rediscovered, and incorporated in order for the characters to become culturally whole.

The alienation that prevents the characters from having healthy relationships is reflected in the separate development of the narrative lines, which eventually merge into a single narrative, as the individual characters form family and social units, demonstrating the possibility of solidarity within the context of difference. In *The Temple of My Familiar*, there is a strong contrast between the clearly identified, subjective voices of the narrators and the supposed objective voice of the traditional omniscient narrator. The multiple voices orchestrated by Walker offer different perspectives of the same or contiguous histories without privileging any one character. In the structure of the novel, the voices are often dissident, and in fact the narrative must first break traditional bonds before characters can recreate authentic bonds. For example, Carlotta and Arveyda's marriage and Fanny and Suwelo's are disrupted so that the characters can complete their personal quests. As the text itself breaks down traditional narrative boundaries, the characters must redefine bonds established on the lines established by the hegemonic traditions—mother, father, sister, husband, wife—in order to create their own cultural and sociopolitical identities. As Carlotta states, "I'm *still* married to

Arveyda . . . but the bond is no longer the primary basis of our relationship" (374).

The characters and their stories unite at the end of the novel and solidify their union with shared memories and the vision of a future. This is similar to what Christian identifies as "Walker's pattern of interrelated illumination" (229), in that the struggles of all the characters for self-knowledge and integration are stitched together in the design of the novel. This stitching creates what Christian refers to as the "pattern for change" in Walker's novelistic quilts—*Meridian, The Third Life of Grange Copeland*—in which the individual struggle of the characters is linked to the greater social struggle (137).

Both *The Joy Luck Club* and *The Temple of My Familiar* question the destruction of authentic cultures as a means of survival and adaptation in the hegemonic culture. The Chinese-American children need to become "American" to *make it* in the mainstream culture, forgetting their Chinese selves. The Central American children need to become North American, confining their cultural background to the creation of artifacts to sell. The black woman's rejection of her African father forces her to deny her own African self, focusing her anger toward a white world to which she refuses to conform. By returning to China, Central America, Africa, in both physical and spiritual quests, these women are able to *choose* to incorporate the cultural difference into their identity. Again, these narratives also suggest a positive resolution for the future in the incorporation of the past and present, the residual and the emergent, in keeping the past alive in the present and the other active in the self.

In some ways, Louise Erdrich's *Tracks* seems like a radical departure from *The Joy Luck Club* and *The Temple of My Familiar,* partly because of the shift in locale, from the San Francisco Bay area to North Dakota, from the struggle of urban minorities to lives on the margin of the United States. In *Tracks,* however, Erdrich also deconstructs the traditional narrative to reveal alternative and multiple perspectives. In this novel, chronologically first in the cycle of novels that includes *Love Medicine* and *The Beet Queen,* she explores a Native American community in North Dakota. The narrative jumps between the confused, hysterical remembering of a young half-breed woman and the passing on of history by an old Chippewa, Nanapush, to Lulu, the granddaughter he claims in naming. He is giving his memory to her, partly to convince her not to marry a man from an opposing clan, but also so that she will not forget who she is and who they were. As chronicle of the end of a family and the dismembering of a Native American cultural center, the passing on of history in terms of a specific, nonhegemonic memory is underscored. The old man is acutely aware that his perspective, his particular memory will not be recorded in the *official* history. Having worked as a translator for the government, he knows words lose their sacred and real meaning in dealings with the government: "My girl, listen well. Nanapush is a name that loses power every time that it is written and stored in a government file" (32). This weakening of meaning leads as well to a weakening of the cultural identity.

His storytelling is also an act of healing, a medicine, to bring back together the mother, Fleur Pillager, a source of cultural power, very much connected to the "old ways," the land, and her daughter, Lulu, born of Fleur's violent rape by white men and sent by her mother to a government school to save her from the disintegrating community. Nanapush tells Lulu: "But you, heartless one, won't even take off your pointy shoes, walk through the tough brush, and visit her. Maybe once I tell you the reason she had to send you away, you will start acting like a daughter should. . . . Perhaps when you finally understand, you'll borrow my boots and go out there and forgive her, though it's you that needs forgiveness" (211). He sees his stories as a possible medicine to remember the mother/daughter self that is at the core of the culture.

The contrast in the narrative between the two very distinct voices and perspectives emphasizes the effect of ideological and personal necessity in the interpretation of events, one voice working to heal, one to destroy. Distortion works on the memory and understanding of Pauline, in her own confused and pressured position as an outsider, contrasting with the clear remembering and sometimes conscious manipulation of language and memories of Nanapush; in his words, "She was worse than a Nanapush, in fact. For while I was careful with my known facts, she was given to improving the story. . . . Because she was unnoticeable, homely if it must be said, Pauline schemed to gain attention by telling odd tales that created damage" (39). Pauline's own desire for recognition restructures her memories, creating images and stories that she herself begins to believe. From the beginning of the novel, we see her begin to create her own mythology of the powerful Fleur Pillager that will conflict with the Christian mythology in which she eventually finds a permanent means of obscuring her memories. Pauline's obsession with memory stems from the day following Fleur's rape by three white men when she was working in Argus. She and her brother, Russell, in their own revenge at the men's violence, lock the men into refrigerated meat lockers where they have taken shelter during a tornado, leading to the death of two of the men. Although Pauline's memories are very clear and detailed about the rape, she falters in remembering her own involvement: "It was Russell, I am sure, who first put his arms on the bar, thick iron that was made to slide along the wall and fall across the hasp and lock. He strained and shoved, too slight to move it into place, but he did not look to me for help. Sometimes, thinking back, I see my arms lift, my hands grasp, see myself dropping the beam into the metal grip. At other times, that moment is erased" (27–28). Pauline learns that she can manipulate the truth. When she tells the story to Margaret, she molds it to her own ends, and Margaret accepts the distortion because it suits her desire to discredit Fleur: "Fleur had enticed the men to her and killed them for her amusement" (55). Erdrich writes Pauline's story as individually and importantly her own, true according to her own despairing vision. At the same time, Erdrich demonstrates the danger in the town people's motivated appropriation of Pauline's stories, imbuing them with their own "collective authority," regardless of their relationship to events as they really happened. These stories, then, fuel the antagonisms in the already divided community.

Remembering as oral transmission is especially important in *Tracks,* as Nanapush keeps himself alive by talking and keeps his culture alive by telling stories. Because of the nature of oral storytelling, unlike written *histories,* the subjective role of the narrator is clear; at the same time, in the sense that the individual storyteller is a depository for cultural memory, the story takes on the sanctity of a spiritual history. In telling this story to Lulu, Nanapush gives form to the events as he witnessed them: "There is a story to it the way there is a story to all, never visible while it is happening. Only after, when an old man sits dreaming and talking in his chair, the design springs clear" (33–34). Like the epic poets who evoke the muse of memory, Nanapush, in the act of remembering, reveals the design or form of seemingly unrelated incidents in the past. As all histories are products of selective remembering and narrative ordering from a specific perspective, so Nanapush is giving his perspective. But as he tells Lulu, "Perhaps you've heard what I'm going to tell you now, I don't know. If so, you've heard it on the lips of others and never from one who witnessed" (219). Nanapush's perspective is that of one who witnessed and participated in the memories he is narrating. The design of Pauline's account unfolds as she tells it and follows the development of her madness; she seems not to be remembering as much as struggling against the truth that memory can reveal.

In *Tracks,* Erdrich makes clear that memories are products of individual processes that are never unmotivated. Nanapush's story is clearly motivated, both by the desire to give Lulu the history of her mother and her culture and by the desire to counter other stories. Pauline's memories are also shaped by motivations, on the one hand her longing to find a place in the community, on the other to escape a painful memory that lies at the base of her madness. In addition, the history of the dominant culture is motivated by its appetite for land, money, and power, and the need to repress and manipulate the Native Americans in order to obtain these. In order to evaluate historical narratives, understanding of these motivations is essential. Pauline's memories, as Nanapush points out, are harmful to the community and the culture because they are motivated by personal obsession. In juxtaposing the two voices within the context of the struggle to maintain a way of life, Erdrich provokes a critical reading of all history and the importance and sanctity of memory for marginal cultures, based on shared cultural values and historical imperative.

As in the two novels discussed earlier, the narrative in *Tracks* alternates voices, shifting from one perspective to another in order to undercut the authority of the narrative structure. In this way, these novels seem to reproduce formally what Gloria Anzaldúa defines as the perspective of *la mestiza:* "she has discovered that she can't hold concepts or ideas within rigid boundaries" (378). Tan, Walker, and Erdrich are all confronting the effects of the confrontation of different cultures within the individual and the community. The deconstruction of the narrative exposes gaps between cultural perspectives and the difficulties of individuals who must straddle these gaps and live with contradiction. The power of *la mestiza* (or *el mestizo*) rests in the ability to come to terms with these differences: ". . . She learns to juggle cultures. She has a plural personality, she operates in a pluralist mode—nothing is thrust out, the good, the bad, and the ugly, nothing rejected, nothing abandoned. Not only does she sustain contradictions, she turns the ambivalence into something else" (379). Jing-Mei is able to let her Chinese blood flow through her veins; Suwelo discovers the plurality of black history through the memories; Nanapush becomes a tribal bureaucrat in order to bring Lulu home. These multivoiced narratives all reject the false unity of the hegemonic, patriarchal narrative that demands the reproduction of reality according to one transparent metalanguage, recognizing instead the positive nature of the polyphonic, polycultural world.

With Sandra Cisneros's *The House on Mango Street,* the fracturing of the narrative line takes on still another function. The narrative voice, that of a young girl as she remembers her coming of age in the tenement on Mango Street, remains constant. What is fragmented is the process of remembering itself. Each memory is told as a distinct narrative unit, without artificial narrative cohesion. Although the narrator supplies connections between the incidents through her own subjective remembering, she does not emerge as a main or privileged character in the narrative. As in the other novels examined above, rather than one or even a few main characters, Cisneros's book emphasizes the multitude of characters present in the narrative re-membering of the young girl: bedridden Aunt Lupe, who listens to her stories and poems; Alicia, who wakes up early to make the tortillas and takes two trains and a bus so that she can attend the university; Minerva, who writes poems and excuses her husband's abuse; Earl, the jukebox repairman, with all his different wives; Marin, with the boyfriend in Puerto Rico and the dreams on the corner. As Ellen McCracken points out, the text rejects the "privileged status of introspective texts and individualistic notions of self," placing the self in a "broader socio-political reality of community" rather than on an internal individual conflict (Horno-Delgado et al. 66).

The novel is composed of a series of forty-four vignettes, short stories, memories told from the perspective of the child, Esperanza Cordova, as she loses innocence and gains the consciousness to select and organize memory, without the overly motivated analysis that characterizes many omniscient narrators. Through these series of memories, the reader is able to observe the coming of age of a young Latina woman and her growing awareness of her position in the society that surrounds her. The text reproduces that initial sense of disconnected incidents that eventually provide the basis on which the subject in society learns to "see" herself. The reader pieces together the social fabric along with the narrator, in an almost voyeuristic sense, seeing the community through the vision of one of its members.

The main principle of organization is chronological juxtaposition, events and memories ordered in the sequence in which they occurred, not necessarily thematically, although one can deduce thematic coherence as well. For example, the section "Our Good Day" ends "Down, down Mango Street we go. Rachel, Lucy, me. Our new bicycle. Laughing the crooked ride back" (18). The following section is titled "Laughter" as though the child narrator uses association as an unconscious organization. But there is also a sense that each experience adds to the growing perception of the narrator as she tries to make sense of her world and her role in that world. The memories shift in focus from the terror of scolding nuns and the obsession with heavy shoes to serious attempts to understand the pain and oppression she sees around her on Mango Street.

The lack of explicit narrative or explanatory connectives leaves the creation of overall narrative coherence to the act of reading, which may be what leads some critics to deny the novelistic nature of the work. However, the overall movement of the text becomes clear as the reader, along with the narrator, pieces together the elements of the story to arrive at an understanding of the past and its relationship to a present and a future. As the narrator relates her different perceptions, she emphasizes certain themes through repetition and variation. The dominant theme is the loss of innocence, which in this particular social situation means the awakening of Esperanza's understanding of what it means to be both a member of a minority and a woman in a white patriarchal culture. The memories and stories she chooses to relate all focus on the social, cultural, and sexual alienation she experiences as a child.

The first sections of *The House on Mango Street* relate Esperanza's sense of displacement, which memory can only generalize: "We didn't always live on Mango Street. Before that we lived on Loomis on the third floor, and before that we lived on Keeler. Before Keeler it was Paulina, and before that I can't remember. But what I remember most is moving a lot" (7). The house becomes a symbol for permanence and belonging: "They always told us we would move into a house, a real house that would be ours always" (7), but one which the awakening consciousness of the child narrator finds elusive, "But I know how those things go" (8). The absence of a permanent home signals her alienation from that other world of the dominant white culture outside the boundaries of Mango Street. By the end of the novel, she is still determined to acquire the house, but she sees it more in terms of the symbolic space; in "A House of My Own," she writes, "Only a house quiet as snow, a space for myself to go, clean as paper before a poem" (100). The house, as a container of identity, will be her own, with her porch and pillows and petunias. It will be a house she creates and imagines, not one created and imagined for her.

The most powerful theme woven through this text is that of a young girl's growing sense of sexual alienation and the resulting assertion of self. In their introduction to the critical anthology *Breaking Boundaries*, Eliana Ortega and Nancy Saporta Sternbach write: "Whether Latina writers express themselves in English, Spanish, or interlingual, they live in a society defined by male paradigms; for this reason, Latina literature frequently confronts sexual inequality in both Anglo and Latino cultures" (Horno-Delgado et al. 15). Through her description of the lives of the women on Mango Street, the narrator gives a clear, graphic description of patriarchy as it affects her community. In the section "Alicia Who Sees Mice," she writes: "Is a good girl, my friend, studies all night and sees the mice, the ones her father says do not exist. Is afraid of nothing except four-legged fur. And fathers" (32). Alicia has inherited her mother's rolling pin, but "studies at the university for the first time" to escape the limitations of that role. Fathers and husbands are frequently the judges and jailers of the women's limited lives, almost as though by restricting the women's roles—wife, mother, sister, whore—they can maintain control over their own lives.

Sally is the most prominent character in the novel, introduced toward the end and dominating more sections and memories than the other characters. She is also the most poignantly portrayed character. She is "the girl with the eyes like Egypt and the nylons the color of smoke" (77), whom the narrator originally looks up to and wants to imitate, even as she senses Sally's pain. She transfers her own desire for a house to Sally, her own dreaming: "Do you ever wish your feet would one day keep walking and take you far away from Mango Street, far away and maybe your feet would stop in front of a house, a nice one with flowers and big windows . . ." (78). At this point the narrator seems to identify with Sally, almost as a type of alter ego, the other she might become if she does not say goodbye to Mango Street.

As Sally continues to develop as a victim of cultural oppression and patriarchal domination, the narrator becomes increasingly separate from her. In "What Sally Said," the narrator confronts the abuse that Sally suffers from her father. Immediately following, establishing a thematic link, is perhaps the pivotal section, "The Monkey Garden." Sally flees from her father to the false love of the Monkey Garden, where the narrator describes her vision of Sally's torment as she acquiesces to the desire of the neighborhood boys. This is the longest section of the book, the most detailed memory, in which the narrator remembers her anger, her frustrated will to save Sally, who does not want to be saved.

Sally's actions are also the cause of Esperanza's sexual humiliation and rape in the next section, "Red Clowns." As she becomes aware of Sally's true plight, gaining through the experience her own direct knowledge of Sally's desperate and alienated vision of sexuality, she also moves away from Sally and her world; emphasizing this disillusionment, the narrative repeats the refrain, "you lied." Sally escapes from her father's house into a marriage with the marshmallow salesman, but she has clearly exchanged "one repressive patriarchal prison for another" (Horno-Delgado et al. 68), in which her husband does not allow her to talk on the phone or visit with her friends. Although she has "her husband and her house, her pillowcases and her plates" (95), clearly she has given up any chance at her own life.

But as Sally falls, Esperanza rises, gaining consciousness of her own need to resist. The narrator gradually becomes an active participant in her community, analyzing the world around her and taking a stance. In the section "Beautiful and Cruel," she plans her rebellion, choosing her model from the outside: ". . . I have decided not to grow tame like the others who lay their necks on the thresholds, waiting for the ball and chain. . . . I have begun my own quiet war. Simple. Sure. I am one who leaves the table like a man, without putting back the chair or picking up the plate" (82). The memory that follows immediately on the pitiable description of Sally's wedding is "The Three Sisters," an echo of the three fates, who "had the power to sense what was what" (96). The sisters focus on the narrator's name, Esperanza (hope), repeating it as though to manifest the power of its meaning: "She'll go very far" (97). These sisters are Lissie from *The Temple of My Familiar,* Suyuan Woo from *The Joy Luck Club,* Nanapush from *Tracks,* reminding Esperanza that she is her past, that she is "special," but that she must "remember to come back. For the ones who can not leave as easily as you. You will remember?" (98). Indeed, *The House on Mango Street* is a remembering, a coming back for all those who were not able to leave. As Ortega and Saporta Sternbach state in their analysis of Latina writing, "Because Latinas live in a context of having to juxtapose several oppressions simultaneously, articulating their anger and breaking those silences constitute pithy components of their literary discourse. . . . At the same time, another constant of their work is their view of themselves as preservers of history, documenters of their own lives, as well as those of their community" (Horno-Delgado et al. 16). *The House on Mango Street* tells the story of a young girl's coming of age, of her recognition of the oppression of her community, her growing anger and commitment to saving herself as she cannot save Sally. At the same time, it is the story of the creation of a storyteller, one who will not forget and for whom remembering the lives of the men and women on Mango Street is a means of understanding herself as well as her community.

Narrating Memory

The deconstructive act that these minority women's narratives perform demonstrates the importance of recognizing the type of control that the traditional narrative form exercises over the material it contains. The traditional narrative voice, regardless of its position, implies unity of vision, linear progression, a comfortable beginning, middle, and end. Perspective is always centered in the individual with whom the narrative originates. John Berger's analysis of perspective in the visual arts points to the importance of drawing attention to the subjective nature of perspective in narration: "Perspective makes the single eye the centre of the visible world. . . . The visible world is arranged for the spectator as the universe was once thought to be arranged for God" (10). By choosing to open up the narrative form, dispersing the points of origin and denying artificial cohesion, these minority women writers are challenging the very nature of patriarchal authority. Unseating the singular eye or I, they are acknowledging, and often celebrating, differences between cultures and even within themselves.

Perhaps even more importantly, however, these writers are providing models for marginalized groups for recovering and revising their own history, based on a respect for memory and a recognition of the subjectivity of all narrative. Their works disorder and decenter the narrative without losing track of the primary task of telling the stories. The fragmented narrative creates the possibility that the other, the past that has been repressed or unknown, is emerging into the story in spite of the power inherent in the typical narrative voice. This produces the impression that multiple voices can disrupt or interrupt the narrative flow, inserting their own voices and stories. Although this is clearly only, in a sense, an impression, and the writer is still selecting and ordering these disruptions, in the novels included in this study the narrative acts as a mimetic representation of the way in which other voices have inserted themselves into the writer's consciousness and contribute to an understanding of the structure of society.

These writers—Tan, Walker, Erdrich, and Cisneros—counter in their work what Fredric Jameson in *The Political Unconscious* calls master narratives: "ideological paradigms which contain within their plots a determined ending." Minority women writers, like other marginalized writers, reverse this process, producing works that openly examine the economic, political situations in which they are writing. Writing against established narrative patterns becomes a way of questioning the way in which these master narratives shape our ways of seeing. Remembering is the process of reclaiming and protecting a past often suppressed by the dominant culture, and in this sense, as re-visioning, it is essential in the process of gaining control over one's life. As Rich states, it is an act of survival.

Works Cited

Anzaldúa, Gloria, ed. *Making Face, Making Soul = Haciendo Caras: Creative and Critical Perspectives by Women of Color*. San Francisco: Aunt Lute Foundation Books, 1990.
Berger, John. *Ways of Seeing*. New York: Penguin, 1972.
Christian, Barbara. *Black Women Novelists: The Development of a Tradition, 1892–1976*. Westport, CT: Greenwood, 1980.
Cisneros, Sandra. *The House on Mango Street*. Houston: Arte Público, 1988.
DeShazer, Mary K. *Inspiring Women: Reimagining the Muse*. New York: Pergamon, 1986.
Erdrich, Louise. *Tracks*. New York: Holt, 1988.
Harlow, Barbara. *Resistance Literature*. New York: Methuen, 1987.
Horno-Delgado, Asuncion, Eliana Ortega, Nina M. Scott, and Nancy Saporta Sternbach, eds. *Breaking Boundaries: Latina Writings and Critical Readings*. Amherst: U of Massachusetts P, 1989.
Jameson, Fredric. "Modernism and Imperialism." *Nationalism, Colonialism and Literature*. Minneapolis: U of Minnesota P, 1990.
———. *The Political Unconscious: Narrative as a Socially Symbolic Act*. Ithaca: Cornell UP, 1981.
Knapp, Steven. "Collective Memory and the Actual Past." *Representations* 26 (Spring 1989): 123–49.
MacCabe, Colin. "Realism and the Cinema: Notes on Some Brechtian Theses." *A Critical and Cultural Theory Reader*. Ed. Anthony Easthope and Kate McGowan. Toronto: Toronto UP, 1992. 35–39.
Rich, Adrienne. "When We Dead Awaken: Writing as Revision." *On Lies, Secrets and Silence, Selected Prose, 1966–1978*. New York: Norton, 1979. 33–49.
Tan, Amy. *The Joy Luck Club*. New York: Putnam's, 1989.
Walker, Alice. *In Search of Our Mother's Gardens: Womanist Prose*. New York: Harcourt, 1983.
———. *The Temple of My Familiar*. New York: Harcourt, 1989.
Williams, Raymond. *Marxism and Literature*. New York: Oxford UP, 1977.

Rereading Photographs and Narratives in Ethnic Autobiography: Memory and Subjectivity in Mary Antin's *The Promised Land*

BETTY BERGLAND

Ethnic Autobiography, Photographic Representation, and Subjectivity

In 1969 Houghton Mifflin republished Mary Antin's autobiography, *The Promised Land*. The 1969 jacket cover stated, "the original text of 1912 is reprinted without change." The re-edition, however, failed to include the eighteen photographs present in the original, nor did it mention the omission. In 1985 Princeton University Press reissued *The Promised Land*, reproducing the 1969 volume. Again, the photographs were excluded.[1] While the photographs were omitted in both re-editions, the 1985 paperback edition avoided all visual images, excluding not only the original photographs, but also rendering an abstract design on the paperback cover. On the other hand, the 1969 edition incorporated a visual image on the front jacket cover—a cameo portrait of an unidentified young woman on what appears to be the bridge of a ship. Small and indistinct, without historical or geographic markers in the photograph, this portrait suggests ocean passage and a single individual—not specifically Mary Antin, but an image presumably to signify the immigrant. This image, representing no specific time or place, suggests the way in which the Antin narrative has been representative of all immigrants. What significance, then, might we attach to the publishers' omissions of the photographs found in the original text? Would the narrative story be altered if the visual images had been included in subsequent editions? Did readers of the 1912 text with the photos read a different Antin than readers of the 1969 or 1985 editions? More generally, how do visual images affect the messages readers take from an autobiography? And, perhaps most important, how has the absence of any scholarly discussion of the photographic texts in the Antin narrative affected our understanding not only of *The Promised Land* but of immigrants presumed to be represented there?

These two republications by major presses that ignore the photographic images integral to the original text while claiming to reproduce the original alter possible meanings late-twentieth-century readers might derive from reading the 1912 version. The publishers, however, have only reproduced the scholary tendency to overlook the visual. Significantly, scholars writing about ethnic literature and autobiography have omitted reference to or discussion of the photographic images in Mary Antin's *The Promised Land*. Specifically in the Antin case, but also generally in the discussion of the ethnic autobiographies, scholars have concentrated on the verbal texts, not the visual texts; consequently, meanings associated with visual images are lost in these readings. Why the presses omitted the photographs and why scholars have overlooked the omissions can be treated as separate questions, though they are also connected.[2] The larger issue, and that which connects these two questions, remains the neglect of photographs and visual images in discussions of literary studies generally and in ethnic literature and autobiography specifically. That neglect means scholars, as well as readers, overlook the way meaning is conveyed through visual codes. Along with the printed text, visual images contribute to comprehension and thus meanings associated with subjectivity, ethnicity, and memory. Therefore, the issue here is not simply scholarly oversight, nor is it simply a matter of Mary Antin's autobiography. In the past two decades we have witnessed a resurgence of interest in both ethnicity and autobiography, yet an examination of visual texts in autobiography has been ignored, despite the fact that photographs frequently appear in ethnic narratives. Because of the power of visual images to frame the boundaries of meaning, they serve a critical function for readers in the construction of the ethnic identity, personal and collective, and thus the construction of ethnic memory and meaning. This is especially so for the late twentieth century, when American culture is primarily a visual culture, and when reproductions of earlier manuscripts often include photographs, for example in the case of Hilda Satt Polacheck.[3]

The tradition of including photographs in autobiographies can be found throughout the twentieth century, particularly among immigrant groups, suggesting that Mary Antin's incorporation of photographs was

Photographs and Narratives in Ethnic Autobiography

well within an established tradition. Jacob Riis, a Danish immigrant perhaps most known for his documentation of the poor in *How the Other Half Lives,* released in 1890, published his autobiography, *The Making of an American,* in 1902 and included eighty-four photographs. Riis included a greater number and range of visual images than was traditional, including documentary photographs he had taken of poor urban immigrants, aerial photographs of tenement blocks, and immigrant portraits, in addition to self-portraits and sketches of Denmark. Certainly, Riis's own professional interest in photography can explain the quantity of photos in his autobiography; nevertheless, the inclusion of a significant number of photographs interspersed in the narrative represented an established tradition. Andrew Carnegie's narrative, *The Autobiography of Andrew Carnegie,* published in 1920 by Houghton Mifflin, eight years after Mary Antin's autobiography, included thirty-one photographs, twenty-six of which represented portraits of himself or male associates—in short, photographs signifying patriarchal power. Though Carnegie had amassed an enormous fortune during his lifetime, his origins as a poor Scottish immigrant were humble: the photographs presumably provided critical evidence of proximity to privilege and power. Also, two years after Carnegie's publication, Scribner's published *The Americanization of Edward Bok,* an autobiography of the Dutch immigrant and editor of the *Ladies Home Journal.*[4] Though this narrative incorporated fewer photographs than Carnegie's, it included what seems to represent a standard iconography of the genre: the man (on the frontispiece), the child, the father, the birthplace in Holland, the mother, the present home, Bok in his office, and Bok at home—in his garden. Noteworthy here are the photographs of the female, signified by the images of the mother and the grandmother, often absent in autobiographical representations. Presumably, a man editing a woman's magazine had to demonstrate relationships with and proximity to the female.

On the other hand, a tradition of excluding photographs in autobiographical writing also existed—notably among the elite. Henry Adams's *The Education of Henry Adams,* for example, does not include photographs.[5] One can reasonably argue that at the turn of the century the New England patriarch required no photographic documentation to demonstrate his place in the universe, as Carnegie presumably may have felt he needed, since he included not only numerous portraits of himself juxtaposed with Anglo-American patriarchal power, but also an image of palatial environs at Skibo Castle in Scotland, where he retired. Significantly, though exceptions exist, autobiographies in which photographs

47

emerge in the early twentieth century tend to be autobiographies of immigrants or ethnics, not those whose positions in the American culture are secure. In other words, the elite figures like Adams required no affirmation of existence; the immigrant and the ethnic, however, may have required photographic evidence of existence in America.

How does the appearance of these visual images then affect the reader? How is our perception of ethnic subjectivity affected? These questions become important as we look at the renewed interest in autobiography in the last twenty-five years. The resurgence of interest in ethnicity in the last two decades has emerged alongside a parallel interest in autobiography by scholars of literature, history, folklore, women's studies, and ethnic studies. Thus, many scholarly studies have focused on the speaking "I" of autobiography, while publishers have reissued out-of-print narratives (as in the case of Mary Antin's *The Promised Land*) or published original manuscripts heretofore considered uninteresting (Hilda Satt Polacheck's *I Came a Stranger: The Story of a Hull-House Girl*), at the same time as memoirs and autobiographies, published by small, independent, as well as major national presses, are emerging with photographs. Another pattern in publishing ethnic autobiographies, even if no photographs are used within the text, is to place a portrait of the autobiographer on the cover, presumably to demonstrate or to authenticate the ethnicity of the autobiographer: Richard Rodriguez's *Hunger of Memory: The Education of Richard Rodriguez* and Anne Moody's *Growing Up in Mississippi* are examples of this.[6] Given the long tradition of incorporating photographs in autobiographies, the virtual absence of scholarly studies on these images is remarkable.[7]

How do we explain this neglect? Scholarly emphasis on the printed word and the logocentrism of Western culture certainly reside at the core of this neglect. Despite the fact that photography and the visual media generally have become primary instruments of knowledge about the world for most people in Western cultures, the knowledge industries—schools, universities, libraries, publishers, archival repositories, and so forth—emphasize the printed word. Further, the assumption that the photograph is transparent, reflecting a reality out there, contributes to this neglect. Given that assumption, photographs are often perceived as simply illustrating knowledge conceptualized through words. On the other hand, scholars have not wholly ignored the photograph in Western culture; however, studies emphasizing photography exist primarily in two arenas—photography as social documentation and photography

Photographs and Narratives in Ethnic Autobiography

as art. These traditions have served as the two poles of scholars' interest in photography in the United States.[8]

One consequence of this polarized conceptualization of photography is that scholars outside the disciplines of art history and journalism have tended to ignore the ways in which visual codes both construct and reinforce cultural narratives encoded in verbal languages. As a result, Allan Sekula argues in his essay, "On the Invention of Photographic Meaning," that we have created a series of either/or propositions concerning photography: the photographer is either a seer or a witness; photography is viewed either as expression or as reportage; photography is theorized either as representing imagination (and inner truth) or as the empirical truth; photographs are evaluated either for their affective value or for their informative value; and, finally, photographic signification remains either metaphoric or metonymic.[9] In other words, photography is linked to art *or* life, to history *or* fiction, to the real *or* the imaginary. This kind of polarized thinking represents the larger dualisms embedded in Western culture, keeping us from seeing how cultural narratives and ideologies reside in all cultural productions and function in the culture to secure certain social relationships. Further, these views inhibit scholars from examining the way photographs and visual images contribute to meanings associated with being human. More precisely, and significantly, we have failed to consider how visual representations shape meanings for readers, both generally and in the contexts of verbal narratives, and therefore how these images shape meanings surrounding issues of identity and memory for Americans and ethnics.

Importantly, photographs have also been neglected generally in studies of ethnicity. The development of photography in the nineteenth century coincides with mass immigration to the New World from Europe and Asia. Since by the early 1840s replacement of the daguerreotype with the positive-negative process in photographic development made it possible to copy an infinite number of prints from one negative, the mechanical reproductions became inexpensive and widely accessible just at the time when millions of immigrants from Europe and Asia were arriving on these shores.[10] Thus, immigrants as well as American tribal peoples, migrating Blacks, and slaves in the antebellum era could record their lives. Further, because photographs might provide an index of Americanization, they often became significant in documenting not only geographic but also economic and social mobility.[11] At the same time, photographs could serve as evidence challenging prevailing views;

for example, the photograph of five generations of a slave family frequently duplicated and found on the cover of Herbert G. Gutman's *The Black Family in Slavery and Freedom, 1750–1925* helps critique the assertion that the institution of slavery destroyed black families.[12] This scholarly neglect needs to be reversed, since those without the memory of experience do turn to photographs for images of the past. How we read those images affects our memory and understanding of the past.

In this context, then, we require theories and strategies of reading photographs, and we must resist prevailing views that photographs are "unmediated copies of the real world." If we assume that they transparently and instrumentally point us to an objective world, then we fail to see how photographic images exist within a complex system of cultural signification. Rather, we require some theoretical framework if we are to "read" these images as part of the text, as contributing the subjectivity of the autobiographer. We might think of photography as another language system or discourse, producing cultural codes or messages. Like other languages, photographic images are "ideologically saturated," to use Mikhail Bakhtin's expression, with other people's meanings.[13] What this means is that photographic images, like words, are embedded with cultural meanings, no more transparent than words are transparent. Thus, in examining cultural discourses, including photographic discourses, we need to consider the unstated messages and meanings conveyed by the image, often presented as natural or given, though sometimes only implied. The purpose of such discourse analysis, suggests Diane Macdonell in *Theories of Discourse,* is "to unmask discourses and knowledges which, from various institutions, and in the face of all the inequality that divides our society . . . claim to speak on behalf of everyone, saying in effect: 'we are all the same; we all speak the same language and share the same knowledge and have always done so.' "[14] If we consider photographs, like words, as parts of culturally encoded systems of meanings, we can read in the photographs in ethnic autobiographies elements of the meanings associated with ethnic and American subjectivities.[15]

Photographs commonly seen to represent immigrants might serve to illustrate the historically and culturally embedded meanings that must be decoded. Photographs of immigrants, especially those made by Lewis Hine at the turn of the century, frequently serve to signify immigrant status. For Hine, Ellis Island provided a common setting for representing immigrants and non-American ethnics. Essentially, they were represented in transition from one world to another: they were photographed

Photographs and Narratives in Ethnic Autobiography

arriving in boats, waiting on ships, and along the shore or in the halls; these images are frequently reproduced in the culture to represent the mass of immigrants who arrived on these shores around the turn of the century.[16] Generally these photographs frame immigrants outside of any communal or historical context. This is particularly evident in what I will call the passage or transition photographs, which capture immigrants in steerage, on a gangplank, approaching Ellis Island, or in the receiving hall. Such photographs, because they might represent any number of ethnic groups, frequently serve as representatives of the aliens entering America. Lewis Hine's 1905 photograph "Immigrants Going down the Gangplank" and Alfred Stieglitz's 1907 "The Steerage" serve as examples of this genre of photographs. Representing the two dominant modes of photography in this country—photojournalism or social document, and the photograph as art—by two well-known photographers, these images have come to signify the non-American.[17] Similarities exist: both of these images are taken aboard transatlantic ships and reveal passengers disembarking or awaiting that moment. While Stieglitz's image views the new arrivals from a perspective apart, above, and separate, and in Hine's image the photographer and the photographed remain on the same plane and much less separate (the distinction in the angle of vision is one of Sekula's central points in discussing these images), both photographs mark the moment of passage, representing the immigrant in transition, outside of any particular time, place, history, or community. The images, however, serve as significant cultural representations of the immigrant and so reinforce prevailing ideologies that objectify those perceived as the cultural Other.

The passage photographs frequently appear to signify the immigrant or alien. Most recently, the paperback publication of John Bodnar's *The Transplanted: A History of Immigrants in Urban America* includes a passage photo on the cover of the volume. A woman, presumably a mother, stands with three children ranging in age from about two to ten years on an undefined boardwalk, surrounded by bundles, satchels, and suitcases. Significantly, they are white, presumably from Europe: they have come to stand for all immigrants.[18] Because these images signify the universalized immigrants, they can be appropriated for a variety of uses, signifying huddled masses seeking entry to the promised land, erasing culturally specific worlds from which the immigrants came, and leveling all difference to what Allan Sekula terms an "abstract humanity." In the conclusion to his essay "On the Invention of Photographic Meaning," he writes: "The celebration of abstract humanity becomes, in any given political situation, the celebration of the dignity of the passive victim. This is the final outcome of the appropriation of the photographic image for liberal political ends; the oppressed are granted a bogus Subjecthood when such status can be secured only from within, on their own terms" (109). In this context, it is striking that the jacket cover of the 1969 edition of *The Promised Land* reproduces a passage image, de-historicizing and de-contextualizing Antin's narrative. That image evokes an immigrant from somewhere, going somewhere: abstract humanity is represented, not a subjectivity secured from within. Because that image serves to represent Antin's narrative visually, and the narrative presumably represents millions of immigrants, this image comes to represent abstract humanity coming to America. What is particularly noteworthy is that narrator Antin did not represent that passage of the journey with photographs: the chapter tracing the transatlantic journey, entitled "The Exodus," goes unrepresented by visual images. Because so many of these images were available at the time of publication in 1912, certainly Antin (and her editors) could have included a passage photograph to illustrate the ocean journey—but passage images of abstract humanity remain absent in *The Promised Land*.

In this way, photographs in *The Promised Land* might imply a "Subjecthood from within," as Sekula suggests, and so offer a meaningful case study for examining the images in ethnic autobiography. Because contemporary American and Western culture has become dominated by the visual message, ethnic scholars must begin to consider the visual images and meanings that accompany ethnic narratives and contribute to the meanings readers associate with those images. Recent developments in culture studies, American studies, media studies, and feminist film theory, as well as folklore and the so-called new social histories, have led scholars to decode visual messages in new and provocative studies emphasizing how photographic images function in the culture.[19] These studies generally focus on arenas where the visual abounds—in media studies, in film studies, in photojournalism. From these approaches, however, we can learn strategies for considering the visual in the context of verbal narratives. Such an approach seems fruitful in examining the autobiographies of ethnic groups. The kinds of visual images selected by a writer, the order in which these appear, and the relationships established between the visual images and the written text all affect the way the reader reads, and so our memory of ethnic subjects and communities is affected. How an autobiographical subject is perceived—young, old, alone, aligned in a community, where he or she is situated in time and space, whether that changes, how and why—are perceptions influenced by the inclusion, sequence, and subject matter of the photographs. For this reason, a study of photographic representation is a critical dimension of understanding the construction of ethnic subjectivity and memory.

Photographs offer a rich cultural source for examining cultural narratives and ideologies and thus memories surrounding ethnicity. If we view photographs as part of a system of signification, shaped culturally and historically, as cultural representations that we can decode, we can explore the kind of subjects posited in photographic images and so develop a more complex and meaningful understanding of ethnic memory and subjectivity. Allan Sekula uses the expression "photographic discourse," which he defines as "a system within which the culture harnesses photographs to various representational tasks" (87). This means that photographs carry messages, that there is no universalized meaning in a photograph, but that they acquire meaning within the contexts in which they appear. What he calls for is a "historically grounded sociology of the image, both in the valorized realm of high art and in the culture at large" (87). What I propose in this essay is that we consider the photograph within ethnic autobiography as an integral part of the meaning of the narrative and the subjectivities posited. As we examine meanings surrounding photographic representation in ethnic autobiographies, we might discover not only the way visual images construct certain kinds of subjectivities and thus convey ideologically loaded meanings, but also ways to critique these, to rethink, and re-remember, ethnic identities and multicultural histories.

Mary Antin's The Promised Land

Immigrants from the Pale of Settlement in Eastern Europe in the late nineteenth century, the Antins arrived in the United States at the peak of mass immigration but also during the peak of the Americanization movement, a movement intended to make the burgeoning foreign populations into good American citizens. In this context, the narrator of *The Promised Land* identifies with America and defines her subjectivity primarily in relation to American discourses.[20] Albert E. Stone writes in *The American Autobiography* that the narrative "dramatizes the historical experience of Americanization in frankly mythic terms."[21] Throughout much of the twentieth century, the Antin narrative has been reproduced in school anthologies, and scholars have focused on her narrative as prototypical of the huddled masses, the non-American becoming American. Thus, Mary Dearborn can write in *Pocahantas's Daughters: Gender and Ethnicity in American Culture* that the autobiography has become "an immigrant classic."[22] While it is read as an immigrant autobiography, it is also read as a Jewish autobiography, an ethnic autobiography, and an American autobiography.[23] Because of the cultural signification surrounding the narrative, a discussion of this text and its photographs evokes the "photographic discourse" surrounding American and ethnic (as well as gendered) identities.

Mary Antin was born Mashke Antin in 1881 in Polotzk, Russia, to Jewish parents forced by oppressive czarist policies to live within the Pale of Settlement. In 1891 Israel Antin emigrated to Boston and after three years sent for his wife and children, including Mashke/Mary, who was then about fourteen. The family settled in Boston, moving several times within the environs as Israel Antin pursued various businesses. While the family lived within modest means, Mary Antin excelled in her schooling and was encouraged to attend the Boston Latin Grammar School. Upon completion of her schooling, Antin attended the Teacher's College at Columbia University and Barnard College, though she did not complete a degree. In 1899 her first book, *From Polotzk to Boston,* was published. She married in 1901 and bore one daughter, Josephine Esther. *The Promised Land,* written when Antin was "nearly thirty," was published in 1912. Two years later, her third and last book was published, *They Who Knock at Our Gates,* in opposition to the xenophobic developments during the first two decades of the century, an appeal to keep the gates open to immigrants. By the end of the decade, Antin and her German-American husband separated (he later departed for China, where he lived out his life), and she suffered from what was diagnosed as neurasthenia, a common diagnosis for women. After the publication of her three books, she wrote only a few articles, and little is known of her life after 1900. She died in 1949 and probably remains best known for *The Promised Land.*[24]

The narrative text of *The Promised Land* consists of twenty chapters, roughly divided between the Old and New Worlds. The first seven chapters focus on life in the Pale, particularly Polotzk, Russia; a transitional chapter, "The Exodus," documents the journey to America; and the remaining twelve chapters (nine to twenty) focus on life in America, ending with autobiographical Antin's school-leaving and transformation

Photographs and Narratives in Ethnic Autobiography

into an American citizen. The Old World chapters emphasize the collective experiences of Jews in the Pale of Settlement, documenting economic hardship and religious persecutions, as well as the daily life of the Jewish community in Polotzk. The Antin family serves as a focal point for that narrative development and its emphasis on communal experience. The New World chapters, however, emphasize the individualized experience of Antin, distinct from father, mother, and siblings—the "I" of autobiographical Antin. Although the narrator states in the introduction that "its chief interest lies in the fact that it is illustrative of scores of unwritten lives" (xiii), the autobiographical "I" primarily stands alone—apart from siblings and family, community and peers in the majority of the New World chapters. The individualized "I" is primarily situated in the schools—both temporally and spatially—and the school success of the autobiographical "I" becomes a metaphor for the potential success of all immigrants. Therefore, the school chapters emphasize the transformation into an American citizen, while the last three chapters address a second transformation—the discovery of Nature and the alteration that brings. The narrative autobiography closes spatially and metaphorically linking these two transformative experiences of Americanization in school and nature: autobiographical Antin is left on the steps of the Boston Public Library after a natural history outing with a specimen jar of the day's collection in hand. (Significantly, the last photographic image is a nature scene, discussed below.) The discourses on Americanization, signified by the library, and the discourses on nature, signified by the specimen jar, merge as young Antin contemplates the meaning of being an American. Temporally, the moment signifying her ontological transformation to American occurs in adolescence. The narrator writes that everything that happened after this moment is a repetition of what has gone before—in other words the significant change is completed, yet the autobiographical "I" has not yet achieved adulthood. Thus, for readers who imagine the autobiography represents the essential self, Mary Antin becomes frozen as an adolescent.

Like many autobiographies, *The Promised Land* includes extensive photographic representations in the original, in this case the 1912, publication. Like other narratives, the images contradict as well as reinforce the narrative texts. The photographic representations in *The Promised Land* provoke the reader in a variety of ways, especially because of the tensions between words and images within the texts and because of the opposition between the two verbal and visual narratives. *The Promised Land* includes eighteen photographs. Nine focus on her life in Polotzk, in the

Pale; nine represent her life in Boston. Generally, each chapter is illustrated by a photograph: five chapters lack photographic representation; two chapters contain two images each. Selected, ordered in a sequential pattern, they suggest a progressive meaning in the narrative, a meaning presumably to complement the narrative text. Who did the selecting and sequencing is unclear; however, we must assume that Antin and the editor collaborated: her presence is suggested in the personal nature of many of the photographs.[25] The photographs generally correspond to central concepts of each chapter (see table 1).

I will discuss these photographs in the order in which they appear, emphasizing in my analysis the cultural codes in the visual cues, the subjectivity evoked, and relationships (complementary and contradictory) to the narrative texts. Both the verbal and the visual narratives move chronologically and geographically from the Old World of Antin's childhood to the New World of her adolescence—from immigrant to American. The narrative and photographic texts together possess, thus, a degree of symmetry: both use the metaphor of the Old and New World, and they are equally divided between them. Tensions also exist between the subject in the narrative and visual texts: if the verbal narrative affirms Antin's transformation to American citizen, the visual text challenges those affirmations by evoking the emptiness of the American spaces in the promised land; these are not only spaces that the autobiographical subject does not occupy, but also spaces in which the reader would have difficulty locating the autobiographical Antin. Therefore, examining the photographs in the autobiography might lead to a radically altered reading of the narrative, a counterreading that implies a critique of the very discourse she presumably celebrated.

The first photograph, found opposite the title page, is labeled "Mashke and Fetchke," (fig. 1) and refers to Mary (Mashke) and her older sister (Frieda). Aged about four and six in the photograph, the girls are dressed similarly in long-sleeved, ruffled dresses, bloomers, boots, and long dark stockings, and they stand in a full-length pose. The inclusion of Mashke and Fetchke opposite the title page seems significant: the photograph demonstrates Antin's attachment to her sister (whose arm the young Mashke holds in the photo), but the image also evokes the close alliance narrator Antin felt toward her sister in the autobiography—Frieda went to work in the New World, enabling the younger Mary to continue her schooling. The childhood image also evokes beginnings, reflecting the linearity of the narrative. Interestingly enough, although the autobiographical "I" suggests the singularity of a historical individual, reflected

Table 1
Photographic Representation in Mary Antin's *The Promised Land* (1912)

Chapter and Title	Corresponding Photo and Caption
[Old World Photographs]	
Frontispiece	Mashke and Fetchke
1. Within the Pale	The Grave Digger of Polotzk
2. Children of the Law	Heder (Hebrew School) for Boys in Polotzk
3. Both Their Houses	The Wood Market, Polotzk
4. Daily Bread	My Father's Portrait
5. I Remember	Grandfather's House, Where I Was Born
	The Meat Market, Polotzk
6. The Tree of Knowledge	Sabbath Loaves for Sale (Bread Market, Polotzk)
7. The Boundaries Stretch	Winter Scene on the Dvina
8. The Exodus	————
[New World Photographs]	
9. The Promised Land	Union Place (Boston) Where My New Home Waited for Me
10. Initiation	————
11. "My Country"	Twoscore of My Fellow Citizens—Public School, Chelsea
12. Miracles	————
13. A Child's Paradise	————
14. Manna	Wheeler Street, in the Lower South End of Boston
15. Tarnished Laurels	————
16. Dover Street	a) Harrison Avenue in the Heart of the South End Ghetto
	b) I Liked to Stand and Look Down on the Dim Tangle of Railroad Tracks Below
17. The Landlady	————
18. The Burning Bush	The Natural History Club Had Frequent Field Excursions
19. A Kingdom in the Slums	a) Bates Hall, Where I Spent My Longest Hours in th Library
	b) The Famous Study, That Was Fit to Have Been Preserved as a Shrine
20. The Heritage	The Tide Had Rushed In, Stealing Away Our Seaweed Cushions

Figure 1. Mashke and Fetchke

also in the New World segment of the narrative, no single portrait of historical Antin is found among the images.

The first photograph in the narrative text representing the Old World, "The Grave Digger of Polotzk," signifies death. Because of his primary position in the text and because of the close, three-quarter-frontal portrait of the grave digger, prominence is given to death in the Old World representation in the autobiography. The narrative does not make specific reference to the grave digger; however, Antin's description of life within the Pale resonates with death. The grave digger signifies that mortality, but the details—the grave digger's cap turned sideways, the furrowed brow, hands buried in the folds of clothing, the deep-set eyes, the sympathetic resignation in his visage, the buildings in the background,

Photographs and Narratives in Ethnic Autobiography

and its reproduction in Antin's autobiography—prevent a universalized reading of a memento mori. These details specifying time and place ground mortality with historically and culturally specific meanings linked to life in the Pale. Roland Barthes argues that while visual imagery communicates denotatively and connotatively, the "link between signifier and signified remains historical."[26] Here, with the prominence of the grave digger and the use of that image to represent this chapter, autobiographical Antin underscores the brutality, oppression, and suffering of the Jews living in the nineteenth-century Pale of Settlement.

If the grave digger connotes the pervasiveness of death, patriarchy is connoted in the photograph illustrating the second chapter, "Children of the Law," captioned "Heder (Hebrew School) for Boys in Polotzk" (fig. 2). In this photograph, school boys are seated on benches around a table, heads bowed over their books, while the three schoolmasters stand at both ends of the room and oversee the boys' studies. The narrator emphasizes the religious community as the focus of resistance to the oppression in the Pale, stating that the religious integrity became "a fortress

Figure 2. Heder (Hebrew School) for Boys in Polotzk

erected by the prisoners of the Pale, in defiance of their jailers; a stronghold built of the ruins of their pillaged homes, cemented with the blood of their murdered children" (29). The notion of religious knowledge as the focus of resistance is also contained in the photograph. Yet the patriarchal dimension of that knowledge and resistance becomes powerfully evident in that visual image. Clearly, the children of the law are male children: male domination of that study, evident in the photograph, is reinforced in the narrative text. Yet Antin's own narrative contradicts the prevailing evidence of the photograph: Antin's father, encountering liberal ideas outside the Pale, resigned to live as far as possible "the life of a modern man" (76). This meant his daughters studied Yiddish, Russian, and German, subjects well beyond the usual schooling for Jewish girls; later, economic circumstances, not ideological ones, halt their study. Here the photograph supports the prevailing view of an androcentric educational system, while the narrative text challenges that view.

The following chapter, "Both Their Houses," focuses on Antin's parents—Esther Weltman (Antin) and Israel Antin. The Weltman family is engaged in various business enterprises and represents property and economic status, while Israel Antin, who studied for the rabbinate, represents scholarship and religion. Together, these two families in both their houses represent communal values. Thus, the photograph accompanying this chapter, "The Wood Market, Polotzk" (fig. 3), evokes a communal sensibility. The image signifies a communal effort in the collection and distribution of wood, important for both food and warmth. In short, the question of survival was a communal one. This sense is conveyed by the fact that three generations are represented: the intergenerational labor signifies a communal undertaking. This image becomes particularly striking when contrasted with Antin's New World photographs, where there is a virtual absence of intergenerational links. Also significant is the implied relationship between the photographer and those photographed: at the wood market, the subjects in the photograph gaze at the photographer; in the New World photographs such a direct gaze is absent. Communal values are evoked in the image of the wood market; however, the image also evokes the gendered division of labor—here only men appear at the wood market.

If the male dominates in the image of the wood market and the heder, suggesting a patriarchal order, this is made explicit in the next two photographs. The next chapter, entitled "Daily Bread," contains a single image, "My Father's Portrait" (fig. 4). Absent is an image of the mother or the maternal family, despite the fact that the narrator tells us the

Photographs and Narratives in Ethnic Autobiography

Figure 3. The Wood Market, Polotzk

mother's family possessed wealth, while the father possessed learning, and that economic survival was contingent on both parents. Thus, Antin employs only the image of the father to represent daily bread, meaning economic survival, despite the fact that the mother and the mother's family not only contributed to that survival, but at periods were vital to survival. Furthermore, the next photograph, "Grandfather's House, Where I Was Born" (not illustrated), again emphasizes patriarchy as one of two images in the chapter "I Remember," addressing childhood memories. This house of her birth does not signify *grandparents*, but the *grandfather*. Though the grandfather died when Antin was four, and thus memory of him would have been minimal, the house is possessed by *him*. The home, within Judaic tradition, signified a sacred space where women assumed some degree of power; however, ownership of that space is allocated to men, and ownership implies power. Thus, if a woman would give meaning discursively to her presence in a patriarchal discourse, she must identify with male ownership, which confers legitimacy and power. How can we explain this omission of the mother's portrait and the maternal ancestors and the female presence in the birthplace?

61

Figure 4. My Father's Portrait

Roland Barthes argues that those excluded from power are forced "to steal a language—as men used to steal a loaf of bread" (167). What this means is that if Antin, the narrator, wished to represent a legitimate "I" to the reader, one the culture sanctioned, she must use—or steal— discourse considered legitimate, meaning a patriarchal discourse. For the Antin narrator to give legitimacy to her subjectivity, to write herself into personhood in Western patriarchal culture, she must align herself with the male discourse, here signified by the father's portrait and the absence of the mother. She quite literally had to steal, because the discourse of the self was not hers. Here we must think not only of the image of the heder, in which religious knowledge is associated with the patriarchs,

Photographs and Narratives in Ethnic Autobiography

but we must think of the tradition of the autobiography, which Sidonie Smith argues has remained androcentric over five hundred years.[27] Androcentric here means not simply focused on the male, but signifying the detached and atomized individual whose humanity is linked to maleness. In other words, in order to be intelligible within the autobiographical narrative, narrator Antin is forced to speak in the familiar discourse of autobiography—which is to say in codes familiar to a patriarchal worldview. This does not mean she consciously "chose" such a strategy.

This chapter of reminiscences also includes the image "The Meat Market, Polotzk." Unlike the image of the wood market, the meat-market image represents both males and females and several generations. While the clothing and display racks denote humble surroundings, the image is communal, an evocation reflected also in the narrative text of childhood reminiscences. The communal sensibility of the meat market evokes a sense of egalitarianism, while the grandfather's house, along with the father's portrait from the preceding chapter, visually preside over these childhood memories and suggest patriarchy.

"Sabbath Loaves for Sale (Bread Market, Polotzk)" (fig. 5) illustrates the chapter "The Tree of Knowledge." With this image in the narrative on epistemology, knowledge is associated with the sacred as well as with dailiness, with the spiritual world of the Sabbath and the economic and physical world of food. The image becomes quite complex, however, in the context of Western narratives about religion. When I spoke with Loren Hoekzema, the editor of the Princeton volume, regarding the absence of the photographs, he mentioned that he had wished to include on the cover of the volume an image representing Jewish life in late-nineteenth-century Eastern Europe, and he had hoped to find a synagogue. He found none. And Antin's photographs include no synagogues. Does this lack mean a lack of synagogues in Polotzk? The linked forces of official anti-Semitic policies and Christian domination within czarist Russia suggest that is a reasonable reading. Nevertheless, that a building represents the most significant site of the religious may be a cultural phenomenon. Here, the narrative text that addresses questions of religion, knowledge, and doubt situates the religious not within an institution, but within certain practices. In this chapter, the narrator describes her growing religious doubt and recalls defying certain religious practices to test the consequences—for example, she carries a handkerchief beyond the boundaries of the house on the Sabbath. Nothing happens. She also narrates in this chapter that in order to save oil, her father extinguished

Figure 5. Sabbath Loaves for Sale (Bread Market, Polotzk)

the Sabbath candle before the end of the Sabbath—forbidden—but heavenly retribution did not come. The narrator's religious sensibilities, thus, become more complex: readers are led to believe that Antin no longer associates the religious simply with rules. Noteworthy also, the religious practices narrated remain linked to the home, not in a place apart. The photograph, then, seems to signify a rich and complex notion of the sacred—represented not as a place apart, but a place intimately linked to livelihood, to daily life, to food, to the complexity of lived religious knowledge. In the absence of a house of worship the unsaid of the photograph also communicates the religious persecution of the Jews in Polotzk. Nevertheless, the representation of the religious in that visual image reinforces the assertion of the narrative text that for Jews in Eastern Europe, faith meant not only suffering but also shared knowledges and practices that gave comfort in the intimate spaces of the home and the communal market.

The last photograph of the Old World, "Winter Scene on the Dvina" (fig. 6), centers on women and represents the chapter "The Boundaries

Photographs and Narratives in Ethnic Autobiography

Figure 6. Winter Scene on the Dvina

Stretch." In this chapter Antin recounts the privations, personal and collective, primarily economic, that led to the eventual emigration of the Antins. The photograph of women washing clothes in the middle of winter, made possible by a hole cut in the ice, demonstrates the harshness of that struggle, yet the photograph also conveys a collective struggle. The collectivity evoked by the women's labor suggests that the difficulty of the harsh conditions may have been made endurable by the shared struggle. And we see adult women engaged in meaningful activities, occupying positions in society as adults. In addition, the women seem aware of the photographer—they are linked, we might assume, by a shared history. Juxtaposing this last representation of the Old World with the first one of the grave digger, we might consider that the first connotes death and the last, a cleansing; death is represented by a solitary grave digger, the regeneration by a collective labor.

Though the photographs representing the Old World in Antin's narrative do not include her, except as she appears in the foreground of the whole narrative in the image with her sister opposite the title page, the reader might imagine Mary Antin taking a position in this adult world, despite the harshness of the conditions. This is a communal world, conveyed both in the narrative and in the photographic texts. Of the eight photographs signifying the Old World that are interspersed in the narrative, five represent communal scenes (the heder, the wood market, the meat market, the sabbath loaves, and the scene on the Dvina). While the single portraits of the father and the grave digger signify patriarchy and death, the single image that is unpeopled, her grandfather's house, represents, contradictorily, not only the grandfather, and thus patriarchy, but a family and generational links to the past. Thus, though they signify oppressive forces from outside the community, which eventually led to emigration, as well as patriarchal forces within the community—the law, the father, and daily life—the Old World photographs nevertheless portray a historical and contextualized world signifying a communal life. In that world the Antins and their neighbors are not represented only as objects of czarist anti-Semitic policy or as bogus subjects, but they are subjects on their own terms in a complex sensuous and seasonal world, a communal world of labor and struggle as well as celebration. These photographs representing the Old World from which the Antins emigrated contrast significantly with prevailing images of the immigrant and the ethnic generally reproduced in the culture.

As noted before, no photographs represent Antin's passage from Polotzk to Boston, and the narrative of this passage is also brief; however, that journey is detailed in her first published volume, *From Polotzk to Boston*. Certainly it is significant that no passage photos represent the immigrant or immigration itself.

Antin begins her visual representation of the New World in the chapter entitled "The Promised Land," with the photograph captioned "Union Place (Boston) Where My New Home Waited for Me" (fig. 7). In Union Place, the narrator writes, she saw not "a short box of an alley," but rather "two imposing rows of brick buildings, loftier than any dwelling I had ever lived in. Brick was even on the ground for me to tread on, instead of common earth or boards" (183–84). However, this image of Antin's New World home remains ambiguous, despite the imaginary transformations of this space in Antin's narrative text. Home as an empty space signifies promise; yet the empty space here evokes an alley, that which the narrator insists it is not. Yet, in a culture where dwellings signify the character of the inhabitants, this image of home as emptiness haunts the viewer—especially because Antin includes no other visual representation of a home in which she resided in the promised land.

Photographs and Narratives in Ethnic Autobiography

Figure 7. Union Place (Boston) Where My New Home Waited for Me

While narrator Antin affirms her transformation into an American throughout the autobiography, the absence of photographic representation of a home in America is striking. Later, writing about Dover Street, identified as a slum, the narrator affirms: "Dover Street was never really my residence—at least not the whole of it. It happened to be the nook where my bed was made, but I inhabited the city of Boston" (340). Thus, the city itself becomes the narrator's home, though within that cityscape, no site or space signifies actual or possible residence. Not finding an adequate material home in the promised land, the narrator resides in an imaginary one.

Perhaps because the New World homes were uninhabitable, autobiographical Antin takes up residence for much of the narrative in the schools. "Twoscore of My Fellow Citizens—Public School, Chelsea" (fig. 8), illustrating the chapter "My Country," signifies the school as a vital space in the New World Americanization process. For millions of immigrants at the turn of the century, the school was the primary vehicle of Americanization: the narrator wrote that the public school served foreigners best when it made good Americans, and she was glad "to tell how the miracle was wrought in one case" (222). Consequently, much of the narrative, including the first chapters on the New World, focuses on the school. For autobiographical Antin, this miracle of transformation to American is signified in her imagined link with George Washington. As fellow citizens of America they were linked, an alliance that ennobled her, and because of his greatness, Antin writes, "I could not pronounce the name of George Washington without a pause. . ." (223). The shared citizenship with Washington discussed in the narrative text, coupled with the photograph of the school children, suggests a democratic and egalitarian vision. Nevertheless, the image helps expose the contradictions in the American citizenship the author celebrates. In her

Figure 8. Twoscore of My Fellow Citizens—Public School, Chelsea

Photographs and Narratives in Ethnic Autobiography

position as a woman, she was denied the rights of citizenship, namely the franchise, at the writing of the autobiography in 1912. Further, although the Chelsea school picture signifies a collectivity—and the only one in the New World—it represents childhood and a single generation. In other words, this communal vision of young Americans never translates into an image of an adult community: the reader gets no sense of what it means to Antin to be American, or how this noble alliance with Washington translates into an adult life. Significantly, the image of American citizenry linked to "My Country" represents school children. Democracy for these American "citizens" never moves beyond the schoolroom.

The public spaces represented in the New World convey a striking opposition to the Old World public images and further evoke the contradictions of the promised land. This is especially evident in the next two photographs, which represent chapters 14 and 16. (Chapters 12, 13, and 15 contain no photographic representation.) "Wheeler Street, in the Lower South End of Boston" illustrates the chapter called "Manna" and signifies the crowded conditions and economic struggles of poor urban enclaves such as the one where the Antins lived. The narrator writes, "On Wheeler Street there were no real homes, . . . there was no common life in any form that means life" (272). That lack, and the emptiness implied, is evoked in the photograph of a virtually empty street, except for the young boy and an onlooker gazing out from a passageway. The image also speaks by what is not shown: though Antin identifies streets and neighborhoods where she lived, no structure represents her dwelling, her home in the New World, as her grandfather's house did in the Old World. Dover Street (where the Antins lived) intersected at "Harrison Avenue in the Heart of the South End Ghetto" (not illustrated). Like Wheeler Street, this image connotes residence, but both evoke depersonalized public space and contrast with the personalized and communal representations of Polotzk; whereas the Old World markets showed an intergenerational and collective labor, the New World market portrays individuals disconnected from each other as well as from the photographer, emphasizing isolation and alienation.

The chapter "Dover Street" contains a second image, called "I Liked to Stand and Look Down on the Dim Tangle of Railroad Tracks Below" (fig. 9), which invites the viewer to take a perspective similar to that of the Antin narrator gazing from the South Boston Bridge, a place referred to as "a favorite resort," connoting, ironically, both pleasure and escape. The narrator's desire for a sense of place in the promised land, and a

Figure 9. I Liked to Stand and Look Down on the Dim Tangle of Railroad Tracks Below

means of getting there, is evoked in the reference to the search for her own "proper track" (298). This longing expressed in the narrative text contrasts radically with the surrealism in the photograph of these railroad tracks. The dimness of night, the clouded sky, and the smoking chimneys of the train engines create a blurred and darkened image, only partially lit by illumination in the railroad yard. That faint light exposes the tangle of tracks and a few trains, and the angle of vision from a bridge above the yard offers a broad view conveying an emotional isolation and a loneliness that has a chilling effect. That this image comes to represent Antin's longing, a "resort," is certainly striking. Juxtaposing the verbally articulated longing with the visually evoked, blurred, and complex vision of the urban landscape in the New World makes explicit the contradictions between the subjectivities evoked in the narrative text and in the photographic text.

In the context of these contradictory messages in the narrative and visual texts, we might also situate what the narrator labels her second transformation—the discovery of Nature. This the narrator examines in

Photographs and Narratives in Ethnic Autobiography

the chapter entitled "The Burning Bush," with obvious allusions to the transformation of Moses in the divine presence. Through the settlement house Antin frequented, she encountered "The Natural History Club Had Frequent Field Excursions" (not illustrated). Here the narrator explains her burgeoning interest in Nature—with all the mystification and reverence signified by the capital N. In this image, five people (presumably five members of the Hale House Natural History Club on an outing) explore a stream and collect specimens, to describe, classify, organize—in short, capture—Nature. So preoccupied with nature, the individuals remain isolated in their collecting, oblivious to the photographer or each other. While adult females occupy this space, their leisure activity contrasts with the Old World water photograph and the labor of women washing clothes in the Dvina in winter. Further, we learn in the narrative that Antin was referred to as the mascot of this group, suggesting the way in which because of her gender, ethnic background, class, age, or level of education (or all of the above), her place in the group was trivialized. Yet, America was identified with Nature; so alliance with Nature suggested a way of possessing America, for becoming American. Consequently, Antin's second transformation of discovering America through Nature is linked to the first transformation of becoming American in the schools.

The visual images depicting these transformations provide few meaningful clues about what precisely this means. However, the penultimate chapter, "A Kingdom in the Slums," hints at that meaning in the two images that signify Western knowledge: Boston Public Library's "Bates Hall, Where I Spent My Longest Hours in the Library" (fig. 10), and "The Famous Study, That Was Fit to Have Been Preserved as a Shrine" (fig. 11), the study of Dr. Everett Hale. Antin writes that she felt ennobled within the monumental beaux-arts architecture, surrounded by the courtyard columns and gallery prophets of the Boston Library, especially in the reading room, where she felt "the grand spaces under the soaring arches" (342). Referred to as The People's Palace, the Boston Public Library evokes a democratic spirit, making the autobiographical subject feel like a privileged citizen. The yearning for knowledge and understanding, and its promise of fulfillment, leads her there; however, the privileged nature of that knowledge appears in the juxtaposition with the next photograph—the only domestic interior space in the narrative. The carpets, tapestry, statuary, precious artifacts, and spaciousness speak of privilege and contrast dramatically with Union Place. The female figure in the image, seated at a desk, remains unidentified, and may conceivably represent Hale's daughter who painted Antin's portrait, or

Figure 10. Bates Hall, Where I Spent My Longest Hours in the Library

Antin herself, for the narrator writes that she came to Hale's study before school and on Saturdays, while attending the Boston Latin Grammar School. The unidentified male figure—white-haired, bearded, seated at a desk behind the female, and presumably Hale—faces the same direction as the female figure, evoking the image of a mentor guiding the young woman. However, like the other peopled images of the New World, even here in this presumably intimate and personal space, the same impersonality prevails. Whether or not the female image in Hale's study represents Mary Antin, readers presume the narrator aligns herself with that space, in a sense denying that Dover Street was her residence, as she claims: "anyone could be happy a year on Dover Street [residence in the slum], after spending half an hour on Highland Street [site of Hale's home]" (345). The privilege of temporarily occupying Hale's study makes the poverty of Dover Street tolerable and masks the contradictions of identification with America.

Photographs and Narratives in Ethnic Autobiography

Figure 11. The Famous Study, That Was Fit to Have Been Preserved as a Shrine

The final photograph, a seascape, is captioned "The Tide Had Rushed In, Stealing Away Our Seaweed Cushions" (fig. 12). In the last scene of the narrative, Antin describes the Natural History Club outing at the sea, after which she was left in front of the Boston Public Library with a specimen jar in her hand. Thus, the visual and narrative text link nature with the Boston Public Library, link the discourses of scientific rationality and Western knowledge, and link Antin's two transformations—allied with America and Nature. The image challenges the affirmation of the narrative—that Antin became an American—for the closing image of the promised land lacks the specificity that could identify it with America, except to the degree that America was linked with Nature. Even so, the abstract representation offers no indication of how this space could be occupied: it represents America as an abstraction. While Antin's Old World images are all peopled, except the grandfather's house (which names a person) images in the New World remain strikingly unpeopled, or when peopled, represent disconnected persons in impersonal settings.

73

Figure 12. The Tide Had Rushed In, Stealing Away Our Seaweed Cushions

Thus, this final image reminds the reader of the other empty spaces among the photographs, most strikingly, the first image at Union Place and the view of railroad tracks. In images that are peopled (Wheeler Street and Harrison Avenue), anonymous persons are signified as in the image of Bates Hall in the Boston Public Library. In the images that might represent more intimate relationships—in Hale's study and in the Excursion—individuals exist in solitary pursuits, linked neither to each other nor to the photographer, nor might we say they represent any shared or communal activity. The only collective image remains the school picture at Chelsea—of children. Explanations for the selection must be speculative. Since the economic condition of the Antin family in the New World probably meant they neither owned a camera nor could afford professional photographers, photos selected to represent the promised land might reasonably have been other than these.

Antin's visual images signify a range of temporal and spatial arenas—from the Old World to the New, from the public worlds of market places, libraries, and the seashore to the private world of Hale's library. Perhaps

Photographs and Narratives in Ethnic Autobiography

what is most striking about the photographic narrative in opposition to the verbal narrative is the way in which the photographs contradict the prevailing message of the narrative. The autobiographical Antin asserts in the verbal narrative that she is transformed into an American; further, in the last chapter she asserts that everything in her life that followed this transformation to American is repetitious. Yet what is remarkable about the New World photographs is that not only does Antin not emerge as an adult figure, but also it becomes difficult to imagine her in the spaces that represent the visual terrain of the New World signified in the photographs. Becoming an American remains an abstraction that can best be represented by empty spaces—and significantly the closing photograph is a seascape, in which the reader finds it difficult to imagine Antin. Consequently, the photographs reveal the abstract nature of the assertion "I am an American"—which not only cannot be represented visually, but the attempts at visualization reveal the contradictory nature of that Americanizing discourse. Further, in none of the New World photographs does an exchange exist between the photographer and the persons photographed. In the only photograph that might be said to represent a community, the school in Chelsea, the group represents children, and the only reason they are grouped together is the compulsory nature of American public education. How these children should grow up and be citizens—that which the autobiographical Antin longs for—cannot be suggested by these spaces. Thus, the representations of the Americanization process remain abstract (empty spaces and seascapes), absent any human or communal world, and the only representation of democracy is the school picture of children.

What meanings do we associate with the photographs? Do they alter the reader's perception of Antin's subjectivity when read in conjunction with the narrative text? I would draw several generalizations from the photographs in Mary Antin's *The Promised Land*, which I believe might be applied to other ethnic autobiographies containing photographs. The photographic images affect our reading of Antin's subjectivity and the ideology embedded in the autobiography, both complementing and contradicting the narrative text in several ways. First, the autobiographer is represented most concretely as a child, in both the narrative and the visual texts. Second, while the female presence is documented in both Old and New World photographs and narratives, in significant moments representing a life, the female (as adult) is absent both in Old World portraiture and in New World rites of passage. Third, complementing the narrative text, the Old World photographs detail a specific and localized ethnic memory and identity, in opposition to the abstract humanity frequently representing the immigrant, while the New World memory remains abstract and impersonal. Fourth, while the Old World represents a collective identity in both visual and narrative texts, the New World narrative emphasizes individual achievement in the promised land, yet the photographic images document unpeopled spaces, making the promises of the New World ring hollow. Finally, if the photographic images belie the promise of the narrative text and expose the contradictions of the American Dream, perhaps we can read these images as the yearning, the longing of Antin the immigrant for something promised and hoped for in the New World—a yearning that might be represented in other ethnic narratives as well. I will elaborate on each of these below.

First, the (ethnic) autobiographer as a child. The photographic images of Mary Antin represent her as a child: in the frontispiece, she is about four years old; in the school picture, she is perhaps thirteen; if the unidentified female image in Hale's study is Antin, it evokes a young woman. Nevertheless, the visually represented Antin remains a schoolgirl, reinforcing the image of the narrative Antin in which she never leaves adolescence. Thus, as the narrative text leaves her in adolescence, at her school-leaving, so the visually rendered images of Antin also freeze her in childhood or adolescence. The reader cannot imagine the adult Antin—what it means to be an adult American is not conceptualized. Adults that are represented in the New World engage in individual pursuits—studying Nature and studying books—or they are found in impersonal street crowds, for example on Harrison Avenue. Significantly, the adult Antin is not identified in any of these images.

The emphasis on childhood and youth in ethnic autobiographies can be found in numerous other autobiographies as well, for example, in that of Hilda Satt Polacheck, *I Came a Stranger,* published by the University of Illinois Press in 1989. The posthumous publication includes twenty-three photographs. Both the narrative and the photographs represent most of Polacheck's life and the multiple subject positions she occupied as daughter, sister, factory worker, teacher, wife, mother, peace activist, playwright, drama critic, and reformer. The jacket cover of the volume, however, shows a cameo portrait of a young Hilda superimposed on an image (above and slightly off center) of what represents the street market near Hull House. Thus, despite the multiplicity of adult subjectivities within the text, the cover signifies a young girl. The cameo portrait appears again on the title page. The repetition of the dominating cover image, the cameo image of the girl, reinforces adolescence, especially in combination with the subtitle, "The Story of a Hull-House Girl." This dominant image, coupled with the term "girl" in the subtitle of the narrative, tends to freeze the autobiographer in a particular moment in time—in youth, in girlhood—despite the other images. Consequently, that visual imagery dominates and reinforces the subjectivity of childhood. To see the female, the ethnic as childlike is to perpetuate patterns of domination and submission, patterns of exploitation and oppression. Such cultural knowledge resides not only in the more overt examples of culture, but also in more subtle patterns, including these photographic discourses. That women are not the only ones to be constructed as the child in the culture is powerfully suggested in the title of Claude Brown's autobiography, *Manchild in the Promised Land*.

The emphasis on youthful images can be found, therefore, also in African American autobiographies. The cover of Ann Moody's *Coming of Age in Mississippi,* published in 1968, reveals an adolescent Moody, in black and blue tones, gazing off into a distance. The camera angle extends upward, directing the reader's eyes from Moody, off the page, suggesting a visionary youth. Also, in the introduction to the second edition of *Angela Davis: An Autobiography* (1988) (and on the back cover of the 1974 edition), the four cameo photographs, not found in the original 1974 editon, evoke childhood: inside the cover, opposite the title page, four small oval images of Davis signify childhood and youth: one image represents an infant of fifteen months, two images evoke Davis at the ages of six and seven, and one image represents her as a junior at Brandeis. Again, the preponderance of images of youth and adolescence seems remarkable. Images of childhood and adolescence presumably do not threaten the readers as the passionate and political adult, and communist, Angela Davis, evoked on the cover, may. These interior cameo photos thus serve to remind the reader that this radical, like the reader, was also once young, vulnerable, and innocent. Further, since the photos represent single portraits, with one exception, they signify an individual, not a collectivity or movement, nor do they evoke the political commitment central to Davis's life.

Second, the absent female. Mary Antin as adult, as female, is not embodied in these photographs. The virtual absence of the historical and embodied adult female Mary Antin in the spaces represented by America, the promised land, is significant and contributes to a radical rereading. Because of that absence, we do not see change, growth, and maturity—change in subjectivity over time is not posited. Even the photographs of Hale's study and the Natural History Club Outing signify adolescent activities—whether or not Antin is to be read into these images. Thus, Antin is suspended in adolescent Americanness, and femaleness remains absent. In the Old World photographs, readers are presented with an image of the lives and labors of the adult female. In America, adult (adolescent) females collect specimens and study. Beyond that we do not know from the photographic images what spaces or subjectivities females might occupy. The images expose the contradictions of the narrative text. Although the New World photographs include adult *females*—in Hale's study and the nature outing, although Mary Antin is not identified in either of these images--the female presence is temporary, tenuous, and contradictory. Antin's presence in the Hale study is linked to her being a student; reasonably, when she ceases to be a student her place in Hale's study may end. And in the photograph at the stream, the subject positions seem trivialized—for both male and female. Furthermore, the discourse of Americanization in which Antin identified herself promised personhood; however, in her position as woman, citizenship is denied. Thus, the school child, ennobled in her alliance as citizen with George Washington, reaches neither adulthood nor womanhood. The fault here is not in a deficient essential Antin, but in the ideologies of the discourse in which the narrator would make the autobiographical Antin inhabit America. By declaring Americanness, by articulating "I am an American," the autobiographical Antin claims that subjectivity, but she cannot occupy the spaces signifying (patriarchal) America; thus, the absent (female) subject. Further, those empty spaces signify the impossibility of her ever occupying those spaces—the narrative in which Mary Antin is the classic immigrant remains an abstraction and thus unpeopled. The abstractions of the visualized promised land suggest no spatial arena in which the immigrant female might dwell. Thus, the photographs permit us to see more clearly the contradictions in this classic autobiography.

Third, Old World ethnic memory—in opposition to abstract humanity. Photographs serve as powerful representations of a past that can challenge prevailing assumptions about history—offering a counter-memory. What the Old World photographs of Antin's *The Promised Land* do is to open up a historical, contextualized, and personalized world of these Russian-Jewish immigrants, a specificity generally absent in dominant cultural images. When Loren Hoekzema sought an image of a synagogue for the

Photographs and Narratives in Ethnic Autobiography

cover of Antin's autobiography, he went in search of a visual representation of a past only dimly imagined and remembered, and outside of memory for the second, third, and fourth generations of immigrants. Thus, the Old World visual images serve an important function for contemporary readers—to visualize an ethnic memory. These photographic images make explicit certain meanings in the verbal narrative: (1) they concretize historical phenomena, such as the existence of the grave digger and the old shtetl schools; (2) they demonstrate the communal dimensions of work and religion through the meat and wood markets, as well as through the women washing clothes and the preparation for the Sabbath; and (3) they illuminate the dailiness in a life of struggle before emigrating toward America. The world represented in these photographs is personal, local, immediate, complex, harsh, and meaningful. Therefore, these photographs offer a significant challenge to the de-historicized and depersonalized photographs that represent an abstract humanity, not only those that are found in the popular media such as the *Time* and *Life* examples, but also those that represent immigrants and ethnics on the cover of the 1969 edition of Mary Antin's autobiography and on the paperback cover of Bodnar's recent monograph, *The Transplanted*. Ethnic memory remains specific, local, and personal; also it is historical, geographical, and material. Thus, that ethnic memory risks challenging the abstract promises of America, for to be American is to forget that past. However, the visually rendered memory of the New World exposes the contradictions of the promised land.

Fourth, the empty spaces of New World individualized achievement. Autobiography literally means "self-life-writing," emphasizing the individual "I." Most scholars have stressed the way in which Antin writes of her individual experience, although she claims to speak for millions. However, when we consider the photographs, we discover that in the narration of the Old World experiences, she documents essentially a collective experience. Save for the childhood picture opposite the title page, her own portrait is absent, something exceptional in autobiographies that incorporate photographs. On the other hand, in the New World section in which Antin focuses on her school experience, the portraits of Antin again are noticeably absent, and in the two pictures that may include her—the school picture and that of Hale's study—she is neither identified nor is she the central focus. If the Old World photographs are said to represent a collective, the New World photographs signify the absence of any community. While the narrative text emphasizes the achievements of Antin, primarily school achievements, the photographic images expose the emptiness of the spaces Antin occupies and thus the hollowness of those affirmations about the promised land. Perhaps this emptiness is most poignantly revealed in the image "Union Place (Boston) Where My New Home Waited for Me," and in the "dim tangle" of railroad tracks. Both of these images suggesting the New World are haunted by emptiness, darkness, and spaces devoid of real promise or even humanity. The final image of the seascape, evoking the natural world, certainly is less bleak, and the presence of the sailboat suggests life. Still, the image represents no specific place and no community, and the subject is absent. That emptied space contrasts significantly with the Old World photographs. Furthermore, the absence of the Antin subject in this final image contrasts sharply with the tradition of portraiture, especially in immigrant autobiographies, such as those of Jacob Riis, Andrew Carnegie, and Edward Bok. Individualized achievement of the adolescent girl may be represented in the narrative, but meaningful subjectivity cannot be visually rendered for the female immigrant, the female ethnic.

Fifth, ethnic memory and yearning. If we might read the empty spaces of Antin's New World as exposing contradictions in the American Dream, we might also see these as representing a longing for the promises embedded in the ideologies of the New World—freedom to live in peace, a longing for equality and justice, the ability to participate in the democratic life of one's community. In the opening chapter of her book *Yearning: Race, Gender, and Cultural Politics,* bell hooks explains how she came to the title. She writes,

> ... as I looked for common passions, sentiments shared by folks across race, class, gender and sexual practice, I was struck by the depths of longing in many of us. Those without money long to find a way to get rid of the endless sense of deprivation. Those with money wonder why so much feels so meaningless and long to find the site of meaning. Witnessing the genocidal ravages of drug addiction in black families and communities, I began to "hear" that longing for a substance as, in part, a displacement for the longed-for liberation—the freedom to control one's destiny. All too often our political desire for change is seen as separate from longings and passions that consume lots of time and energy in daily life. Particularly the realm of fantasy is often seen as completely separate from politics. Yet I think of all the time black folks (especially the underclass) spend just fantasizing about what our lives would be like if there were no racism, no white supremacy. Surely our

Photographs and Narratives in Ethnic Autobiography

desire for radical social change is intimately linked with the desire to experience pleasure, erotic fulfillment, and a host of other passions. Then, on the flip side, there are many individuals with race and gender and class privilege who are longing to see the kind of revolutionary change that will end domination and oppression even though their lives would be completely and utterly transformed. The shared space and feeling of "yearning" opens up the possibility of common ground where all these differences might meet and engage one another. It seemed appropriate then to speak this yearning.[28]

Though nearly a century separates Mary Antin and bell hooks, as well as racial categories, the concept of yearning also seems to open up the photographs in Antin's autobiography. Though the narrative text articulates the prevailing ideology of the promise of America, the photographs provide no evidence of the fulfillment of that promise. Rather, the photographs seem to evoke only a yearning for the fulfillment of that promise in the new land.

Ethnic Memory, Subjectivity, and Meaning

In the introduction to the second edition of *Angela Davis: An Autobiography* (1988) Davis writes that when she wrote her autobiography in 1974 she disagreed with the white feminists who so glibly linked the personal and the political. In 1974, she explains, police violence could not be equated with domestic quarrels. Since then, with the burgeoning knowledge about extensive and brutal domestic violence, Davis writes, "domestic violence is no less an expression of the prevailing politics of gender because it occurred within the private sphere of a personal relationship. I therefore express my regrets that I was not able to also apply a measuring stick which manifested a more complex understanding of the dialectics of the personal and the political" (viii). We construct the world through the lenses and memories of a particular historical, cultural, and social context: white, middle-class women at the forefront of feminism in the late 1960s possessed little experience or memory of police violence as a daily phenomenon and could not imagine the violence to which Angela Davis alluded. However, in 1991 the widely televised violent beatings of Rodney King by members of the Los Angeles Police Department became a persistent reminder to television viewers living outside the range of racially motivated attacks, and now white and middle-class audiences can better imagine the brutality of racism.

Furthermore, in the 1990s, with the widespread exposure of violence directed at women, and the changed laws responding to this, few questions anymore the public and political dimensions of domestic violence. So, too, Angela Davis, after fifteen years and with the perspective of feminists speaking the unspoken—that the patriarchal system privileging males over females promotes male abuse of the female—rethinks the political associations between police brutality and domestic violence. The systems of domination and subordination based on gender and race lead to violence and oppression and thus look more alike in 1991 or 1988 than they did in 1974. Central to Davis's rethinking is the expanding notion of the political.

If we acknowledge the meaning of the political in the broadest sense, then that which refers to the citizen and to the public arena remains political.[29] This means that practices that define and identify the domain of the citizen serve political ends, so cultural practices and cultural productions that define the boundaries of America and American—as citizen—belong to the political. This means ethnic autobiographies that aim to articulate the meaning of the citizen, the American, the human, belong to the political and serve ideological functions in the culture. If meaning is associated with effects, then we must ask what are the effects, culturally and politically, of messages (stated and unstated) in ethnic autobiography?

Central to the political dimension of ethnic memory is the question of subjectivity and identity: that is, what constitutes the ethnic and the non-ethnic, individually and collectively? Ethnic autobiographies often serve dual and contradictory functions: autobiographers may write to prove their Americanness, as Mary Antin seems to do, or they may write "to demonstrate individual membership in the human community," as Henry Louis Gates argued slaves did.[30] On the other hand, ethnic autobiographers may write to counter a dominant culture, to document submerged cultures, as Malcolm X, Ralph Ellison, and Angela Davis seem to do. Whereas individual autobiographies may counter dominant cultural ideologies about a melting pot, liberal democracy, and freedom for all, we might also reread and rethink old stories to gain new perspectives, and considering photography within autobiography may aid us in that process. George Lipsitz discusses counter-memory in a way that is meaningful for this rethinking of autobiography and ethnic memory: "Counter-memory is a way of remembering and forgetting that starts with the local, the immediate, and the personal. Unlike historical narratives that begin with the totality of human existence and then locate

Photographs and Narratives in Ethnic Autobiography

specific actions and events within that totality, counter-memory starts with the particular and the specific and then builds outward toward a total story. Counter-memory looks to the past for the hidden histories excluded from dominant narratives. But unlike myths that seek to detach events and actions from the fabric of any larger history, counter-memory forces revision of existing histories by supplying new perspectives about the past."[31]

Ethnic autobiographies and memories begin with the local, the immediate, the personal. They have served, and continue to serve, as a counter-memory to the so-called grand narratives of Western civilization and American culture, offering revisions of the past. However, our reading of cultural texts also remains historically and culturally situated, affected both by our own memories and by the prevailing cultural ideologies. Thus, revising memories of the past as new information and strategies emerge makes revision of the past possible and meaningful. The photographs in *The Promised Land* do precisely that. Rereading Mary Antin's narrative by incorporating the original photographs into the entire autobiographical text—heretofore omitted—provides new perspectives about the Antin text and our own reading of ethnic autobiography. The contradictions presumably invisible to Antin become visualized and concrete for the reader. Juxtaposing Antin's visual rendering of her "promised land" with the narrative that embraces Americanness illuminates the contradictions of the text and so permits us to rethink this classic narrative and the past it evokes. Because photographic images situate memory and subjectivity in time and space, historically and geographically, they provide a meaningful site for examining cultural meanings associated with ethnicity and subjectivity, not only in Antin's autobiography, but in other ethnic autobiographies as well. Rereading narratives and photographs can provide new perspectives on the past and on our decoding ethnic memories and meanings.

Notes

Earlier versions of this essay were presented in papers entitled "Constructing Subjectivities in the New World: Reading Photographs in Mary Antin's Autobiography, *The Promised Land*," read at the American Studies Association Conference in Toronto, Canada, in November 1989 and at the 1990 MELUS Conference in Chicago, Illinois. I wish to thank especially George Lipsitz and Wendy Kozol for their support and constructive comments on these earlier drafts. Also I wish to express gratitude for the encouragement on this work expressed by Jules Chametzky and Werner Sollors at the MELUS conference.

1. See Mary Antin, *The Promised Land* (Boston: Houghton, 1912; 2nd ed., Boston: Houghton, 1969; Princeton, NJ: Princeton UP, 1985).

2. The two issues, I believe, remain both linked and separated. Why exactly the photographs were omitted in 1969 and 1985 remains unclear; however, those omissions seem related to the generalized exclusion of visual images from literary studies, which accounts for the scholarly neglect. In a telephone conversation with Loren Hoekzema, 3 October 1989, Hoekzema, editor of the 1985 Princeton edition, stated that they had no intention to exclude anything, that they had used the Century edition of 1969 from Houghton Mifflin, which did not include photographs, and that he had no knowledge there were photographs in the 1912 edition. Although the Princeton editors had sought a photograph for the cover of the volume to represent the Old World, one could not be found; he noted that he had sought particularly an image of a synagogue and had gone to the New York Public Library's photographic collection on Eastern European Jews. He also mentioned he had consulted with Oscar Handlin. Regarding the exclusion of the photographs in the 1969 edition, Mr. Handlin explained in a letter to me, dated 7 December 1989, that despite the fact that he wrote the introduction to the volume, "the production process was entirely in the hands of the publishers." He had no further information about the photographs and also failed to locate the Antin papers. Thus far, my inquiries and correspondence with Houghton Mifflin to determine why the photographs were excluded from the 1969 edition have produced no verifiable or satisfactory explanation.

3. I am not aware of any studies that address photographs in ethnic autobiographies.

4. See Jacob Riis, *The Making of an American* (New York: Macmillan, 1902); Andrew Carnegie, *The Autobiography of Andrew Carnegie* (Boston: Houghton, 1920); and Edward Bok, *The Americanization of Edward Bok: The Autobiography of a Dutch Boy Fifty Years After* (New York: Scribner's, 1922).

5. Henry Adams, *The Education of Henry Adams* (Boston: Massachusetts Historical Society, 1918). The manuscript was first distributed privately in 1907, which may account for the omission of photographs; however, by 1918, when the Massachusetts Historical Society published the autobiography, the tradition of including images was established.

6. For example, the Ojibwe novelist, teacher, and trickster Gerald Vizenor includes more than fifty photographs, representing a range of subjects, times, and places in *Interior Landscapes: Autobiographical Myths and Metaphors* (Minneapolis: U of Minnesota P, 1990); Hilda Satt Polacheck's *I Came a Stranger: The Story of a Hull-House Girl* (Urbana: U of Illinois P, 1989), published posthumously, includes nearly as many; and the republication of Angela Davis's *Angela Davis: An Autobiography* (New York: Random, 1974) by International Publishers in 1988 includes photographs not found in the original. See also Richard Rodriguez, *Hunger of Memory: The Education of Richard Rodriguez* (New York: Bantam, 1982); Malcolm X, with Alex Haley, *The Autobiography of Malcolm X* (New York: Grove, 1965). A notable exception to the pattern of including photographic representation in ethnic autobiography can be found in the various publications of the widely acclaimed autobiography of the Chinese-American woman Maxine Hong Kingston,

Woman Warrior: Memoirs of a Girlhood among Ghosts (New York: Knopf, 1976; New York: Vintage, 1977).

7. I am unaware of any studies that include a discussion of Antin's photographs or that consider generally the photographs in immigrant and ethnic autobiographies. Marilyn F. Motz, "Visual Autobiography: Photograph Albums of Turn-of-the-Century Midwestern Women," *American Quarterly* 41.1 (March 1989):63–92, addresses the concept of the autobiographical in photography; however, the analysis focuses on a genre that is exclusively visual, the photo album. In this way Motz's essay reflects the attention feminist scholars have given to film. For a provocative study on how the narrative and visual codes interact in the constructing of dominant ideologies in *Life* magazine of post–World War II America, see Wendy Kozol, *Documenting the Public and Private in Life: Cultural Politics in Postwar Photojournalism* (Philadelphia: Temple UP, forthcoming).

8. Alan Trachtenberg, in his important work, *Reading American Photographs: Images as History, from Matthew Brady to Walker Evans* (New York: Hill and Wang, 1989), traces the development of photography in America in the late nineteenth and early twentieth centuries, emphasizing the continuity and discontinuity from Matthew Brady's photographic documentation of the Civil War to Walker Evans's representation of America in the 1930s—the continuity in their efforts to record the *real* America and the discontinuity, particularly in Evans's ambivalent attitude toward art photography and his efforts to escape the earlier formulations of document photography and art photography. The oppositions between these two polarities in conceptualizing photography emerge especially in the early twentieth century. That opposition is particularly evoked in Trachtenberg's chapter "Camera Work/Social Work," signifying the two poles in American photography, represented by the work of Alfred Stieglitz and Lewis Wickes Hine. Stieglitz's "Gallery, 291" and his journal, *Camera Work,* represent the earliest efforts in this country to see photography as artistic expression, as meaningful as painting. On the other hand, Lewis Hine, photographing child labor, used photography as a kind of social work, in an effort to end the economic and social practices that exploited children. In his photographs, as in those of the earlier works of Jacob Riis, Hine imagined that the brutality to children would be self-evident and transparently conveyed in the photographs and would contribute to outrage and so to the end of the brutality.

9. Allan Sekula, "The Currency of the Photograph," *Thinking Photography,* ed. Victor Burgin (London: Macmillan Education, 1982) 108. The provocative essays in this volume demonstrate the value of examining photographs as cultural objects that operate powerfully in the culture to encode and circulate meanings.

10. See Susan Sontag, *On Photography* (New York: Noonday, 1973) 125.

11. Photographs have been an integral part of documenting certain groups of Americans. Jacob Riis in *How the Other Half Lives* documented the immigrant poor on the Lower East Side. Lewis Hine's images of immigrants at Ellis Island still serve as signifiers of the immigrant. From another—rural and midwestern—perspective the itinerant photographer Andrew Dahl (whose work is housed at the Wisconsin Historical Society) traveled through the Midwest in the last quarter of the nineteenth century photographing farmers, recently settled immigrants. Those photographed often sent their images to relatives back home to

demonstrate successes, usually material, in the New World. Thus, farmers brought their prized possessions outside to the yard of the frame house, which always stood in the background as a signifier of stability and material achievement and comfort. In addition to draft horses and farm equipment, which inevitably appeared in the photographs, the proud new Americans would bring outside the dining table, covered with linen and china cups and plates; in some the new Singer sewing machine would also appear before the camera. Whether or not the family chose to display its wealth so conspicuously and thus demonstrate its inclusion in the prevailing bourgeois culture, Dahl may well have informed his subjects of the photographic convention, indicating that this was the way photographs were made in the Midwest rural communities in the late nineteenth century.

12. Herbert G. Gutman, *The Black Family in Slavery and Freedom, 1750–1925* (New York: Vintage, 1976).

13. Mikhail Bakhtin, *The Dialogic Imagination,* trans. Caryl Emerson and M. Holquist (Austin: U of Texas P, 1981).

14. Diane Macdonell, *Theories of Discourse* (New York: Basil Blackwell, 1986) 7, 45.

15. The current debates emerging in the press regarding multiculturalism and the critique of ethnicity through the trivialization of the term in "the cult of ethnicity" suggest that this meaning is accepted by many within the academy who seem threatened by the visibility and volume of voices representing non-Europeans. The cover story of *Time* magazine, 8 July 1991, "Who Are We?" addresses the question of multiculturalism in American society and particularly in the schools. Arthur Schlesinger, author of *The Disuniting of America,* writes in that issue an essay entitled "The Cult of Ethnicity, Good and Bad": "The eruption of ethnicity is, I believe, a rather superficial enthusiasm stirred by romantic ideologues on the one hand and by unscrupulous con men on the other: self-appointed spokesmen whose claim to represent their minority groups is carelessly accepted by the media" (21).

16. See, for example, Lewis Wickes Hine, *Reproductions from Original Lewis W. Hine Negatives,* in the George Eastman House Archive (Rochester, NY: George Eastman House, 1970); Lewis Wickes Hine, *America and Lewis Hine: Photographs 1904–1908* (New York: Aperture, 1977); Lewis Wickes Hine, *Lewis Wickes Hine's Interpretive Photography: The Six Early Projects* (Chicago: U of Chicago P, 1978).

17. For a discussion of these, see Allan Sekula, "On the Invention of Photographic Meaning," *Thinking Photography,* ed. Burgin, 84–109.

18. John Bodnar, *The Transplanted: A History of Immigrants in Urban America* (Bloomington: Indiana UP, 1985). The photograph by Lewis Hine is entitled "Italian Family" and was made at Ellis Island, 1905. This same image is used to present the "European Immigrant Wave" in the cover story, "Whose America?" in *Time,* 8 July 1991, 17.

A recent example of mainstream media representation illustrates the phenomenon in the popular culture. To celebrate the reopening of Ellis Island to the public after major renovations of this turn-of-the-century gateway for millions of European immigrants to the United States, *Life* magazine devoted its cover story and picture for September 1990 to that event. (*Life* magazine identifies the photograph with the Brown Brothers, yet the image reminds us of the many taken by

Photographs and Narratives in Ethnic Autobiography

Lewis Hine at Ellis Island, and of the kind of images often reproduced to signify aliens in America as a nation of immigrants.) The photograph shows an adult woman and a child of about five years of age, presumably a mother and child. Though no one else is in the photograph, the benches and background suggest the Great Hall which received immigrants on Ellis Island. Mother and daughter are dressed in heavy woolen coats with thick scarves wrapped securely around their heads; skirts and long stockings are visible under the heavy coats and suggest layers of dress; their durable, leather boots lace to mid-thigh and imply warmth and sturdiness. Taken together, the clothing suggests handmade, pre-industrial garments of the turn-of-the-century, tailored and sturdy clothing representing rural folk of modest means whose clothing must last. The woman holds papers in her left hand, presumably her entry documents, and gazes into the camera with an expectant look, at once both anxious and pleased. The caption in bold print states, "How We Came to America: Ellis Island Reopens—and Brings our History Back to Life." (The word AMERICA stretches across the page, measuring over an inch.) The caption tells us how we should read the image. The pronouns *we* and *our* juxtaposed with the bold lettering signifying America, tell us that these are Americans. The *we* linked to the photograph signifies American, including the woman and child, meaning the female is incorporated into the definition of American. But also, the mother and child evoke an image of the Madonna and child, the sacred. Significant, though, these immigrants are European, and they are white. The *our* in *our history* signifies European immigrants and white Americans. Americans may not be Anglo-Saxons, but they are Europeans by descent, suggests the image—the photograph along with the text defines the boundaries of America. The meaning implied here, though unsaid, includes the corollary: that others—from Africa or Asia for example, or indigenous peoples—are not Americans.

For a provocative study of the construction of the female with children in photographic images, see Wendy Kozol, "Madonnas of the Fields: Photography, Gender and 1930s Farm Relief," *Genders* 2 (Summer 1988): 1–23.

19. See, for example, John Berger, *Ways of Seeing* (New York: Penguin, 1972); Burgin, ed., *Thinking Photography*.

20. This essay will focus on Mary Antin's autobiography. The discussion of the photographic and narrative texts in this autobiography is not intended to represent all ethnic autobiographies; rather, the analysis is intended as a theoretical approach that might be used in examining other ethnic autobiographies. For development of theoretical assumptions surrounding autobiography and ethnicity, and a more thorough discussion of Mary Antin's *The Promised Land*, see Betty Bergland, "Reconstructing the 'Self' in America: Patterns in Immigrant Women's Autobiographies," diss. U of Minnesota, 1990. Also, for a comparison of the photographs in the autobiographies of Mary Antin and Emma Goldman, see chapter 7 of the dissertation.

21. Albert E. Stone, introduction, *The American Autobiography: A Collection of Critical Essays* (Englewood Cliffs, NJ: Prentice, 1981) 4.

22. Mary V. Dearborn, *Pocahontas's Daughters: Gender and Ethnicity in American Culture* (New York: Oxford UP, 1986) 10.

23. Distinctions between immigrant and ethnic autobiographies sometimes

blur, as Sau-ling Wong noted in "Immigrant Autobiography: Some Questions of Definition and Approach," *American Autobiography*, ed. Paul Eakin (Madison: U of Wisconsin P, 1991) 142–70. For example, in James Craig Holte's *The Ethnic I: A Sourcebook for Ethnic-American Autobiography* (New York: Greenwood, 1988), he includes immigrants born outside the United States (such as Mary Antin and Jacob Riis), as well as Native Americans and African Americans born in the United States (Black Elk, Malcolm X, and Zora Neale Hurston), but also second-generation immigrants born in the United States (such as Maxine Hong Kingston, Chinese-American; Jerre Mangione, Sicilian-American; and the very successful Lee Iacocca, Italian-American). Mary Antin's *The Promised Land* is discussed by literary and ethnic scholars both as an immigrant autobiography (she emigrated from Russia to the United States in 1894) and as an ethnic autobiography (she was a Russian, Jewish-American woman). The terms *ethnic* and *ethnicity* remain complicated and have generated decades of discussion about their meanings; the *Harvard Encyclopedia of American Ethnic Groups*, ed. Stephan Thernstrom (Cambridge, MA: Harvard UP, 1980) documents 107 different ethnic groups in the United States, employing fourteen different criteria for determining ethnicity. In this essay, the terms *ethnic* and *ethnicity* will refer generally to a sense of peoplehood, which may be internally or externally defined but distinguishes itself from Anglo-American (or Yankee—a category in the *Harvard Encyclopedia*) identity. However, *immigrants* are frequently equated with *ethnics*, with the *alien*, the *cultural other* within the cultural productions.

24. Biographical information on Mary Antin can be found in her obituary in the *New York Times*, 18 May 1949, 27; in *Notable American Women 1607–1950: A Biographical Dictionary*, vol. 1 (Cambridge, MA: Harvard UP, 1971) 57–59; and in Oscar Handlin's introduction to the second edition of *The Promised Land*.

25. We cannot know whose intent is represented by these photographs—their selection, organization, content. However, to emphasize individualized intent and motivation is to ignore the cultural dimensions of the visual signification and the effects on readers.

26. Roland Barthes, *Roland Barthes*, trans. Richard Howard (New York: Noonday, 1977) 27.

27. See especially Sidonie Smith, *A Poetics of Women's Autobiography: Marginality and the Fictions of Self-Representation* (Bloomington: Indiana UP, 1987).

28. bell hooks, *Yearning: Race, Gender, and Cultural Politics* (Boston: South End, 1990) 12–13.

29. The *Oxford English Dictionary*, vol. 7 (Oxford: Clarendon, 1978) 1074, defines *political* in the first and broad definition as "Of, belonging to, or pertaining to the state or body of citizens, its government or policy, especially in civil and secular affairs; public, civil; of or pertaining to the science of art or politics."

30. Henry Louis Gates, Jr., "James Gronniosaw and the Trope of the Talking Book" *Studies in Autobiography*, ed. James Olney (New York: Oxford UP, 1988) 52.

31. George Lipsitz, *Time Passages: Collective Memory and American Popular Culture* (Minneapolis: U of Minnesota P, 1990) 213.

The New Man and the Mediator: (Non-)Remembrance in Jewish-American Immigrant Narrative

GERT BUELENS

Early Jewish-American fiction and autobiography have most often been analyzed as a reflection of the "immigrant experience."[1] In this essay, I wish to argue that these narratives rather constitute active interventions in a specific and changing social reality profoundly marked by relations of power and the often-conflicting interests of the population of the United States. The rhetorical strategies immigrant narratives employ are to be regarded as at least implicitly participating in what Jameson calls an "antagonistic class discourse." What therefore needs to be examined is how these texts do not just reflect the immigrant experience, but embrace a politics of nonremembrance, which serves to stabilize subjectivity, contain social dissent, and legitimize the immigrant as acceptable to the dominant order.

The essay focuses on Jewish-American narratives that, in recalling the immigrant experience, aim to represent the American Jew as a rightful aspirant to an American identity. Protagonists are carefully groomed so as to appear acceptable in the eyes of an Anglo-Saxon Protestant norm, which is always, at least implicitly, present in the text. The religious and/or emotional predicament of the assimilating Jew is foregrounded, and, if expressed at all, his desire to escape from social marginality is hinted at only vaguely. However, what is really at stake is the American Jew's attempt to represent himself as part of an economically privileged class.

The texts rely conspicuously on two conceptual figures, the new man and the mediator, which are linked to the contradictory cultural roles in which America casts the immigrant. As new man he reenacts the traditional part of the American Adam, is reborn in the crossing of the Atlantic, and comes to share in the American belief in opportunity for all—a belief that serves to stabilize the overall social status quo by the antirevolutionary promise of individual ascent. But if the immigrant should actually demand the realization of that promise, then the cultural role of new man could become a powerful challenge to the prevailing economic system, based as that was on the exploitation of underpaid and overworked laborers. The economic expansion of the turn-of-the-century northern United States was dependent on the availability of a cheap work force. The new immigrants provided a constant supply of poor and often naive workers, who could be exploited—and therefore kept unfree and unequal—with fewer qualms of conscience the more ethnic, the more different, the less natural, the less like "us," they remained. In Jewish-American immigrant narrative, the figure of the new man consequently appears with double connotation. For one, this figure can indicate a desire and a willingness to assimilate to the dominant American ideology of rebirth in the New World, the immigrant voluntarily shedding his or her former identity; for another, it can be associated with an aggressive claim to equal rights and a rejection of the subservient role into which a capitalist order tried to place the immigrant.

The alternative figure of the protagonist as mediator corresponds to the exceptional immigrant who, by virtue of an intimate understanding of both Old World and New, is able to stand between the immigrant ghetto and the so-called Real America. This conceptual figure is to an extent less disturbing to the established economic order than the potentially aggressive new man, since it endorses the existing social divide and offers a pragmatic strategy for life in the United States—assimilating the best of old and new. However, as the new man can carry dual connotations, so the mediator can work to support quite a different social message: Real America and immigrant ghetto can become hypostatized wholes in these texts, seen to exist side by side in a disunified, culturally pluralist United States.

The conceptual figures of new man and mediator also signify distinct relationships to the immigrant past. If the new man rejects the past as "a heavy garment that clings to your limbs when you would run" (Antin, *Promised Land* xxii), the mediator tries to translate an Old World heritage into Real American terms. In both cases, remembrance is a problematical affair. New manhood implies a break with the past that results either in complete silence about it or in a recollection of the Old World that provides a foil for the United States as a haven for "starved and eager souls who have elsewhere been denied what here we hold to be, as a matter of

The New Man and the Mediator

course, rights free to all" (Roosevelt 7). Narratives that focus on a mediating role for their part aim to rewrite the Jewish past in such a way as to remove from it all ideological obstacles to integration in the New World. Both new manhood and mediatorship frequently result in a veritable politics of remembrance, the burden of which is the social legitimation of the American-Jewish immigrant.

A key text in this discussion is Mary Antin's *The Promised Land*, an autobiographical novel that turns around the contradiction between the new-man and mediator figures and as such provides the richest elaboration of their role in American-Jewish immigrant fiction. It is enlightening to consider the cultural context in which Antin's book appeared, since new manhood and mediatorship shaped novels before and after *The Promised Land*. The essay closes with a closer analysis of Elizabeth Stern's work, which leads us beyond Antin's achievement to a recognition of the limitations of new manhood and mediatorship.

Mary Antin's *The Promised Land* (1912) is the only piece of Jewish immigrant writing to have become a big popular success: it topped the nonfiction bestseller list for 1912 and still came seventh in the subsequent year (Hackett 108, 112). It is not surprising to learn of the warm reception the work received, when one takes into consideration the predominant belief in America's fundamental freedom and limitless opportunity that it expresses. Recent criticism of the autobiography has often found fault with the "excessive assimilation and submissiveness" that *The Promised Land* preaches (Sollors 45). Yet contemporary critics were alive to the subtlety of Antin's project. If the story describes a Jewish immigrant enthusiastically embracing the values of the United States as a full-fledged new woman,[2] it also endeavors—in true mediating style—to demonstrate the inherent non-American qualities of the immigrant. This dual aim is reflected in the book's reception. While the *New York Times* reviewer, addressing the work's mediating aspect, praised it for proving "the benefit of America and the immigrant, each to each," Boston patrician Barrett Wendell objected to Antin's "irritating habit of describing herself and her people as Americans" (cited in Sollors 88).

In assessing Antin's work, it is important to consider the historical context in which it appeared. The early 1910s saw "[t]he traditional policy of unlimited immigration . . . seriously questioned" (Handlin vi). The public climate was swinging perceptibly against allowing further immigrants into the country: "Strange new unassimilable people, crowding the cities, threatened to degrade all Americans" (Handlin vi). Antin's autobiography indirectly displays its awareness of the ongoing debate by portraying an allegedly typical eastern European immigrant who becomes an entirely assimilated American citizen. Thus this new-woman story serves a legitimating function aimed at allaying native American apprehensions about the allegedly unassimilable "new" immigrants. "The argument for immigration," wrote the *New York Times* reviewer, ". . . is implicit in every chapter of 'The promised land.'" The book has indeed been called "one of the strongest expressions of the myth of America as ideal and vision" (Girgus 14), and this is clearly the way the American public read the book when they gave it "an enthusiastic reception" (Handlin v).

Yet there is a different side to Mary Antin's autobiography that a recent study of the text has aptly described as its "darker metaphor of the self as 'Wandering Jew'" (Wardlaw 87). While part of Antin's project in *The Promised Land* is to show how an immigrant becomes a new man, without any ties to the Old World, the text's mediating aspect, emphasizing the inherent qualities of the immigrant, results in a strong undercurrent of doubt with regard to its protagonist's ability to forget the past and become a permanent resident of the promised land. A note of worry is manifest in the narrative from beginning to end. "A long past vividly remembered," the introduction remarks, "is like a heavy garment that clings to your limbs when you would run" (xxii). Antin expresses the hope that the telling of her life story will serve a therapeutic end and release her from her memories: "I will write a bold 'Finis' at the end, and shut the book with a bang!" But the insistent negations that mark the closing page of the text seem to indicate that the narrator is still struggling with the Russian Jewish past. "My spirit is not tied to the monumental past," the final paragraph emphasizes. "The past was only my cradle, and now it cannot hold me. . . . No! it is not I that belong to the past, but the past that belongs to me" (364). As Dittmar comments on this passage: "One senses that this position is taken up more in the spirit of a declaration of intent than in that of an emotionally secure self-definition" (*Assimilation* 74).[3]

The problematical status of the past in *The Promised Land* clearly rests on the double bind in which the protagonist finds herself due to the conflicting demands of the two cultural roles in which the text inscribes her. Antin's new womanhood means that she must represent herself as successful in her educational and social career, the typical ghetto Jew—product of the past—acting as a foil for her success. But the legitimating

The New Man and the Mediator

intention of *The Promised Land* requires that this narrator act also as mediator between the new and the old, interpreting and even acting the part of the typical immigrant and his past. The selection of the possessive pronoun "his" in this context is not neutral. As Aranzazu Usandizaga has argued, Antin's text needs to be understood as an early experiment in women's autobiography, writing for and against a public expectation that an immigrant autobiography would have as its hero a male character.

The tension that this complex situation gives rise to is apparent from the fault lines in Antin's narrative: those instances where her exultant "life story" of a new woman needs to be adjusted in order to arrive at a memoir that is more representative of the life of a typical immigrant. This tendency becomes most conspicuous in the part of the text that deals with the experience of immigration. Antin finds that she "might properly borrow" official statistics and observations on the immigrant experience "to fill the gaps in my recollections" (181). She refrains from doing so, she claims, "prevented by my sense of harmony. The individual, we know, is a creature unknown to the statistician, whereas I undertook to give the personal view of everything." Yet the next paragraph is already departing from the experiences of the Antin family into generalization that applies to the Russian Jew at large. Mr. Antin's "history for that period," we learn, "is the history of thousands who come to America like him. . . ."

At a crucial point the text is even led to revise an earlier description of a character when its unconventionality threatens to disrupt the "typical" thrust of the narrative. No lesser figure than Mary's mother has to be thus recast. At first, she is shown to possess a remarkable hunger for intellectual development and sufficient willpower to persuade her parents to allow her to achieve a considerable level of schooling for a girl in an East European Jewish community. "My mother was fifteen years old," Antin writes, "when she entered on a career of higher education. For two hours daily she was released from the store [where her "devotion, ability, and tireless energy" had made her "indispensable"], and in that interval she strove with might and main to conquer the world of knowledge" (52–53). After a year her promising career was truncated by the necessity of marriage, but Mary's mother had still managed to distinguish herself by culture and enterprise. Nevertheless, arrived in America, she too has to serve as the exemplary immigrant Jewish woman in Mary's illustration of statistical facts: "My mother, like the majority of women in the Pale, had all her life taken her religion on authority . . .," Antin now claims (245): "Considering how the heavy burdens which she had borne from childhood had never allowed her time to think for herself at all, but had obliged her always to tread blindly in the beaten paths, I think it greatly to her credit that in her puzzling situation [in the New World] she did not lose her poise entirely" (246). The picture of Mrs. Antin we now get is the product of an imagined past, a past that has been constructed in line with the ideological requirements of the narrative: Mary's mother has conveniently become the average Jewish matron, sluggish and docile, uncultured and conservative.

The recasting of Mother Antin should not be seen only as a product of the narrative's general need to represent "typical" immigrants. Rather, it is part of a specific emphasis on the break between the generations, which alone allows the heroine to appear as both new and typical. Indeed, the generational split makes it possible to create two sets of typical immigrants: on the one hand are the typical ghetto inhabitants, for whom immigration has come too late; on the other are the typical new Americans, who are peculiarly well placed to profit from the opportunities the United States offers. Not only Antin's mother is cast into the former category. Discussing the life of her father, the narrator recalls the hopes he cherished when he contemplated emigration. She highlights the heightened significance of American freedom to one for whom it meant "far more than the right to reside, travel, and work wherever he pleased; it meant the freedom to speak his thoughts, to throw off the shackles of superstition, to test his own fate, unhindered by political or religious tyranny" (202). Mary Antin waxes indignant as she paints the picture of her father in the past, forced to spend his days acquiring "useless learning," married off and "bidden to multiply himself," in short: "led about as a creature without a will, a chattel, an instrument" (203). When Antin's father arrived in America at the age of thirty-two, for "most of his life he had been held in leading-strings. He was hungry for his untasted manhood" (202). Mary Antin is here reinscribing the initiation of her father's emigration within the initiation of her own adolescence.[4] The Jewish pale is represented as an emasculating place, where men in their early thirties have yet to become gendered adults. The text thus implicitly lends literal meaning to the promised new manhood of the United States. But, significantly, *The Promised Land* claims that Antin's father never really managed to make a success of things in the New World, never became a true man.

If the parent figures can still be fit more or less inconspicuously into

The New Man and the Mediator

the text's politics of remembrance, the representation of the autobiographical "I" as typical immigrant is a greater challenge. While claiming that the "chief interest" of her own story "lies in the fact that it is illustrative of scores of unwritten lives," the narrator cannot, in actual fact, adhere to the details of her own experience, since that would lead her to present a persona who is exceptional rather than typical (xxi). That is the main reason why, at the end of her autobiography, Antin chooses to remain silent about her marriage to Lutheran Amadeus Grabau, which had taken place in 1901. Antin's heroine must remain celibate to demonstrate the purity of her love for (Christian) America. For similar reasons, the narrative is broken off the moment she begins to frequent the houses of "the distinguished men and women who busied themselves with the humble fortunes of a school-girl" (61). The truth about Antin's life is that, at a young age, she had already established "impressive connections," as Oscar Handlin notes: "She was by no means a lonely or helpless stranger; even as a school girl she had spent her holidays with the Phillip Cowens [editor of the authoritative weekly *American Hebrew*] . . ." (ix). This aspect of Antin's life fits in neither with her role as privileged interpreter of the existence of the poor Russian immigrant, nor with that of the independent new woman whose personal virtue has made possible her emancipation. Rather, it points to a much more realistic picture of a woman who, through coincidence and favorable circumstances, managed to bring herself to the attention of the important group of primarily German-Jewish American philanthropists whose support was instrumental in affording Antin the opportunity to become an "American." It was this aspect of the book that met with the scorn of a Jewish reviewer. "To me," Salpeter wrote in *The Menorah Journal*, "[Antin] reveals herself as a smug, parvenu snob of the East Side, the sycophantic protegée of the nice and respectable persons who patronized her, a person to whom the East Side existed as inspiration for her writing moods" (177–78).

If Antin's role as mediator between the old and the new results in characters rewritten to suit the narrative's representative requirements, it also leads to a confusing image of the immigrant poor who are alternately presented from the perspective of middle-class America and from that of the ghetto itself. American negative images of the ghetto are systematically juxtaposed with Antin's inside knowledge of immigrant qualities as these are ultimately epitomized in her own exemplary career. Seeking the middle ground between immigrant and Anglo-Saxon, Antin admits that it is only a "certain class of aliens" who are capable of making use of the freedom that America offers everyone (359), while others, "stupid and unteachable," will fail in America (55). That is why she seems to agree with the "well-versed metropolitan,"—meaning the person familiar with the structure of the modern metropolis—who "knows the slums as a sort of house of detention for poor aliens, where they live on probation till they can show a certificate of good citizenship" (183). It is in such passages that the reassuring role of the mediator is clearest: the ghetto is presented not as a moral scandal, but as a necessary protective buffer. Moreover, the description implicitly establishes a natural link between poverty and crime that is not challenged by the rest of the chapter. Poverty is thus approached from a moralistic basis that sees it as a problem that will disappear when the poor arrive at the insight that they need only show enough willpower to live as good citizens to put an end to their miserable situation.

Antin maintains this philosophy of individual moral achievement in the face of such notable evidence to the contrary as the life of her sister Fetchke. In the Antin family, money came not only from the work done by the two parents, but also from the income brought home by Mary's slightly older sister Frieda, as she is called in the New World. Although the text discusses Frieda's fate more than once, it never explicitly admits that it is thanks to the labor put in by her sister that the family has sufficient funds to allow its studious young member to embark on a full educational career. Yet, at one point the narrator does express a sense of guilt: "I remember that I accepted the arrangements made for my sister and me without much reflection, and everything that was planned for my advantage I took as a matter of course. I was no heartless monster, but a decidedly self-centered child. . . . it was I that ran away [to school], on winged feet of joy and expectation; it was she whose feet were bound in the treadmill of daily toil" (201–2). There then follows a remarkable little sentence, which manages to mystify the real inequality between the siblings, instead pointing a self-critical finger at the protagonist's failure to appreciate the moral heroism implicit in Frieda's fate: "And I was so blind that I did not see that the glory lay on her, and not on me" (202). Dittmar has commented perceptively on the function performed by this sentence: "In other words: the injustice no longer appears to be lodged in the actual imbalance of burdens and privileges, but has been displaced to the (now corrected) way the author perceived it at the time" (*Assimilation* 73).[5]

Remembrance here functions at a micropolitical level, recall from a particular perspective affording the narrator an opportunity of disguising the untranscendable socioeconomic fact that the poor ghetto family could not afford to send Frieda, "the only one who was of a legal age to be put to work," to high school. Instead it manages to single out the ethical quality of one immigrant individual. The figure of Frieda moreover brings into focus the contradictory nature of Antin's characterization of the immigrant: Frieda, the typical immigrant, "bound in the treadmill of daily toil," on the one hand serves as a contrast to exceptional Mary, the carefree schoolgirl, yet, on the other hand, Frieda is also the moral heroine of the situation, proving that "typical" immigrants need not, after all, be morally deficient. Once again, we can observe the roles of mediator and new woman in intricate interaction.

In Mary Antin's work the new (wo)man and mediator figures take on their most interesting guise, as the two are locked in a contradiction from which the narrative desperately tries to escape. Antin was not, however, writing in a cultural void. Around the time when she published her "Autobiography of a Russian Immigrant," as *The Promised Land* is subtitled, American-Jewish fiction was appearing that approached the ethnic situation of the Jew in the United States through a reliance on similar conceptual structures. In the earlier of these novels the protagonist is more often seen as a new (wo)man, aspiring to membership in the Anglo-Saxon dominant class; in the later ones—published after *The Promised Land*—he or she more often seeks a middle position between the Real America and the Jewish metropolitan ghetto. It is tempting to conjecture that Antin's influential narrative was read by subsequent Jewish authors as above all a mediating story: the heroine stands with one foot in the Old World—the past she is trying to negate—and the other in the New—marrying Grabau and becoming a big success in gentile circles. But Antin's narrative must also have served to make later writers aware of the complicating factor that her heroine can only turn into a success because her audience can see in her the exceptional immigrant—the new woman, profiting from the beneficent influences of a healthy America. Undoubtedly, these other texts, like Antin's, struggle to define a clear position within the American sociopolitical landscape. They are marked above all by their desire to reduce the complexity of that landscape to the manageable proportions of new manhood or mediatorship, though few if any achieve a convincing resolution. I shall first consider an example of narratives that inscribe their protagonists in a new manhood and then go on to examine novels that can be better understood from the perspective of mediatorship. Finally, two autobiographical narratives by Elizabeth Stern will be discussed that interestingly display a recognition of the limitations of new manhood and mediatorship.

Typical of the new-manhood novels published in the first few decades of the twentieth century,[6] Ezra Brudno's *The Fugitive* (1904) centrally deals with the proposed intermarriage of Jew and Christian, as a young shtetl Jew—more than half of the novel is set in late-nineteenth-century eastern Europe—falls in love with an aristocratic Christian girl. The basic ingredients of the plot interestingly anticipate Zangwill's influential 1908 play *The Melting-Pot* (which he conceived in 1905 [Sollors 66], when Brudno's novel had just appeared). In both works a relationship between Jew and Gentile is complicated by the fact that the girl's father is responsible for the death of the boy's. In each case America resolves the problem by signaling an end to all Old World prejudices, leaving the lover-protagonists happily married. As David Fine comments: "History, in Brudno's vision, if not irrelevant, is escapable and erasable. Past grief, pain, alienation are shed, for the protagonist at least, as easily as earlocks and prayer shawls. There are no yokes or tethers" (20). Nonremembrance enables the hero's acculturation.

At the end of the narrative, Israel and his gentile wife Katia Bialnick "live in harmony with God and man" (390), but in order to reach this conclusion the text has to manage a number of persistent problems. Katia's father, for example, a disturbing reminder of the Old World past, conveniently dies on the eve of his daughter's marriage to Israel. The novel's penchant for melodrama is clear here. Bialnick, who had been instrumental in framing Israel's father with the alleged ritual slaughter of a Christian child, reappears in Israel's life just in time to ask with his dying breath the boy's forgiveness (386).[7]

Another problem is dealt with in a more interesting way: America's anti-Semitism poses a serious challenge to the harmony sought by the protagonist, a challenge that is eventually met by the inventiveness of the narrative. In the chronology of the story, "the Land of Liberty" is at first used as an ironic term, and America is attacked for the "merciless poverty and suffering" it inflicts on the immigrant Jew: " 'This misery is the work of cruel persecution,' " Israel reflects (277). Anti-Semitic taunts are the order of the day (275–76), and American justice serves to support the rich (German) Jews against the immigrant (Russian) ones (318–20). Developing this contrast provides a first solution to the disappointment with "the Land of Liberty," ultimately enabling the protagonist to wonder " 'What have I in common with the Jews?'. . . . 'Why not cut myself loose from these people? The Christians, indeed, have treated the Jews cruelly in the past, but what is that compared to the prejudice which the well-to-do American Jews have shown against the poor Russian refugees?' " (351). In this way Israel can convince himself that there is no longer any reason to refrain from marrying his aristocratic gentile bride. The novel thus presents the protagonist's choice as an essentially moral one, the repudiation of his Jewish heritage being justified by the ethical failings in German Jewish behavior.

Yet this moral criticism of German Jewish sweatshop owners, which was functional in the context of the contemplated intermarriage, is conveniently put aside from the moment that Israel and his friends can share the socioeconomic opportunities that America offers.[8] Jewish "fugitives from the land of bondage" are now said to "enjoy the liberty of our glorious country; they, too, have thriven in the great land of freedom" (389). The novel's epilogue notably singles out the socioeconomic success of its protagonists: formerly exploited Russian-Jewish friends of Israel's are now themselves the proud owners of "the prosperous factory of Levando & Son, who are the most prominent in one of the western States. . . . I have been successful in my profession, and also in gaining the respect and friendship of my good American neighbours" (389–90). The novel does not clarify how the Levando factory can lead the field without itself seeking recourse to methods similar to the ones so reviled earlier.

Neither does it turn the weapon of moral criticism against the practitioners of anti-Semitism, which continues to cloud the sky of glorious America. Instead, *The Fugitive* deals with this issue rhetorically. When Israel's son in turn is taunted with his Jewishness, his father sighs at the " 'cross' " he has to bear while the boy's gentile mother, Katia, "murmur[s]": " 'Father, forgive them, for they know not what they do' " (392). The Christian discourse is here used with reversed roles, the Jew suffering the fate of the Crucified, while the Christians now become tormentors. Israel experiences a "revelation" that enables him to interpret his own father's victimization as expressing "the symbolism of my race, the symbolism of the Christ. It showed me that the Crucified was the symbol of His people as my father was of his generation and as I am of mine. It showed me that . . . none but the fugitive race are the eternal bearers of the cross" (387). The symbol of crucifixion redeems the past, uniting both father and son, the one killed by Christian prejudice, the other exploited by German Jews and tormented by anti-Semitic intolerance, with Christ himself, a Jew killed by Romans. The essence of crucifixion thus becomes social persecution—the cross borne by the fugitive—rather than religious conflict.

This recuperation of Christian imagery for the self-definition of the Jewish "race" enables the narrative to complete its resolution of the problem of anti-Semitism. *The Fugitive* boldly seeks to inscribe its protagonist in the role of the persecuted Christ, transforming his Jewish heritage of suffering into a source of alignment with gentile America by appealing to the latter's historical identification with the Crucified. The novel's appropriation of Christian rhetoric is subtly made to serve the social aspirations that motivate the narrative. Those tendencies within American society that try to exclude the (Russian) Jews are now themselves paradoxically marginalized into the persecuting position the Jews historically occupied. Israel's new manhood thus in effect brings about a whole reorganization of the novel's social field, which allows the protagonist to achieve socioeconomic success—to join the American dominant class—without apparently denying his Judaism. Rewriting the cultural past, Brudno is able to realize his hero's assimilation with ideological integrity.

If Brudno's *The Fugitive* offers the best embodiment of the new-manhood strand in Jewish-American immigrant narrative, the clearest expression of mediatorship is to be found in Edward Steiner's appropriately entitled novel *The Mediator: A Tale of the Old World and the New*, published in 1907, five years before Antin made use of the two cultural roles. As a mediator, Steiner's hero will stand between the Jewish and Christian traditions: the novel evenhandedly exposes the horrors of Christian anti-Semitic violence and the harshness of a law-centered Judaism. But if the notion of mediation has practical consequences for the personal life of the protagonist, impelling him to refrain from pursuing the typical new-man path to private happiness through marriage to a gentile woman, mediation is here also synonymous with Christian conversion work among recent Jewish arrivals. While, at the end of the novel, the death of the hero's father at the hands of American anti-Semitic hoodlums acts as a strong enough reminder of his own membership in a Jewish community of suffering to stop him from marrying the Christian woman he loves, the mediator remains firm in his resolve to go out to recruit new men, who appreciate the moral superiority of an essentially

The New Man and the Mediator

love-based Christian religion over a legalistic Judaic faith. More implicitly the novel also suggests the need for the immigrant Jews' social emancipation. Mediatorship thus serves as the conceptual figure that organizes the main biographical narrative, while new manhood appears as the ultimate goal of the hero's mediating work. Unlike *The Promised Land,* in which the protagonist herself had been locked into a double bind between the roles of mediator and new woman, *The Mediator* is a simplistic, and heavily melodramatic, work, which adopts the guise of mediator to perform its real conversionary ideological mission.[9]

A curious work, which is mainly mediatory in intent, while displaying a certain kinship with Brudno's and Antin's new (wo)manhood resolutions, is Louis Pope Gratacap's *Benjamin the Jew* (1913). The main aim of this novel is to legitimize immigrant Jews on the ground that they should be acceptable to the observer because morally and aesthetically pleasing. The text is written very much from the point of view of such an external onlooker, and throughout treats Jewishness from a sympathetic distance. In *Benjamin the Jew* the narrator takes up an Anglo-Saxon attitude of initial unfamiliarity with the Jewish culture that turns into pleasant surprise at its richness and passionate indignation at the injustices inflicted on it. The book provides a clear illustration of the ideal of a mediatorship between Judaism and Christianity that is motivated by a desire for Jewish social emancipation.

Joseph Nassi, the protagonist's father, is described as an influential person in eastern Europe, where his position "had hitherto saved [his village] from the Pogram [sic]" (24). Nevertheless a pogrom scene, graphically depicted, is introduced as the reason for the family's departure for the United States (19–20). The manner of their crossing again emphasizes the Nassis' class status, though the exceptional nature of their treatment is nowhere identified. Consequently, the account of landing in New York comes across as incredibly naive, the immigrants waving goodbye to the ship's crew and simply walking off the ship to do some sightseeing before they make their way to their friends' home (97–99). A semblance of realism enters the narrative by way of a beautiful understatement when Joseph Nassi "began to feel that they were not entirely congenial to all citizens of his new home" (100). Soon the Nassis are lodged with their friends, at home in their habitual well-to-do surroundings. Their host, "Abraham Charles Loetter[,] was an admirable example of success, achieved in a country of limitless chances" (117). This success is not due to luck or won through exploitation of unexperienced immigrants (greenhorns), as it will be in Cahan's *Rise of David Levinsky* (1917). "Of course," the text quickly assures its readers, "he had swung up the ladder of material promotion by the exercise of inherent powers . . ." (117).

Yet the New York Jewish upper middle class is criticized for its lack of spiritual values, and the ideal the novel projects is symbolized by the place where the Nassi family will choose to live. Neither the Upper West Side nor the Lower East will do. Eastern Broadway, however, on the edge of the Jewish ghetto, is still Jewish in spirit, but "with its wide, well kept thoroughfare, its tidy shops" created a "pleasing" (the novel's key word) atmosphere: "the people grew here, . . . assimilated a finer culture, and keeping within the precincts of their religious separateness looked out on a fresher world" than the ghetto (148). Protagonist Benjamin, who, as youngest member of the family, holds the key to the future, is dubbed the "REDEEMER," who "should grow up in the midst of his own, drinking in from the fountains of Jewish literature and Jewish religion . . . and gathering to them too (should he confess it?) the polish and dignity of the Gentile individualistic isolation" (145). Trying to fuse within himself the best of the two traditions, Benjamin incorporates the dream of mediation, which seeks to achieve material success without surrendering—as would the pure new man—the heritage of the past. Yet the novel is at the same time reminiscent of the new-man resolution of *The Fugitive*, emphasizing as it does not so much the unification of Judaic and Christian ideology as the social rise of the Jew without loss of his religious and cultural specificity. What Benjamin's example is meant to achieve, we learn, is the "self-correction" of the Jewish poor (144). The highly atypical social situation of the novel's immigrant protagonists serves to underscore the imaginary and ultimately conservative nature of its proposed resolution.

Elias Tobenkin's *Witte Arrives* (1916) for its part is remarkable in that its mediatorship is not only dramatized at the level of the hero's actions but that it is also enacted at that of literary style in a form of cultural mediation between Old World and New. The most striking aspect of the novel, which distinguishes it from most other immigrant narratives, is that it devotes less attention to the milestones in the protagonist's encounter with America and more to day-to-day life. The actual arrival in the United States, for instance, is over before any of the immigrants notice it. "Masha Witkowski and her three children had been admitted to

The New Man and the Mediator

America, and they were not aware of it" (1). When the family meets father Witkowski, who had traveled ahead of the others to make a beginning in the New World, the actual encounter itself is reported only from the perspective of fellow train passengers, who, at first unpleasantly aroused by the un-American behavior of "the little group of stampeding aliens," soon regard the scene with "a kindly, understanding look" (13). What little Jewish emotionalism occurs in the text is safely filtered through an unimpeachably American point of view.

Seen in the context of the contemporary reception of immigrant fiction, Tobenkin's style appears to constitute an attempt to avoid the kind of criticism that had been leveled by reviewers only two years earlier at Edward Steiner's *From Alien to Citizen:* "The pictures which he draws are, many of them, too florid and too highly colored with emotion to be very palatable to a people, the reading section of which is still largely Teutonic. . . ." Indeed, the same newspaper, the *New York Times*, commended Tobenkin's novel "because it interprets [the Russian Jew] as he has never been interpreted before." But Tobenkin's restraint earned him the scorn of a prominent Jewish review, the *Menorah Journal*, which noted that "[t]he author hastens through the episodes in as unemotional a manner as if he were making a report to a charitable organization . . ." (Schwab, 108). Tobenkin's "error [was to try to] "write like Emerson, and [show] none of the earmarks of a foreigner" (109).

In fact, Tobenkin's aspiration to a New England intellectualism, free from alien emotional effusiveness, was counterbalanced by a desire to write what he calls "the book of life" (chapter 22). Tobenkin puts into the mouth of a publisher the praise that he would no doubt have liked to receive: " 'You have a story here that is different from anything that has been written in years. There is heart in it. . . . things one has lived through, sufferings one has experienced in one's soul' " (287). *Witte Arrives* aspires to an emotional restraint that does not obscure the heartfelt quality of its concerns. As such, the novel aims at a middle course between "Teutonic" detachment and "Russian" passion.

This mediatory aim is equally apparent in the character of the protagonist. While Witte's "political leanings" had struck the anxious *Springfield Republican* reviewer as "frankly socialistic," the nature of his social criticism is, as in so many of these immigrant novels, actually vaguely moral rather than politically radical. A typical observation runs as follows: " 'there is no reason why men who want work should not find it. There is no reason why work should be made hateful by mismanagement, by improper surroundings, by indifferent or brutal treatment of the worker.

... there is no reason why culture and refinement should be the heritage of the few' " (289). The novel follows the pattern of earlier work in mapping out a trajectory for its hero that leads to his personal accession to wealth, culture, and refinement through individual social climbing.

Although the hero marries a woman of "evident high breeding," "great culture and refinement," who contrasts strongly with Witte (he felt "'decidedly plebeian" next to her [220]), the only " 'problem' " the text singles out in their relationship is the partners' different "race" (298). In the final scene, Zangwill's *Melting-Pot* resolution of intermarriage is at first explicitly rejected because Witte's experience taught him that "Jew and Christian alike still cherished age-long prejudices against one another" (299). Yet, eventually, the text moves to the same conclusion as Brudno's *The Fugitive*, which, as we have seen, prefigured Zangwill's piece, marshalling "love" at the level of the innocent young people, the new Americans, as the only answer to "this muddle of religious bigotry and persecution. . . . this blind, unreasoned race hatred" (*Witte Arrives* 302). The title of the last chapter, "Old Sorrows and a New Life," captures the essence of Tobenkin's answer: his Jewish hero will always be bothered by the past sufferings of his people; a fresh start as a member of the New England intellectual and social aristocracy holds the promise of a solution. The staccato-style thoughts that occur on the penultimate page indicate that this avenue leaves the hero's Jewish identity far from unchallenged. As in *The Promised Land*, insistent negations point to an attempt to make the true purport of the resolution "innocent . . . , so that consciousness . . . must not accept it in its real meaning": "His father would understand him. . . . He was not surrendering. . . . He was not deserting . . ." (Buelens 327; *Witte Arrives* 303).[10] The conclusion is a typically mediatory one, with the protagonist rather desperately trying to reconcile unsettling memories of an Old World past and all it stood for with an urgent desire for participation in a New World future and all it holds in store.

The limits of both new manhood and mediatorship as strategies for coping with the promised land are exposed in the autobiographical work of the little-read Elizabeth Stern.[11] Her *My Mother and I* (1917) is above all a moving account of the growing estrangement between an immigrant mother and her rapidly Americanizing daughter. The overt tone of the book is that of the assimilated immigrant who looks back with some sadness on the cost of acquiring "a new self" but who is simultaneously convinced of the inevitability and rightness of her striving for rebirth

(117). In a foreword to the text, which had also prefaced its original appearance in the *Ladies Home Journal* (1916) (Umansky v), Theodore Roosevelt emphasized this latter aspect: "When we tend to grow disheartened over some of the developments of our American civilization, it is well worth while [sic] seeing what this same civilization holds for starved and eager souls who have elsewhere been denied what here we hold to be, as a matter of course, rights free to all . . ." (7). Yet contemporary reviews of the work were quick to recognize that it was "at once an idyl and a tragedy" *(New York Times)*, a book alive to the "pain and separation" involved in Americanization *(Cleveland)*.

An autobiographical novel in the tradition of Antin's *The Promised Land, My Mother and I* displays a similar desire to be at one and the same time the story of a mediator between the immigrant and America and that of a new woman who has entirely shed her Old World self. In her role as mediator, the narrator is able to draw a loving picture of the immigrant ghetto and its inhabitants. A long chapter devoted to the protagonist's activity as a scribe of letters for the illiterate members of the community remarks how she "could never have written one letter for [a usually loud-voiced peddler], if mother had not translated his grunts and embarrassed blushes, and extracted by sympathetic questions and tactful suggestions the information he wished to send to his father and to his sweetheart in Europe" (33). However, as soon as the narrator is aware of "the ideal of the new women which we, the college girls of this country were to be" (136), she begins to resent the ghetto and its "women who came in their slovenly dresses, content in their stupidity and their cloth, . . . the pale girls who simpered and toiled with the one aim of a dreary married life" (135).

Although the narrator is at pains to assure her mother "that it could never be she or father who would be 'strange' to me [but] the house, the dirty street" (139), her fundamental attack on the deficiencies of the ghetto cannot avoid censuring the woman who is, simultaneously and throughout the novel, made the object of such warm respect. In comparison to the women she meets outside the ghetto, the narrator's revered mother comes to seem a disappointingly pitiable drudge. Sally Drucker correctly observes that Stern "defines Americanization in terms of alienation from her parents, particularly her mother" (66). The ideal of motherhood that the protagonist encounters among her classmates, a "white-gowned, laughing, young mother," is, of course, unattainable to a woman who has to continue with her bonnet sewing even when visitors call round. That such economic realities constrain her mother's choices is something that neither the young protagonist nor the adult narrator consciously seem to appreciate. Writing at the age of thirty, Stern's selective memory does not recall such facts in the context of the new ideal she is worshiping. Yet, emotionally, there is a realization that the heroine is treating her mother unfairly in blaming her for occupying a class position that lies outside her power to change: the "I" figure "could not endure to see that strange look which for the first time in my life, mother turned to me": "something cut into my heart at the thought of hurting her" (111).

If *My Mother and I* and Antin's *The Promised Land* both struggle with the conflicting demands of new manhood and mediatorship, "Stern's motive for writing is connection with, rather than exorcism of, the past," as Sally Drucker has noted (65). Stern's book at times comes across as the more interesting because it thematizes the very tension between its protagonist's desire to become a Real American and her love of a mother who, the text acknowledges, cannot ever share her daughter's journey. Thus we read the new woman noting that "nothing . . . seemed to me more wonderful than to have been born of parents that were Americans" (107). "My mother country had always been—America," the heroine says elsewhere, "It was only my home that had not been American" (147). Her central aim in life becomes the creation of such an American home.

By the closing scenes of the story a deep rift has appeared between mother and daughter. Some reviewers perceptively noticed the contrived nature of the denouement, in which the protagonist marries "an American," whose exclusive command of the English language makes it impossible for him to communicate with his wife's mother, who knew "only Yiddish" (160). Ellen Umansky has in fact demonstrated persuasively that Stern's real husband must have been a Jew by descent, with whom the heroine's mother would have possessed at least that common plane (ix). In the early years of their marriage husband and wife even worked for some time on Jewish philanthropist Jacob Schiff's project "to reroute American Jewish immigration from New York to the Southwest" (Umansky ix).[12]

The climax of the sense of alienation between mother and daughter arrives when the former, full of expectation, comes to visit her daughter's first-born, exclaiming: " 'Now I can find the joy of all mothers again. I can find my lost young motherhood in your child' " (162). Her predicament is described with such great feeling that the reader's emotions are entirely directed toward sympathy for the poor old woman, ill

The New Man and the Mediator

at ease in the modern, sanitary world of her grandchild, "afraid to touch the crib, to soil the spotless rugs" (164–65). Above all, though, "son has been taught that he must play without demanding help or attention from adults about him" (164). The new, American standards demand that people be raised to become self-sufficient, atomized units in an efficiently organized labor process. "[Mother] felt alien, unnecessary" (165).

Despite the sympathy with which this stark contrast between the hopes and ideals of mother and daughter is presented, the final recuperative movement of the text rings quite false. "I wonder," the narrator exclaims, "if, as the American woman I strive to be I can find a finer example than my mother!" (168). In its attempt to reestablish the family link that had formed the structural basis of the work, the narrative ultimately can do little more than affirm the mother's worth as one of those who "do not understand America [b]ut have made their contribution to America—their sons and their daughters" (169). The conclusion of *My Mother and I* cannot outbalance or neutralize the impression left by the fundamental ideological split it has portrayed. On one side is situated a deprived but close-knit community that fends off poverty by hard work and mutual charity and that can make room for pleasure and emotional fulfilment only during the working day. On the other side of the rift are prosperous individuals who distinguish strictly between their paid jobs, including the social work that Stern embarks on, and their leisure time when there is room for pleasure and emotional values. In the later work *I Am a Woman—and a Jew* (1926) Stern discusses her unfitness for social work, which, she realizes after having left the profession,

> did not need—nor want to have—intensity of feeling, a burning desire to help one's neighbors, a great love for humankind, sympathy and unquestioning faith. It needed a cool mind . . . , it needed skepticism. . . .
> That was not ever mine to give. It was not in me to do work of the mind, without personal interest and affection. (35)

Though the criticism of social workers' attitudes is only muted, it is clear that Stern has abandoned much of her earlier belief in "efficiency" as a means toward the better life. Compared to the community tasks that the mother figure self-evidently fulfills in *My Mother and I,* American social work is presented as a heartless activity that rigorously seeks to exclude the very inspiration that should fire it.

The narrator's disappointment in her job is but the first step on a ladder of changes that gradually return the protagonist of *I Am a Woman— and a Jew* to the values of her parents. Her earlier moral criticism of the "slovenly" ghetto women is now implicitly reversed when she expresses her distaste for women, "middle-class Americans," who "lived for pleasure," caring for neither home and children, nor job. Whereas early in *I Am a Woman—and a Jew* the narrator's children are still described as " 'adorable little Gentiles,' " (123) the admirable product of the individualist education they received, later on the narrator registers her desire to see her son "tied" to his home, "even with bonds that would mean pain for him if they were broken . . ." (289). The narrator now does not hesitate to admit that she "hungered for the comfort of some religion, some way in which my father and his philosophy of life would be near to me and my life" (234). While the overt project of *My Mother and I* had still been to defend an individualistic Americanism, by the time Stern came to publish *I Am a Woman—and a Jew*, a strengthened sense of Jewishness leads her to conclude that ". . . I belong to my people" (362). Drucker has related the different attitudes expressed in the two works (she calls the ending of the later "diametrically opposed to the ending of her first" [69]) to the distinct historical context in which they appeared. If the early book "emphasizes the immigrant's contribution to America even if it also describes some alienation and loss," it does so because it appeared during World War I, when Americans rallied together against a common enemy (69). In the later work, "despite the descriptions of social and material gains, the emphasis appears to be on what America has taken from the immigrant Jew: a sense of spiritual wholeness" (69). The change can be linked to the upsurge of "American nativism and anti-immigrant feeling that followed World War I. Stern and other writers were no longer as optimistic about the possibilities of American pluralism" (69).

In her introduction to *I Am a Woman—and a Jew*, Ellen Umansky provides details about Stern's subsequent development. Rather than return to a religious Judaism, a step that did not seem impossible to the narratorial voice of the 1926 text, Stern in the early 1940s joined the Quaker movement, which Umansky aptly circumscribes by its alternative designation the "Religious Society of Friends" (xv). Umansky maintains that Stern in this way seemed "to have turned away from her earlier struggle to forge a bond between her world and the world of her father" (xvi). I would argue that in joining a community that places friendship so centrally Stern did return to the example of her immigrant mother and made clear her ultimate dissatisfaction with the atomized, efficient America she courted as a young adult. The strong mediatory emotional undercurrent that could be identified throughout her writing in the end

The New Man and the Mediator

managed to gain the upper hand over the new woman stance that she at first quite ruthlessly attempted to adopt.

To conclude this essay, I should like to describe how the two cultural roles that organized Mary Antin's *The Promised Land* in such a complex way further appeared in the author's life and writing. Before the end of the decade that had seen the publication of her autobiography, Antin suffered the simultaneous disappointment of seeing her beloved country turn against even its assimilated immigrant citizens and of losing her "ideal gentile husband [who] removed himself, alone, to China" (Gartner 47). The eventual breakdown of the marriage in 1920 seems to have been accelerated by the tensions of the "World War and the xenophobic, isolationist period which followed" (Handlin xiii). Antin's "attack of neurasthenia" in 1918 (Handlin xiv) is explained by Wardlaw on primarily cultural grounds: her flight into depression was a reaction to the "deception" that Antin felt had replaced the promise of the American dream and new (wo)manhood (89).

Antin's subsequent silence was broken only briefly, once in 1937 and a second time in 1941, when she published "House of the One Father," an essay in which the mediating role that had figured implicitly in her autobiography becomes more prominent. Antin here assumes the role of mediator by displaying, as a Jewish woman, an active interest in alternative religious traditions, most notably the Christian; at the same time she emphasizes her renewed allegiance—as an American who "[f]or decades . . . had lived cut off from Jewish life and thought"—to her own "Jewish fold . . . in a time of virulent anti-Semitism" (41). This mediatorship is vividly illustrated by an anecdote that features Antin as an invited lecturer in a Protestant church serving as lecture hall:

> With a shock I realized that I was standing in the pulpit itself, the place of authority of a Christian house of worship. . . .
> Open your eyes, America, and see a miracle. I stand before you *healed*, I sang, with a great and final healing that spreads to a whole people. Centuries of Jewish history are atoned for in this moment you have created. The dark abyss of separation between Jew and Gentile is closed by my presence in this pulpit. (39)

The exultant tone magnifies the isolated occurrence all out of proportion. It is, moreover, placed in the context of Antin's discovery of the New Testament and her growing awareness of "the supreme role of Jesus of Nazareth in *mediating* the Hebrew tradition to the modern world" (38) (emphasis added). The near juxtaposition of the two statements seems to cast Antin in the part of a new Messiah, but, crucially, it fails to appreciate the full thrust of the comparison. Jesus was, of course, not simply a mediator between the old and the new but was, in a sense, a new man, seen from the perspective of the new religion of Christianity. Antin has not yet managed to resolve the confusing double bind in which she finds herself as one who desires to mediate and one who would fully belong to the New World. A further complicating parallel is that the historical consequences of Jesus' supposed mediation were, as Antin acknowledges indirectly in the essay, the Jews' " 'bloody persecution in all Christian lands' " (38). The new religion largely supplanted and tried to extinguish the old in the same way that, in *The Promised Land,* the narrator wanted to forget the past in order to become a full-fledged member of the present. The figure of the mediator, we can conclude, ultimately cannot disguise the aggressive effect the new (wo)man has on the cultural past.

Antin's relationship to her cultural past, fraught with anxiety, epitomizes the problematical dimensions of the narratives here considered. Most of these display a basic disposition toward new (wo)manhood, protagonists attempting to inscribe themselves in the American ideology of individual social ascent. Concurrent with this orientation is a desire to reject the ties that bind to the past. Yet, a mediatory recollection of the Jewish history of suffering is rarely absent from these works, producing an often uncomfortable complexity. In the most interesting texts, such as *The Promised Land* and *My Mother and I,* remembrance occupies the heart of the narrative, as the protagonist seeks to untangle the conflicting hold of the two immigrant roles by rewriting the past in such ways as make it rationally and emotionally acceptable to the new (wo)man holding the pen.

Notes

1. See, e.g., Dittmar, Guttmann, and Sherman.

2. The term new woman is used throughout the essay as the feminine variant of the new man figure, as defined earlier.

3. The original German comment runs as follows: "Man spürt, dass diese Positionsbestimmung eher den Charakter einer Absichtserklärung hat als den einer affektiv gesicherten Selbstdefinition." See also Freud's work on negation, which concludes that "Negation is a way of taking cognizance of what is repressed; indeed it is already a lifting of the repression, though not, of course, an acceptance of what is repressed" (235–36). The repressed is thus "rationally negated,

The New Man and the Mediator

i.e. its true meaning is made innocent . . . , so that consciousness . . . must not accept it in its real meaning" (Buelens 327).

4. I must register here my indebtedness to Stephen Fender's discussion with me of the significance of initiation rituals to *The Promised Land.* See also his *Sea Changes.*

5. The original German comment runs as follows: "Mit anderen Wörten: Als ungerecht erscheint nicht mehr das faktische Ungleichgewicht der Lasten und Privilegien, sondern nur dessen damalige (jetzt korrigierte) Beurteilung durch die Verfasserin."

6. Other examples are Wolf, Brudno's *The Tether,* Sterner, and Nichols.

7. As Louis Harap aptly characterizes *The Fugitive:* "[it] mechanically winds through coincidence . . ." (19).

8. Dittmar points to *The Fugitive* as an illustration of the fact that before World War II Jewish immigrants' scrupulous pursuit of social success mostly does not appear as the epitome of an American mentality but rather as personal failure of character ("In der Zeit vor dem zweiten Weltkrieg erscheint die skrupellose Jagd jüdischer Immigranten nach gesellschaftlichem Erfolg indes meist noch nicht als Inbegriff amerikanischer Mentalität sondern eher als persönliche Charakterlosigkeit") (*Assimilation* 159).

9. In view of the author's position as professor of theology at the Protestant Grinnell College, Iowa, these are hardly surprising aspects. Steiner's autobiography *From Alien to Citizen* recounts his ideological trajectory.

10. Rideout's comment on Tobenkin's later novel *The Road,* in which ethnicity plays no part—is apt here too: "the book is dated in technique despite the liberal use of three dots in the passages reproducing the characters' thoughts" (118).

11. None of the standard overviews of Jewish-American literature and culture (such as Fischel and Pinsker or Fried et al.) refer to Stern. Brief remarks are offered by Dittmar, "Jüdische Gettoliteratur"; a more substantial though flawed discussion is Drucker's (see below).

12. Little is known of Stern's life, however. There is even some confusion over her maiden name, Umansky giving it as Elizabeth Gertrude Levin (ix), the author's son T[homas] Noel Stern listing Elizabeth Gertrude Limburg in his own *Who's Who* entry. Noel Stern's entry also mentions that he is preparing a "combination autobiography and family history," which holds the promise of more information. By treating *My Mother and I* as a straightforward autobiography, Sally Drucker mistakenly assumes that all the events it mentions are actual facts, including the marriage to a gentile.

Works Cited

Antin, Mary. "House of the One Father." *Common Ground* 1 (1941): 36–42.

———. *The Promised Land.* Boston: Houghton, 1912; Princeton: Princeton UP, 1985.

Brudno, Ezra Selig. *The Fugitive: Being Memoirs of a Wanderer in Search of a Home.* New York: Doubleday, 1904.

---. *The Tether*. Philadelphia: Lippincott, 1908.
Buelens, Jan. "Negation in Freud." *Logique et Analyse* ns 57-58 (1972): 319-31.
Burch, Connie B. S. "Women's Voices, Women's Visions: Contemporary American Jewish Women Writers." Diss. Purdue U, 1987.
Burchell, R. A., and Eric Homberger. "The Immigrant Experience." *Introduction to American Studies*. 2d ed. Ed. Malcolm Bradbury and Howard Temperley. London: Longman, 1989. 158-80.
Dittmar, Kurt. *Assimilation und Dissimilation: Erscheinungsformen der Marginalitätsthematik bei jüdisch-amerikanischen Erzählern (1990-1970)*. Frankfurt: Lang, 1978.
---. "Jüdische Gettoliteratur: Die Lower East Side, 1890-1924." *Amerikanische Gettoliteratur: Zur Literatur ethnischer, marginaler und unterdrückter Gruppen*. Ed. Berndt Ostendorf. Darmstadt: Wissensch. Buchges., 1983. 50-112.
Drucker, Sally M. "Autobiographies in English by Immigrant Jewish Women." *American Jewish History* 79 (1989): 55-71.
Fender, Stephen. *Sea Changes: American Literature and British Emigration*. Cambridge: Cambridge UP, 1992.
Fine, David M. "In the Beginning: American-Jewish Fiction, 1880-1930." Fried et al. 15-34.
Freud, Sigmund. "Negation." *Standard Edition*. New York: Norton, 1990. Vol. 19. 235-39.
Fried, Lewis, et al., eds. *Handbook of American-Jewish Literature: An Analytical Guide to Topics, Themes, and Sources*. New York: Greenwood, 1988.
Gartner, Carol Blicker. "A New Mirror for America: The Fiction of the Immigrant of the Ghetto, 1890-1930." Diss. New York U, 1970.
Girgus, Sam B. *The New Covenant: Jewish Writers and the American Idea*. Chapel Hill: U of North Carolina P, 1984.
Gratacap, Louis Pope. *Benjamin the Jew*. New York: Benton, 1913.
Guttmann, Allen. *The Jewish Writer in America: Assimilation and the Crisis of Identity*. New York: Oxford UP, 1971.
Hackett, Alice Payne. *70 Years of Bestsellers: 1895-1965*. New York: Bowker, 1967.
Handlin, Oscar. Foreword. *The Promised Land*. By Mary Antin. v-xv.
Harap, Louis. *Creative Awakening: The Jewish Presence in Twentieth-Century American Literature, 1900-1940s*. Contributions in Ethnic Studies 17. New York: Greenwood (in cooperation with American Jewish Archives), 1987.
Jameson, Fredric. *The Political Unconscious: Narrative as a Socially Symbolic Act*. Ithaca: Cornell UP, 1981.
Mann, Arthur. *The One and the Many: Reflections on the American Identity*. Chicago: U of Chicago P, 1979.
Nichols, Anne. *Abie's Irish Rose: A Novel*. New York: Grosset, 1927.
Rev. of *From Alien to Citizen*, by Edward Steiner. *New York Times* 1 November 1914: 477.
Rev. of *My Mother and I*, by Elizabeth Stern. *Cleveland* July 1917: 100.
Rev. of *My Mother and I*, by Elizabeth Stern. *New York Times* 8 July 1917: 255.
Rev. of *The Promised Land*, by Mary Antin. *New York Times* 14 April 1912: 228.
Rev. of *Witte Arrives*, by Elias Tobenkin. *New York Times* 27 Aug. 1916: 334.
Rev. of *Witte Arrives*, by Elias Tobenkin. *Springfield Republican* 9 Dec. 1916: 3.

The New Man and the Mediator

Rideout, Walter B. *The Radical Novel in the United States 1900–1954: Some Interrelations between Literature and Society.* Cambridge: Harvard UP, 1956.

Roosevelt, Theodore. Introduction. *My Mother and I.* By Elizabeth Stern. 7.

Salpeter, Harry. "The Jew as Autobiographer." *Menorah Journal* 5 (1919): 175–78.

Schwab, Rosalind Ach. "Two 'First Novels.' " Rev. of *Witte Arrives*, by Elias Tobenkin, and *The Abyss*, by Nathan Kussy. *Menorah Journal* 3 (1917): 108–10.

Sherman, Bernard. *The Invention of the Jew: Jewish-American Education Novels (1916–1964).* New York: Yoseloff, 1969.

Sollors, Werner. *Beyond Ethnicity: Consent and Descent in American Culture.* New York: Oxford UP, 1986.

Steiner, Edward. *From Alien to Citizen.* New York: Revell, 1914.

———. *The Mediator: A Tale of the Old World and the New.* New York: Revell, 1907.

Stern, Elizabeth Gertrude. *My Mother and I.* New York: Macmillan, 1917.

Stern, Elizabeth Gertrude. (as Leah Morton). *I Am a Woman—and a Jew.* 1926. Masterworks of Modern Jewish Writing; New York: Wiener, 1986.

Sterner, Lawrence. *The Un-Christian Jew.* New York, 1917.

Tobenkin, Elias. *Witte Arrives.* 1916. Upper Saddle River, NJ: Gregg, 1968.

Umansky, Ellen M. Introduction. *I Am a Woman—and a Jew.* By Elizabeth Stern. 1986. v–xvi.

Usandizaga, Aranzazu. "Two Versions of the American Dream: Mary Antin's *The Promised Land* and Agnes Smedley's *Daughter of Earth.*" *Deferring a Dream: Literary Sub-Versions of the American Columbiad.* Ed. Gert Buelens and Ernst Rudin. ICSELL Ser. Basel: Birkhäuser (forthcoming).

Wardlaw, Ruth. "Recastings of the Self: The Interaction of Metaphor and Personal History in American Immigrant Autobiography." Diss. Emory U, 1976.

Wolf, Emma. *Other Things Being Equal.* Chicago: McClurg, 1892.

Zangwill, Israel. *The Melting-Pot.* New York: Macmillan, 1908.

Memory and Silences in the Work of Tillie Olsen and Henry Roth

JULES CHAMETZKY

Henry Roth's *Call It Sleep* (1934) and Tillie Olsen's *Tell Me a Riddle* (1961) explore and demonstrate in complex ways how personal is the personal, how political the political, and how difficult to assess the relationship between the two, when seen against the contingencies of time, circumstance, and individual histories. Despite the political nature of the authors' early commitments (both were Communists in the 1930s) and the social aspects within their texts—rooted in a certain kind of immigrant Jewish experience and history, the poverty they came out of and write about—as I read them there is something irreducibly personal in the lives central to these works.

What has intrigued discoverers of Roth is the long creative silence after the achievement of this novel. Was the "silence" specific to Roth as a person, or was it the result of the times he lived through, the restraints of his political commitments, and the larger social and political milieu in which he lived? Not surprisingly, the answers to this riddle have come down on both sides. Roth himself has thought about and attempted to answer these questions in a variety of ways, as will be seen later in this inquiry.

In her important collection of essays and reflections entitled *Silences* (1978), Olsen outlines the reasons for her long period of removal from literary pursuits after her early recognition as a writer on the left in the 1930s until her return in the late 1950s as a writer and the success of *Tell Me a Riddle* in 1961. Since that time she has become one of the most influential feminist writers, although the Jewish, political, and existential elements of her most famous story could as easily be foregrounded. Olsen seems less tentative than Roth in her self-appraisal, though that, too, requires some interrogation.

In the pain of their personal lives within the painful political era they traversed will be found reasons for their long literary silences—for many years *after* significant utterance by one, both before and after a major literary achievement for the other. There was loss and, in Olsen's case (perhaps lately in Roth's case as well), recovery, but the lacerating effects of a total or deep recall cannot be underestimated—so when it occurs, one can understand the deep need for silence. Indeed, that "need for silence" is profoundly bodied forth in each of their most significant fictional works.

There is much that is revealing, suggestive, and complicated in these writers' lives and in the production, reception, and impact of the works in question.

Henry Roth was born in 1906 in Galicia (now Austria), brought to the United States when he was eighteen months old, much the same as David Schearl, the protagonist of *Call It Sleep;* Tillie Olsen was born in 1912 in Nebraska, the second of seven children of Ida and Samuel Lerner (a longtime socialist). They now live in New Mexico and California, respectively.

As a student Roth became the protégé of his teacher, the writer Eda Lou Walton—the first of several maternal women he was to become attached to—to whom *Call It Sleep* is dedicated. He joined the Communist Party in 1933, three years after he began the novel. When exactly he left the party is not clear, though interestingly enough, 1956 was the year of Khrushchev's revelations to the Twentieth Congress about Stalin's crimes, the year of the Hungarian uprising, and the year in which revived interest in *Call It Sleep* began. In *The Radical Novel in the United States* (1956), Walter Rideout called it one of the most distinguished proletarian novels, after it had gone virtually unmentioned in literary histories for twenty years. In that same year Alfred Kazin and Leslie Fiedler both named it in an *American Scholar* survey of undeservedly neglected books of the past twenty-five years (the *only* book to receive more than one mention). In that year Roth suffered a severe and incapacitating depression.[1]

The book was republished in hardcover in 1960 (Cooper Square Publishers) but did not then get noticed in any appreciable fashion. The "breakthrough" came with Irving Howe's front-page *New York Times Book Review* piece on the 1964 Avon paperback edition. Giving such space and prominence to a paperback reprint was and remains, according to Bonnie Lyons, unprecedented for the *Times*.[2]

What has intrigued almost everyone who has rediscovered Roth is the long silence—the hiatus in his career after the generally acknowledged achievement of his until then only published writing. From then until

1990 (about which more later) there are a few scattered periodical publications: two short pieces in *The New Yorker* in 1939–40, another in the year of his resurrection, a couple of parables in *Commentary* in 1959–60, and another *New Yorker* piece in 1966. There were occasional *segments* of an apparent work in progress and interviews, but essentially a long *literary* silence. In the late 1930s or early 1940s he destroyed manuscripts of two aborted, more proletarian, less personal novels in progress. For twenty years there were jobs as a metal worker and as a psychiatric aide in Maine—where he also raised geese and ducks for years. After that there were bouts of travel, some research, and short and scattered pieces. Only lately, in his 85th year, has there been a significant change—a veritable outpouring of writing, though his first wish was that none of it was to appear in English until two years after his death.[3] He has changed his mind, however, and *A Star Shines over Mount Morris Park,* the first volume of a longer project called *Mercy of a Rude Stream,* appeared in 1994.[4] More on that later.

How much did the political climate of the times and his own commitments stifle or otherwise affect him? A difficult question to answer definitively. There was a negative reception in a party organ that wounded him—and who knows what kind of behind-the-scenes criticism. A one-paragraph unsigned review in *The New Masses* attacked *Call It Sleep* for being "too long, too impressionistic, too introspective" and for overemphasizing "the sex phobias of a six-year-old Proust."[5] It should be pointed out, however, that this attack was quickly followed by many left-wing defenses of the novel (albeit often in political terms), and in fact, the book had rather a good reception overall and a good sale (two printings) in its original publication.[6]

Roth did attempt a more stalwart proletarian fiction afterward, but because it was not to his satisfaction, he ultimately destroyed it. In one of his later parables he suggests that the wilderness through which he wandered all those years of silence was indeed part of the public, political scene of those years.

On my reading of the novel, however—and those elements of his life available to a researcher—I have to come down on the side of claiming the silence was built into and in a sense emerges from the events and sensibility bodied forth in the text. To read *Call It Sleep,* judging from personal experience and the responses of students and critics over decades, is invariably to experience an almost unbearable pain in and with it—the pleasures in its subtleties, craft, even occasional *opera buffa* qualities come later. There is the difficulty and pain of simply reading the

Memory and Silences

dialects, but more significantly the feeling of raw, exposed nerves, in David Schearl and behind him in the author. Above all, there is the pain and terror of the almost unmediated Oedipal conflict that is at the heart of the book—the incredible threat of the at times crazed father Albert Schearl and the incredible sensitivity and vulnerability of the child David Schearl who endures and lives it (though barely).[7] The core of the book is an extraordinary case study, the resolution of which might require a psychotherapeutic solution, not a political or social one.

Perhaps that suggests why *Call It Sleep* received such appreciation in the Eisenhower and anti-Communist 1950s and in the years of the Kennedy rapprochement with American ethnicity. Insofar as its emphasis and impact were so clearly psychological, here was a definitely ethnic book in its setting, language, and ambience, by a onetime Communist (who had already paid the price of marginalization common to other early political radicals), that called for no serious ethnic or other social-political assertion. Perhaps, too, one could observe in it the ugliness of the immigrant's enforced English, so masterfully recorded in the book, and lament the loss of the richer selves revealed in the immigrant's own first language—the occasional Yiddish and the lyrical English of its translation associated with the mother's tender talks with the son. This would represent an early and covert affirmation of "roots"—and an ambiguous one, because on the evidence of David's life and experience, there was also much that was ugly, painful, and destructive in the early ethnic experience, much that one would just as soon forget or abandon.

Although this largely autobiographical novel is steeped in the Jewish-American experience and depends heavily on the rhythms, vocabulary, and speech-act uses of Yiddish, Roth broke early in his life with Judaism and Jewishness. According to Bonnie Lyons in her fine piece, he was recommending as late as 1963 the total assimilation of Jews in America. Only with the Six-Day Arab-Israeli war of 1967 did Roth discover a strong sense of concern with and acknowledge a Jewish identification. But then his identification was with the Israelis, not with American Jewry.[8] To me, this is a clear case of denial—repressing and enforcing silence about an important dimension of his own life and background. This repudiation is not incompatible with the "need for silence" I find prefigured in *Call It Sleep*.

2

In *Silences* (1978), Tillie Olsen observes that she "did not publish a book" until she was fifty, and she says that she was for most of her life "as distant from the world of literature . . . as literature is distant from my world." That refers to the roughly twenty-year period of silence (like Roth's) that began about 1934–35, when she was a promising young Communist writer (she joined the Young Communist League in 1933) publishing under her maiden name. As Tillie Lerner she appeared in *Partisan Review* when it was an organ of the John Reed Club. At the time she was one of the few woman writers, and perhaps the *only* one, speaking at the 1935 American Writers congress (to judge from its printed program). In 1955 she enrolled as a student of writing at Stanford and began the process that led to *Tell Me a Riddle*. In *Silences* she lists the reasons why she effectively stopped writing during this period: married in 1936, soon thereafter the mother of three children, years spent answering family demands, political activity, and work, work, work at a variety of working-class jobs to make ends meet. A writing fellowship in 1956–57 gave her the time and money to begin and finally publish the four stories that became the 1961 book.

Tell Me a Riddle was an almost instant success (the title story won a first-place O. Henry Award in 1961) and of great influence ever since. The women's movement was at the time nascent, the left practically nonexistent—what many of us were struck by in those waning days of the New Criticism was the *political* intelligence and concern that informed this subtly and brilliantly crafted collection of stories. The Woman Question was seen as unmistakably and boldly there, and one was also very aware that the people in the title story were of the old Jewish left (at the Haven, the husband says, there is "a reading circle. Chekhov they read, that you like, and Peretz. Cultured people . . ."), and that Eva, the grandmother, like Olsen's own parents, was a "1905-er." It is, finally, to the vision of luminous idealism and purposefulness embodied in that failed 1905 Russian revolution that Eva returns in her late moments. That experience, that past, is the yardstick that measures the loss that she (and they, and we) have experienced in this century, in this place.

The best single essay on Olsen that I know underlines her political roots and attachments, establishing her in a line of *socialist* feminism.[9] As the women's movement has grown in force through three decades, "Tell Me a Riddle" has become almost a sacred text, and the influence of Olsen's writing, teaching, and discoveries cannot be overstated. As Rosenfelt says, "Her work has been particularly valued by contemporary feminists, for it has contributed significantly to the task of reclaiming women's achievements and interpreting their lives."[10]

Memory and Silences

Read as a text of a certain kind of feminist politics, the story powerfully foregrounds the ways in which woman's autonomy, self, capacities for development and life (so much "unused life" is a refrain through the story) have been denied by traditional and, at the time of its publication, relatively unquestioned man/woman, mother/children, woman/family relations. That is perfectly clear, but in this reading and use, which have assured the story's power and influence, the older political meanings and its Jewishness—in a recent interview Olsen has affirmed her "Yiddishkayt," from a Jewish left, secular humanist perspective—as well as a certain bleak existential quality (the personal confrontation with age and death) may be overlooked or undervalued.

The feminist view of both the story and Olsen, when it downplays the political side (narrowly considered), has bestowed a feminist identity upon the writer that may have filled an emotional and political vacuum left by the failure of the old left. Her situation would seem more promising than Roth's, for whom an oblique return to a form of Jewish identity may serve to fill a similar vacuum. Her fictional breakthrough in 1961, while followed by the production of several extremely significant texts, has not, however, been followed by much significant new fiction.

Olsen has produced since then a stunning essay on Rebecca Harding Davis's *Life in the Iron Mills* (1972) and the important meditation on women and writing, *Silences*, already cited. There is a manuscript called "Requa," a novel about Native Americans in northern California, as yet uncompleted, although a section of it first appeared in 1970 (in the *Iowa Review*). That and *Yonnondio: From the Thirties* (significant subtitle!) in 1974 appear to be the only sustained fictional works since *Tell Me a Riddle*—and *Yonnondio* is the first section of a novel begun in the 1930s, put away, and revised some forty years later. If one were to inquire into the sources of the "slowness" (which Olsen herself has recognized and tried to understand as a legacy of a lifetime, as a woman, of having to put things off), the almost obsessive perfectionism of Olsen that seems to limit her productivity, one would have to address the personal, the psychology of the writer as well as the gender-related social roots she so well defines in *Silences*.

3

Henry Roth's would seem to be the "harder" case, but it is intriguing to note that the long drought since *Call It Sleep* has ended—the much-celebrated "block" overcome as Roth passes his 87th year. First of all,

Mario Materassi helped Roth assemble in 1987 the extremely useful and interesting collection of all of Roth's published pieces, however small or scattered in time, along with informative interviews and correspondence, in *Shifting Landscape: A Composite, 1925–1987*.[11]

Since then, Materassi has translated and published in Italy in March 1990 a slim volume of some one hundred pages from *Mercy of a Rude Stream*, a novel/memoir-in-progress that Roth has worked on over the past decade and that may contain over three thousand pages in manuscript form. Materassi is at work translating an additional three hundred pages for later publication. Roth meanwhile has written several hundred pages of another memoir that is projected to be of equal length. These pieces were originally intended to appear only in Italian translation, and possibly at some point in German, Roth earlier having stipulated that nothing of this work was to appear in English until two years after his death.[12] And so, even as he writes and publishes again, with a new-found prolificity, a kind of cat-and-mouse game with silence continues—although he has now decided to allow U.S. publication of some of this material (as noted earlier).[13]

As mentioned previously, Roth has attempted to anatomize the reasons for his silence and alludes to other well-known one-book or merely repetitive authors, but with a less assured locus for it than Olsen has suggested in her reflections on the subject. His theories about it have been many and keep changing, he said in 1975.[14] On the one hand, to compress many of Roth's observations, he couldn't believe (he said in 1969) that someone as talented and disciplined as he was *could* stop writing. It must have been the 1930s, he suggests—it wasn't his particular affliction. "The cases," he concludes in these reflections, "are personal, but they were also much bigger than any of us."[15] Such a statement would be hard to disagree with—the legacy of a 1920s modernist aesthetics, then the era of the leftward turn of so many writers in the face of economic collapse and the rise of fascism were indeed events of surpassing importance.[16] Yet he clearly points to the paramount role of personal conflict when in the first interview in *Shifting Landscape* he talks about "a counterdrive *not* to write." That, he says, was his dybbuk.[17] Toward the end of *Shifting Landscape*, Roth says that before the 1970s when, for various reasons (his new-found commitment to Israel, more leisure, encouragement from Materassi and others), his work began to flow again, whenever he considered writing again, everything inside "turned to jelly, turned to fluid" as he thought about the events of his life, the putative subject of his writing.[18] There we may have the bedrock anxiety, whose true roots probably require some form of depth analysis.

Memory and Silences

In one of the latest published interviews with Materassi (1986), he comments on the parable "The Dun Dakotas," which he published in *Commentary* in 1960. In the parable—which is transparently about his "block"—a scout in Indian country is waiting for a chief to let him through. Finally, after a period of seeming petrification, he is told he can pass. Roth tells his interviewer that at the time he wrote this "the guy was trapped by history, in the same way Joyce was trapped by history. . . . But in actual fact, when it comes down to the reality of the thing, I don't think Joyce was trapped by history: I think Joyce was trapped by himself, just as I was by myself."[19]

In *Silences,* Olsen locates the primary if not the sole source of silence in the circumstances of social life. In one of the first introductory paragraphs of the book she notes that "literary history and the present are dark with silences: some the silences for years by our acknowledged greats; some silences hidden; some the ceasing to publish after one work appears [Roth's case]; some the never coming to book form at all." "This book," she writes, "is about such silences. It is concerned with the relationship of circumstances—including class, color, sex; the times, climate into which one is born—to the creation of literature."[20] After that early 1960s statement, which also includes male writers who suffered significant silences, Olsen writes more strongly in the 1970s about the special and more overriding (in numbers, depth, extent) of the silences imposed upon women. In the strong essay called "One Out of Twelve: Writers Who Are Women in Our Century" she cites the women who took years and years to get one book done or whose production, though distinguished, was limited. Compared to men writers of like distinction and years of life, few women writers have had lives of unbroken productivity or leave behind a "body of work." "Early beginnings, then silence; or clogged late ones (foreground silences); long periods between books (hidden silences); characterize most of us. A Colette, Wharton, Glasgow, Millay, Lessing, Oates, are the exceptions."[21] She talks a little later, in what is very personal, given the anguish and slowness of her own production, about the habits, the weight of years, that press in upon women, not easily broken, so that what should take weeks takes months, what should take months takes years.[22]

All of this is powerful, true, and one would hope by now familiar. Yet we must also try to assess the irreducibly personal—even as we admit in the obvious cases cited above that the personal, when repeated in large numbers, as C. Wright Mills instructed us years ago, is political (or at least a *social* fact).

A close look at the key fictional texts, the two master works produced by these writers, is in order—not to crudely or dogmatically psychologize from them, but to search for a clue to the perhaps unexpressed psychic *need* as well as *burden* of silence. I will focus only on some of the elements that illuminate the pain of memory and its double-edged quality—on the one hand redeeming and validating lives and histories, on the other its potentially paralyzing quality. As much as there is a need to remember there may be a need to forget.[23]

4

The story "Tell Me a Riddle" is divided into four sections, enumerated but not titled, though I believe the controlling idea, metaphor, or theme in each ultimately leaps out at one.[24] In section 1, Eva's cancer is discovered and certain key themes are announced: "the stubborn, gnarled roots of the quarrel" between husband and wife through forty-seven years of marriage, now bursting out, distressing their grown children. Section 2 ends with the italicized line *"Goodbye, my children"*—a fit title as we delve deeply in this section into Eva's values and her history of being forced to put *self* aside. She will let it all out now, bitterness included, sticking to her guns, as it were, in all areas of present confrontation. She declines the ministrations of a rabbi in her sickness, recalling her old and fundamental antireligious attitudes (not to teach "superstitions," she spits out. "Race: human, religion none" she says defiantly and proudly); she declines to play "the good grandmother," refusing the embrace of a child—*not* being conventional, living according to others' needs and definitions of one. One great source of pain in the story, besides the acutely physical, is the pain of all her repressed and deflected life. Who can recall it, where did it go? The waste. The bitterness. Section 3 could be called "In the dwelling places of the cast-off old" (its first sentence), in which Eva, after recognition of all the unused life around her, in her, *everywhere*, knows she is dying.[25] Section 4 presents "The Death" itself, in all its harrowing physical agony. All the earlier themes recur—the reawakening of old values, mourning for unlived life in herself and others, but recalling vividly its promise and potential. It and she are full of the sorrow and pity of our century and its horrors, its "monstrous shapes," of this kind of life and death. We can now begin to tell or ask the riddle she evaded earlier—"What is the meaning of your life, Grandma?" The meaning is in *this telling* and if there is *any redemption*

Memory and Silences

that has to be it—a heavy burden, given that the full story is too horrible, let alone too *much* to recall in its entirety.

Call It Sleep is also divided into four parts, albeit each much longer and more complex than in the Olsen story. Each is designated with a title based on a concrete place or object that has an important and unifying meaning in the section and ultimately in the story as a whole. Various themes in each are linked and cumulatively grow toward a powerful resolution and denouement. The titles are symbolic, combining and compressing meanings, emotions, and values.

Part 1, the "'Cellar," is, early on, part of David Schearl's experience, the cellar that he has to walk past daily in the immigrant slum tenement, about 1908, and a fearful, mysterious place. Later a cellar is the scene of a climactic near-sexual assault on David's cousin (not by him). It is a place where "rats" live. Its associations are dark, dirty, frightening—linked to his sexual initiation in a dark closet with a lame neighbor girl, "playing bad" she calls it, and it is associated for him with fear, loathing, and near castration.

The second is called "Picture"—which refers to a print of blue cornflowers in a field that his beloved mother Genya purchases and hangs up to brighten the drab apartment. It embodies a memory of the Old Country, as we learn, and recalls his mother's youth and sexuality—as David learns when he overhears his mother and her sister Aunt Bertha exchange confidences. It is revealed that Genya had a love affair (whether consummated or not is unclear) with a Gentile before she married Albert Schearl.

Part 3 is called "Coal"—and a central symbol is introduced. Ordinarily associated with dirty, dark cellars, coal becomes a magic instrument of potential cleansing when David hears in his cheder a story connected with the prophet Isaiah. According to the tale, the prophet cleansed his lips with a hot, glowing coal, achieving purgation and apparently angelic transcendence. It should be noted, however, that such purgation and transcendence invokes great and *silencing* pain. Finally, the last section is called "The Rail"—which becomes another rich, ambiguous symbol based on a concrete part of David's experience. As if on the rails of a streetcar, the story is now brought inevitably to a structurally fixed resolution—crashingly in this case. The section is more "literary" than the others, with reflections in it of Joyce, Dos Passos, Michael Gold, T. S. Eliot, a whole modernist and politically engaged tradition that also provides a distancing from the intense personal center that characterizes the earlier sections.[26] At the end of the section, the distraught boy runs from a horrible scene between his parents in which the father claims he is not the true father of Genya's child (David) and then beats him with a whip the child himself hands him (surely one of the most awful scenes I can recall in American fiction). The boy runs out toward the electrified rail of the streetcar line. David thrusts a metal ladle into it, with the wild idea that it is equivalent to Isaiah's act with the burning coal—hoping for an act of cleansing and transcendence of his all-too-human life. It could also result in a final and absolute silence. It seems at first as if he were dead, electrocuted, but he is rescued, taken home by his parents—Albert admitting to the authorities that the boy is his son, and David slips off to sleep under the gentle ministrations of his loving mother.

The mere outlining of these tales suggests, I think, the reasons they have moved so many readers. They are big subjects, lovingly, artfully, but not sentimentally rendered, their meanings haunting and resonant.

The strength of each rests in the hard, unblinking look at the pain in these lives and the act of *memory* that recalls it. They eschew sentimentality, refuse concessions to rhetorical formulations of hope—that staple of socialist realism and kitsch. Each seems to suggest something redemptive in its beautiful concluding prose, but I am not sure this suffices to dull the painful and tragic qualities embodied in the depicted events. Both works evoke memory, are about memory in some respect, as the precondition for art/writing. But the writing does not necessarily exorcise or ameliorate the ache of the lives and experiences recreated, represented. Insofar as it perpetuates or recalls a dead-end quality in the represented reality, it would be better perhaps, from a human, personal (not the literary) side of things, *not* to remember, not to write. As Roth has said in his most recent interview, his inability to deal with the "sordid" matter of his unconscious incestuous feelings, his "evasion" of it, may have accounted partly for his difficulty in writing a novel that would be a sequel to *Call It Sleep*. This late comment strikes a convincing note.[27]

Eva awakens everything—she refuses pills, painkillers. "Let me feel what I feel,"[28] she says fiercely and then laughs. There is strength there; some critics cite it as an affirmation of the life principle. In fiction yes—in life, I think one might well take and give the pills. The old husband remonstrates bitterly at the end: "Who wanted questions? Everything you have to wake?" Then, dully, he says, in a move and sentence that show why Olsen is so incredibly feeling as a writer and person, "Ah, let me help you turn, poor creature." In the moving last two paragraphs of the story, Jeannie is meant to represent the hope—the future—carrying the torch of memory onward, redeeming the agony of her grandmother's death and life. Jeannie is an artist, and it should be noted that her act of memorializing is partial at best, selective. The Chagall-esque vision captured on her sketch pad at the end, loving and poignant, of the two old people lying hand in hand is indeed part of the reality of her grandmother's life: ". . . their hands, his and hers, clasped, feeding each other." But the fundamental quarrel of those forty-seven years, all that unused life, remains as an aching wound. There is an affirmative gesture in Jeannie's being there to capture what is positive and beautiful in these lives, but obviously she cannot get it all, as the story itself tries to. The story suggests, too, that nothing can repair the losses to this lived life—even if Jeannie evokes an image of the old woman at her last moment envisioning a return to innocent girlhood, "when she first heard music."

When we approach the conclusion of *Call It Sleep*, despite the apparent peace and reconciliation of the ending, a kind of despair at memory/art, with the possibility of continuing to remember and making this kind of art, reveals itself when it must confront a shattering experience and a traumatized life.[29] As with the coal applied to the lips, or the electric current through the body, the shock *may* be cleansing, presumably restorative, but it is quite obviously maiming and can bring one close to death. As David learns in an earlier scene when a tugboat almost crushes him as he sits by the river, God holds us in his hands, but we can be destroyed in a flash. In another part of the book, David must *forget* or he will scream.[30] Recalling *everything* before his swoon into sleep/oblivion is almost too much. It is not just prelude to sleep; it might as well be sleep. "It was only toward sleep one knew himself still lying on the cobbles, felt the cobbles under him, and over him and scudding ever toward him like a black foam, the perpetual blur of shod and running feet . . . shoes, over one and through one, feel, not pain, not terror, but strangest triumph, strangest acquiescence. One might as well call it sleep. He shut his eyes." Thus the novel ends, with the boy at last able to shut his eyes to pain and terror. David seeks oblivion, a perfect silence or nothingness—a mystic place beyond the concrete realities that are simply too much to bear.

I conclude with the observation with which I began—that in the pain of their personal lives, within the painful political era that they traversed, will be found the reasons for their long silences. There was loss, and in Olsen's case recovery and triumph, as Blanche Gelfant has astutely argued,[31] but the lacerating effects of a total or at least deep recall cannot be underestimated, so that I can understand, when it occurs, an equally deep need, if not of forgetting, then of a silence that we might as well call sleep. Why Roth after so long a literary sleep has apparently awakened in the twilight of his life might be the fruitful subject of another study—the lineamints of which I hope I have suggested in this essay.

Notes

1. Bonnie Lyons, "Henry Roth," *Dictionary of Literary Biography*, vol. 28, *Twentieth Century American-Jewish Fiction Writers*, ed. Daniel Walden (Detroit: Gale Research, 1984) 263. Much of the data above and that follows is drawn from this excellent study.

2. Howe, "Life Never Let Up," *New York Times Book Review*, 25 Oct. 1964: 60–61. Lyons 263.

3. The information about this phase of Roth's recent work comes from two telephone conversations with Mario Materassi, professor of American literature at the University of Firenze, 20 May 1990 and 5 June 1991. Materassi has played a vital part in reactivating Roth's literary life and recalling his life in the past, about which more later.

4. Leonard Michaels, "The Long Comeback of Henry Roth: Call It Miraculous," *New York Times Book Review*, 15 Aug. 1993: 19.

5. Lyons 260.

6. Lyons 260.

7. Many critics have seen the ending as hopeful and redemptive—including Bonnie Lyons (above) and Sam B. Girgus, who argues strongly for an idea of regeneration (through pain the central character emerges reborn, accepting himself as a Jew in a triumphant acceptance of life). See his *The New Covenant* (Chapel Hill, U of North Carolina P, 1984). The most convincing case has been made recently by Thomas J. Ferraro, in an essay called "Oedipus in Brownsville," in *Ethnic Passages* (Chicago: U of Chicago P, 1993) 89–122.

8. Lyons 263.

9. Deborah Rosenfelt, "From the Thirties: Tillie Olsen and the Radical Tradition," *Feminist Studies* 3 (Fall 1981): 370–405.

10. Rosenfelt 372.

11. Henry Roth, *Shifting Landscape: A Composite, 1925–1987*, ed. and with intro. by Mario Materassi (Philadelphia: Jewish Publication Society, 1987). There is an arch and wrong-headed refusal to see the utility of this collection by Donna Rifkind in *The New Criterion*, Feb. 1988: 75–76.

12. Conversation with Materassi.

13. Murray Schwartz has called to my attention a note by Sandor Ferenczi on

the folk proverb "Silence is Golden" in which silence is tied to retention in response to deep unconscious fears of "childish accidents in which the patient was 'too weak' to retain the motion ['movement'?]" (*Further Contributions to the Theory and Technique of Psychoanalysis*, vol. 2 [London: Hogarth, 1926] 250–51). An intriguing suggestion, but impossible to follow up. I am more inclined to see a release taking place, but along with it a prohibition upon publishing, after the death of various people close to Roth (including his wife) who might be sensitive to the material he is now writing about.

14. Roth 75–76.
15. Roth 77.
16. A most interesting essay on the full range of the question of modernism and its relation to power (personal, literary, political) in our time that deals with almost every major theorist and text touching on the issue, begins and ends with a cogent analysis of *Call It Sleep* (Bruce Robbins, "Modernism in History, Modernism in Power," *Modernism Reconsidered*, ed. Robert Kiely and John Hidebidle [Cambridge: Harvard UP, 1983]). Daniel Aaron, *Writers on the Left: Episodes in American Literary Communism* (New York: Harcourt Brace and World, 1961), remains the standard work on the leftward turn of writers in the '30s.
17. Roth 77.
18. Roth 257.
19. Roth 110.
20. Tillie Olsen, *Silences* (New York: Delacorte/Seymour Lawrence, 1978). All references are to this text.
21. Olsen 38.
22. Olsen 39.
23. In her 1990 doctoral dissertation (University of Massachusetts) on psychological "splitting" in four novels of the 1930s including *Call It Sleep*, Deborah Schneer, to whom I am indebted for rethinking the ending of the novel, uses a telling subtitle: "The Right to Forget."
24. Tillie Olsen, "Tell Me a Riddle," *Tell Me a Riddle* (New York: Dell/Delta, 1961).
25. Olsen, "Riddle" 108.
26. See the brilliant essay by Wayne Lesser, "A Narrative's Revolutionary Energy: The Example of Henry Roth's *Call It Sleep*," *Criticism* 23.2 (Spring 1981): 155–76.
27. Michaels 19.
28. Olsen, "Riddle" 144.
29. Toni Morrison solves the problem beautifully in *Beloved* (New York: Knopf, 1987): "not a story to pass on"—this horrific tale of slavery—she says several times at the end, but pass it on brilliantly she does and the pain is somehow accommodated and presumably does not have to be paralyzing. In the Passover Haggadah Jews are enjoined to remember that "we were slaves in Egypt"—a knowledge each generation is to take unto itself, remember it as if it had happened to the recreator of the story. It might, finally, be easier to remember and be reborn (and free) if one did not suffer the slavery *in fact* but only in recreated and newly constituted *memory*.
30. Henry Roth, *Call It Sleep* (New York: Avon Bard, 1964) 359.
31. Blanche Gelfant, "After Long Silence: Tillie Olsen's 'Requa,' " *Women Writing in America: Voices in Collage* (Hanover: UP of New England, 1984) 59–71.

Nostalgia, Amnesia, and Grandmothers: The Uses of Memory in Albert Murray, Sabine Ulibarri, Paula Gunn Allen, and Alice Walker

WOLFGANG KARRER

> A tail of a comet is a memory. Grammar may be fortunately within a call. Consider grammar.
> —Gertrude Stein, *How to Write*

> Memory fails.
> —James Welch, *Winter in the Blood*

Memory, Recall, and Recoding

It will be useful to distinguish memory and remembrance, the stored content and the access to it. "Recall" is a synonym for remembrance. This distinction allows us to reformulate Proust's distinction between *"mémoire volontaire"* and *"mémoire involontaire."* It is really the recall that is either voluntary or not; the memory is there, whether conscious, preconscious, or unconscious, to use Freud's terminology. Recall can be blocked through repression or suddenly released through new experiences of introspection. Memories can be stored in traces, obliterated, or overwritten.

Poetological distinctions in the uses of memory (Bergson, Benjamin) tend to repeat to a certain extent Coleridge's romantic efforts to separate imagination (tapping the unconscious) from fancy, a purely mechanical and combinative faculty. These efforts at dichotomizing mental faculties

Nostalgia, Amnesia, and Grandmothers

or processes usually serve to distinguish "higher" poetic processes from ordinary everyday experiences. *"Mémoire involontaire"* or *"Erfahrung"* (practical experience) were claimed to be superior to *"matière," "mémoire volontaire,"* or *"Erlebnis"* (lived experience) much as imagination was claimed to be superior to fancy.

Freud has tried to overcome such problems. He postulated that both the intensity of the experience (the cathectic charge of the memory trace) and the frequency of recall may have to do with the availability of memories. He also postulated a distinction between infantile amnesia (those years of early childhood we cannot remember) and hysterical amnesia and attributed both to repression, a mechanism of censorship that stops us from recalling certain memories, painful but important, in our pasts. Detailed memories of our adolescence may be a cover for infantile amnesia, illusionary as in paramnesia or invented to fill a gap as in confabulation. Freud's distinction between infantile and hysterical amnesia and the relation between them have gone a long way to explain some of the processes hinted at by Coleridge. And modern ethnic literature has taken up the hints of Freudian psychology. It has also developed it further.

Modern experimental psychology has added some answers to our questions on memory or it has offered reformulations of the very questions by making additional distinctions between short-term and long-term memory and testing the capacity of both, as well as the conditions under which sense impressions enter into storage. (Memory here means the storage place itself rather than its content.) Research has also pointed at the importance of encoding images and thoughts in memory traces and of decoding them during recall. Thus it seems not only a matter of storing and recalling information in our brains, but the code systems with which it is stored and retrieved are equally important in accounting for remembrance and amnesia (Horn 1985). It is here, in the encoding and decoding process of perceptions and thoughts as images and concepts, that language and literature play a significant part (for a general theory of coding processes see Eco 1976, 48ff.). Literary memoirs are not only a reproduction of earlier perceptions and thoughts, but an often carefully and always culturally complex recoding of earlier experiences of life. The adult rewrites the experiences of the child. And from ethnic autobiographies and memoirs we can expect a particularly rich interplay of different codes for experience and remembrance, storing and recall. For the following discussion I shall distinguish the following phases and concepts:

experience —→ encoding —→ memory trace —→ decoding —→ recall

If the encoding is rewritten after recall I shall call this recoding.

Postmodernist criticism has added yet another dimension to the debate on memory. The term "nonsynchronous memory" (Hicks 1991, xxiii) refers to a specific sense of deterritorialization in modern ethnic literature. This includes more than just the question of displacement and return. For many minority writers deterritorialization also includes the experience of nonsynchrony, or closer to Ernst Bloch's nonsimultaneity *(Ungleichzeitigkeit)*. The ethnic community one remembers or returns to is not only a different space. It is also a different social time, with a different pace and pattern. And for many postmodern writers, recall includes the "conscious decision to embrace deterritorialization and to resist the temptations of nostalgia" (Hicks 116).

Individual and collective arts of selecting, storing, and recalling experiences are finally related to the development of media—their technical extensions—and to each other. In other words, the individual recall of memories is framed by a complicated set of social and mechanical factors that feed into it and/or from it. With modifications, this holds for storing perception and thought as well. All four of these relations involve questions of power and social control. And this is exactly the situation multiethnic literature in America has to confront implicitly or explicitly. And if personal or collective identity depends to a large degree on memory and recall, but also on innovating both, then literary strategies of individual and collective recall become crucial to ethnic communities.

Recall and Recoding in Train Whistle Guitar

Let us look at a first example. *Train Whistle Guitar* (1974) by Albert Murray is an early attempt at a multicultural memoir in fictionalized form, a genre that next to the rewriting of the autobiographical conventions may be one of the lasting contributions by minority authors to U.S. literature in the second half of this century. Murray's novel is firmly based in African American blues traditions, as I have shown in an earlier contribution (Karrer 1982). *Train Whistle Guitar* retells the story of young Scooter's progress into manhood in Gasoline Point, Mobile, Alabama between 1926 and 1930. It is the classical initiation story with male heroes as father surrogates and role models. Scooter's innocence in his father quest leads to experience and the discovery of his mother. While the male

Nostalgia, Amnesia, and Grandmothers

heroes stand for the African American blues culture, Miss Tee, Scooter's mother, embodies the values of education and upward mobility. Scooter leaves Gasoline Point behind to go to college. He has passed his tests of experience and interpretation and has become a man.

Murray chooses the first-person narration, closest to the memoir and autobiographical matrix, with its well-known device of splitting the "I" into a narrative and a discursive one, a past and present state of one and the same person (Blasing 1977, xxvi f.). Scooter the adult recalls, selects, and organizes memories of his youth into an overriding structure, that of the apprenticeship or initiation formula (Suleiman 1983, 63–100). In Murray's own words, Scooter creates a myth with its corresponding values in order to transmit them to his community:

> It is the storyteller working on his own terms as mythmaker (and by implication as value maker), who defines the conflict. . . . The story teller works with language, but even so he is a song and dance man (a maker of *molpês*) whose fundamental objectives are extensions of those of the bard, the minstrel, and the ballad maker which, incidentally, are also those of the contemporary American blues singer. . . . The song and dance ritual, whatever its extensions, whether as drama, lyric, poem, ode, hymn, lay, epic, ballad or blues, is not only a reenactment-creation, but also a reenactment illustration, demonstration, and initiation. (Murray 1973, 21f.)

Thus the storyteller makes myths and values, and these values are clearly multicultural, or "Omni American" as Murray prefers to call them. The omni-American values guide Scooter slowly out of his black blues culture into the dominant white culture of college, record playing, and writing. (Murray has since published a major biography of Count Basie.) Thus, the adult Scooter, the narrator, is the result of the very recoding process he describes, and his strategies of recall show this. Recall, for Murray, becomes ritual reenactment.

I have called the resulting hybrid form of ethnic recall the "syntax of nostalgia" (Karrer 256). Like Faulkner and much of the southern "literature of memory" (Gray 1977), Murray foregrounds the act of remembrance as part of the narrator's discourse. "I cannot remember," "I always remember," "I remember when I remember," "I will never forget" are expressions that recur many times in *Train Whistle Guitar* (7, 14, 19, 104, 136, etc.). And with other key words, like "sometimes," "also," "always" the words of remembrance and forgetting structure sentences, paragraphs, and sometimes whole chapters in the novel. Here is the first paragraph of chapter 1:

> The color you almost always remember when you remember Little Buddy Marshall is sky-blue. Because that shimmering summer sunshine blueness in which neighbourhood hens used to cackle while distant yard dogs used to bark and moskito hawks used to flit and float along nearby barbwire fences, was a boy's color. Because such blueness also meant that this was whistling time and rambling time. And also baseball time. Because that bright silver bright afternoon sky above outfields was the main thing Little Buddy Marshall and I were almost always most likely to be wishing for back in those days when we used to make up our own dirty verses for that old song about it ain't gonna rain no more. (6)

The incantatory repetitions of "remember," "almost always," "used to," "also," "because" and the accumulation of visual and auditory images enrich both the memory and the act of recalling. They are aided by the sentimental split of self address (I-you), retrospective naming (Little Buddy Marshall) and enrichments of meanings ("also," "as if," etc.). These procedures create nostalgia, because they serve to enhance the cathectic value of the memory traces and of the act of recalling them. Repetition simultaneously ritualizes recall and the past, and it tends to obliterate time and change: "But then such is the difference between legendary time and actuality, which is to say, the time you remember and the time you measure" (28).

But as the reference to the old song demonstrates, there is more than repetition to remembering. By inventing new words for old songs, Scooter and Little Buddy incorporate as well as change the collective and oral traditions of their community. And both individual nostalgia for childhood innocence and collective oral tradition come together in *Train Whistle Guitar*. Murray recodes his childhood as a song; more precisely, he recodes his recall as blues, and thus—as a kind of secondary elaboration—also transforms Scooter's earlier encoding of experiences as blues. His narrator's syntax freely follows the AAB structure of classic blues stanzas (Karrer) and overcodes it with a white syntax of nostalgia, completely alien to the blues tradition. Murray's strategy of ethnic recall is clearly multicultural, embodying Tin Pan Alley, brand names of the twenties, Native American legends, and bedtime stories. It is also clearly male.

Summing up, like his literary model, Ralph Ellison, Murray ritualizes not only the events he recalls but also the very process of recall itself. The recurrent activities that fill most of our everyday lives superimpose themselves in our memories, and recollecting those recurrent and singular events of the past borrows a high emotional charge (the Freudian cathexis) from them. A similar claim has been made for contemporary films and their power to transform everyday life, especially urban life, into highly oneiric ritual experiences, a profane mythology of ourselves (Biro 1982). Scooter recreates himself by recoding his past experiences and thus makes them come alive again. In other words, he tries to deny the difference between himself as an adult and the child by recoding both as omni-American. It is not necessary, it would even be harmful to return to Gasoline Point as an adult. It has to remain what it was. With this, he tries to deny history, not only that which has elapsed since 1930 and the writing of the memoir, but also that between 1926 and 1930. As the structure of the apprenticeship or initiation story emphasizes the change in the individual, it often tends to blot out the changes in the community within which the initiation takes place. Gasoline Point is saved from time like a fly in amber. Communal and individual values can be reaffirmed and held up to the present community as an antidote and inspiration at the same time.

Recall and Decoding in Tierra Amarilla

Chicano writer Sabine Ulibarri's book *Tierra Amarilla* (1964, bilingual edition 1971) at first sight seems to follow the strategies of recall chosen by Murray. A New Mexico childhood of the twenties and thirties is reconstructed in its emotional highlights and singular events and embedded in the ritualized practices of the Chicano community, and the hero's changes follow the well-known conventions of the initiation or apprenticeship formula, including the male donors or father surrogates that help the youthful hero on his way.

Ulibarri also encodes his recollections in a first-person narrative, and he makes the recollecting process a central theme of his stories. The first of the six stories exposes the theme. It is about a magical horse: "Era blanco. Blanco como el olvido. Era libre. Libre como la alegria. Era la ilusión, la libertad y la emoción." (He was white. White as memories lost. He was free. Free as happiness is. He was fantasy, liberty, and excitement) (5). Whiteness, symbolically associated with forgetting, leads to liberty. And liberty leads to illusion. These three steps dramatize much of the central hero's dilemma. His freedom from the past derives from partial amnesia and turns out to be illusionary in the end. When he returns as an adult to the community and scenes of his childhood, he suffers from a nervous breakdown, an advanced case of schizophrenia. He experiences a dual personality in which his dead father, whom he came to honor, threatens to take over his personality. This leads to a flight back home to his wife and collapse, followed by total amnesia. Only after patient attention of his wife and the reading of his own manuscripts does the writer tentatively reconstruct his own identity. The loss of identity through amnesia in the last story, "Man without a Name," points at the problem of this writer's initiation. His earlier reminiscences are not so much faulty for what they omit—blocked or censored memory traces—but for the way they are encoded.

Especially in the early stories, Ulibarri's narrator, Alejandro Turriaga, transforms his memories into legend and myth. He uses the strategies of ritualized recall to enhance and valorize his memories. The white horse becomes magical and pagan and transcends time and space: "an ideal, pure and invincible, rising from the eternal dreams of humanity. Even today my being thrills when I remember him" (6). And the anecdotes about Padre Benito, no doubt often retold in the community and family, fuse into a portrait of an "angelical" person with biblical sandals and a beatific smile who brought life and light to the community of Tierra Amarilla (20). These legendary transformations achieved in the oral retelling of past experiences follow certain conventions, deeply embedded in the community's legends and beliefs. And no doubt the narrator, who applies the same transformations to a local blacksmith in another story, has learned these legendary encodings from Don José Viejo, who tells him he has fought with bears and was born of a queen bee. Both the persons recoded in the reminiscences and the valorizing recoding itself firmly belong to the Chicano traditions of storing, recalling, and transmitting the past. And both are male or symbols of virility, like the horse. But as the stories proceed toward their shattering end, the narrator's discourse increasingly shifts into a realistic and critical mode, which uncovers how these very modes of encoding and reconstructing the past are engendered and how they help to keep women under control. In story 3, an embarrassing incident at a wake keeps two women unmarried and excluded from the community which keeps this incident alive for more than thirty years through an insulting name. In story 5, the community, including the narrator's parents, wrecks a happy marriage because they are not willing to forget rumors about the dubious past of the wife. All this and his earlier training as a man finally lead to Alejandro's traumatic confrontation with his father and with the patriarchal traditions of his community. The discovery that he has become his father and through him an embodiment of a patriarchal past that has badly prepared him for World War II and for marriage triggers his breakdown and hysterical amnesia. His personal and ethnic identities are blotted out, and the chances for a rebirth are ambiguously hinted at but never fulfilled. The total identification with a legendary past, based on a gender-encoded and ritualized recall of crucial moments, destroys the present. Murray celebrates nostalgia; Ulibarri questions it.

Retelling the past displaces the present. But it also may contain the cure for a future in which the strengthened writer returns to his community to witness, accompany, or help to bring about its changes. Writing *Tierra Amarilla* is part of the way. The book is the medium of change. The writer is able to challenge some of the functions of the oral transmission of the past by showing it to be a basically male discourse of gender control. The sequel to *Tierra Amarilla, Mi abuela fumaba puros* (My Grandmother Smoked Cigars) (1974) picks up the ambivalent heritage of male and female sex roles in the Chicano community but groups it around the hero's grandmother, a significant move that many women writers would also make in the seventies and eighties.

The flight from the ethnic community to return to it as well as the ambivalent relation to it that it implies have become a central tradition in contemporary multiethnic writing. To go home again is the spatial equivalent of recall; the community signifies the memories and their storing place. And to continue the analogy, the childhood passed in the community is its encoded experience. Toni Morrison's analysis of the seamless web of stifling family and community relations (Diedrich 1990) or Sandra Cisneros's attempts in *The House on Mango Street* (1988) to create a space for Chicana writings in her community (Bus 1990) come readily to mind. Both authors make their heroines or heroes return and confront the communities they originally came from. Gloria Anzaldùa's ambivalent attempts in *Borderlands* (1987) to return to her origins in Hargill, Texas, are another case in point. One could multiply this prodigal son or daughter theme with further examples, but the theme and its function have often been described. It is the old dilemma of regional writing and the myth of return (Christensen 1981–82). This development of a fictionalized memoir literature often dramatizes the individuals' ambivalent relationships to their respective ethnic communities and firmly belongs to the liberal tradition of rewriting America as displacement and a conflict between individual and society (Robertson 1980, 127ff.).

Recall Through Recoding in The Woman Who Owns the Shadows

By questioning the underlying gender conventions in his community—especially in "Juan P.," "La fragua sin fuego," and "Hombre sin nombre," Ulibarri anticipates feminist strategies from within the different ethnic communities by several years. Paula Gunn Allen's first novel, however, *The Woman Who Owned the Shadows* (1983), takes an approach directly opposite to that of Murray and Ulibarri. Allen, who is of mixed Laguna Pueblo/Sioux/Lebanese-American descent, uses a mythic and ceremonial approach to her theme, something she had earlier developed in an article contributed to *The Remembered Earth* (1979):

> The great mythic and ceremonial cycles of the American Indian peoples are neither primitive in any meaningful sense of the term, nor are they necessarily the province of the folk; much of the material on the literature is known only to educated, specialized persons who are privy to the philosophical, mystical, and literary wealth of their own tribe.
>   Much of the literature that was in their keeping, engraved perfectly and completely in their memories, was not known to the general run of men and women. Because of this, much of that literature has been lost as the last initiates of particular tribes and societies within the tribes died, leaving no successor. (Allen 1979, 222)

Allen clearly points at the social and biological limitations of oral traditions but also emphasizes their central role in preserving an idea of wholeness in Native American life: "The two forms basic to Native American literature are the Ceremony and the Myth. The Ceremony is the ritual enactment of a specialized perception of cosmic relationships, while the Myth is a prose record of that relationship" (Allen 227).

The sacred hoop of memory and community is embodied in myths and ceremonies of cosmic wholeness, and it is menaced by oblivion and destruction. In *The Woman Who Owned the Shadows* Allen seems to recreate a case of hysterical amnesia that leads to a gradual recovery of personal and collective recall through ceremony and myth. Both phases are firmly tied to gender and ethnicity. And the two processes, therapy and ceremony, overlap and finally come together.

The book is dedicated to Spider Grandmother, Thought Woman, who thinks the stories Allen writes down. The main story focuses on Ephanie Kawemie Atencio, from Guadalupe, New Mexico, who goes to San Francisco, marries a Nisei, divorces him after the death of a child, and falls into a deep depression that leads to an attempt to kill herself. She slowly recovers by recalling a traumatic childhood experience with Elena and Stephen—a dangerous jump and fall—and by suddenly understanding the myths of Old Spider Woman, Sun and Corn Woman, and the War Twins. Ephanie thus simultaneously recovers her individual and collective past as a Native American woman. She had tried several ways to overcome her despair and to find herself: group therapy in San Francisco, work at the local Indian Center, the reading of esoteric books, a new friendship with Teresa. But it is her solitary remembering and dreaming that finally brings the solution: Old Spider Woman appears to instruct her:

> The story of the people and all the spirits . . . is the story of what moves, what moves on, what patterns, what dances, what sings, what balances, so life can be felt and known. The story of life is the story of moving. Of moving on.
> Your place in the great circling spiral is to help in that story, in that work. To pass on to those who can understand what you have learned, what you know. . . . Give it to your sister, Teresa. (210)

On a psychoanalytical level, Ephanie recovers a blocked memory trace that deals with an experience that has strong sexual overcodings: the decision between male and female bonding, between Stephen and Elena, and the dangerous fall. On a Native American level, however, Ephanie (Epiphany) is on a vision quest to recover the feminine traditions of her tribe: Spider Woman and the grandmothers are the creators of the universe, and all diversity develops from their wholeness and unity. "Separation was against the Law" (174). Allen's double strategy of recall by recoding the psychoanalytical into the ceremonial thus significantly deviates from those of Murray and Ulibarri.

Neither ritual nor legendary transformation, but a patient weaving of recurrent key words that finally fall into place to open a way into the collective memory provide the texture of this novel. Spider Grandmother and her incessant weaving are the obvious prototype for this strategy. Each of the four parts of *The Woman Who Owned the Shadows* begins with a mythic prologue that forms a current story. Each of the words of the first story—a creation myth—is then carefully woven into part 1 to form a dense net of symbolic references to singing, water, sun, twinning, and above all women: She Who Matters and She Who Remembers, Corn Woman and Sun Woman. Only these words now appear as part of a realistic and contemporary narrative. And only the reader who remembers their function in the creation myth will recognize the overcoding of these words. Ephanie thus reenacts the old sacred stories by rediscovering their gendered meanings. The twins she had and her relationships with Elena and Teresa acquire new meanings. The spider in her room saves her life. And her own life suddenly makes sense in terms of the central myth. Each part adds more to the myth and the dense nets of references that stabilize Ephanie's new ethnic and gender identity.

By weaving an ever denser pattern of verbal echoes intermeshing with the sacred creation story of the Lagunas, through rites of exorcism, and through dreams, Allen's heroine frees herself from her stifling present and draws strength from a collective tradition of Native American women that helps her to master her memories and future (Georgi-Findlay 1990). Allen's explorations of ethnic memory take place in a truly multicultural setting that intersects with the issues of class and gender. Therapy, the unlocking of personal and collective memories, blends ritual and modern psychoanalysis. Leslie Silko had done the same for storytelling in *Ceremony*. Both writers innovate the stylistic repertoire of recall, and they ambivalently regress into myth without denying deterritorialization.

Total Recall and Amnesia in The Temple of My Familiar

A final example—there are so many—of amnesia and recall, also feminist and innovating contemporary fictional discourse: Alice Walker's *The Temple of My Familiar* (1989). Walker decenters the central hero(ine) convention and freely interweaves the life stories of at least twelve major characters. Though structured around the four central characters of Suwelo and Fanny, Arveyda and Carlotta—in a way a feminist and multiethnic answer to D. H. Lawrence's *Women in Love*—the book has its hidden center in a figure named Lissie, whom Alice Walker in a talk on the book in 1989 called "the last human goddess." Lissie has total recall, stretching not only to her various past lives as white or black women or men but also through the whole history of mankind, even beyond the "Lucy" discovered in Africa and probably the oldest human skeleton discovered so far. Lissie's memory extends into a distant past where animals and human beings lived as familiars, and the keeping alive of that tradition—Native American as well as African—is one of her main functions in the world of the eighties.

Walker's conventions are those of magic realism. She freely interweaves different styles and strategies to recover the past. There is the voyage of Carlotta's mother into her past, the manuscript and museum studies of Mary Ann Briden, Fanny's return to Africa, her therapeutic session with Robin Ramirez, Carlotta's dreams, Arveyda's evocative music, and most important of all, the stories of Lissie and Hal, told for the benefit of Suwelo, who is estranged from Fanny and himself.

The novel opens with Carlotta: "In the old country in South America, Carlotta's grandmother, Zedé, had been a seamstress, but really more of

Nostalgia, Amnesia, and Grandmothers

a sewing magician. She was the creator of clothing, especially capes, made of feathers. These capes were worn by dancers and musicians and priests at traditional village festivals and had been worn for countless generations. When she was a young child, Carlotta's mother, also called Zedé, was sent to collect the peacock feathers used in the designs." (3)

This introduces important themes such as grandmothers, feminine arts, magic realism, history, and partial recall (because Carlotta's limited point of view ignores why the priests wore feathers and what went on before the "countless generations"). Later we learn through Carlotta's mother that the priests destroyed matriarchy out of envy and decorated themselves with feathers to compensate for their incapacity to have children. Zedé explains: "Our mothers taught us that in the old, old days, when they were their grandmothers and their grandfathers were old—for we are our grandmothers, you understand, only with lots of new and different things added—only women had been priests. Yes! This is what they said. But really, in the beginning they were not priests to themselves; it was the men who made them so. But then the men forgot that they had made them so" (48).

"Really," as in the first quote, points at the recoding of history and individual memories: both are gender specific, and women have an important stake in recalling as men have in forgetting. Grandmothers are crucial in keeping herstory alive and adding to it (Minh-ha 1989).

The archetypal grandmother in the book is, of course, Lissie. She opens her third story with: "In the dream world of my memory, however, there is something. I do not remember this exactly, as I remember the other things of which I have told you. But the memory, like the mind, has the capacity to dream, and just as the memory exists at a deeper level of consciousness than thinking, so the dream world of the memory is at a deeper level still. I will tell you of the dream on which my memory, as well as my mind, rests" (82).

And she tells of a dream memory in which she lived peacefully as a pygmy with her cousins, the apes in a tree. Grandmothers in *The Temple of My Familiar* thus recall large parts of human history. Lissie's dream about the temple in which she tried to enclose her familiar can be read as an allegory of memory and repressed history. And much of the novel is dedicated to the efforts to recall at least part of that history.

All four major figures suffer from traumatic amnesia related to their parents and childhood, and all free themselves with mutual help from this past to create a new and truly intercultural, intersexual, and intergenerational present and future. This is mainly done by talk. There is no common syntactic encoding of experience or recalling it. Anything goes: massage, storytelling, dreams, even music. But it has to be shared in a truly intercultural way to get back to our common origins. By abolishing the individual hero or heroine, Walker also establishes recall as something social and thus breaks with the dichotomies of oral/written or individual/collective recall and recoding. Recall is work where memories fail, and men and women have to work together in reconstructing the past for a better present and future.

Mary Ann Briden serves as a white counterexample. She sheds her past identity like a snake sheds a skin and rediscovers a new life for herself by researching her great-aunt. She also discovers matriarchy through diaries, letters, and museums. Both her two ships, *Recuerdo* and *The Coming Age*, and her activities in Africa to honor M'Suktu, the last of her tribe, underline the possibilities for change and new ethnic relations.

Walker refuses to ritualize recall or to mythify the past. Both are full of gender and race conflicts, and though all characters are firmly middle class and intellectuals—in fact, most of them are writers or artists—their past contains enough of colonial and imperial struggles to keep history or herstory from relapsing into myth. Walker thus seems to be pointing at a strategy of recall that goes beyond the confines of the personal or even ethnic memory stores. Her novel expands the themes of memory and recall even beyond national or continental limitations. Hers is a truly intercontinental book. She seems to have opened a new way of writing multiethnic memories for the modern increasingly global world. Though Lissie is the archetypal grandmother of the oral minority cultures (Minh-ha), she owns a by-no-means exclusive access to the past.

Going Home

Maybe it is too early for a conclusion, but I would like to generalize from my examples. All four writers come from the South, Paula Gunn Allen the Southwest. So maybe some of my conclusions are restricted to that cultural area of the United States.

The male writers seem to prefer the initiation story moving from innocence to experience and guided by male mentors and role models. The two women tell stories of hysterical amnesia, moving from forgetting to recall with the help of grandmothers who are storytellers and role models at the same time. Ulibarri seems to anticipate this move. If these narrative frames are not gender specific, the role models are. *My Grandmother Smoked Cigars* (1974) seems an exception. The return to the places of origin may dramatize displacement and aid recall (Ulibarri, Walker). But the myth of return can be replaced by an interior journey into dreams and myths (Allen, Walker) or by the very act of remembrance itself (Murray). And the different strategies of encoding recall—the syntax of nostalgia or blues structure, the legendary transformation and its undercutting, therapeutic ceremony, and collective consciousness raising—all embody the dominant and the ethnic code at the same time. Whether this happens in harmony (Murray, Allen, Walker) or in conflict with the cultural codes (Ulibarri) tells us something about the authors' stances. And here only Walker deliberately transcends ethnic boundaries between minorities. Ephanie's marriage to Nisei Thomas Yoshuri fails.

The spatial metaphors for remembrance are the ethnic community, displacement, and return. Christensen has described the classical convention very well:

> The native writer has roots in his community and has come to take possession of his land as a defence against the amorphous freedom and mobility he experiences as a national citizen. . . . The native writer sees himself as the memory of his people, and he *writes* because he fears the disappearance of things around him; he *records* because his world is fading away.
>
> Native women writers also wish to preserve their region; they write against that part of their history which, like the myth of manhood, belittled their sex. To that degree, they empathize with other denied people, the racial and cultural minorities whom they sometimes embrace in a common political struggle . . .
>
> At the bottom of everything in a region is the desire of the best to go away, like Odysseus, and return with the world in their head, to better the place—and keep it native. (2,6)

Against this pattern, the difficulties of going home in our four examples stand out clearly. Murray's Scooter substitutes ritualized recall for going home. His remembrance saves Gasoline Point from change. Ulibarri's narrator Alejandro Turriaga returns to Tierra Amarilla only to discover he has never really left it. He was not equipped for change in the outside world, because he has not understood the legacy of his ethnic community. Allen's Ephanie Atencio leaves Guadalupe behind for San Francisco. She violently rejects the truth about the uranium mines on the reservation when she learns about it from white ecologist women on a return visit. The myth she discovers is a substitute for going home; Ephanie stays in San Francisco. Alice Walker, who had tried a similar patterning in *Meridian* (1976), allows her major characters no such retreat. They may travel to South America or Africa or even Baltimore, but their true home is their common history, the history of humanity embodied in the matriarchal human goddess Lissie. By refusing her characters a geographic homecoming, Walker makes them citizens of a multicultural and interethnic world where going home means going forward into new relationships.

It seems to me that my four examples fall into four important types of ethnic recall in contemporary fiction:

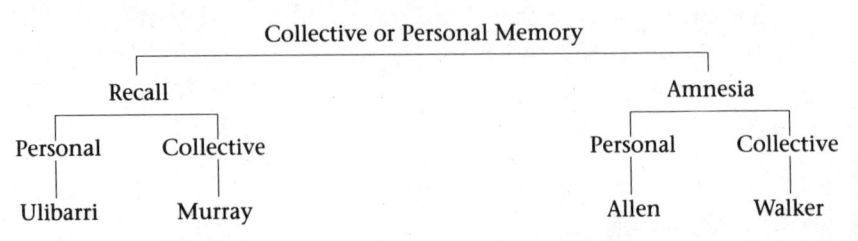

```
                    Collective or Personal Memory
          ┌──────────────────────┴──────────────────────┐
                Recall                          Amnesia
          ┌──────┴──────┐                 ┌──────┴──────┐
       Personal     Collective         Personal     Collective
          │             │                 │             │
       Ulibarri       Murray            Allen         Walker
```

The discursive strategies of recoding experience through nostalgia, therapy, ceremony, or oral tradition support different types of recall and amnesia.

First, there is a world of change surrounding the ethnic communities of Gasoline Point, Alabama, and Tierra Amarilla and Guadalupe, New Mexico, that affects both the hero(ine) and the community. The wish to honor, preserve, or change the community or simply to return to it displaces a rapidly changing United States where wars and media bombardment, but also the awareness that there are other Guadalupes, Gasoline Points, and Tierra Amarillas, stifle or further such wishes. This outside world of change, the urban ghettos of the 1970s, are obliterated in *Train Whistle Guitar*. But at the same time they are omnipresent in the affirmation of the past idyl in Gasoline Point. Albuquerque and San Francisco are present as a foil to Tierra Amarilla and Guadalupe. In Ulibarri, who also mentions Berlin, and in Allen, life in the cities throws a new light on the ethnic communities they come from, and commemorating them becomes a dubious endeavor. Walker, finally, uproots her characters thoroughly and never allows them to go home again. They visit to discover their past or to sell their inheritance. And the change has also reached the places they go home to. The characters in *The Temple of My Familiar*, once they recall, become actively engaged in that change instead of deploring it. And the change is toward increasing multiculturalism in all communities, African, North American, and South American.

Second, there are no ethnically pure strategies available. Myth and

Nostalgia, Amnesia, and Grandmothers

Freud, blues and Tin Pan Alley, tape recorders and dreams overlap, blend, and may serve equally well to recode past or to restore lost experiences. What matters is the loss. Ethnic writers have discovered that recall and amnesia are intimately connected with power relations between cultures—collective amnesia results from hegemony of one culture over another—and gender traditions within each culture. And they have devised several strategies, some of which I have mapped out, to counteract such amnesia. In all the strategies, grammatical and literary recodings of memory traces play a major role. In all, the language of the dominant Anglo-American culture disturbs the ethnic decoding or blends with it. The absence or presence of conflict between the two modes reveals a lot about the narrator's strategies and aims. And whether the fight against amnesia is won through solitary reminiscence or collective talk, the solution opens different positions for writers in their respective ethnic communities and beyond.

Third, this "beyond" is increasingly characterized by the "corporate takeover of public expression" (Schiller 1989). And this includes public memory. The electronic storing of information has not only provided new models for memory research. It has also enabled private corporations, mainly the very media that control so many images and signs that we take in daily, to collect and sell information on past events. Data banks and private media control much of this information flow and thus our images of ourselves and others. And this control always includes a process of cultural selection. Thus the memory work of minority authors, though easily absorbed into the information flow once it is published, also serves to preserve memories normally pruned from electronic storage and to reorient people exposed to that flow. Only Walker includes television and radio in her fictional world, but the modern media also stand behind much of what Murray, Ulibarri, and Allen tried to do: to restore to their people a sense of place and remembrance of their past.

Amnesia and recall, ethnic versus dominant or oral versus written encoding, as individual or collective effort, with or without return to the community, these are some of the underlying options. Though writers will without doubt develop new ways of tapping their personal and collective memories to (re)create the struggles for ethnic and multiethnic identities, a considerable amount of contemporary minority writing in the United States and maybe elsewhere could be read with such divisions in mind.

Works Cited

Allen, Paula Gunn. "The Sacred Hoop: A Contemporary Indian Perspective on American Indian Literature." *The Remembered Earth: An Anthology of Contemporary Native American Literature.* Ed. Geary Hobson. Albuquerque: U of New Mexico P, 1979.

———. *The Woman Who Owned the Shadows.* San Francisco: Spinsters/Aunt Lute, 1983.

Biro, Yvette. *Mythologie profane: Cinéma et pensée sauvage.* Paris: Lherminier, 1982.

Blasing, Mutlu K. *The Art of Life: Studies in American Autobiographical Literature.* Austin: U of Texas P, 1977.

Bus, Heiner. "Sandra Cisneros, Gary Soto, and the Chicano/a Autobiography." Karrer and Lutz. 1990. 129–42.

Christensen, Paul. "The Fall of Texas." *Pawn Review* 5 (1981–82): 2–7.

Diedrich, Maria. " 'When You Kill Your Ancestor You Kill Yourself': Africa and the Modern Black Identity in Toni Morrison's Novels." Karrer and Lutz. 1990. 94–114.

Eco, Umberto. *A Theory of Semiotics.* London: Macmillan, 1976.

Georgi-Findlay, Brigitte. "Concepts of History in Contemporary Native American Fiction." Karrer and Lutz. 1990. 159–74.

Gray, Richard. *The Literature of Memory: Modern Writers of the South.* London: Arnold, 1977.

Hicks, D. Emily. *Border Writing: The Multidimensional Text.* Minneapolis: U of Minneapolis P, 1991.

Horn, Gabriel. *Memory, Imprinting and the Brain.* Oxford: Clarendon, 1985.

Karrer, Wolfgang. "The Novel as Blues: Albert Murray's *Train Whistle Guitar* (1974)." *The Afro-American Novel since 1960.* Ed. Peter Bruck and Wolfgang Karrer. Amsterdam: B. R. Grüner, 1982. 237–61.

Karrer, Wolfgang, and Hartmut Lutz, eds. *Minority Literatures in North America: Contemporary Perspectives.* New York: Lang, 1990.

Minh-ha, Trinh T. *Woman, Native, Other: Writing Postcoloniality and Feminism.* Bloomington: Indiana UP, 1989.

Murray, Albert. *The Hero and the Blues.* Columbia: U of Missouri P, 1973.

———. *Train Whistle Guitar.* New York: McGraw, 1974.

Robertson, James Oliver. *American Myth, American Reality.* New York: Hill, 1980.

Schiller, Herbert. *Culture Inc.: The Corporate Takeover of Public Expression.* New York: Oxford UP, 1989.

Suleiman, Susan Rubin. *Authoritarian Fiction: The Ideological Novel as a Literary Genre.* New York: Columbia UP, 1983.

Ulibarri, Sabine R. *Tierra Amarilla: Stories of New Mexico* [Cuentos de Nuevo Mexico]. Albuquerque: U of New Mexico P, 1971.

Walker, Alice. *The Temple of My Familiar.* New York: Harcourt, 1989.

X Rays of Irish America:

Edwin O'Connor, Mary Gordon,

and William Kennedy

WILLIAM KEOUGH

> The fact is that the values and traditions fed to the furnace of American life never disappear altogether—at least not quite. There remains always, in every ethnic tradition, in the generational legacy of every individual family, a certain residue, a kind of ash, what I would call "ghost-values": the tag-ends and shreds and echoes of the past calling to us generations after their real force has been spent, tantalizing us with idealized visions of a stability or order or certainty of meaning that we seem never to have known, and that we imagine can somehow be restored.
> —Peter Marin, "Toward Something American"

One morning a few years back, I was greeted at the mailbox by a flier from the Irish American Cultural Institute that featured a bearded farmer on the return envelope (scythe braced like a rifle over the shoulder of his torn Aran sweater) above the text, "We are our ancestors." That farmer's image was being proffered as a talisman to remind us Irish-Americans that our identity is inextricably entangled with his, his story ours.

But what does this mean? How can we Irish-Americans, often three or four generations removed, relate to this farmer? What is in us still that is in him? What "ghost-values" do we still carry in us, what do we remember?

In asking what Irish-Americans "remember" or what values they have maintained, however, it is difficult to find a meaningful umbrella (a Big Top really) to cover the over forty million Americans who claim Irish descent. For the purpose of this study, I will limit my inquiry to postfamine Catholic Irish immigrants and their descendants, who form the majority of Irish America and provide more recent and distinctive immigrant identity. But even here, there is a difficulty; the real story is often conveniently overlooked. "It is part of the problem of Irish-Americans that their history remains an unread book," as Shaun O'Connell has observed, "the scrap paper for a fake treasure map" (*Recorder* 38). Flooded by a plethora of Irish-American kitsch (leprechauns, shamrocks, darlin' Barry Fitzgerald movies, and so forth), many Irish-Americans prefer to view "the Auld Sod" through a "green fog" of sentiment, as novelist James Carroll has aptly put it. The Ring of Kerry, the Lakes of Killarney, and the Cliffs of Moher may be as pretty as postcards, but they are *only* postcards. The real Ireland, off the beaten track of tourist buses, contains a terrible beauty as much our inheritance as the landscape of mist and dreams.

Though many of us claim links to Tara and Norman chieftains, our ancestors, more commonly, were subsistence farmers who survived the harrowing immigrant experience because of their toughness: Brian Boru just wouldn't have cut the mustard. For chronicler William Shannon, the Irish village "was cutting peat on a rainy morning, gathering in the hay on long, warm August days, going to the spa for the fair. It was the picture of grandma churning butter by the door or making bread by the open hearth. It was the memory of Father coming home drawn and exhausted from a long day in the fields.... It was overhearing the old men around the fire, talking of British foreclosures and chewing over political gossip months old" (24).

But *was* it? Is this not an overly sentimental picture, a construct of a lost Eden? Memory, we know, is imperfect, and memories are the creation of familiar consent rather than eidetic photographs. Perhaps the most familiar theme of social history, observes David Thelen, "is that people have resisted rapid, alien, and imposed change by creating memories of a past that was unchanging, incorruptible, and harmonious" (1125). Is "home" not rather, as Marin suggests, a place "for us, as it is for all immigrants, something to be regained, created, discovered, or mourned—not where we are in time or space, but where we dream of being" (18).

Certainly, Ireland, for most Irish Catholics, was no Eden; they emigrated because they were dying. The central disaster was the famine of 1845–50; and tales have been handed down of victims, huddled in ditches, their mouths dripping with the green ooze of nettle soup; of

X Rays of Irish America

emigrants embarking from Cobh and Galway who died en route, their bones deposited in the deep Atlantic or in shallow fever graves along the St. Lawrence; of those fortunate enough to reach "Americay," only to find more discrimination lying in wait. It is a familiar, if bitter, story. But these immigrants, if empty-handed, did not come empty-headed. As a persecuted majority that had maintained a specific identity for over three hundred years, this cotter class brought from Ireland a sense of distinct community, bundled in rural memories. Many of these early immigrants remembered Erin vividly, memorializing it in poetry and song, sending back "American letters" stuffed with bills, and contributing, coin by painful coin, to the building of cathedrals. But most could not and did not return and often reacted to the pain of exile with silence.

Because of nativism, Irish Catholics did not "melt" easily. Second- and third-generation McGuires and Currans regarded themselves as Irish by choice, American by accident: *Irish*-Americans rather than American Irish. Memory of an *ur*-Ireland remained, but so diluted over time and blended in generational struggle as to be largely a fictional construct. "The challenge of history," asserts Thelen, "is to recover the past and introduce it into the present. It is the same challenge that confronts memory" (1117). So now, too, in "remembering" his grandparents' or parents' "memories" of an Ireland that no longer exists, the third- or fourth-generation Irish-American still clings to his own diminishing sense of something "Irish," as opposed to "American," within himself.

But where *does* one go to discover the truth of the past? In "the grand scheme" of history, the minor players from whose loins most of us spring often are overlooked. I have chosen to focus on three novelists—Edwin O'Connor, William Kennedy, and Mary Gordon—who have concentrated on Irish-American society and whose works serve as X rays of that society, exposing the bone truths, the health or cancer therein. Their work reveals the persistence of certain "ghost-values" formed by memory, experience, and education, which still haunt and define Irish-Americans, whether they care to admit or receive, like the Ash Wednesday smudge on their foreheads.

2

"I wanted to do a novel on the whole Irish-American business," Edwin O'Connor remarked. "What the Irish got in America, they got through politics; so, of course, I had to use a political framework" (qtd. O'Connell, *Recorder* 31). In *The Last Hurrah,* O'Connor does just that, drawing on the character and career of James Michael Curley, Boston's "Rogue King," to provide us with a rich portrait of Irish-American political life in 1950s Boston through the "last hurrah" of mayoralty candidate Frank Skeffington.

Skeffington's memories give the novel its breadth and depth—"a benign journey" flashing across seven decades of Boston politics and torchlight parades. Skeffington remembers "the small and shabby tenement in which he had been born" and "the astonishing, unlettered, shrewd old men who, from oilcloth-covered tables in their own kitchen, had ruled their wards like czars" (383). He also recalls "the grand freak show" that transformed the city: "A hundred years ago the loyal sons and daughters of the first white inhabitants went to bed one lovely evening, and by the time they woke up and rubbed their eyes, their charming old city was swollen to three times its size. The savages had arrived. Not the Indians; far worse. It was the Irish. They had arrived and they wanted in. Even worse than that, they got in" (75).

For Skeffington, there is bitterness in these recollections of rejection and servanthood. His own mother, he recalls, was fired from working in an elegant Beacon Hill townhouse for pilfering (an accusation, he admits, her poverty drove her toward). Skeffington views his election as an empowerment of his people; like Chekhov, he is determined to squeeze the last drop of the slave out of himself and his people. Yankee morality embodies hypocrisy; for the Boston Irish, Skeffington reasons, there has never been a level playing field. In fighting for his "savages," Skeffington acts as a tribal chieftain, revengeful toward the enemy, compassionate toward "his own kind."

For Skeffington, memory *is* history: to forget is to die. When Skeffington loses his "last hurrah," his dignity belies Strabo's observation, "The Celts are unbearable in victory and completely downcast in defeat." Skeffington's victory is his nobility in defeat; his virtues and vices—loyalty and compassion, ruthlessness and venality—are a final salute, a *last* hurrah to the Boston Irish immigrant past.

But if *The Last Hurrah* is nostalgic, even (as some critics would have it) sentimental, O'Connor's *All in the Family,* his portrait of the Kinsella clan, reveals a less "charming," more feral Irish America. The novel opens with Jack Kinsella relating how his father took him, as a boy of eleven, to Ireland, determined to search out exotic places like the Giant's Causeway and the Poisoned Glen, to meet the tinkers and the whalemen of the Aran Islands. Romantic Ireland, however, is not what they find: "The funny thing was that when we got to Ireland, none of these things my father talked about ever really happened" (32).

What Jack and his father come upon is an Ireland in decay. Pointing to a "long and strange-looking dog" lounging about their fancy Dublin Hotel, Jack's father says, "An Irish wolfhound. They're trying to revive the breed" (32). Like the wolfhound, this Ireland is much in need of revival. What is left of the "real" Ireland is in the fields, with the men spading in bogs. Jack's father offers a paradigm of the immigrant story; he talks of his great grandfather, born "in a cottage with a dirt floor and a roof made of straw, who had come to America as a very young man and had got a job putting down railroad tracks; about his son, my grandfather, who had left school before finishing and had run away to sea, and then a few years later, had come back home wearing a very handsome suit and with more money than an ordinary sailor could have hoped for" (47). But Jack is not charmed; he wishes his grandfather had been different, a pirate perhaps, somebody more romantic than the dull real-estate magnate he actually became. Significantly, Jack remembers how modestly his grandfather lived at home, concealing his real worth—as if at any moment he might be stripped of his wealth, just as Irish Catholics were once denied the right to own a horse worth more than five pounds. The traits of the old country—fear and suspicion—are carried over to the new.

Jack and his father visit Uncle Jimmy, a successful American entrepreneur, now returned to live with his three boys in a modern bungalow next to a ruined Norman castle. "How do you like that: three dummies!" he sneers at his sons. "In a country where every feeble-minded little bum can get up on his two hind legs and spout poems, all these three can do is clam up! A swell ad for America you are!" (57). But Jimmy is an Equal Opportunity abuser, with no illusions about "the auld sod": "There's nothing to do but go out in the rain and get wet. . . . A Mick farmer and his wife look after it for me. God knows what they do when I'm not around. Throw potatoes at each other, I guess. And sleep: everybody sleeps fifteen hours a day. At least!" (198). It is with detachment, even scorn, that these Irish-Americans confront Dublin and "the very green and hilly country a hundred miles or so to the southwest." They make few connections; their hearts remain in America.

Back home, Jimmy's "dummies" distinguish themselves: James becomes a priest; Phil, a lawyer; and Charles, governor. But when Phil threatens to bare the shady deals Charles has made to advance his senatorial candidacy, Jimmy accuses Phil of the ultimate Irish sin—disloyalty. "Stop all the God-damned bushwa! Stop acting like some thick-headed Mick son of a bitch. Stop sticking the shiv into your own brother! Stop double-crossing your own family" (371). In the Gospel according to Jimmy, revelation is betrayal, decency be damned; disagreements are to be kept "all in the family."

This is far from Skeffington's world—his sense of duty undertaken out of personal and communal honor. Skeffington's passing, we see, has signaled the onset of a new era of television candidacies, of smiling faces with Irish names but little racial memory. Reflecting on Skeffington, Charles shrugs: "Nobody's got that kind of popularity any more. It was a personal thing that depended on tribal loyalties, immigrants on the way up, racial spokesmen, Communion Breakfasts—there's some of that still around, of course, but in Skeffington's campaigns it was the big thing. You could do very well for yourself if you could get up and tell a few funny stories, quote Robert Emmet, and shout 'Ireland must be free!' for a finish. Today it's slightly more complicated" (182). For Charles, Skeffington's world is as dead as Skeffington. His Brave New World not only scorns Irish racial memories but is amoral, brutal. With Jimmy's approval, Charles commits Phil to a mental hospital and wins the senatorial race. But in winning the world, O'Connor seems to be suggesting, Irish-Americans like Charles are in danger of losing their souls.

All in the Family ends, as it began, in Ireland, with an older and wiser Jack back at the old hotel, which now has "an American wing designed by Finnish architects" and is, as the daft manager describes it, "half hotel, half hospital": "The convertible room: you can sleep in it at night and be operated on in it in the morning . . . ether will replace the breakfast tea. Snip snip snip and the offending organ is removed! Oh, yes, everything up to the minute in Holy Ireland. Ah ha ha ho!" (426). So, in a reverse curve (through a screwball in effect), we see how Ireland is being affected by returning Yanks. The emigrant/immigrant circle, if not unbroken, is closing quickly and ironically. Jack bumps into "Walshie," a Boston political hack who offers his own acidic view of Ireland: "Give me home sweet home any day! Everywhere you go in this country the grub is lousy. And the hotels! Down in Parknasilla the wife found a bug in her bed!" (429) No dirt-floor, *Erin-go-bragh* nonsense for Leo J. Walsh.

Jack's response is more resonant, if ambiguous. He recalls that first trip when he and his father swam naked in a "freezing pool" and were purified. He makes a last pilgrimage to Jimmy's abandoned castle, now overseen by a churlish Irish caretaker, but then prepares, with wry acceptance, for return "to the city I had always loved, to the house which had always been my home": Boston.

With *All in the Family*, O'Connor seems to be suggesting Irish-Americans can go home again, but that home, for whatever it is worth, is America. O'Connor's Irish-Americans, as Shaun O'Connell has suggested, are caught on the horns of a dilemma, equally doomed either as parochial chauvinists like Skeffington with "no future in the city, only memories" or as "hollow-men" like Charles, who turn their backs on their cultural heritage" (*Imagining Boston* 126). O'Connor certainly thought hard and deep about acculturation. Through the prism of politics, his work details the changes he witnessed in the Boston Irish; and he offers a lament for "Irish" values gone by the boards. Charles Kinsella, like Skeffington, is a political success; but his cynicism betrays his roots. For Charles, Ireland is merely a place across the sea, "Irish" politics an anachronism. But, in rejecting "tribalism," O'Connor suggests, Kinsella is also rejecting the life of the past; and *All in the Family* is a novel of deracination and assimilation that disturbs rather than comforts: a portrait of loss.

3

William Kennedy praised O'Connor for his insights into Irish-American political history. But he also criticized what O'Connor omitted, "either to be polite to the Church or to Irish society, or out of squeamishness," and vowed, in his own work, to present Irish America with all its "wit, anger, sexuality, deviousness" (Griffin 296). Certainly, Kennedy's own Albany novels include the hard truths—the obscenities of racism, crime, despair—that Kennedy felt O'Connor had omitted; and they can make the reader wince. Perhaps as Irish-Americans grow more secure, they are more free to criticize their own.

Legs, set in the bootleg era of the 1920s, rehearses the saga of gangster Jack "Legs" Diamond, alive far beyond ordinary mortals like the mythic Irish hero Cuchulain, so "his phlogiston itself burnt its way into your own spirit" (36). For Jack, there is just the burning present, the *what-is*.

Narrated by Jack's lawyer Marcus Gorman, in interwoven fashion much like the curlicued scroll of *The Book of Kells*, *Legs* is replete with broad anecdotes, Gaelicisms, portraits of Irish Catholic kitsch. The walls of Jack's home, for instance, are filled "with framed calendar art and holy pictures—a sepia print of the Madonna returning from Calvary and an incendiary, bleeding sacred heart with a cross blooming atop the bloody fire" (43). Jack and his hoodlum buddy Goose play variations of the Irish dozens; when Jack says, "Polacks shit in Church," Goose rejoins, "Then I see two Irishmen takin' shits up on the altar all at once. I seen one Irishman shit during a funeral. Irishmen don't know any better" (77). Jack smiles—and kicks Goose's eye out. *Game, set, match.*

In this "gangster-time," Irish-American relics abound. Packy Delaney's Parody Club is festooned with

> a four-globed chandelier and a four-bladed ceiling fan and photos on the walls of old railroad men, old politicians, old bare-knuckled fighters, dead Maud Gonne's likeness sketched on a handbill announcing her appearance at Hibernian Hall to raise funds for a free Ireland, defunct Hibernian Society marching down State Street on a sunny St. Patrick's day in '95, disbanded private fire companies standing at attention in front of their pumpers, K. of C. beer drinkers, long in their graves, tapping a keg at McKown's Grove clambake. (261)

These mementos function as the warp and woof of Irish Albany. At Packie's, Jack joins a *caeli*, an Irish songfest, where they sing "profoundly out of the musical realm of their Irish Catholic souls, 'There's an old time melody / that I heard long ago / Mother called it the rosary / she sang it soft and low'" (262).

But not all is soft and low. Jack, according to Marcus, is an "ancestral paradigm for modern urban political gangsters"—unlike Richard Nixon, however, because "only boobs and shitheads rooted for Nixon in the troubled time; heroes and poets followed Jack's tribulations with curiosity, ambivalent benevolence, and a sense of mystery at the meaning of their own response" (216). Jack's devil-may-care attitude mirrors what we now know about Jack Kennedy's fatalism—he similarly thumbs his nose at fate and predicts his own assassination; and after he is gunned down, his friends share stories of the mythic hero, embellishing: "Jack could turn on the electric light sometimes, just by snapping his fingers. Jack could tie both his shoes at once" (311).

Jack may be dead, but he is still around, somewhere. But in Kennedy's Albany, the ghosts are more neighborly—phlegmatic and casual. Jack (age 34 years, 5 months, 7 days) is surprised to find the yellow fluid of death oozing out of his body: "Honest to God, Marcus," he says, "I really don't think I'm dead." In its strange blend of the just-stopped-living and the about-to-be dead, *Legs* keens for a rougher, more colorful, pagan Celtic world.

Billy Phelan's Greatest Game continues the saga. Billy's Albany, Kennedy's Albany, is not mainstream America. When amanuensis Martin Daugherty tells his wife she is the embodiment of Ireland in female flesh, she fills the kitchen with laughter: "You're mad entirely," Mary Daugherty said [in] the lilt of Connacht, a callous response to madness in her morning kitchen.

"You can bet your sweet Irish ass I'm mad," Martin said. "I dreamed of Peter, carried through the streets by pederast priests." (15)

Torn between the competing realities of the new amalgamized Albany and the old Irish neighborhood, Martin is struggling to throw off the yoke of his Irishness, to accept what Henry James called the complex fate of being an American. Where his father "was possessed by concrete visions of the Irish in the New World, struggling to throw off the filth of poverty, oppression, and degradation, and rising to a higher plane of life, where they would be the equals of all those arrived Americans who manipulated the nation's power, wealth, and culture," Martin is "bored with the yearnings of the immigrant hordes and [seeks] something more abstract: to love oneself and one's opposite" (24).

But Martin, like his creator, remains fascinated with the complexity of America's ethnic reality—keeps turning it over like a prism to expose its multifaceted horrors. When a Jewish friend relates a moment of "monstrous ethnic truth"—"the persecuted Irish throwing a persecuted Jew [his grandfather] out the window in protest against drafting Irishmen into the union Army to help liberate the persecuted Negro," Martin shoots back, "You can't blame the Klan on the Irish. I could match grand-fathers with you. One of mine was killed at Antietam, fighting for the niggers" (113).

The Albany Irish are not only perpetrators and victims of racial stereotyping, but embodiments of these very stereotypes. To be Albany Irish, Martin laments, is to be "Pis-ant martyr to the rapine culture, to the hypocritical handshakers, the priest suckups, the nigger-hating cops, the lace-curtain Grundys and the cut-glass banker-thieves who marked his city lousy. Are you from Albany? Yes. How can you stand it? I was there once and it's the asshole of the northeast. One of the ten bottom places of the earth" (272–73).

It is thus a complex fate to be an Albany Irishman as well, as we see with Billy Phelan. Like Jack, Billy is vibrant, "pure energy in shoes," crazy enough to kidnap a scion of Albany's "Irish American potentates of the night and day." His humor is morbidly tough. When a friend observes of a corpse, "He don't look so bad," Billy rejoins, "He don't look so bad for a corpse" (74). Raking in a poker pot, he smiles: "My mother thanks you, my sister thanks you, and above all, Lemon, I, William Francis Irish Catholic Democrat Phelan, I too thank you" (123). Billy recognizes his Irishness, but that identity contains little dignity. When Daddy Big asks what he's doing in his all-black cafe because he "ain't a nigger," Billy shrugs, "I'm an Irish Catholic. Same thing to some people" (193). But under the tough-guy front, Billy is ashamed of his shanty-Irish roots. When his alcoholic father yearns to come out of the bum-Irish cold to bring a turkey home for Thanksgiving, Billy schemes to get his old man a new outfit so he can "look like an American citizen again." At the end, we see Billy Phelan, alive if not exactly flourishing, back at the pool hall, "the only cosmos in town."

Ironweed, Kennedy's sequel, continues the story from the perspective of Francis Phelan, Billy's father. The novel opens in the Catholic cemetery where Frannie comes upon his mother weaving Brigid's crosses. In this Dantean world, "the neighborhood of the Phelans" as Frannie calls it, where "the dead, they got all the eyes," he is on familiar terms with many of the spirits, including his own baby boy whose death, after Frannie dropped him, precipitated his long day's journey of exile and penance. His wife has long ago forgiven Frannie; he just cannot forgive himself. Frannie may be a bum, but (as even Billy admits) he is a bum with soul.

For Frannie, the past is a heavy weight, not that he complains. Ironweed, a sunflower deriving its name from the toughness of its stem, is an appropriate symbol for Frannie. Typically, Kennedy's Irish are beyond complaint, yet curious about the meaning of it all and determined to remember details of the past and to chew them over as a squirrel with acorns. The Banshees are still around: Francis chats on a streetcar with a man he killed by accident and with an old flame who died in a fire; at one point, he imagines his mother's wedding night from her viewpoint; during one rare visit home, he dons old clothes from an attic trunk and is flooded with memories of his youth.

Despite its grimness, *Ironweed* contains certain tender mercies. When crazy Rudy philosophizes, "There must be a God. He protects bums. They get up out of the snow and they go up and get a drink. Look at you, brand-new clothes. But look at me. I'm only a bum, a no-good bum,"

Francis soothes him: "You ain't that bad. You're a bum, but you aint that bad" (188). Offering the communion of his whiskey bottle to another bum, Francis says: "Have a drink, pal. Lubricate your soul" (209). For Kennedy, "soul" is a term of spiritual praise, if not formally Catholic, similar to the "soul-brother" bonding of blacks. In a final epiphany, Francis senses the forces of darkness coming to extinguish "great souls" like his longtime drinking companion, Helen, while over him a question hovers: *How should this man pray?*

Indeed, Kennedy seems to be asking, how may *any* of us pray? *Ironweed* presents an irreverent, oddly poetic, portrait, tinged with fatalism. The Banshee is within as well as without, remorse of conscience as well as terror. Through confronting his sins, through suffering, Francis passes through his own Gethsemane; and, having experienced so much of hell and purgatory, he dreams, at the end, of heaven, of home, of sleeping "in a mighty nice little room." Not a bad dream. We root for him.

Throughout Kennedy's novels, there is constant cross-referencing; his characters live in the same neighborhood, know the same people, will fill the same graveyard. He continues to produce work imbued with historical facts and real-life figures, a scrapbook of the past for the benefit of the living. Just as Joyce intended the Dublin of 1904 to be reconstructable from the pages of *Ulysses,* Kennedy recreates the actual historical Albany the Irish wrested, slowly and painfully, from the Dutch. *Quinn's Book,* his "nineteenth-century" Albany novel, composed along Dickensian lines, with fortuitous escapes, lugubrious letters, and whores with hearts of gold, includes poignant portraits of shanty-Irish famine immigrants persecuted by the "American Irish"; *O Albany!* provides a poignant and lively testimonial to his beloved city and that world now strangely passed and "passing strange."

Kennedy's underworld reveals its Irish roots. Legs and Billy may be gangsters, Frannie a bum; but still they respond with stoic honor to what has to be done and that which stirs, fitfully, in their souls. They may not talk about "The Auld Sod" much, yet they seem quintessentially Irish, full of humor, ingenuity, even faith of a sort; and they also reflect, as Anthony Burgess once observed of Irish writing, "the presence of a kind of grace, a moral elegance that frames all sorts of wretchedness" (Forkner 18). Despite the outrages that bedevil them, they refuse to stay limited within neat or demeaning definitions as they prepare to go over to the "other side," which may be death or Ireland.

4

For Mary Gordon, the "other side" is not just Ireland, but the truth about women, ignored or slighted in the primarily male writing of Irish America. "Growing up," says Jean, the wife of Jack Kinsella, in O'Connor's *All in the Family*, "I heard only two sounds in our house: screams and prayers, I got a little tired of both" (234). Mary Gordon, too, is tired of screams and prayer. If O'Connor's Irish Boston is both treasure trove and trap, where humor functions as a reprieve, and Kennedy's Albany a gangster world that crucifies and, occasionally, redeems, Gordon's Queens is a stifling parochial society where ridicule wounds and cripples. For Gordon, secrets are the most oppressive element of Irish Catholicism; and she has determined to reveal that personal and racial history Irish Catholics refuse to acknowledge.

Final Payments is a fable of repression characterized by sacrifice and self-denial. For eleven years, Isabel Moore has devoted herself to nursing her father, a professor of medieval history, through his last lingering illness. She summarizes an article he once wrote for *Catholic World* entitled "The Catholic Temper": "Protestants, it said, thought about moral issues, drank water and ate crackers, took care to exercise and had a notion that charity was synonymous with good works. Catholics, on the other hand, thought about eternity, drank wine and smoked cigars, were sometimes extravagant, but knew that charity was a fire in the heart of God and never confused it with that Protestant invention, philanthropy" (40). Dr. Moore's Catholicism defines and defies everything wrong, that is, liberal, in the modern world; but his faith is narrow, quirkily right wing, full of fury, of little use to Isabel.

Only after her father's death does Isabel venture out, at the age of thirty-one, with an often comic sense of moral probity. Sharing "Catholic" jokes with an old schoolmate, Isabel suddenly realizes her life is rooted in stop-time 1960s Catholicism: "I was the only one who understood Liz's jokes about the peace movement: nuns in Ship'n Shore blouses who made her want to join the Green Berets just to be on the opposite side; priests with no sense of irony losing their virginity in their forties; concerned laity, all overweight or underweight, with bad taste in shoes and bad complexions. . . . Eugene McCarthy the man every Catholic girl had dreamed of marrying, as Dan Berrigan was the priest we yearned to seduce" (19). Liz matches Isabel tartness for tartness: "Look at the shoes on the wife. Can you believe it? Bows. Manhattanville 1962.

I bet she has a miraculous medal pinned to her bra" (26). Of one friend of her father, she observes:

> Father Mulcahy was clean as a piglet bathed in milk. His black hat was brushed as smooth as the skin of a fruit; his white hair, so thin that the hard, pink skull showed beneath it like a flagstone floor, looked as though the color had been taken out of it purposefully, through a series of savage washings. He gave off the odor of an impossibly chaste talcum powder; they all did. I'm sure they buy it where they buy their vestments. But over it all, like a tropical storm over Norway, was the secular smell of his Old Spice. (55)

There is a crisp, albeit malicious, rightness to such portraits, and the ridicule often spills over into self-mockery—an essential moral ingredient. But Isabel realizes these in-jokes perform "the Catholic high school girl trick" of substituting comedy for intimacy, thereby distancing feeling.

Isabel's own feelings are complex; she is constantly discovering that the real world is more complicated, more devious, than the moral platitudes for which her Catholic childhood prepared her. Having lived so long out of the world, she is constantly playing catch-up. She is chaste, though many years before she slept with her father's prize pupil. Now in the world she is unprepared for passion or coarseness; and her reemergent desire has tragicomic undertones. Drunk, excited by the coarse red hair of his arms, like a teenager Isabel has sex in the front seat of a car with Ryan, her best friend's husband, whom Liz herself has described as "a six-foot walking penis with a social conscience." Afterward, Ryan gropes her breast "as if making a meatball" and offers her a handkerchief so as not to stain the upholstery. There is a further irony when Isabel learns that Liz herself has a lover, and a woman at that.

When Isabel does find "Mister Right," Hugh, a compassionate social worker from whom she learns to mouth the word pleasure "like a plum," he is unhappily and irrevocably married. Isabel once again "does the right thing," giving him up because they are both "good people" and denial of pleasure is the duty of every good Catholic woman, guilt pleasure's reward, only penance worthy. Isabel thereupon serves as handmaiden to her father's former housemaid Margaret, who hates her for being young, pretty, and bright (all the things she most certainly is not); she grovels in front of the loutish Margaret and eats junk food to get fat and ugly. Finally, enraged by Margaret's life-denying (even Jesus-denying) spite, Isabel calls her girlfriends to come get her and sets about rejoining the larger, nonparochial world.

"There is a great deal I wanted to say, "Isabel Moore announces at the end—a statement that might apply to Gordon herself. By placing Isabel in a sort of time capsule from which she emerges no more prepared than Woody Allen in *Sleeper,* Gordon suggests the ambiguous worth of the parochialism at the heart of Irish Catholic life in the fifties and sixties. Such values, she suggests, are anachronisms, time bombs, in contemporary America; Irish-Americans should rethink their reality—come out of the closet.

If *Final Payments* signaled the arrival of a writer with a fresh vision (or re-vision) of Irish-American life, particularly female Irish-American life, her less-than-flattering portrait of the parish upset many "fellow parishioners." In 1989, in "A Writer Goes Home," Gordon wrote of her experience at a beloved uncle's wake where several relatives let her know just how much they hated her books and announced that (except for her mother, one cousin, and possibly one aunt) all in the family considered her an "embarrassment or a lost soul." Gordon connects their displeasure to her having revealed secrets, because "to reveal for the Irish is to put oneself and the people one loves in danger" (32). Yet is it not, she asks, the duty of a writer to reveal?

In *The Other Side,* a twenty-four-hour time capsule of the thoughts of four generations of the MacNamara clan, Gordon reveals more. The novel opens in New York with the immigrant patriarch and matriarch doddering in various debilities: Vincent in a nursing home, recuperating from being pushed and toppled by Ellen, who has misread a comforting gesture as a sexual advance; Ellen at home, in and out of dark madness. Aging has so contracted the both of them that they are now nothing *but* memories, sometimes faulty, mainly unspoken; and the novel, through memory, addresses the costs and gains of passage, the struggle to forge an American identity.

Vincent's memories are various, ambiguous, shifting from his American past to his Irish roots. He recalls being intrigued by Irish neighbors' reference to America as "a place you could stretch your legs and take some giant steps, not like this godforsaken country, where your every movement was hobbled both by priests and by poverty" (246). He remembers Ellen's beautiful anger "at the Irish countryside, the harsh soil and scrub growth, the gorse she hated. She'd no memory of tilled field, of the elm or the potato, tender when in leaf. Anger had been Ellen's chief food. . . . She'd never believed in happiness. The mention of it put her in a fury" (41). Vincent recalls "the lit-up Past" of Ireland and his early greenhorn days in America—Fanny Breyton singing at Tara Hall:

> My heart is heavy in my breast, my eyes are full of tears
> My memory is wandering back to long departed years

> To those bright days long, long ago
> When nought I dreamed of sordid care, or worldly woe
> But roved a day, light heart boy, the woods of Kilaloe.
> (246)

But, no longer a "light heart boy," Vincent is terrified by the shiftiness of time. "When is now? When is it becoming the not now, the past? I am nothing. Nowhere I stand is firm" (268).

Ellen remembers leaving Ireland with a "pain like a spike through the center of her chest." But her Ireland, far from Shannon's construct or Vincent's recollections, is a rural horror show: she recalls her father's public affair, for which she feels terrible shame, and her mother sitting in the cold darkness of a stone cottage, gibbering in Irish, "God take me from this life." Ellen remembers Ireland as terrible and terrifying; and she enjoys mocking Vincent's fond memories:

> Pigs and dirt and begging relatives. No thanks, none of that 'I'll Take You Home Again Kathleen' cod for me, thank you. That's my husband's department. Say the word bog only and he's drowning in the water of his tears. . . . Yes, Dad, 'tis little enough ye knew of it. You left at fifteen and lucky for you. 'Twas a lovely life you had. Breaking your back on the farm that went all to your brother, then apprenticed out at twelve. 'Twas what ye wanted for yer children, wasn't it. The lovely bread, the lovely singsongs by the peat fire. Everybody slaving till they died or wore out. 'Twas wonderful. If only I could have it back. (86, 160)

Ellen sings of "the starving tinkers out to steal me blind back, back to the auld sod of my dreams." She prefers jokes, songs, toasts, speeches, and passionate political arguments—all distancing performances, like Isabel Moore's Catholic jokes, rather than invitations to intimacy. For Ellen, secrecy is the greatest virtue: "Display was what she hated. You kept things to yourself. You kept them hidden. You took them out in privacy, you hugged them to your body. You did not show off. You kept your feelings to yourself. Anger only was allowed" (250). Ellen hides newspaper clippings under the bed (to have "a sense of things," as she says); but now when she searches her memory, she finds "[e]verything is simply, for no reason, gone" (105–6). As she pores over the "lucid rhomboids of the past," she vows never to share the truth of her life with her children; her coldness is her only joy, though she knows her begrudging is "[a] slave's trick . . . [a] slave's gratitude" (120). Now, in darkness and silence, with the final outrage of death bearing down on her, she offers her family a terrible legacy: *"I will remind you how frail your grasp is upon what you determine to be human. At any moment you can be the animal I am"* (342).

Their children, perhaps because of Ellen's bitter legacy, have died or disgraced themselves. Only Magdalen, a bedridden, agoraphobic alcoholic, shares her father's rosy view of the past. Looking at an old photo, she thinks: "This is exactly how it was. We were like that. I remember, we were lovely. I remember every morning we were just like that. I never understood: we could have been like that forever" (314). But Magdalen's testimony, because of her condition, is flawed, untrustworthy; we are not to believe it was "just like that."

The grandchildren, the third generation "caught on the moving staircase of upward American striving" (50), find themselves distanced from their grandparents' immigrant reality and their parents' disasters. They sense, however, a "ghost-ash," a legacy of self-hatred and spite they cannot quite wash out of their souls. Even Cam, the most sympathetic of the lot, recognizes in herself "the taste for condemnation, a racial trait she guessed, of preserving, self-preserving Irish women"; she views "her own kind," Teddy Kennedy, Phil Donahue, as a "bunch of third-raters or self-destructors" (57). She asks (and answers) her own question: "Why weren't the Irish interested in pleasure? It's no accident [they] built the subways. And then stayed there. It was the perfect place for them, dark, underground, dangerous, hidden" (250).

Her cousin Dan, returning from a visit to Ireland, cites "the sickle cell anemia of the Irish . . . bred into the bone" (160) and speculates whether that unhappiness might spring from the fact that "they were a colonized nation and had taken from their colonizers all their symbols of prosperity and of success" and had "an obsession with concealment" (161). His final assessment is a double-edged sword: "He felt they were his people, the Irish, and he pitied and admired them. He enjoyed them, but he felt that, like him, they had no idea how to live" (163).

The plot of *The Other Side*, twenty-four hours of cycling and recycled memories, explores the themes of shame, guilt, secrecy, and denial, the ambivalent legacy Gordon feels is that of the American Irish. Through Vincent, we experience loss; through Ellen, we question the "green fog" surrounding the "real" Ireland; through Cam and Dan, we come to sense the confusion of the Americanized Irish most of us have become. Once again, as with Isabel Moore, we see the damage that denial and secrecy can bring, particularly in sexual matters. At the end, as we follow Vincent tottering home fearful of Ellen's fury, his journey contains all the novel has revealed of the three generations: "He believes that she can see him, but he's not quite sure." A small step, if not for all mankind, for Irish-Americans anyway.

In her work, Mary Gordon has explored the Irish connection and delved into the dark to expose "the other side" of the Irish-American soul. Gordon speaks of her Irish "cousins" with fondness, but with some reservations: "I just have this incredible, unreasonable soft spot in my heart for them, despite the fact that there are things about them too that I can't stand. I think they are very idealistic and I love that about them. I know they have a great sense of humor and I love Irish wit. I also think they have a wonderful gift for language. They have a humility which can sometimes do them in: a sense of the absurd in the human condition. They can be very kind and cruel at the same time" (Burns 80). She pinpoints a certain doubleness, a "schizophrenia": "On the one hand, they have an almost obsessive love of privacy and secrecy. On the other, they love to talk and tell stories" (Burns 74).

In her own work, Gordon is determined to tell stories *and* to tell the truth, and it is obvious she views her novels as acts of liberation. It may be argued that her portrait is too grim: "Mirror, mirror on the wall, who is the fairest of us all?—Not you, *mauvereen!*" But Gordon's Irish-Americans confront the ambiguities of their lives and act with anger, honesty, and (on occasion) faith, hope, and charity. If much of the action is internal, this brooding has a rare intensity. She reminds us of the courage embodied in those Irish who "see the human condition in its clearest, most undiluted colors, feel its starkest music in the bone" ("A Writer Goes Home" 41). Gordon's world, too, as she wrote of Edna O'Brien, is a "vale of tears where ghosts jostle the beautiful fleshly living for a place in the fanatic heart" ("Edna O'Brien" 51); it is also a moral proving ground, in which the act of memory, in opening up a dialogue with the grave and with oneself, forges a healthier, more open future.

5

In chronicling the American Irish, O'Connor, Gordon, and Kennedy reveal how the core of belief early emigrants transported to America has become transformed, at first unconsciously, later consciously—even resolutely, into something less Irish, more American, so that the core is now the remnant. *Sic transit,* one might say, whatever transits. But the "ghost-values" remain and include piety, humor, secretiveness, courage, fatalism. These writers also reveal much else, how the fierce and conflicting loyalties of family and religion and the notion of "our kind" can suffocate as well as comfort. As Andrew Greeley has shrewdly observed, "The two most devastating things that can be said to the young Irishman who attempts to move beyond the rigid norms are 'Who do you think you are?' and 'What will people say?'" (190). O'Connor, Gordon, and Kennedy have photographed the shadows at our backs to liberate us from such belittlement. For each of these writers, the engine of truth is individual and collective memory, however painful.

Their fiction, grounded in the historical present, reveals the distinct flavor of an Irish Catholicism bubbling within the American crucible. O'Connor's world is external, even grand; his scenes are most often public events—wakes, political rallies, church services; and if we learn much about what his Irish do, we learn less about why they do it. In recalling Old World virtues such as loyalty and compassion, O'Connor reminds us of what has been lost and suggests we beware making pacts with the devil in order to "make it" in America. Gordon's world is internal, and we learn more about what her characters think and feel, fear and resent. For Gordon, the solution is seen to lie in disclosure—opening the heart, telling the truth—in order to rid ourselves of false piety, emotional sterility, and spite. From the bones of Albany, Kennedy has proffered a hardscrabble world of immigrant striving—through ditch digging, hustling, crime, and politics—for both survival and respectability. For Kennedy, the "ghost-ash" is a Celtic core of emotion, antimaterialist, pagan, which reveals a complicated softness in the struggle to claim America.

Time itself, the Irish proverb reminds us, is also a good storyteller. The Irish-American story, which, Daniel Moynihan claims, includes "a past of heroic or at least colossal travail; a present shading from lace-curtain respectability to *le comfort bourgeois* and further to the higher indulgences with which the American well-to-do have experimented of late" (Greeley vii) has new chapters still to be written. Today many "Yanks," fleeing hectic corporate jobs, are opting for cottages in the quiet Irish countryside. Niall Williams and Christine Breen's *O Come Ye Back to Ireland,* the story of one such couple who took to farming in County Clare, is dedicated "to all those whose dreams we carried in us"; thus the immigrant dream comes full circle. The more we rush pell-mell into the future, it seems, the more our ancestors call out to us, as they do to Frank Skeffington, to Frannie Phelan, to Ellen MacNamara, to signal not only remembrance of the dead but the honorable ways of the tribe. "So we beat on," Nick Carroway remarks at the end of Fitzgerald's *The Great Gatsby,* "boats against the current, borne back ceaselessly into the past."

To recall that Irish farmer I began with. To insist, "We are our ancestors," means, of course, that we are of their blood. But it also suggests something more profound, that the collective soul of those who have gone before survives in us: we are the offspring of their most profound dreams. To live unreflective of one's roots, as the work of O'Connor, Kennedy, and Gordon suggests, is to be cut off from one's soul as well as one's ancestors. To tell their stories, and our own, involves not only an act of homage and fealty but of self-discovery. We are, then, not only our ancestors but also our descendants, at least insofar as we might bequeath something to apprehend—X rays of our lives—bone truths that are in the end the true legacy.

Works Cited

Burns, Veronica. "An Interview with Mary Gordon." *The Recorder* Summer 1987: 71–81.
Carroll, James. "Beyond the Dream." *Boston Globe Magazine* 17 Mar. 1985: 44ff.
Forkner, Ben. *Modern Irish Short Stories*. New York: Penguin, 1982.
Gordon, Mary. "Edna O'Brien: A Fanatic Heart." *Irish America* July–Aug. 1991: 49, 51.
———. *Final Payments*. New York: Random, 1978.
———. " 'I Can't Stand Your Books': A Writer Goes Home." *New York Times Book Review* 11 Dec. 1988: 1ff.
———. *The Other Side*. New York: Penguin, 1990.
Greeley, Andrew M. *That Most Distressful Nation: The Taming of the American Irish*. New York: Quadrangle, 1972.
Griffin, William D. *The Book of Irish Americans*. New York: Random, 1990.
Kennedy, William. *Billy Phelan's Greatest Game*. New York: Penguin, 1983.
———. *Ironweed*. New York: Penguin, 1983.
———. *Legs*. New York: Penguin, 1983.
Marin, Peter. "Toward Something American." *Harper's* July 1988: 17–18.
O'Connell, Shaun. "Irish America's Red Brick City: Edwin O'Connor's Boston." *Imagining Boston*. Boston: Beacon, 1990, 108–40.
———. "The Red Brick City." *The Recorder* Summer 1987: 31–40.
O'Connor, Edwin. *All in the Family*. Boston: Atlantic Monthly, 1966.
———. *The Last Hurrah*. New York: Bantam, 1957.
Shannon, William. *The American Irish*. New York: Collier, 1966.
Thelen, David. "Memory and American History." *Journal of American History* 75.4 (1989): 1117–29.
Williams, Niall, and Christine Breen. *O Come Ye Back to Ireland: Our First Year in County Clare*. New York: Soho, 1987.

Expanding the Collective Memory: Charles W. Chesnutt's *The Conjure Woman* Tales

SANDRA MOLYNEAUX

> Well, suh, you is a stranger ter me, en I is a stranger ter you, en we is bofe strangers ter one anudder.... Wid strangers dey ain' no tellin' w'at mought happen.
> —Uncle Julius

The post-Reconstruction South, humiliated by civil war, economic stagnation, and social confusion, desperately sought to remember its past as chivalrous. Consequently, the history of slavery was being rewritten as a myth of the "Lost Cause," claiming kinship in Western literature's heritage of heroic narratives. While Southern Negroes were learning to read the white man's texts, Charles Waddell Chesnutt (1858–1932), a self-taught educator who knew both North and South, Black and White, desired to broaden the cultural record by teaching Whites to read Negro "texts." In an 1880 journal entry, Chesnutt recorded plans to fulfill "a high, holy purpose" (H. M. Chesnutt 21), anticipating Anna Julia Cooper's "Voice from the South," through which the cultivated black man would cure the white man's barbarity by civilizing him (210). To both writers, art would educate people to new feelings and a new point of view by "honestly and appreciatively portraying both the Negro as he is, and the white man . . . as seen from the Negro's standpoint" (Cooper 225). At the same time, Chesnutt reminded Blacks they were accurate recorders of the past, competent readers of the present, and responsible shapers of the future.

The Conjure Woman, whose structure and rhetoric is as complicated and subversive as were the times in which it was written, is Chesnutt's challenge to forgetfulness. The work validates oral testimony within a

Expanding the Collective Memory

literary tradition, models dialogue aiding memory, and illustrates how story acts as a civilizing process that "creates culture by discovering and reinforcing tales to be told not only twice, but continuously" (Fryer 227). By tracing Chesnutt's changes to earlier short stories and by seeing how additional stories alter the final collection, we follow the author's own retelling as his memory sharpens and challenges deteriorating social and political conditions. Remembering, Chesnutt tells a story that reminds us to remember.

Between 1885 and 1889 Chesnutt published thirty-four sketches and short stories, the success of which led to the 1899 publication of *The Conjure Woman*, a collection of seven "conjure" tales, each embedded within a framing narrative. A product of much rethinking and coordination, *The Conjure Woman*'s artistry lies in the adjustments Chesnutt made in transforming individual stories into a continuous series.[1] The stories are not a loose aggregate: they form a complex network of interlocking themes reflecting "an interconnected pattern of life" (Whitt 42). Like people talking, each story both responds to the preceding and anticipates the next, and the whole moves forward in a recursive pattern that gathers the chaotic past into a hopeful future.

The interior tales are parables, mysterious transformations brought about by Aun' Peggy, a free black "conjure woman" who mysteriously intervenes on behalf of her people. They are drawn from an ex-slave's "memory—or imagination" (C. W. Chesnutt, *The Conjure Woman* 41 [hereafter cited as *CW*]) and contain timeless morals that comment, like a voice from the past, on conditions in the contemporary frames. Chesnutt temporally displaces the new slavery of post-Reconstruction economic exploitation and social segregation—and revenge as the only viable option to both—onto the antebellum conjure tales and simultaneously applies African American "folk" wisdom to "progressive" America's ills. The complex interplay between "oral" interior narrative and "recorded" exterior frames links black and white voices to past and present experiences, and it differentiates between individual experience and official records and between intuitive and rational versions of reality.

By diffusing the point of view, Chesnutt mutes his own bilingual voice, allowing the tale tellers to match wits in a verbal duel—a competition for narrative control that models the author's entry into contemporary dialogue. Uncle Julius, an elderly, shrewd, witty "conjurer," can, from a lifetime of experience, read the lay of the land. Julius knows his audience. He also knows how to tell a story and knows how story functions as a cooperative medium that unites a community of talkers and listeners who can subsequently share future memories. The framing narrator, John, a young displaced Northerner, is the "cultivated" white reader. But Chesnutt denies him the expected controlling voice, which would have diminished the interior tales' power. John interprets actions and motives and tries to direct the force of Julius's transformation tales, but his continual misreading and failure to comprehend connections turn him into an ironic foil: he is blind, lacking a receptivity that can suspend protective accretions of overrationalization and lofty rhetoric.[2]

In each narrative, John's stated desire—purchasing land, using schoolhouse lumber, dismissing Julius's grandson, purchasing a horse, curing Annie, draining the swamp, forcing submission—triggers Julius's memory, and the old man recalls a story, which he repeats in order to deter or redirect John's action. The interior conjure tales, however, disguise their competition with the exterior narration, just as slaves "in those horrid days before the war" (*CW* 159) had conjured their white masters in verbal wordplay. Chesnutt's Negro audiences, whether sophisticated readers or illiterate listeners, would have recognized his subversive attempts to maintain memories threatened by silence, denial, or debasement.[3]

By liberating Julius from white paternalism and by asserting wisdom over subservience, experience over a rigid system, Chesnutt exposes the false sentimentality of the "faithful old servant" formula popularized in the plantation genre, and he undercuts the pejorative connotations of dialect stories as marginalized expressions of African American experience. Dialect, for Chesnutt, is the key to the "stolen voice" of Negro free speech and of African-based storytelling ripped from its original cultural context ("Superstitions" 376).[4] Chesnutt permits the Negro voice he remembered as a child to speak in its own right, and he emphasizes the effects of orally transmitted traditions, which, in folk cultures, are the occasions for keeping history alive and for promoting social cohesion.[5]

Cultures in flux need new collective myths if they are to remain vibrant. As storyteller, Chesnutt differentiates between "superstition," which fixes a culture in cyclical time, and the "high, holy purpose" of his art, the roots of which are found in a religious sensibility that accepts the supernatural. The "so-called conjuration" material originates in "African fetishism," yet, as he reminds his white readers, it bears resemblances to debased moral practices found in white American culture. To Chesnutt the "quaint combination of ancestral traditions . . . which in the place of their original had all the sanctions of religion and social custom, become, in the shadow of the white man's civilization, a pale reflection of their former selves. In time . . . they were mingled and confused with the witchcraft and ghost lore of the white man, and the tricks and delusions of the Indian conjurer" ("Superstition" 371). Chesnutt lamented society's forgetting "these vanishing traditions," and he wanted to reassert a moral imperative by reinstating the power of folk forms into the contemporary world.[6] Chesnutt's conjure stories exemplify the mythic power of original tales transposed to a new historical reality. By holding up the "magic mirror" of truth ("Superstition" 376), Julius/Chesnutt would coax, seduce, or trick readers who recalled only what they wished. They would tell stories to strangers and expand the collective memory.

In rewriting his individual stories, Chesnutt seems to be remembering, almost in spite of himself as his later essays might indicate (Ferguson 109), the strengths of his own folk roots. He significantly expanded the frame for the opening story, "The Goophered Grapevine," by more clearly establishing the Southern landscape and by escalating the dynamics between narrators. The new material locates *The Conjure Woman* and its narrators in the center of overlapping metaphors rooted in the land itself—where "lines of rotting rail fence" contrast with "the solemn aisles of the virgin forest, where the tall pines . . . wrapped [John] in cloistral solitude" (8, 7). John seeks security in an impoverished system, a "more equable climate" for his wife's physical condition, and, incidentally, a somewhat settled environment where "labor was cheap" (1, 2). Benevolent paternalism and economic interests cohere immediately.

The new material quickly signals that John, a product of Northern economic energy, professional medical expertise, and Western literary tradition, is densely literal-minded. His "coolness of judgment desirable in making so radical a change" (4) enables him to learn "what [he] wished to know" (7); but, as a stranger to the area, John lacks any memory of place that could reorient his thinking in a new society. His "judgment," limited to reading texts, prevents his reading the signs that signify other, deeper meanings to his "unaccustomed eyes" (3–4)—such as the curfew bell on the market-house tower, a locally familiar holdover from slave days (Whitt 45). At an unfamiliar crossroads, John does not know what turn to take; he must depend upon a "little negro girl" (7).

Julius, too, becomes a more complex character in the revision because Chesnutt adds that Julius "was not entirely black." Julius's "not altogether African" blood does not, as John infers, cause the "shrewdness in his eyes," but reinforces the stereotype that morals and wisdom have their source in white blood, an assumption undercut by the tales' moral messages and by John's perceptual limits. Julius as mulatto also adds another parallel between Negro exploitation during slavery days and the contemporary, post-Reconstruction setting of the frames. John could never have conceived of Julius as a "disputing heir" "involved in litigation" over the land John wanted to purchase, nor that Julius might have either hereditary claim or emotional investment in the land he had tilled under slavery. Without aid, Julius had cultivated and profited from an annually rejuvenating crop until John's claim intervened (5).

The added references to ownership also strengthen links between stories, anticipating "Po' Sandy's"[7] tragedy in which the desire for self-possession and rootedness contrast with capricious exploitation of resources. In a new story, "Mars Jeems's Nightmare," John delights in Julius's usefulness yet judges his "peculiar personal attitude [to John's property as] . . . predial rather than proprietary." John interprets Julius's feelings and appropriates his memories, claiming that Julius's attachment stems from a change in his status defined by others, not from choice: "He had been accustomed . . . to look upon himself as the property of another. When this relation was *no longer possible,* owing to the war, and to his master's death and the dispersion of the family, he had been unable to break off entirely the mental habits of a lifetime, but had attached himself to the old plantation" (65, emphasis added). John's words expose brilliantly his own previously unchallenged "mental habits," which continue to see the former slave as property without independent resources, family ties, or self-discipline.

The first three stories progressively explore the right of possession: identifying the source of personal power in nature itself, claiming resources for communal use, and seeking entry into economic productivity. Julius gets what he wants. Although he loses to John any legal claim to the grapevines, Julius remains as coachman (driver) and storyteller, and he benefits the Negro community by engaging Annie's emotions: identifying with Teenie's loss when Po' Sandy was cut into lumber, she donates the wooden schoolhouse to the Sandy Run Colored Baptist Church; placing herself in Mars Jeems's nightmare, she rehires Julius's grandson after her husband has dismissed him. More importantly, however, the added material sharpens the thematic shift from economic competition toward the corrective power of story as a cooperative, civilizing medium that would fulfill Chesnutt's original goal of changing feelings (H. M. Chesnutt 21) and, subsequently, society. As he remembers, language, memory, and intuitive wisdom become his new subjects: Chesnutt "restore[s] the lost voice."

Expanding the Collective Memory

This focal shift becomes clearer by comparing the two versions of "The Conjurer's Revenge" in which the heavily revised frame realigns the relationships among Annie, John, and Julius. Chesnutt removes Annie's institutional religious activities. In the original, Annie "exchange[d] religious experiences" with Julius, presented him with a hymnbook, was a "zealous missionary" among the Negroes, and (according to John's interpretation) objected to Julius's tale on the ground that he disseminated a "fictitious narrative on the Sabbath day" ("Conjurer's Revenge" 628). The revision radically shifts from Annie's influence as an ineffective teacher, giving Julius what he can neither read nor use, to that of a resisting student and centers Annie at the site of misunderstanding. Annie, in her own voice, now objects to the revenge tale, claiming "it is n't [sic] pathetic, it has no moral that [she] can discover" (*CW* 127).[8] Julius, on the other hand, counters her objection: "he did not seem to understand. . . . 'I can't make out w'at you means by some er dem wo'ds you uses, but I'm tellin' nuffin but de truf. . . . I be'n hearin' de tale for twenty-five yeahs, en I ain' got no 'casion fer ter 'spute it. Dey's so many things a body knows is lies, dat dey ain' no use gwine round' findin' fault wid tales dat mought des ez well be so ez not'" (127–28). Julius challenges Annie to clarify her words, insists on the veracity of experience and oral tradition, responds directly to her failed appreciation, and becomes her teacher. He, like Chesnutt, teaches as he remembers, drawing Annie into his community of hearers where stories are reinforced by their repeated telling.

The revision also diminishes John's influence as truth arbiter. Chesnutt parodies John's reading habits and challenges the source of his knowledge exclusively from books. Both versions of the frame open with John reading the "impossible career of the blonde heroine of a rudimentary novel" (104); but the revised tale ends with a staple literary convention, the sentimental deathbed scene that fails any truth criteria: "I sees de good angels waitin' fer me up yander, wid a long w'ite robe en a starry crown, en I'm on my way ter jine 'em" (126). The conjure man's testimony is taken from the type of novels John prefers, those "happy-ending" books that debase genuine mystery.

At the same time that Julius's characters desire loving, yet unattainable, attachments, Chesnutt distances John from his "wife," whom he had called "Annie" in the original. Chesnutt's revision also denies the husband entry into his wife's interior state of mind and prevents John from making claims that Annie ostensibly endorses. John becomes a far more consistent character, who clearly misjudges motives and actions; he is also denied access to an invisible authorial voice.[9]

In addition, Chesnutt removed a large section in which John persuaded Annie to attend to the "lantern-jawed, tallow-faced" poor whites who also suffered from slavery ("Conjurer's Revenge" 623). While the original account may well reflect the historically accurate effects of the Civil War on poor Whites, the adjustment focuses more squarely on those who are excluded from property by law; and it realigns the pivotal balance between spirit and law, forgiveness and justice, intuition and reason.

Throughout "The Conjurer's Revenge," more than in any other story, Chesnutt questions cause and effect, appearance and reality—related assumptions that lead John to purchase a "worthless, broken-winded, spavined quadruped," which seemed a "very fine-looking animal" (*CW* 130). Because of "the deceitfulness of appearances," John has no way to assign value to unfamiliar acts using traditional methods. Furthermore, John and Julius seem to be talking at cross purposes: no clear connection exists between the responses Julius gives to John's persistent probing for rational explanations. To Julius, not deceived by appearances, there is nothing magical about men seen as mules although he "don ha'dly 'spec' fer [John] ter b'lieve it" (107). However, John willingly accepts negative criteria: because John had "not recently paid Julius any money, and as [Julius] had no property to mortgage," the coachman, therefore, *must* have been in collusion with the horse trader. But John could not "charge [Julius] with duplicity unless [he] could prove it, at least to a moral certainty" (131). John sees himself as Julius's financial, legal, and moral overseer—the source of Julius's wealth—whereas, in reality, he is "not a very good judge of horseflesh" (130). John insists upon narrowly interpreting events based upon his own learned codes; but, as Julius cautions, even "de mule seed de sense" (124) in listening to another point of view. Parodying the idea that Negroes can be classified as children or animals and, therefore, legitimately treated as work horses and mules, Chesnutt transforms the unsympathetic, ideal reader into a "metamorphosed unfortunate" who, like the horse he bought, is "blind in one eye" and whose sight is defective in another. John is the child who cannot read.

By contrast, even though Annie and Julius find it difficult to accept each other's mode of apprehending truth and to understand each other's language, they nonetheless continue to talk with each other. They remember and correct failures exposed in the preceding story, "Mars

Expanding the Collective Memory

Jeems's Nightmare," in which dialogue keeps the story alive and adjusts one story to another—Aun' Peggy depends on Solomon to tell her "w'at is gwine on roun' de plantation" (77, 78); Mars Jeems admonishes Solomon not "ter say a wo'd ter nobody" (92) yet encourages Mars Johnson to "tell [him] some mo'" (94–95); Annie "forgot to tell" John that she rehired Julius's grandson; Julius "told" John and Annie the moral of the tale: "dat w'ite folks w'at is so ha'd en stric', en doan make no 'lowance fer po' ign'ant niggers w'at ain' had no chanst ter l'arn, is li'ble ter hab bad dreams" (100). Furthermore, oral forms link generations: Julius had "heard dat [nightmare] tale befo'" Annie and John "wuz bawn" (101).

The Conjure Woman tales move from issues of fecundity to self-possession and the desire for family unity toward more complex patterns of social organization that require sensitive regulation and greater effort in communication. "The Conjurer's Revenge" holds a critical position in this progression. Not only is it the central story, and not only does it end in a fragile equilibrium, it also realigns the remaining stories away from economic usefulness, secular social contract, rational law, and the reliability of the written word toward the power of oral testimony, intuitive wisdom, and sympathetic identification as reliable authorities. "The Conjurer's Revenge" is the only segment in which Julius profits directly. As a fledgling entrepreneur, the "Conjurer" takes revenge and dupes John, turning his capitalistic practices against him. Julius buys "a new suit of store clothes" (131). Having profited by trading horse stories with John, however, Julius abandons "revenge," a cycle with no satisfying conclusion, as a meaningful option; and he tells the remaining tales more for his hearers' benefit than for his own.[10]

To overcome revenge as the only available arbiter of justice, however, another moral system must be in place. In "Sis' Becky's Pickaninny," the Conjure Woman tricks both Kunnel Pen'leton and the horse trader for swapping Sis' Becky for a horse. But, as the colonel knows, "lawsuits was slow ez de seben-yeah eetch" (154), and he becomes trapped within his own system. Revenge reappears with disastrous results in "The Gray Wolf's Ha'nt," where Dan is at the mercy of a law that is no law for him. Although he seems justified in defending himself and Mahaly against the Conjure Man's son, he can neither find nor offer protection from jealousy or revenge because "dey wa'n't no w'ite folks 'speshly int'rusted" (172), and "Brer Dan could n' do nuffin. . . . [Even] Aun' Peggy . . . did n't know de wolf langwidge, en could n't 'a' tuk off dis yuther goopher nohow, even ef sh'd'a' unnerstood w'at Dan wuz sayin" (190). A law that could break revenge patterns—here respected as white man's code—refuses to hear claims of the disenfranchised and is incapable of recognizing an inarticulate cry from the heart.

"Sis' Becky's Pickaninny" and "The Gray Wolf's Ha'nt" continue to contrast written reflection and oral performance. Before Sis' Becky's story, neither John's novels, plantation serenades, friends' talking, nor letters from the North could dispel Annie's depression as do Julius's tale and his rabbit's foot, talismans he would share with "anybody [he] sot sto' by" (136). Becky's memory of her little boy, who appears disguised as song birds, reduces her pain and keeps her alive long enough to effect a permanent reunion. Annie, too, is cured when she recognizes that Becky's "story bears the stamp of truth. . . . [It] is true to nature, and might have happened half a hundred times, and no doubt did happen, in those horrid days before the war" (159).

Only after Julius's talismans touch Annie does John, in a momentary lapse, grudgingly admit that although "fancy doubtless embellished" Julius's "exhaustless store . . . even the wildest [story] was not without an element of pathos,—the tragedy, it might be, of the story itself; the shadow, never absent, of slavery and of ignorance; the sadness, always, of life as seen by the fading light of an old man's memory" (167–68). To John, "ignorance" and faded or unreliable memories in old age may account for Julius's "fancy"; but to Chesnutt/Julius, the "pathos" stems from memories of the lived story itself, the true stories of slavery that are in danger of being severely distorted or entirely erased.

In "Gray Wolf" Chesnutt again parodies John's taste in literature, this time a philosophical treatise analyzing "transformations . . . which all existences have undergone" (163–64); and he satirizes the proliferating scientific studies in anthropology, ethnology, and sociology that justify racism and condemn as "fanciful" transformations occurring within stories. Although John understands his text as "presented in the simplest and most lucid form," he cannot connect his readings to his experiences. John claims to understand that "the genesis of the rearrangement of every evolving aggregate is in itself one, [as] it presents to our intelligence—" (164), but he breaks his reading to describe Julius not as a human being but as an arrangement of aggregates, as "a huge faded cotton umbrella" progressing "toward the house, and beneath it a pair of nether extremities in trousers." Novels that are untrue to people's nature and dry, philosophical tracts that lack emotional engagement fail to connect those who do not share the same past, language, culture, or opportunity. Neither do they foster an evolving society's meaningful rearrangement.

Expanding the Collective Memory

As with Po' Sandy, however, neither desire nor love alone can overcome the effects of recalcitrant will or willful blindness; and Sis' Becky's successful restitution to Mose through Aun' Nancy's and Aun' Peggy's efforts is not repeated with Dan and Mahaly. "The Gray Wolf's Ha'nt" is indeed a "harrowing tale," which takes its hearers into the hell of vindictive behavior. The only adequate response is silence as the forces of nature threaten revenge on the couple's heretofore secure structure: "The rising wind whistled around the eaves, slammed the loose window-shutters, and, still increasing, drove the rain in fiercer gusts into the piazza. . . . The blast . . . bore to our ears a long, wailing note, an epitome, as it were, of the remorse and hopelessness" (192–93).

The story affects both Annie and John, but their long-term responses differ. When John "recalled the story" a year later, he looked for facts, proof that Mahaly's grave or Dan's bones existed on his land. But "the hand of time had long since removed any evidence" (193–94) necessary to prove to John the truth of Julius's story. Annie, however, having been healed by Julius's conjuring, needs no further legitimation; she internalizes the stories' emotional truth, the recollection of which enables her to act. Her sympathy engaged, she, in turn, heals others. Although she has no economic power to alter conditions substantively, she effects small changes within her social sphere.

In the final story, "Hot-Foot Hannibal,"[11] the separation caused by Chloe's and Jeff's harsh words in the interior tale can be overcome if people in the frame willingly exchange healing words.[12] Annie responds to Julius's jealousy tale, commands John's unwitting cooperation, and repairs the threatened dissolution between her sister and her fiancé. Black and White, male and female work together to reconcile the estranged Northerner with the neighboring Southerner.

Because John determines the boundaries in which he accepts or rejects experience as valid—and employs only dogmatic and rational criteria—he cannot adjust his character from that of paternalistic overlord. Annie, however, responds as the child who participates in the stories' emotional truth, yet she matures enough to act upon her new awareness. Annie becomes one of Chesnutt's "elevated whites," and he suggests that future relations between races depend upon awakening a feminine sensibility through telling living stories to one another. He claims, at any rate, that it is the "old black aunties," now driven to the "remote chimney corners" by the preacher's "stern frown" and the teacher's "scornful sneer," who remember and keep alive the oral, ancestral traditions ("Superstitions" 371).[13]

The Conjure Woman shows that human relations cannot be legislated by rational systems alone, particularly when they originate from and apply to only one segment of society. Educating and civilizing needed to proceed in two directions simultaneously; Whites needed to recognize that Blacks already possessed culture, intelligence, and high character but not equal access to education, property, and respect. But transforming hearts can be a slow process, and Julius contents himself with small advances. He prefers the "long road" (199). Julius never reaches John as he does Annie. John remains unsympathetically dense, never knowing "exactly what motive influenced the old man's exertions" in Mabel's reconciliation with Murchison. More significantly, just as John "had never imagined" his ward's passion (196), he never knew what "reason or other" Julius had for remaining with Annie and him rather than with the newlyweds (228–29). Julius had not only invested in the land but also in people. John, however, can neither acknowledge nor understand new relations and will not invest himself in forming them. Julius knew that so long as John and he remained "strangers ter one anudder" (11), each could learn only what he wished to know (7).

Chesnutt's "conjuring" voice negotiates a delicate course between clashing cultures—challenging faded memory, stubborn blindness, and divisive discourse. Chesnutt demonstrates that it is essential to remember the content of one's heritage, the collective experience; it is equally important to break the process of restrictive "mental habits" that harden as superstition. The extended boundaries of a new social reality could not—cannot—be structured on only one set of memories or habits. Storytelling, however, creates a new kinship in shared experience. *The Conjure Woman* remains a recorded legacy and model for a new generation willing to civilize itself—to extend beyond an alien dialect and into the "magic mirror" of story, where the "act of catching the voice has a simplicity which stamps it as original" ("Superstitions" 376) and therefore true.

Notes

1. In addition to the four previously published stories—"The Goophered Grapevine" (1887), "Po' Sandy" (1888), "The Conjurer's Revenge" (1889), and "Hot-Foot Hannibal" (1899)—Chesnutt added three new works: "Mars Jeems's Nightmare," "Sis' Becky's Pickaninny," and "The Gray Wolf's Ha'nt." He also removed several stories from consideration: "A Victim of Heredity," in which the conjure woman intervenes directly in the economics between Whites; "Tobe's

Tribulations," in which the relationship of the thin framing story to the conjure tale is almost nonexistent; and "A Deep Sleeper" (previously published in 1893), which lies too close to the lazy, watermelon-loving Negro stereotype to prevent any misunderstanding by its readers. "Tobe's Tribulations" and "A Victim of Heredity" were subsequently published in 1990. See C. W. Chesnutt, *Short Fiction;* H. M. Chesnutt; and Andrews.

2. My position on John's ironic role agrees with those taken by Britt (271) and Hemenway (300–301); for alternate readings see Winkelman (133) and Burnette (442). Chesnutt's naming his white narrator "John" cannot be accidental. The name inverts the identification of slave and master in a cycle of Negro folk tales recovered by Zora Neale Hurston—verbal or physical contests between John, "one smart nigger," and the outwitted Ole Massa (75–90). Furthermore, John is a common name assigned to male children, and John's wife, "Annie," is clearly a diminutive: neither character is dignified by a last name, recalling slaves' lack of family names.

3. As Robert Hemenway notes, "Chesnutt's idea of his own audience is important" (301–2), but one must be careful not to assume that Chesnutt wrote for a homogeneous Negro audience: some prosperous, educated Blacks, particularly in the North, dissociated themselves from rural, uneducated Blacks, a theme sparklingly dramatized in *Jelly's Last Jam*. Also, some of Chesnutt's "cultivated" white readers would enter the dialogue and respond to the truth within. Others, like John, would not. Chesnutt wrote to them all.

4. Others call dialect either a mask or a veil. Henry Louis Gates calls the African mask a "metaphor for dialect," a "form of masking, a verbal descent underground," which "exploits the metaphor against its master. . . . Dialect is our only key to that unknown tongue, that lost, mythical linguistic kingdom" (89–94). Lorne Fienberg states that Julius's "mask enables him to tell the 'truth' and . . . the veil permits the dynamic interplay of relationships between black and white" (171). Also see Babb, Foster, Render, and Wideman.

5. Robert Pelton's description of the West African trickster figure's cultural function also seems strikingly similar to that of Uncle Julius: the trickster problem is ultimately "one of language. The trickster speaks—and embodies—a vivid and subtle religious language, through which he links animality and ritual transformation, shapes culture by means of sex and laughter, ties cosmic processes to personal history, empowers divination to change boundaries into horizons, and reveals the passages to the sacred embedded in daily life" (3). Also see Melvin Dixon on "Chesnutt as teller and trickster for his wider literary audience" (187).

6. Robert Hemenway properly cautions that Chesnutt does not use folklore but writes literature with an understanding of how folkloric elements function: "folklore in literature" means a "literary transformation, representation, or simulation of a folkloric event"; and Chesnutt engages in "the dialectics of legend transmission," a communicative phenomenon special to oral tradition (285, 303). Susan Feldmann stresses African folk traditions' performance nature, explaining that "the oral tale lives in the telling" and in an environment in which "the world has not yet been divorced from the act of personal communication" (12). For Chesnutt's position see "Superstitions" (371–72), "Post-Bellum" (193–94), and H. M. Chesnutt (107).

7. "Po' Sandy" (previously published; only dialect changes were made).

8. Chesnutt strengthened Annie's objections to the story by adding two more confrontations between Dan and Primus the mule, thereby continuing a pattern of revenge and confusion until the "cunjah man" wants "ter ondo some er de harm [he] done" (123). While Annie cannot identify with revenge as a valid motive for action, she also overlooks the African's sharing values of Christian repentance, which, even belatedly, recognizes his need to restore the natural order.

9. In the original, John claims knowledge he would have had no access to when he says of Annie: "her conscience, released from the spell of the storyteller's art, warned her..."; and of Julius: "The expression of conscious guilt that involuntarily came into the old man's face..." ("Conjurer's Revenge" 628). The revision also eliminates a long section in which Julius indicates his aversion to the hymnbook's red edges because "folks is alluz sayin' cullud people lubs red" (624). Just as Chesnutt avoids undercutting John's literal responses, he is careful that Julius not subscribe overtly to stereotypes. Only John applies the stereotypes.

10. Julius's redressing (an addition in the final version) and rejection of revenge reflect significant aspects of Chesnutt's philosophy. Not only did Blacks need to redress themselves through education, but also justice demanded that Whites redress continued economic and social enslavement. At the same time, Chesnutt acknowledged the short-term catharsis from revenge but cautioned Blacks—and simultaneously reassured Whites—against revenge as a profitable, long-term tactic. Revenge closes off dialogue and keeps people strangers to one another.

11. "Hot-Foot Hannibal" was published just prior to *The Conjure Woman* (January 1899); the texts are identical.

12. My position here disagrees with that of Eugene Terry, who claims that "Chesnutt undercuts his own book with this last tale" (124). While I agree with Terry's description of Julius as the historian who destroys "the myth of the good master," Chesnutt also suggests a method of cultural reformation that, as Cooper recommends, depends upon civilizing Blacks *and* Whites so that both "will know what is due from man to man" (210). Subsequent disenfranchisement of Blacks may prove Sally Ann H. Ferguson's claim that Chesnutt's goal was a "simplistic vision and illusory hope for a color-blind and racially harmonious world" (117). But the rhetorical strategies of *The Conjure Woman* do offer a "formula for peaceful and equal racial coexistence" (Ferguson 118) that recognizes racism's fundamentally emotional basis and that any solution must acknowledge. Chesnutt cleverly enters a very strident, contemporary debate raging among races and regions for the right to shape America's cultural, political, and economic future.

13. Chesnutt may also infer an alignment of the dispossessed, seeing in nineteenth-century women's position under patriarchy a resemblance to the Negro's untenable position under racism. Just as the "conjure woman" is a force for good in her community, women could be the conduit through which racial reconciliation might take place. Cooper certainly felt the future of America depended upon the educational capacity of its women as teachers of morals, "which strikes ... roots in the individual..." and of manners, which "lubricate the joints and minimize the friction of society" (121). Note also that the disruptive "Conjurers" are male, and the healers are female.

Works Cited

Andrews, William L. *The Literary Career of Charles W. Chesnutt*. Baton Rouge: Louisiana State UP, 1980.
Babb, Valerie. "Subversion and Repatriation in *The Conjure Woman*." *Southern Quarterly* 25.2 (Winter 1987): 66–75.
Britt, David D. "Chesnutt's Conjure Tales: What You See Is What You Get." *College Language Association Journal* 15.3 (March 1972): 269–83.
Burnette, R. V. "Charles W. Chesnutt's *The Conjure Woman* Revisited." *College Language Association Journal* 30.4 (June 1987): 438–53.
Chesnutt, Charles W. *The Conjure Woman*. 1899. Ann Arbor: U of Michigan P, 1969.
———. "The Conjurer's Revenge." *Overland Monthly* June 1889: 623–29.
———. "A Deep Sleeper." *Two Tales* 11 Mar. 1893: 1–8.
———. "The Goophered Grapevine." *Atlantic Monthly* 60 (August 1887): 254–60.
———. "Hot-Foot Hannibal." *Atlantic Monthly* 83 (January 1899): 49–56.
———. "Po' Sandy." *Atlantic Monthly* 61 (May 1888): 605–11.
———. "Post-Bellum—Pre-Harlem." *Crisis* 38.6 (June 1931): 193–94.
———. *The Short Fiction of Charles W. Chesnutt*. Ed. Sylvia Lyons Render. Washington, DC: Howard UP, 1974.
———. "Superstitions and Folklore of the South." *Modern Culture* 13 (1901): 231–35; rpt. in *Mother Wit from the Laughing Barrel: Readings in the Interpretation of Afro-American Folklore*. Ed. Alan Dundes. Englewood Cliffs, NJ: Prentice, 1973. 369–76.
———. "Tobe's Tribulations." *Southern Workman* 39 (November 1900): 656–64.
———. "A Victim of Heredity." *Self Culture Magazine* 11 (July 1900): 404–9.
Chesnutt, Helen M. *Charles Waddell Chesnutt: Pioneer of the Color Line*. Chapel Hill: U of North Carolina P, 1952.
Cooper, Anna Julia. *A Voice from the South*. 1892. New York: Negro Universities P, 1969.
Dixon, Melvin. "The Teller as Folk Trickster in Chesnutt's *The Conjure Woman*." *College Language Association Journal* 18.2 (December 1974): 186–97.
Feldmann, Susan, ed. *African Myths and Tales*. New York: Dell, 1963.
Ferguson, Sally Ann H. "Chesnutt's Genuine Blacks and Future Americans." *MELUS* 15.3 (Fall 1988): 109–19.
Fienberg, Lorne. "Charles W. Chesnutt and Uncle Julius: Black Storytellers at the Crossroads." *Studies in American Fiction* 15.2 (Autumn 1987): 161–73.
Foster, Charles William. "The Representation of Negro Dialect in Charles W. Chesnutt's *The Conjure Woman*." Diss. U of Alabama, 1968.
Fryer, Judith. *Felicitous Space: The Imaginative Structures of Edith Wharton and Willa Cather*. Chapel Hill: U of North Carolina P, 1986.
Gates, Henry Louis, Jr. "Dis and Dat: Dialect and the Descent." *Afro-American Literature: The Reconstruction of Instruction*. Ed. Dexter Fisher and Robert B. Stepto. New York: MLA, 1979. 88–119.
Hemenway, Robert. "The Functions of Folklore in Charles Chesnutt's *The Conjure Woman*." *Journal of the Folklore Institute* 13.3 (1976): 283–309.

Hurston, Zora Neale. *Mules and Men.* 1935. Bloomington: Indiana UP, 1978.
Pelton, Robert D. *The Trickster in West Africa: A Study of Mythic Irony and Sacred Delight.* Berkeley: U of California P, 1980.
Render, Sylvia Lyons. "North Carolina Dialect: Chesnutt Style." *North Carolina Folklore* 15.2 (November 1967): 67–70.
Terry, Eugene. "The Shadow of Slavery in Charles Chesnutt's *The Conjure Woman.*" *Ethnic Groups* 4.1 (May 1982): 103–25.
Whitt, Lena M. "Chesnutt's Chinquapin County." *Southern Literary Journal* 13.2 (Spring 1981): 41–58.
Wideman, John Edgar. "Charles Chesnutt and the WPA Narratives: The Oral and Literate Roots of Afro-American Literature." *The Slave's Narrative.* Ed. Charles T. Davis and Henry Louis Gates, Jr. New York: Oxford UP, 1985. 59–78.
Winkelman, Donald M. "Three American Authors as Semi-Folk Artists." *Journal of American Folklore* 78.308 (April–June 1965): 130–35.

Reading Carnival as an Archaeological Site for Memory in Paule Marshall's *The Chosen Place, The Timeless People* and *Praisesong for the Widow*

ANGELITA REYES

And to us that evening
It was as if it were a masquerade,
It was as if it were a carnival,
A grand-gala fairy-spectacle.
—Anna Akhmatova, "Lethe-Neva"

... these people are my access to me; they are my entrance into my own interior life. Which is why the images that float around them—the remains... at the archaeological site—surface first, and they surface so vividly that I acknowledge them as my route to a reconstruction of a world, to an exploration of an interior life that was not written and to the revelation of a kind of truth.
—Toni Morrison, "The Site of Memory"

There are refrains in Toni Morrison's novel *Beloved* that read, "it was not a story to pass on" and "this is not a story to pass on." Yet these coded messages do not enter the narrative until *after* the story has been told and retold in the context of multiple voices and tales. Morrison's rhetorical strategy consistently says one thing in order to mean something else. It is her way to signify meaning as she depicts the various possibilities for meaning, in the postcolonial African American ethos. That is to say, the story of the fugitive slave mother, Margaret Garner, who kills her three-year-old daughter rather than allow the child to be returned to slavery, needs to be told and retold because it is part of a vital collective force, or what Morrison refers to as rememory.[1] Knowing the New World home, *sweet* home, its cultural community, and its Middle Passage history that affects all people in the Americas—European, Native, and African—is essential for productive survival and sustaining communal integrity through collective memory.

Writing of women whose stories could remain untold, Morrison says they are "disremembered"—they are not only lost and unknown, but their ethos of home is cut off—"dismembered." Thus their memory field, to use Mikhail Bakhtin's notation, has to be ritually evoked, exorcised, and rebirthed. The characters in *Beloved* attempt to excavate memory in order to empower themselves for living and not being lived upon.

Contemporary postcolonial black women writers such as Paule Marshall, Toni Morrison, Gloria Naylor, Simone Schwarz-Bart, Myriam Warner-Vierya, Michelle Cliff, and Maryse Condé depict how for people of African descent in the Americas the "dis-memories" of slavery and the Middle Passage cannot be obliterated into historical amnesia. While Morrison may use either the extended paradigm of the fugitive slave mother or that of young women who are cultural fugitives in contemporary communities to explore ethos and meaning (for example, the latter theme is evident in *The Bluest Eye* and *Tar Baby*), Paule Marshall uses performance ritual and carnival in her novels *The Chosen Place, The Timeless People* and *Praisesong for the Widow* to metonymize the memory field between historical reality and contemporary injustices arising out of the historical tensions of ethnicity, class, and gender.[2]

In *Chosen Place* and *Praisesong* carnival is less the pre-Lenten tourist festival, less the ancient cosmic festival of chaos and order, and more a ritual reenactment of an event from the past—a re-memory of the Fall that displaced and dispersed people of African descent to the Americas and a re-memory of the Revelation that marks the people's hope.

What I propose here is to explore the meaning of ritual carnival in the text and context of the postcolonial archaeological site—that conscious return to an event or place that marks a beginning in the New World. The beginning in this context is not pre-Columbian. It is the beginning that marks European expansion and exploitation in the New World.

Carnival then becomes a trope for intertextuality and a revisitation (or revision) of the memory field. Carnival evokes multiple responses not only because of its simultaneity but also because it is an ancient performance enacted in a new place. Whereas for visitors (the tourist industry as a master discourse) who "jump up" and "play *mas*," carnival is a secular

Carnival as an Archaeological Site for Memory

festival and temporal liminality. For the "little people" in *Chosen Place* and *Praisesong*, local carnival serves as collective counter-memory—a history of recollection that reflects their present social reality and spiritual need. Carnival provides a reciprocal relationship with the historical memory of colonialism and slavery. While Toni Morrison's Sweet Home people may undo the suppression of their emotions in relation to the "sixty million and more" through myth (empowerment derived from "speaking the unspeakable" oracle), Paule Marshall's protagonists reenact those emotions and create an overt dialectic of collective history through ritual performance. Undoubtedly, Marshall is in the postmodernist camp of women writers of color who signify on stories that need to be told through the memory/counter-memory field.[3]

Zora Neale Hurston's profound metaphors of every man, ships at sea, and dreams begin the memory-storytelling of *Their Eyes Were Watching God*:

> Ships at a distance have every man's wish on board. . . . they sail forever on the horizon, never out of sight, never landing until the Watcher turns his eyes away in resignation. . . . That is the life of men.
>
> Now, women forget all those things they don't want to remember, and remember everything they don't want to forget. . . . they act and do things accordingly. (5)

In his work *Time Passages: Collective Memory and American Popular Culture* George Lipsitz discusses how Hurston's metaphor juxtaposes these images in terms of gendering objectivity and subjectivity throughout the narrative: "The world of men in Hurston's account is a world of objectivity and action. It is the world of history, of events and of progress. The world of women . . . is contrastingly a world of subjectivity and sentiment. It is a world of myth, of stories, and of cycles. Men confront their dreams as entities outside themselves, as stories with clear resolutions knowable to all. Women experience their dreams as created constructs . . ." (212). Indeed, Hurston's narrative strategy delves into folklore as the memory field while exploring the intellectual and social tensions between the extended metaphor of the "ship at sea" and its Watcher. Hurston's novel begins with Janie's personal story—the oral "memoir"—and culminates into a collective "herstory" when Phoeby exclaims "Lawd, Ah done growed ten feet higher from jus' listenin' tuh you, Janie" (158). Hurston's discourse thus becomes Lipsitz's assertion of counter-memory as

> a way of remembering and forgetting that starts with the local, the immediate, and the personal. Unlike historical narratives that begin with the totality

of human existence and then locate specific actions and events within that totality, counter-memory starts with the particular and the specific and then builds outward toward a total story. Counter-memory looks to the past for the hidden histories excluded from dominant narratives. But unlike myths that seek to detach events and actions from the fabric of any larger history, counter-memory forces revision of existing histories by supplying new perspectives about the past.... (213)

Their Eyes Were Watching God celebrates an oral tradition even as it identifies a particular ethos ("de nigger woman is de mule uh de world so fur as Ah can see") that "speaks to present day intellectual concerns with time, history, subjectivity, and fragmentation" (Lipsitz 215).

Hurston accentuates Janie's voice—Janie's "memoir"—as part of the narrating voice. In *Their Eyes Were Watching God* the central character does not "write" her story; instead she "tells" or "recollects" and therefore assumes a particular folkloric discourse incorporating both history and myth into the dialectic of counter-memory.

Lipsitz's model of counter-memory begins with the "local, the immediate, and the personal." But these modalities also essentialize an intimacy that provides access to meaning and allows certain truths to surface from what Toni Morrison refers to as the "archaeological site." This archaeological sense of place addresses what the "memory" and its image are really about ("The Site of Memory" 114–15). "Collecting" memory out of an African New World ethos is often arduous and becomes just that—an archaeological process. One returns to the site (personal or communal) searching for an idea in the New World beginning, digging for what was written out of history or suppressed even by the people themselves. Morrison says, "The exercise is also critical for any person who is black, or who belongs to any marginalized category, for, historically, we were seldom invited to participate in the discourse even when we were its topic" ("The Site of Memory" 110–11). Morrison aptly points out that often the truth is "veiled" as, for example, in early slave narratives where many "proceedings were too terrible to relate." Truth turns into erasures because of race and gender subjectivity. In discussing this memory process Morrison uses the image of the river that is engineered, straightened out to make room for modern development. "Occasionally," she says, "the river floods these places. 'Floods' is the word they use, but in fact it is not flooding; it is remembering. Remembering where it used to be. All water has a perfect memory and is forever trying to get back to where it was" ("The Site of Memory" 119). Morrison connects to a personal archaeological locale (for example, the images and

Carnival as an Archaeological Site for Memory

feelings of her childhood home, Lorain, Ohio) and then places that site within the larger context of all those things that changed the history of African people after the 1492 Fall. Foremost, then, is the act of returning to the image, knowledge, and memory of the archaeological site.

Janie's storytelling as memoir is framed by her return to her archaeological site: "Janie mounted the stairs with the lamp. . . . She closed in and sat down . . . Thinking. . . . She pulled in her horizon like a great fish-net"—home is where Janie, where Hurston herself wants to be.

Returning to home allows memories to "flood" for Morrison. This vital act constitutes a discourse of counter-memory. Expanding George Lipsitz's notion, I suggest here that counter-memory not only addresses "hidden histories," but the particular ethos of the history—redefining the "flooding" of an archaeological site.

In her essay "Multiple Articulations or the Discourse of Going a Piece of the Way with Them," Carole Boyce-Davies (1990) provides another model that supports the idea of counter-memory and its relationship to an archaeological site. Boyce-Davies's theoretical idea is formulated from non-Western-based traditions where "the host goes 'a piece of the way' with a friend or visitor, the distance depending on the relationship, and then returning home." When leaving, the guest is always accompanied by the host or a member of the host family, and the host then returns home. Traditional societies placed much value in "going a piece of the way." It was considered rude, if not unheard of, to not go "some ways" with the guest.[4] The relationship is one of special reciprocity between guest and host with the host's return to an inclusive and connective boundary (home).

Recent trends in literary criticism and feminist discourse appear to privilege the master's domain. This is what I refer to as the dominance of *derridada*—and they insist "don't leave home without it." Derridada is a system of dialectical reciprocity, but only between "master and mistress" constructions. Within the context of postcolonial discourse and thought, leaving home, however, should accompany, not privilege these mistress/*massa'* readings (poststructuralist, deconstructive, Jamesonian, postmodernist, semiotic, gynocentric, post-Freudian, et al.).[5] These *can* be left home or, at least, can go a piece of the way with postcolonial readings and appropriations. Henry Louis Gates, Jr. (1987), asserts that the former kinds of discourse "translate theory into the black idiom, renaming principles of criticism where appropriate, but especially [rename] indigenous black principles of criticism and [apply] these to explicate our own texts."

"Home," then, is the construct for an archaeological site for black feminist/postcolonial discourses because "theory as it is reified in the academy," says Boyce-Davies, "still turns on Western 'phallocentric' (master) or feminist 'gynocentric' (mistress) philosophy. Following any of the popular theorists 'home,' inevitably lands me in the 'homes' of Western theorists. . . ." The guest-host paradigm for black feminist/postcolonial discourse simultaneously demystifies as it creates a closer examination of approaches to reading and meaning. This is not to say that the host ceases to accompany the guest. In her essay "Women Warriors: Black Writers Load the Canon," Michelle Cliff writes that "no literature, least of all African-American women's writing, can be understood as discrete from the culture from which it rises. . . . Black women's literature is dense, as it must simultaneously respond to the dominant culture, struggle against it, and attempt to define the world from 'a black-eyed squint'. . . . It is crucial to my own survival, as a Jamaican woman of mixed race, a particular class, a certain history, to state over and over again: this is who I am" (20, 21).

A postcolonial ethos of remembering "who I am" provides reciprocity between host and guest, private and public. There is, however, always the need to return to the archaeological site. The site is a trope for ways of defining and understanding the counter-memory of cultural consciousness and providing spiritual connections to community.

Paule Marshall's construct of her community began with the "Bajan" neighborhoods of Brooklyn, New York. A first-generation American, Marshall fully credits the Barbadian mother-women from her childhood for providing her with a rich source of cultural inheritance: African, African-Caribbean, and American. In her works Marshall lauds the spiritual-cultural presence of her mother. In a 1971 essay that began the groundwork for numerous other lectures and essays to follow, Marshall wrote of the mother, "She laid the foundations of my aesthetic, that is, the themes and techniques which characterize my work" ("Shaping the World" 105). Her childhood was surrounded by the "unknown bards," the mother-women of her youth who compose the memory field. "Marshall insists that the mother-daughter bond, important as it is for revealing character, for allowing women to be the central characters in their lives, the activists, the centres of power, has a significance for Black women far greater than their individual lives" (Washington 166).

The mother-daughter bond is a central theme in Marshall's first novel, *Brown Girl, Brownstones*—a bonding that is arduous to achieve when a community is too involved in the materialistic web of the "white man country." Through owning things the Bajan immigrants legitimize their worth. Selina, the central figure, rebels against those values. Although she claims herself as a child-product of America, she also affirms herself as a child of the Caribbean, and through the spiritual connection, of Africa. Her coming of age is testimony to being an American woman-child with an African heritage. Marshall says of this representation: "The West Indies is so very important to me because it is part of a history that as a girl I tried to deny. I went through torture as a girl growing up in Brooklyn, going to school with those heavy silver bangles on my wrists, and when we went to the West Indies and came back with heavy West Indian accents, the kids used to laugh at us. It was dreadful. Now the West Indies represents an opportunity for me to fill in something I tried to deny, and it provides me with a manageable landscape for writing . . ." (DeVeaux 96).

Thus returning to the site of memory reestablishes order out of chaos. This connection is of primary importance for Marshall: "I'm trying to trace history. . . . To take, for example, the infamous triangle route of slavery and to reverse it so that we make the journey back from America to the West Indies, to Africa . . . to make that trip back. I'm not talking about in actual terms. I'm talking about a psychological and spiritual journey back in order to move forward. *You have to psychologically go through chaos in order to overcome it*" (DeVeaux 128, my emphasis).

Like Toni Morrison, the very act of writing for Marshall is a return to the image that fosters remembrance. Whereas Morrison may find the nurturing site in Lorain, Ohio, Marshall shapes her memory field from the "poets" in the Brooklyn kitchen. "What I did with my mother's voice is to transform it. I was using her approach—her care with telling a story well, finding the telling phrase—I retrieved these things. I am using the voice of the community" (Washington 165).

Paule Marshall then is a storyteller. Instead of telling the saga, Marshall's characters often perform the saga as an *event* that signifies a series of larger events arising out of European exploitation in the Americas. Abena Busia, writing of Marshall's postcolonial consciousness, states, "Marshall's concern is to take us through a journey of self-recognition and healing. Her texts require . . . a knowledge of 'diaspora literacy,' an ability to read a variety of cultural signs of the lives of Africa's children at home and in the New World. Marshall articulates the scattering of the African peoples as a trauma—a trauma that is constantly repeated anew . . ." (197).

"Diaspora literacy" acknowledges the dialogics of a *connected* consciousness for people of African descent in the Americas. Marshall is concerned about the people who may "forget" or care to ignore the archaeological site. My reading of carnival in *Chosen Place* and *Praisesong* advances the trope of "going a piece of the way" and positions the matrix of Toni Morrison's appropriation of an archaeological site. Indeed, how does Paule Marshall frame the dialectic of carnival as an archaeological site between history and collective counter-memory?

The term carnival as it is employed here conveys both the significance of New World performance ritual and ancient European celebration rites. A so-called pagan rite of spring, carnival was celebrated in ancient Greece and Egypt and was introduced into Europe by the Romans. Of the traditional carnival of Europe, Monica Rector writes that "Carnival referred at first to Shrove Tuesday. Beginning on that day, the church forbids the eating of meat (from Latin *levare*). . . . the word carnival comes from *carnelevamen* later modified into *carne vale!* (farewell to meat!). In Pisa they had *carnelevare*, in Naples *karnolevare*, in Sicily *karnilivare*" (39). Brought to the New World by Europeans during the era of colonialism and slavery, carnival took on African characteristics for both the colonized and the colonizers. Errol Hill writes that

> since the first masquerade held in pre-Christian times, carnival has exhibited certain recognizable features wherever it has taken root and flourished. Clearly originating in the worship of a nature deity—whether the Egyptian Isis, the Greek Dionysus, the Roman Saturn, or some other is immaterial—carnival proceedings have included street processions, costuming and masking . . . energetic dancing . . . and general revelry. . . . When the Roman Catholic church adopted carnival as a pre-Lenten festival, it gave religious sanction to a pagan rite too profoundly rooted in the sustenance of life to be effectively suppressed. (22)

The famous carnivals of Brazil were introduced by the Portuguese *entrudo* with colonialism (in the initial era of slavery) and were popular festivals that the upper-class slave owners controlled until slavery was abolished (Rector 1984). *Carnaval* in Cuba was originally celebrated with festivities on January 6, El Dia de Reyes (the Epiphany or day of the kings). In nineteenth-century Trinidad carnival also was exclusively a festival for the upper classes—the whites and free coloreds (Pearse 175–93).

When slavery was abolished in the West Indies (and Latin America) during the 1830s, former slaves began to participate in the public carnival *fête*. They were allowed to "play *mas*" in the streets along with the

Carnival as an Archaeological Site for Memory

white Creoles and colored people. *Mas* is Creole for masquerade or masque—performances dramatized in the carnival. Now, these "bands" often have very political themes ranging from satire on partisan local politics to global environmental issues. For the former slaves, however, carnival was an active and actual performance ritual—a political drama—signifying post- and preemancipation events. The signification was simultaneously spiritual liminality and profane rejuvenation, and as Hill also states, "[w]ithout question, carnival had become a symbol of freedom for the broad mass of the population and not merely a season for frivolous enjoyment. It had a ritualistic significance, rooted in the experience of slavery and in celebration of freedom from slavery. In this sense, carnival was no longer a European-inspired nature festival. . . . it became a deeply meaningful anniversary of deliverance from the most hateful form of human bondage" (21).

By the twentieth century people of all races and ethnic backgrounds participated in carnival in the Caribbean and Latin America. Carnival assumed the traditions of the diverse cultural heritage the New World offered. In the United States one of the main carnivals is the famous Mardi Gras held in New Orleans. However, because of Caribbean migration and cultural influences, places such as Notting Hill Gate (London), Toronto, Brooklyn, New York, Boston, and Miami all have annual carnivals.[6] Despite the fact that carnival in many areas is central to tourism, it continues to remain a very important event of rejuvenation, a ritual passage of *communitas*, and a symbolic "takeover" by the people who have been most negated by colonialism.

In a number of ways carnival signifies both the confirmation and the rupture of order. That is to say, on the one hand, through its ritual stages, it symbolizes order and chaos.[7] On the other hand, it symbolizes an inversion of a prescribed social order. Monica Rector maintains that "[t]he apparent inversion of the social order leads to the identification of Carnival with an appearance of social chaos, due to a 'possible' liberation of repressed behavior by means of the mechanisms that order life in society. Carnival, therefore, establishes a fusion between the world of society and the world of fantasy, in order to suppress the discontinuity between them" (102). The world of carnival becomes a "privilege" for those who ordinarily would not be privileged. Carnival thus speaks as a multivocal performance that creates a historical signifier on many levels. My approach to carnival as counter-memory therefore uses the context and immediate content (the masque and ceremony) to appropriate the meaning of an archaeological "beginning" in the New World.

The epigraph to *Chosen Place,* taken from the Tiv of West Africa, is the following: "Once a great wrong has been done, it never dies. People speak the words of peace, but their hearts do not forgive. Generations perform ceremonies of reconciliation but there is no end." Paule Marshall is well aware of the forces that connect all displaced peoples. How can humanity at all reconcile the "great wrong"? Undoubtedly, the great wrong of colonialism has affected all people; Marshall takes a particular locale in the New World to illuminate possible reconciliations.

Marshall's place name in the novel, Bourne Island, is fictive, but the situation is one that classifies many places of disenfranchised people. Merle Kinbona, British educated and "cultured," a descendant of both a slave owner and a slave woman, is the central character. The novel opens with her return to the island full of tension and ambiguities about her self-worth. Her disconnectedness comes from her being born as an "outside" child, her lesbian affair in England with an English benefactor, and the breakup of her marriage because of the affair. Her ambivalence and identity are framed within the context of her cultural kinship with the Bournehills under-class. Allen Fuso, one of the American "experts" sent to help the islanders, remarks, "In a way I can't explain, she somehow is Bournehills" (127).

Bournehills is the name of the poor community on one side of the island. Despite numerous Third World development projects brought in by American agencies, Bournehills has failed to achieve economic progress. The "irredeemable masses on the other side of the island" refuse to work with the agencies. They are an anathema to the rest of the island people because, according to the island elite, they refuse to "develop" themselves to acceptable class standards and values. Each year at carnival as "timeless" people they perform the same drama that depicts a slave rebellion, flaunting the masque in the faces of the educated islanders, tourists, and foreign development experts. And each year the Bournehills masque upsets the island elite, who make claims such as "those brutes have changed the whole meaning of carnival with their foolishness" or that the masque is "about some blasted slave revolt that took place down there long ago. . . . A bit of history you know" (63).

According to that Bournehills history, Cuffee Ned was a nineteenth-century slave who led the briefly enjoyed Pyre Hill slave revolt on the island. The Bournehills community performs the victory and eventual defeat of the slaves led by Cuffee Ned:

> They sang of how after defeating the small body of troops and sealing off Cleaver's, their forebears had lived for almost three years like the maroons

of Jamaica and bush Negroes of Guiana—free, at peace, dependent only on themselves, a nation apart. . . .

"They had worked together!" . . . under Cuffee, they sang, a man had not lived for himself alone, but for his neighbor also. "If we had lived selfish, we couldn't have lived at all." They half-spoke, half-sung the words. They had trusted one another, had set aside their differences and stood as one against their enemies. *They had been a People!* (308–9)

The Pyre Hill masque is both a celebration of the rebellion and a reminder of the reality that as a people they no longer work together against colonialism. The masque is not a dirge as some of the islanders perceive it to be. For despite the fact that the Pyre Hill maroons are quelled and Cuffee Ned is eventually beheaded by the colonial troops, his spirit lives on in the collective counter-memory of the people. The remembrance is not only historical, but spiritual, for Cuffee Ned was an obeah man. "But Cuffee had died content, the band declared in a final coda. For he had seen his life and deeds as pointing the way to what must be. And obeah man that he was, a true believer, he believed that death was not an end but a return, so that in dying he would be restored to the homeland. . . . 'Him feel joy,' he was known to have said of himself at the end, 'Him ready fuh to die now' " (310).[8]

The masque itself goes against the social grain as it enforces a certain spirit of rebellion in opposition to neocolonialism that produces such economic disparity among the people. Consequently, the Pyre Hill masque embarrasses the island middle and upper classes because they do not want to be reminded about slavery, colonialism, and the island's poverty: " 'Who wants to be reminded of that old-time business? Worse, it's beginning to embarrass those of our visitors who come to carnival every year. . . . The carnival committee should ban them from town, the brutes. . . . sometimes I wish that whole blasted place would just disappear—wash away in the sea or some damn thing. . . . But what the hell ails those people, yes? Why they got to come with the same foolishness every carnival, spoiling the fete? Why they won't change? The vagabonds!' " (63, 301, 302).

Saul Amron, the director of the development project on the island, who becomes Merle's lover, realizes a crucial factor: "It's that people . . . who've been truly wronged—like yours, like mine all those thousands of years—must at some point, if they mean to come into their own, start using their history to their advantage. Turn it to their own good. You begin . . . by first acknowledging it, all of it, the bad as well as the good, those things you can be proud of such as . . . Cuffee's brilliant coup . . .

use your history as your guide" (338). As a Jew he identifies with the "truly wronged" people of Bournehills although he may not understand them. Merle identifies with Bournehills, and she well knows the rural, marginalized community. She explains to Saul Amron: "You know . . . sometimes strangers to Bournehills wonder why we go on about Cuffee Ned and Pyre Hill when all that happened donkeys' years ago and should have been done with and forgotten. But we're an odd, half-mad people, I guess. We don't ever forget anything, and yesterday comes like today to us" (110). By playing the same masque each year Bournehills returns to its self-defined site of preemancipation memory.

In another kind of collective memory site Lebert Joseph raises his coarse voice and sings, "Si mwê merité/Pini mwê . . . Si mwê ba merité / Pa'doné mwê . . . the Big Drum is not just for me. . . . Oh, no! Is for tout moun' " in a lament that solidifies the ritual performance of the Carriacou carnival in *Praisesong for the Widow*. Although the central character, Avey Johnson (who, like Merle Kinbona, is middle-aged), may not understand his language, she finally grasps the imput of "for tout moun'." His chanting signifies the presence of the "Old Parents" and an African heritage of "nations." Singing in Creole is counterhegemonic; Creole asserts his identity in an otherwise disenfranchised reality. The Big Drum ceremony is, indeed, for *tout moun'* (for everyone)—the people of the African diaspora who may or may not know their nations—"the sons and daughters, grands and great-grands in Trinidad, Toronto, New York, London. . . ." By recreating the story-ritual of the Big Drum ceremony, Marshall highlights the festival's ritual structure as it is redefined by the Carriacouns. In this instance of the Beg Pardon festival these islanders make their annual return to the archaeological site. Like the Bournehills people they are conscious of the enactment as collective memory. They understand its meaning both in and outside of a particular ethos.

In *Praisesong* Avey (Avatara) Johnson is a comfortably middle-class widow who, on a Caribbean cruise with two friends, abruptly decides to leave the ship. Significantly, her trip has been disrupted by recurring dreams of her long-dead great-aunt Cuney of Tatem, South Carolina. When the ship docks for a few hours on the Caribbean island of Grenada, she disembarks and plans to fly back to her home, New York City. However, she misses the plane to New York and abruptly, even against her will, gets involved in the annual carnival festival of the "out-island" people—people of the smaller island, Carriacou—who live and work in Grenada. The excursion back to their homeland (Carriacou and by way of myth and ritual, Africa) is in fact their annual ritual performance of

Carnival as an Archaeological Site for Memory

rejuvenation, their rite of remembering the Old Parents and their African "nations." By going to Carriacou and experiencing the ritual performances of New World African dancing and drumming, Avey Johnson rediscovers her own memory of place as an American of African ancestry. When she leaves Carriacou, she resolves to renew her ties with her own archaeological site of memory in Tatem, South Carolina.[9]

Both representations of carnival, the Cuffee Ned masque and the Beg Pardon festival, show reciprocal relationships that New World people have with their history. Both festivals ritualize mythic and spiritual remembering of their connections to Africa in spite of the dismemberment. Both festivals become rituals for psychic and historical impressions as the participants "reach back" into history. Carnival as the specific event that relates to the larger story enacts counter-memory. Marshall uses the ritual motif in the narratives to indicate how carnival interprets meaning from what happened once—the era of African slavery—to what happens now. It becomes the re-creation of the people's memory. In *Chosen Place,* carnival is past and present modalities of rebellion. In *Praisesong* carnival is the rejection of an imposed non-African sensibility and asserts the needs of the collective memory. The story is retold through the annual performance. Both festivals ignore outsiders' (tourists) participation because outsiders masquerade with no spiritual knowledge of or connection to the memory site. As a vehicle of memory carnival is narrative counter-memory. The Carriacouns may not know what "really happened." But the "image" of what happened enables them as a people to remember collectively and to recreate a memory field that sustains their Africanness even as they are reminded about their economic reality. However, as carnival becomes an active memory field it is both mystic and profane. It creates an individual as well as collective connection to remembered history.

One of the slogans of contemporary carnival is "live once, die forever," that is to say, carnival masque is an enactment that is consumed each year, but it is also eternally present (Nunley 85). Historian of religions Mircea Eliade puts it another way. Ritual festivals like carnival are components of what he terms the "myth of the eternal return." Through the ritual process human beings transform reality from chaos to potential order: "Rituals are symbols in acted reality; they function to make concrete and experiential the mythic values of society. . . . Hence rituals act, they perform, modulate, transform" (Beane 164). Eliade's idea of the eternal return includes rites of passage, myths, and symbols. Eliade juxtaposes the sacred and profane in this reality. The ritual process expresses the "religious" desire for control and order (cosmos). Thus every religious festival event, any "liturgical time" represents the reactualization of a sacred event that took place in a mythical past—in the Great Beginning. This beginning is what Eliade calls *illo tempore*. In order to recall and reactualize this time, human beings use myth and rituals that can integrate present and past—profane and sacred—realities.

Carnival in *Chosen Place* and *Praisesong* is characterized by an *illo tempore* of New World beginnings. Obviously, neither the Bournehills people nor the Carriacouns directly remember slavery and colonialism. Remembrance is forced upon Avey Johnson in *Praisesong* through the recurring dream of her deceased aunt, who knew her connections to the past, and then finally through her interactions with the people from Carriacou. However, through the reality of mythic history, this period of time is evoked and actualized through the ritual festival they must undergo.

For the Bournehills people the masque is sacred because it reactualizes the entire community, the *spirit* of a successful, although short-lived, takeover by their ancestors. The Cuffee Ned masque returns them to a beginning:

> It was a silent march in the beginning. Unlike the other carnival bands whose members were singing in an endless refrain the road march song for the year, the Bournehills band was silent. There was only the slow muffled beat of the steelband up ahead, not unlike taps being sounded; and above this, the steady, inexorable tramp of feet on the harsh asphalt of the roadway. They were doing, it was true, the dance called for at this hour, the restrained rhythmic two-step that scarcely brought the foot up off the ground and was meant to see the marcher through the day. But with them it was more pronounced. The slow dragging step that carried them forward was more stated, clearly audible and regularly punctuated by the loud ring of the bracelets the women and girls wore. . . . (303)

The deliberate silence in what is supposed to be a jubilant march activates reverence that they inscribe to Cuffee Ned and what his rebellion still means for them. Although legally not enslaved, they are still being exploited by the descendants of colonialism. This is what they call attention to: their anger and their mourning of the "sixty million and more."[10] They are "aggrieved," "outraged," and "unappeased."

At the same time, the ritual marching evokes the actuality of the past event through music that is characterized as "an awesome sound—measured tread of those countless feet in the dust and the loud report of the bracelets, a somber counterpoint to the gay carnival celebration. It conjured up in the bright afternoon sunshine dark alien images of legions marching bound together over a vast tract, iron fitted in to dank stone walls, chains—like those to an anchor—rattling in the deep holds of ships, and exile in an unknown inhospitable land—an exile bitter and irreversible in which all memory of the former life and of the self as it had once been had been destroyed" (303-4). The irreversible event that took place in the beginning is ritualized through the memory of the site that at this moment echoes, for them, the mythic reality, "the self as it had once been before it had once been destroyed"—those things that existed before the time of the Atlantic Crossing.

The Beg Pardon festival in *Praisesong* is spiritual protection and allows the people to possess a kind of power. They may be economically poor, but they possess a spiritual wealth because they can return to the memory of heritage and sustaining cultural values. Lebert Joseph tells Avey what the primary reason for the "excursion" is:

> "Is the Old Parents, oui," he said solemnly. "The Long-time People. Each year this time they does look for us to come and give them their remembrance...
>
> "That's why," he continued humbly, "the first thing I do the minute I reach home is to roast an ear of corn just pick out from the ground and put it on a plate for them....
>
> "And who's the first one down on his knees then singing the 'Beg Pardon'? Who?... The Old Parents! The Long-time People!" There was both fondness and dread in his voice. "We must give them their remembrance." (165, 166)

Lebert Joseph informs Avey that he is Chamba—his African ethnic identity. He is surprised that she does not know her "nation." That is to say, Avey, as an *American,* does not know her African ethnicity. He points out that the excursion is just that, a carnival festival. But it is more. Through the annual Big Drum that is the climax, the *communitas,* of the festival they sustain a collective and connecting spirituality. The Big Drum as ceremony is, because they "live once and die forever."

> Once Lebert Joseph offered up the opening statement of the song, his relatives behind him on the ground quickly joined in the singing. And the makeshift drums that had been silent all along began a solemn measure. Arms opened, faces lifted to the darkness, the small band of supplicants endlessly repeated the few lines that comprised the Beg Pardon, pleading and petitioning not only for themselves and for the friends and neighbors present in the yard, but for all their far-flung kin as well—the sons and daughters, grands and great-grands in Trinidad, Toronto, New York, London...
>
> ... And invariably them came... "Cromanti. Is Cromanti people you see in the ring now... Congo, oui. They had some of the prettiest dances." (238-40)

And these people do not have to search for an identity, since they already know who they are and from where they come. They make the annual return to the past—to their homeland (the metaphor of the eternal return)—in order to survive the present and the future. Therefore, the Big Drum ceremony serves as an annual rite that confirms spiritual and cultural affinity.

The Beg Pardon festival creates temporal space between reality and the spirit world. By going to Carriacou and experiencing the intensity of neo-African ritual dancing and music, Avey Johnson rediscovers her own site of place in Tatem. Similarly, at the end of *Chosen Place,* Merle resolves to go in search of her estranged family in Uganda. As educated, privileged black women, Merle Kinbona and Avey Johnson reactualize memory through spiritual kinship with rural and politically marginalized people. Like her literary precursor, Zora Neale Hurston, Marshall celebrates the folk's propensity to be more engaged with tradition and its meaning. Her protagonists move from the disrupture of a cultural ethos to a return home. When she participates in the Big Drum, Avey recognizes the "memory." Avey discovers that one of the dances that is performed during the Big Drum is like what she used to do as a child:

> Her feet of their own accord began to glide forward, but in such a way they scarcely left the ground....
> "And look, she doing the 'Carriacou Tramp' good as somebody been doing it all their life!" ...
> And under the cover of the darkness she was performing the dance that wasn't supposed to be dancing, in imitation of the old folk shuffling in a loose ring inside the church.... The Ring Shout. (248)

Note how Marshall connects these movements to all peoples of the Americas. In *Chosen Place* the people dance a similar movement where "they were doing ... the dance ... the restrained rhythmic two-step that scarcely brought the foot up off the ground," and in *Praisesong* Avey learns that this dance, which is a "non-dance," was what her forebears in Tatem, South Carolina, call the Ring Shout. Her personal memory site is that of Tatem, which her mother-ancestor, Aunt Cuney, wants her to recognize as a site of spiritual empowerment. Whether the dance is done in Bournehills, Tatem, or Carriacou, the event is both spiritual rejuvenation and secular festival. The dance and drum are social and spiritual connections with friends and culture. Moreover, the dance negates any alienation that may exist because of the displacement of African heritage.

Carnival as an Archaeological Site for Memory

The memory moves between colonial time and the present; between home and leaving; between order and chaos.

Whereas Merle in *Chosen Place* may immediately recognize what the recurring Cuffee Ned carnival masque means, Avey Johnson in *Praisesong* must be led to an awakening of meaning in the Beg Pardon festival. The Big Drum ceremony (*communitas* of the Beg Pardon) and the Cuffee Ned carnival *mas* are specific enactments of an event that signifies memory. The signification is counter-memory in the context of the New World ethos. Both festivals as carnival are recurring motifs that return memory to an archaeological site.

Notes

1. On my exploration of the 1856 Margaret Garner fugitive slave incident, see Angelita Reyes, "Rereading A Nineteenth-Century Fugitive Slave Incident: From Toni Morrison's *Beloved* to Margaret Garner's Dearly Beloved," *Annals of Scholarship: Studies of the Humanities and Social Sciences* 7 (1990): 465–85.

2. Paule Marshall, *Praisesong for the Widow* (New York: Putnam's, 1983), and *The Chosen Place, The Timeless People* (New York: Avon, 1969). All references are to these editions and are cited in text.

3. For example, in addition to *The Joy Luck Club*, Amy Tan's novel *The Kitchen God's Wife* is based on memories of Asian-American mother stories that "should not be told" even as they must be told.

4. I continue to value this sense of guest-host relationship. I have been in certain "postmodernist" cultural domains where this reciprocity is not valued and often I am not even accompanied to the door by the host! These values, however, still exist in tradition-based cultures, and although modern lifestyles do not permit the host to walk home with the guest, the concept still applies.

5. See Michelle Cliff's essay "Women Warriors: Black Writers Load the Canon."

6. My appreciation to Louise Lincoln, curator of African, Oceanic, and New World cultures, and Susan Jacobsen, supervisor of public programs, both of the Minneapolis Institute of Arts, for materials on contemporary and historic carnival celebrations from the institute's presentation of the exhibition Caribbean Festival Arts (10 February–14 April 1991). The inspiration for and writing of this essay derives in part from the rejuvenating spirit of that exhibit, which was, for me, a kind of return to an archaeological site. See John Nunley and Judith Bettelheim, *Caribbean Festival Arts: Each and Every Bit of Difference*.

7. In *The Ritual Process* anthropologist Victor Turner posits his theory of ritual status elevation and ritual status reversal within the context of liminality and *communitas*.

8. The Cuffee Ned paradigm is similar to the historical mythmaking of the Jamaican Maroon woman called Nanny. In the eighteenth century this woman

helped to lead the Windward Maroons in their military resistance against the British. It was believed that Nanny was killed in 1733, but according to legend her burial was kept secret. The Windward Maroons believed that her death was not the end, but an enactment of an eternal return that would instill hope in the people.

9. In my essay "Metaphors and Politics of Materialism in Paule Marshall's *Praisesong for the Widow* and Toni Morrison's *Tar Baby*," I explore the significance of *Praisesong* in terms of Marshall's commitment to interpreting history as a metaphor for an African-based value system in the New World. Note how both Toni Morrison and Paule Marshall use the triangular connections of Africa, the Caribbean, and North America to illustrate memory and connected consciousness.

10. Toni Morrison remarked to an interviewer that he had not asked her about the meaning of "sixty million and more," the dedication to *Beloved*. Morrison explains that it is the best estimation of the number of Africans who died in captivity before reaching the New World and during the actual middle crossing (Reyes 1989).

Works Cited

Beane, Wendell C., and William G. Doty, eds. *Myths, Rites, Symbols: A Mircea Eliade Reader*. New York: Harper, 1976.

Boyce-Davies, Carole. "Multiple Articulations or the Discourse of Going a Piece of the Way with Them." Madison, WI: African Literature Association, 1990.

Busia, Abena. "What Is Your Nation? Reconnecting Africa and Her Diaspora through Paule Marshall's *Praisesong for the Widow*." *Changing Our Own Words*. Ed. Cheryl A. Wall. Rutgers UP, 1989.

Cliff, Michelle. "Women Warriors: Black Writers Load the Canon." *Voice Literary Supplement* May 1990: 20–23.

DeVeaux, Alexis. "Paule Marshall: In Celebration of Our Triumph." *Essence* May 1971: 96.

Eliade, Mircea. *The Sacred and the Profane*. Trans. Willard R. Trask. New York: Harcourt Brace, 1959.

Hill, Errol. *The Trinidad Carnival*. Austin: U of Texas P, 1972.

Hurston, Zora Neale. *Their Eyes Were Watching God*. 1937. Greenwich, CT: Fawcett, 1965.

Lipsitz, George. *Time Passages: Collective Memory and American Popular Culture*. Minneapolis: U of Minnesota P, 1990.

Marshall, Paule. *Brown Girl, Brownstones*. Chatham, NJ: Chatham, 1959.

———. *The Chosen Place, The Timeless People*. New York: Avon, 1969.

———. *Praisesong for the Widow*. New York: Putnam's, 1983.

———. "Shaping the World of My Art." *New Letters* 40 (1973): 97–107.

Morrison, Toni. *Beloved*. New York: Knopf, 1987.

———. "The Site of Memory." *Inventing the Truth: The Art and Craft of Memoir*. Ed. William Zinsser. Boston: Houghton, 1987.

———. *Tar Baby*. New York: Knopf, 1981.

Nunley, John, and Judith Bettelheim. *Caribbean Festival Arts: Each and Every Bit of Difference*. Seattle: U of Washington P, 1988.

Pearse, Andrew. "Carnival in Nineteenth-Century Trinidad." *Caribbean Quarterly* (1956): 175-93.

Rector, Monica. "Code and Message of Carnival." *Carnival!* Ed. Thomas A. Sebeok. Berlin: Mouton, 1984.

Reyes, Angelita. "Metaphors and Politics of Materialism in Paule Marshall's *Praisesong for the Widow* and Toni Morrison's *Tar Baby*." *Politics and the Muse: Studies in the Politics of Recent American Literature*. Ed. Adam Sorkin. Ohio: Bowling Green State UP, 1989. 178-201.

Tan, Amy. *The Joy Luck Club*. New York: Putnam's, 1989.

———. *The Kitchen God's Wife*. New York: Putnam's, 1991.

Turner, Victor. *The Ritual Process*. Chicago: Aldine, 1966.

Washington, Mary Helen. "Paule Marshall Talking with Mary Helen Washington." *Writing Lives*. Ed. Mary Chamberlain. London: Virago, 1988. 161-68.

"Tell me your earrings":
Time and the Marvelous
in Toni Morrison's *Beloved*

SHARON JESSEE

> No compound of houses, no neighborhood, no sculpture, no paint, no time, especially no time because memory, pre-historic memory, has no time. There is just a little music, each other and the urgency of what is at stake. Which is all they had. For that work [*Beloved*], the work of language is to get out of the way.
> —Toni Morrison, "Unspeakable Things Unspoken: The Afro-American Presence in American Literature"

> She could tell of the Crows, whom she had never seen, and of the Black Hills, where she had never been. I wanted to see in reality what she had seen more perfectly in the mind's eye.
> —N. Scott Momaday, *House Made of Dawn*

> The end is in the beginning and lies far ahead.
> —Ralph Ellison, *Invisible Man*

In Toni Morrison's fifth novel, a mother's killing of her child forms the central event around which memory, yearning, and remorse coalesce. Loosely based on a historical account of one Margaret Garner, who while escaping from slavery killed her baby rather than see him returned to the slavecatcher (Darling 6), the novel *Beloved* unfolds the complex relationship between a past that Sethe believed was "still waiting" for her and her surviving daughter, and a future that weighed the precariousness of love against overpowering numbness and regret.

Time and the Marvelous in Beloved

Not revealing the past, not calling up old memories, is a matter of great care for Sethe in the novel's Reconstruction setting, which not only makes for narrative suspense, but also foregrounds the central theme of time in the novel: the fusing of the African Diaspora with the aftermath of the Civil War, as a slave-ship survivor's memories join with those of the ghost of an infant female's, or as a mother's possessive and violent love reaches back to offend past generations. The success of Sethe and the others in realizing a future beyond the numbness that comes from repressing the past will depend a great deal on their relationship to time, particularly to the restoration of a West African sense of time, death, and redemption.

As the narrative opens in the 1870s, on the outskirts of Cincinnati, Ohio, Sethe and Denver are the only occupants left at the house at 124 Bluestone Road to contend with the ghost of the murdered child whose "venom" filled the house. Baby Suggs, Sethe's mother-in-law, had died ten years earlier, and Sethe's sons, Buglar and Howard, had gone shortly thereafter, driven away by the powerful antics—breaking dishes, slamming the family dog against a wall—of their baby sister's ghost. When Paul D, a friend of Sethe and her husband, Halle, from twenty-five years ago at Sweet Home plantation where they were together as slaves before the Civil War, comes to 124, his presence sets in motion the pain of remembering the past and the possibility of healing. Sethe begins to wonder, with Paul D there, whether she might actually have a future. But the past, represented primarily by the physical manifestation of a possible slave-ship survivor who calls herself Beloved, requires a fuller penalty of Sethe, a final settlement, as it were.

In her most comprehensive context within the narrative, Beloved stands for all the ancestors lost in the Diaspora, demanding restoration to a temporal continuum in which "present" time encompasses much of the immediate past, including several generations of the dead. According to John Mbiti, in some African traditions "the future is virtually absent" and "people set their minds not on future things, but chiefly on what has taken place." "Present" in Swahili is *sasa* or the "now" period and encompasses four or five generations of ancestors; only after these generations do ancestors and their "time" enter into the *zamani* or mythic period, a "final storehouse" of time (23–25). But slavery disrupted the ancestor worship that maintained that continuum, depriving people of their sacred time.

Beloved "haunts" her mother and the others because they work at repressing the painful memories of being under slavery. That she has been "forgotten" is the reason for Beloved's spite, and from certain African perspectives, part of the reason for the disharmony within the family and community in the novel's present (1873) setting. Several readers have noted the emphasis throughout Morrison's works on reconnecting and affirming the ancestral past in order to have a meaningful relationship to the present, and nowhere is that link made more resonant a theme than in *Beloved*.[1] In one of her comments on this novel in an interview, Toni Morrison remarks that "the gap between Africa and Afro-America and the gap between the living and the dead and the gap between the past and the present does not exist. It's bridged for us by our assuming responsibility for people no one's ever assumed responsibility for" (Darling 5). And in *Beloved*, the readers are compelled to share in the effort to restore the time continuum that the girl Beloved's return demands.

Beloved is the return of the repressed, the forgotten ancestor who comes to possess her mother, the ex-slave woman who was so possessive and full of pride—she actually escaped from slavery with all her children by her husband, Halle—that she killed her baby daughter rather than see her taken back into slavery at Sweet Home plantation. But she is also the link to rebuilding *sasa* time and the community, for the two are mutually dependent. In traditional West African groups, the community was responsible for maintaining the temporal continuum; when it was broken, communal sharing, not individual action, restored it (Barthold 10–11). However, "community" had been tentative at best, since under slavery individuals frequently had scant knowledge of where they would be tomorrow or who their family was. Furthermore, few managed to reunite with relatives after slavery, and nobody seemed to want to recall much about that period.

In the process of moving toward freedom, which Cincinnati, Ohio, both literally and symbolically was, Sethe, Paul D, and Baby Suggs had to try to forget the nightmare that was being a slave. But that means forgetting your ancestors—possibly something that in their African religion was problematic, and furthermore dangerous: the forgotten relatives could turn on you in spite. The ghost occupying Sethe's house—the ghost of her "crawling already?" baby—is a spiteful and jealous ghost, and the novel gradually reveals that the young woman Beloved contains that spiteful streak. The dead, in African religion, want to be remembered. For several generations, they are a part of the *sasa* continuum, the present, and are "familiar" to their descendants until they pass away from *sasa* time altogether (Mbiti 22). *Sasa* is a time dimension with its

Time and the Marvelous in Beloved

own "short future, dynamic present, and experienced past," and it feeds or disappears into the wider *zamani* dimension, which is the "graveyard" or "final storehouse" of time (Mbiti 23). But after death, an individual continues to exist in *sasa* time, where, if he "appears" in visual form to his living relatives, he is recognized by name.

That it is tantamount to a punishment to the recently deceased not to be identified by name is underscored in the novel when Sethe remembered something she had successfully managed not to for many years. Her own mother, whom she knew primarily by watching her work in the fields at a distance, took her aside one day and told her to memorize a brand she had on her breast, so that when she died, Sethe could recognize her by that brand. She did not want to be forgotten. And all of the "voices" that clamor for recognition at Sethe's house are the sounds of "people of broken necks, fire-cooked blood and black girls who had lost their ribbons" along with some hair and a part of their scalps, whose names were unknown (*Beloved* 172). The clamoring for recognition on the part of the dead in Morrison's work finds parallels in some West African perspectives. According to John Mbiti (27), to be forgotten at the time of death and afterward is to have one's "personal immortality" destroyed: the recently deceased are "living dead" who are angry at having met with death violently. And E. Bolaji Idowu, in *African Traditional Religion: A Definition,* states that in some African groups, ancestors are still regarded by their living relatives as "heads and parts of the families or communities" to which they belonged when alive. They have merely extended the family life into the "after-life or super-sensible world" (184–5). From such African viewpoints, then, cutting off individuals from their earthly relations through slavery and violent death in *Beloved* caused them insufferable isolation and a seemingly irreparable tear in the cohesion of their world.

Just after Paul D comes into Sethe's house in the opening chapter of the novel, he is met with just such "a wave of grief" (*Beloved* 3) of the forgotten dead, specifically, Beloved's. His presence there, however, opens up a space in which to feel, and remember, for him and Sethe: "Maybe this one time she could stop dead still in the middle of a cooking meal—not even leave the stove—and feel the hurt her back ought to. Trust things and remember things because the last of the Sweet Home men was there to catch her if she sank?" (18). The terror of remembering, however, does not go away, especially as Sethe wonders "if she could just manage the news" Paul D brought about Halle with his face smeared with clabber from the butter churn, about Paul D wearing a bit in his mouth, and about seeing one of his brothers roasted alive. "I don't go inside" (46), she tells him, but her "rememories," as she calls them, come anyway, like those of the beautiful trees of Sweet Home, only with young black boys hanging from them in nooses.

"Rememory" is Sethe's term for describing how a time and place from her earlier history is "out there" in the tangible world of the present (*sasa* dimension) and can "get you" if care is not taken. She also believes that her job is to somehow keep Denver "from a past still waiting for her" (42). This becomes apparent when she tries to explain her concept of "rememory" to Denver:

> I was talking about time. It's so hard to believe in it. Some things go. Pass on. Some things just stay. I used to think it was my rememory. You know. Some things you forget. Other things you never do. But it's not. Places, places are still there. If a house burns down, it's gone, but the place—the picture of it—stays, and not just in my rememory, but out there, in the world. What I remember is a picture floating around out there outside my head. I mean, even if I don't think it, even if I die, the picture of what I did, or knew, or saw is still out there. Right in the place where it happened.
>
> "Can other people see it?" asked Denver.
>
> "Oh, yes. Oh, yes, yes, yes." (35–36)

Sethe's affirmation that the past can be experienced tangibly has its greatest significance in the reappearance of Beloved. That the young woman named Beloved who appears at 124 is actually the baby girl Beloved, in a more mature body, is something Denver figures out almost immediately. It takes Sethe a while to realize or admit this, because it is too good to be true—almost. "Anything coming back to life hurts," observes Amy Denver, the young white woman who doctored Sethe's swollen, cut-up feet when she was pregnant with Denver and walking to escape from Sweet Home (35). Her remark serves as appropriate commentary on the swollen and painful rememories Sethe has repressed and which Paul's and Beloved's arrivals stir up. But it also serves to describe Beloved herself, coming back to her mother after all these years deprived of her flesh. Sethe may have hoped for a future with Paul D, but Beloved had other plans.

When the nineteen- or twenty-year-old woman shows up in front of 124 just a day or so after Paul D's arrival and the disappearance from the house of the baby's ghost, the reader is prepared to assess this as something more than just a coincidence. Yet the circumstances of the baby's death, as well as the young woman's real identity, remain a mystery well

Time and the Marvelous in Beloved

into the novel. From Tzvetan Todorov's perspective in his study, *The Fantastic,* Beloved is both a "real" ghost within the text, and hence "marvelous," and also an "illusion of the senses," something "uncanny" (41). And she exemplifies one set of themes in Todorov's typology of the literary fantastic: themes concerning the "perception-consciousness" system and the "transgressions between matter and mind," such as the "collapse of the limit between subject and object" and the "transformation between time and space" (114, 120). Is Beloved a double reincarnation of both Sethe's dead child and a slave-ship survivor (possibly Sethe's mother)?[2] Or is she a woman-child who actually did witness her mother's suicide aboard a slave ship? Is she a reincarnation of ancestral ghosts, or simply somebody who finds in Sethe a fulfillment of her desire for a mother just as she prompts Sethe's overwhelming desire to lose herself in the "return" of a child?

Morrison is deliberately disorienting the reader, whom she wants to feel what it is like to be "snatched, just as the slaves were from one place to another, from any place to another, without preparation and without defense" ("Unspeakable" 32). The readers actually enter the text much as Sethe, Paul D, Denver, and Beloved do as they begin not only to imagine the losses of black slaves, but also to experience the gaps in knowledge of the past that the text refuses to fill. The desire to know more is joined with a concomitant dread of knowing, just as the characters value their past and yet also work to forget it. Sethe and Paul D, for example, are ambivalent about remembering the past; they require a gradual progression in their revelations of painful and traumatic experiences. As Sethe rubs Paul D's knee after he apologizes for revealing to her the circumstances of his last seeing Sethe's husband, Halle—that he could not speak to him because he had a bit in his mouth—she thinks of how every morning she awakens to begin the "day's serious work of beating back the past" as she kneads quickbread. Her kneading of Paul's knee soothes him and allows him, for the time being, to stop telling her about Halle; it also allows the reader to stop knowing more. Sethe's and Paul D's withholding of information, their truncated eking-out of their stories, establishes a rhythm that is crucial to the narrative.

Beloved is the complex and comprehensive vehicle through which Morrison has her readers, as well as her characters, confront their evasions, uncertainties, and mystifications of a repressed past: the personal experiences of those under slavery. The "disremembered" of Morrison's novel are, in a broad sense, the ancestors we, the readers, have forgotten. Thus a West African framework of *sasa* and *zamani* time—as well as the necessity to revere and recall the ancestors for several generations so that they may pass into the "final storehouse" of time—operates on the level of the novel as a whole. "The art of writing this book" is thus, says Morrison, a "way of confronting . . . and making . . . possible to remember" (Darling 5) the horror of slavery and the Middle Passage.

The dedication for Morrison's fifth novel reads, "Sixty Million and more"; it is the first phrase the reader encounters concerning all those who died violently during the Middle Passage and for whose presence we, the readers, characters, and narrator of *Beloved,* long. Halle, Sethe's husband and the father of her children, is one of the most emphatic examples of such loss, because no one knows what happened to him after 1855, when Sethe and later Paul D escaped from Sweet Home and Schoolteacher's reign of terror. Halle was special because he had worked Sundays to buy his mother, Baby Suggs, out of slavery, but the only indication of what had happened to him after Sethe's escape is Paul D's memory of Halle just sitting at the butter churn, the coddled milk all over his face. "That's the carnage," however, according to the author, for she wants the reader to "have to yearn for their company, for the people who are gone, to know what slavery did" (Darling 6).

Through *Beloved*'s narrative process, Morrison prolongs our desire both for the end, for illumination, and for the delay of the end, just as Sethe seems to want to know and yet not know who the young woman, Beloved, is. The tension between this desire and dread is "textual energy," in Peter Brooks's sense, where "repetition as binding works toward the generation of significance, toward recognition and . . . retrospective illumination" (296). Recontextualization furthermore suggests parallels and linkages between other elements of the novel as well. The aura of wonder surrounding the nineteen-year-old female who rises out of the river and comes to sit on a stump in front of Sethe's house with "new" skin—not even a wrinkle on her knuckles or the bottoms of her feet (50–53)—the aura of the birth or rebirth of this girl who calls herself "Beloved" runs parallel to the mystery of a death. Of course, at that early point in the novel, the mystery is about where the "crawling already?" baby is: all Sethe's other children have been accounted for. We get, in other words, the extenuating circumstances long before we know who died, and how.

When the scene in the shed does come, we feel the anguish but we are also in a position to suspend judgment of Sethe's act. The gradual working up to the revelation of the killing is to prevent the readers from fixing only on its brutality, for as Morrison has said about her first three novels,

Time and the Marvelous in Beloved

she does not want the language to have to compete with the event itself (Tate 125). Furthermore, Brian Finney notes that just as "redundancy, the repetition of fabula events," reflects the problems the characters face "in thinking and talking about the almost unthinkable and unspeakable experience of slavery" (24), repetition allows the readers to respond to Sethe's act with an understanding of its fully complicated historical context. This painful retrieval of a past event for the reader is mirrored in the characters' ambivalance about remembering, for that seems almost more than they can bear.

Their attempts to construct barriers against the flood of the past, though—attempts such as Sethe's dread of running into a "rememory" and Paul D's containment of emotions in a "tin box" where his heart used to be—are shown to be debilitating. Sethe begins to realize this when, the day after Paul D's arrival, she goes into the "keeping room" where Baby Suggs used to lie and ask for colors to be brought to her. Sethe notices that the room is drab and colorless except for two squares of orange on a quilt and reflects that for the longest time, she has not seen any color, not since the pink in the chips of her baby's gravestone. Also, Sethe takes much longer than Denver or Paul D to allow herself the conscious thought that the young woman, Beloved, is possibly her baby daughter "come back" to her. And yet her reluctance to embrace that possibility is reasonable within the context of what happens when Sethe acknowledges Beloved as the daughter she killed.

Recognized, Beloved becomes a violent and repressed "other" who returns to see her mother's face, to punish and also "join" with her. She can "fly apart" at will, lose teeth and body parts if Sethe "disremembers" her a little too much, strangle her mother if she wants to, and seduce Paul D against his will. She succeeds in driving the latter out of the house and finally off the property, getting Sethe and her sister Denver all to herself at last. Deborah Horvitz explains the possessive drive behind Beloved's frequently repeated phrase. What she seeks—"a hot thing"—is an expression of "the desperately writhing and thwarted wish to be both 'self' and 'other' . . . to regain the lost Beloved by becoming her" (162–63). Beloved, the African ancestor lost to her kin, returns to be called by her *name,* and to name her mother the same, the beloved.

Beloved is too "hungry," though, in her merging with Sethe, for she proceeds to devour her. "Chewing" is a frequent descriptor for Beloved's desire for Sethe, who thins, quits work, and becomes weaker as Beloved fattens and grows stronger. In her study, "Memory and Mother Love,"

Barbara Mathieson observes that in order to make slavery comprehensible in terms of what it did to people, Morrison "invokes the complex range of maternal emotion" (19).[3] The initial relationship of Beloved and Sethe was arrested at the stage of "infantile, childish love, its insatiability and the strong mother-infant bond" (5) severed at Beloved's sudden and unnatural death. Sethe tries to "make up" for Beloved's untimely death and separation, but the flood of adoration Sethe opens up to Beloved only intensifies, rather than assuages, Beloved's spite. By overcompensating for past wrongs, Sethe actually enters into the regressed state with Beloved, pulling Denver along with them into a collective withdrawal from the immediate present.

In thinking that Paul D was wrong in telling her there was "anything outside her door" that she could possibly be interested in, Sethe initiates the deepening immersion of the three women into the past. Shutting the door on the world outside the house in the winter of 1873–74 seems to Sethe to be the final solution to all her problems. From the moment she recognizes the song Beloved is singing as the one she used to sing to her babies, she attempts to do what Baby Suggs did, to "lay it all down" and repose. Sethe is no longer afraid to remember or afraid of her "crawling already?" baby because she cuts herself off from her historical present and gives up on future plans. At this point in the narrative, in fact, the three women's thoughts drift far back into the past, and that, combined with the lyrical quality of their internal monologues—unconventional syntax, poetic description—creates a present time much like the *sasa* period Mbiti describes.

The unspoken conversations—"unspeakable thoughts, unspoken" (199)—begin as Sethe walks home from what will be her last day at work. Sethe's is the first of the three, and begins: "Beloved, she my daughter. She mine. See. She come back to me of her own free will and I don't have to explain a thing" (200). Yet while Sethe says "now I can look at things again because she's here to see them too" (201), she eventually looks at only her past memory of Beloved, due to Beloved's growing insistence that Sethe devote herself completely to her. Denver, who has always loved to hear and tell about her own birth, begins her thoughts with "Beloved is my sister. I swallowed her blood right along with my mother's milk." But she quickly acknowledges the fear that will later on cause her to seek help for her mother: "I'm afraid the thing that happened that made it alright for my mother to kill my sister will happen again" (205). Beloved's thoughts are narrated last, and they begin "I am Beloved and she is mine," and end "now we can join   a hot thing" (210, 213).

Time and the Marvelous in Beloved

The bond developing among the three women alone in the house becomes destructive, and the danger to Sethe is what motivates her other daughter, Denver, to reconnect with the world "outside the yard." Importantly, this generosity on Denver's part—she must overcome her terror of the outside world—balances out Beloved's selfishness. Her going beyond the yard also forges the possibility of a future in the community again for Denver and Sethe, but not before Beloved journeys further back into slavery's past, connecting the pain of Sethe and her "crawling already?" girl with the suffering of many others.

Perhaps because the Beloved who is Sethe's daughter thinks that she and Sethe are now one ("we can join"), her memories of dying at Sethe's hands can at this point in the narrative be joined with the memories of a slave-ship survivor about the Middle Passage.[4] The young woman Beloved, who came out of a river to sit in front of Sethe's house, begins to speak as that survivor, remembering the experience of being taken with her mother on the slave ship and what happened there:

> In the beginning I could see her   I could not help her   because the clouds were in the way   in the beginning I   could see her   the shining in her ears   she does not   like the circle around her neck   I know this   I look   hard at her so she will know that the clouds are in the   way I am sure she saw me   I am looking at her see me she empties out her eyes   I am there in the place where her face is and telling her the noisy clouds were in my way   she wants her earrings   she wants her round basket   I want her face   a hot thing (211)

Yet even though the now-doubled Beloved figure has managed, with the help of Sethe, to find her "place" where she can "rememory" some of her own traumatic histories, it does not suffice to appease her hunger for her Sethe/her mother on the ship or her desire to punish.

Beloved-as-survivor remembers seeing her mother jump off the ship just as the dead people were being pushed overboard, and feels abandoned amid the crowding of others, including a man she is "on top of" who dies: "I am always crouching" (211). She remembers trying to see her mother's face, just as Sethe's Beloved is continually seeking to possess Sethe's: "I want her face" (213). Uncannily, the important details of the young woman's narrative of her initial capture and the subsequent horror of the slave ship resemble earlier memories that Sethe and Baby Suggs have of where and when Sethe killed her baby.

As slave-ship survivor, Beloved describes watching her mother tend vegetables on land in Africa, watching the clouds and flowers, and then watching as the "men with no skin" (white men) come to take her and her mother away. Similarly, Sethe and Baby Suggs recall the dreadful scene on that day in 1855 when Schoolteacher, the slave-catcher, and sheriff come to 124 Bluestone Road in Cincinnati to remand Sethe and her children back into slavery. The story, which comes to the reader in scattered pieces throughout the novel, begins with Sethe working in the garden, her "crawling already?" baby beside her, when Schoolteacher and the other "men with no skin" come into the yard. Furthermore, Sethe's "gathering every bit of life she had made that was fine" to take "beyond the veil" parallels the slave-ship girl's mother jumping overboard, in that they both do what they are able—killing, or suicide—to prevent the horror of capture. Sethe would have also killed Buglar, Howard, and Denver, if others had not stopped her, and the mother who jumped overboard might have taken her daughter with her if she could; at least from the daughter's point of view, she had wanted to "join her" (210–13).

Toward the end of part 3, pregnant and sated on her devouring of her mother's self, Beloved disappears, "explodes" from the front porch of Sethe's house, making a dramatic exit from the narrative. Her disappearance, or dissolution, is a mystery, but it, too, draws together histories and geographies. Beloved watches as her mother runs toward a white man driving up to the house; yet her narratized thoughts, reported in another section of the novel, have to do with watching her mother leave her on the slave ship. Sethe, too, has a fused time/space experience as she believed she was running toward Schoolteacher driving into the yard (she would kill *him* this time, she reasoned, not her own child), when it was actually Mr. Garner coming to pick up Denver for work. The women in the community, for whose help Denver had asked in rescuing her mother from Beloved's possession, stopped Sethe from the act, but Beloved only saw a "hill of people" on the ship whom her mother was joining, and knew that she was abandoned again.

As the past reasserts itself into the present and the present returns to retrieve the past, time seems circular. A comment from Ralph Ellison's narrator in *Invisible Man* might parallel this time orientation in *Beloved*: "the end is in the beginning and lies far ahead" (6). Beloved "returns" to initiate the collective sharing of memory. And yet within her return is the seed of her disappearance from narratability, for the collective sharing she requires is what allows her spiteful ghost to dissipate. "This is not a story to pass on," we are told at the end; what has transpired was "not the breath of the disremembered and unaccounted for, but wind in the eaves" (*Beloved* 275). And in between the initial, fierce reassertion of ancestral right that demands a narrative, and the resignation (however ironic) toward oblivion or a state of non-narratability that forms part of the ending (Brooks 288–89), the text involves all who enter in the process of (re)making time.

Beloved could be said to share with much black literature the compelling quality of making time in the face of being, in Bonnie Barthold's sense, excluded from it.[5] And the novel makes clear that neither forgetting and repressing the past, nor the total immersion and retreat into it, will do. It is within this paradox that the characters in the novel must come to terms with who they are: "they must come to grips with the choices they have made, to acknowledge their lost innocence and recover wholeness" (Otten 87). The narrative's gradual weaving of past histories into the present time of the novel (1873–74), its broken chronology of events, is a "rememory" of the past according to the characters' capacities to tell it and an invitation to the reader to participate in piecing together some understanding of it.

"Storytelling," according to Joseph T. Skerrett, Jr., "is the primary folk process in Toni Morrison's fictional world" (193), and it is clearly one piece of the healing process in *Beloved*. Just as in *Song of Solomon*, singing together "functions as a blues, allowing Pilate, Reba, and Haga to finger the jagged edge of their unhappiness as a way of mastering it" (Skerrett 200), so in *Beloved* the characters' rememories—sometimes individually, sometimes together—allow them to confront the horrors of slavery and of their own traumatized behaviors. Indeed, Carla Holloway suggests that another way of reading Morrison's assertion that "this is not a story to pass on" is to emphasize that this story should not pass away: it should be told, in other words.[6]

Like anything else in this novel, however, storytelling is not infallible or a cure-all. Baby Suggs retreated into color because in spite of her tremendous capacity for love, "whitefolks had tired her out at last" (180). That no one is invincible in the novel is perhaps the illumination that takes us through the ending and back to the beginning. This is a story of survivors who need the communal sharing and mutual respect of their selves in order to "leap" away from slavery and have any kind of future, things that are only beginning to be realized, and tentatively so, by the end of the novel. Of the endings to her novels, Morrison has said that "there is resolution of a sort but there are always possibilities—choices," and that, as in classical Greek literature, "the best you can hope for is some realization . . . suffering is not just anxiety. It is also information" (Jones 136). Perhaps this is the nature of the information given when

Paul D tells Sethe that she—not Beloved—is "her own best thing." And Sethe's replying question, "Am I?" puts forth a hope that she can live in time, not outside of it.

Notes

1. See Skerrett, "Recitation to the *Griot*," and Morrison, "Unspeakable Things Unspoken" for some of the discussions of Morrison's emphasis on the significance of community for individuals' senses of self.
2. Deborah Horvitz suggests that Beloved, as the slave-ship survivor, is also Sethe's African mother (158).
3. A revised version of Mathieson's essay appears in this volume.
4. According to Morrison, the two can exist simultaneously in the same person, for "the languages of death and of the middle passage are the same. The yearning for a smiling face is the same" (Darling 5).
5. Barthold argues that Blacks in the United States were cut off from the African past and at the same time prevented from participating in the Western future, and she cites this statement from James Baldwin: "Black people . . . have been simultaneously deprived of time and fixed in it by the color of their skin" (16).
6, Discussion with Carla Holloway, Annual MELUS Conference, Greenville, North Carolina, March 1989.

Works Cited

Barthold, Bonnie J. *Black Time: Fiction of Africa, the Caribbean, and the United States*. New Haven: Yale UP, 1981.

Brooks, Peter. "Freud's Masterplot." *Contemporary Literary Criticism: Literary and Cultural Studies*. Ed. Robert Con Davis and Ronald Schleifer. 2d ed. New York: Longman, 1989. 287–99.

Darling, Marsha Jean. "In the Realm of Responsibility: A Conversation with Toni Morrison." *Women's Review of Books* 5. 6 (March 1988): 5–6.

Ellison, Ralph. *Invisible Man*. 2d ed. New York: Vintage-Random, 1972.

Finney, Brian. "Temporal Defamiliarization in Toni Morrison's *Beloved*." *Obsidian II: Black Literature in Review* 5. 1 (Spring 1990): 20–36.

Horvitz, Deborah. "Nameless Ghosts." *Studies in American Fiction* 17.2 (Autumn 1988): 157–67.

Idowu, E. Bolaji. *African Traditional Religion: A Definition*. Maryknoll, NY: Orbis, 1973.

Jones, Bessie W. "An Interview with Toni Morrison." *The World of Toni Morrison*. Ed. Bessie W. Jones and Audrie L. Vinson. Dubuque, IA: Kendall/Hunt, 1985.

Mathieson, Barbara. "Memory and Mother Love in Morrison's *Beloved*." *American Imago* 47. 1 (1990): 1–21.

Mbiti, John S. *African Religions and Philosophy.* London: Heinemann, 1969.
Morrison, Toni. *Beloved.* New York: Knopf, 1987.
———. "Unspeakable Things Unspoken: The Afro-American Presence in American Literature." *Michigan Quarterly Review* 28.1 (Winter 1989): 1–35.
Otten, Terry. *The Crime of Innocence in the Fiction of Toni Morrison.* Literary Frontiers Edition, 33. Columbia, MO: U of Missouri P, 1989.
Skerrett, Joseph T., Jr. "Recitation to the *Griot:* Storytelling and Learning in Toni Morrison's *Song of Solomon.*" *Conjuring: Black Women, Fiction, and Literary Tradition.* Ed. Marjorie Pryse and Hortense J. Spillers. Bloomington: Indiana UP, 1985. 192–202.
Tate, Claudia, ed. "Toni Morrison." *Black Women Writers at Work.* New York: Continuum, 1983. 117–31.
Todorov, Tzvetan. *The Fantastic: A Structural Approach to a Literary Genre.* Paris, 1970. 2d ed. Trans. Richard Howard. Cleveland: P of Case Western Reserve U, 1973.

Memory and Mother Love:

Toni Morrison's Dyad

BARBARA OFFUTT MATHIESON

The mother-infant dyad, the most elemental of all interpersonal bondings, is renowned for its ability to generate an outpouring of tender ecstasy matched only by the concomitant reverberations of anger and guilt. Infant need and maternal care reciprocate so intensely, many psychologists believe, that they blur the distinction between child and parent. Yet within the intimate web lurk terrors and traumas. Each of Toni Morrison's five novels probes the tension-fraught permutations of this relationship. Eva and Hannah Peace, Nel Wright, Margaret Street, Ruth Dead, Pauline Breedlove—each mother hovers with limited success at her own precarious point of resolution between strength and vulnerability, nurturance and manipulation, self-sacrifice and resistance. The children, particularly daughters, whirl in a vortex of similarly conflicted emotions for the women who bore them. Morrison's fifth novel, *Beloved*, charts the explosive intricacies of the pre-oedipal bond from the simultaneous perspectives of mother and child, exploring their mutual hunger for a loving union as well as their inevitable struggle for control. This powerful portrait, in turn, serves as the metaphor upon which Morrison grounds her meditation on personal memory and historical self-awareness. Still haunted by slavery, *Beloved*'s African American characters confront a legacy of psychological scars. Morrison orchestrates maternal tensions and memory's pain so that each mirrors the other's anguish and ambivalence. A shared avenue for hope and growth emerges from this unlikely pairing.

Paradoxical Maternity

At the novel's emotional climax, a former slave recognizes in the person of a mysterious visitor the re-embodied spirit of her dead baby daughter.

Memory and Mother Love

Many years earlier Sethe, the escaped slave, found herself pursued by the loathed master from whom she and her children had escaped. Cornered, Sethe slit the throat of her beloved daughter rather than see her returned to captivity. Now the baby's ghost has returned. In an extraordinary section that can best be described as a telepathic opera trio, the newly reunited women pour forth their rhapsodic responses to each other and to the events of past and present. Sethe, the spirit child Beloved, and Sethe's younger daughter "sing" separately and then in chorus about the sense of completion and bliss they feel at Beloved's return. Each in turn varies the same phrase, insisting that "Beloved" is "mine." Sethe begins, "Beloved, she my daughter. She mine" (200). The younger daughter, Denver, concludes her variation with "She's mine, Beloved. She's mine" (209). This pattern culminates in the trio, when the three women chant together

> I waited for you
> You are mine
> You are mine
> You are mine (217)

In the ghost's own passage, the conjunction of identification and love reechoes with a distinctive twist:

> I am Beloved and she is mine. I see her take flowers away from leaves she puts them in a round basket the leaves are not for her she fills the basket she opens the grass I would help her but the clouds are in the way how can I say things that are pictures I am not separate from her there is no place where I stop her face is my own and I want to be there in the place where her face is and to be looking at it too (210)

The opening clause asserts the nameless ghost's "name" as well as her state—she is, once again, beloved of her mother. And "she," Sethe, once again "is mine." In an inversion of Sethe's formulation, the *mother* now belongs to the *child,* restoring the connection so abruptly severed nineteen years earlier. As she remembers her mother gathering herbs and flowers, Beloved cannot imagine that she and Sethe are separate; in her understanding, their identities flow into one another as interchangeably as their faces ("her face is my own"). Though Beloved's body evinces the passage of nineteen years, death has locked her psyche in eternal infancy. Her woman's words articulate a one-year-old's consciousness, and Beloved's emotions remain those of a toddler insatiably yearning for its mother. She has returned to claim what every baby demands—the unqualified love and unwavering attention of the mother whose identity she does not distinguish from her own. Sethe, for her part, absorbs herself as fully in Beloved as any mother does in her infant.

Many parents must feel, as I did, an immediate jolt of recognition at Morrison's moment of union and reunion. In the early hours of the morning after my own daughter's birth, I fell into a half-sleep between waves of hospital bustle and routine. On the edge of waking consciousness, a vivid image of her sleeping face crystallized on my closed lids, seemingly recalled rather than seen. My daughter's face suddenly melted into the sensations of my own body. In a synesthesia of minds, her face became my face on my body. This profoundly affective vision resurfaced immediately in response to Morrison's fictional mother-child relationship; although deformed by extreme circumstances—slavery and death—and involving supernatural components of existence, Sethe's bond with Beloved encapsulates common parental experiences.

Psychoanalytic theory also corroborates Morrison's insight into the intense sense of union between a mother and her child.[1] Exploring preoedipal bonds, D. W. Winnicott theorizes that the infant's emerging consciousness comprehends itself as completely submerged in its mother's persona. Because that mother provides food, stimulation, and protection, she serves as the helpless infant's "ego support," a functional extension of the baby that helps to implement its burgeoning desires. Largely because of the mother's support, the baby does not experience only discontinuous instinctual drives and reactions but instead builds a continuous, stable sense of personal power and identity. The infant's early sense of total immersion in the mother serves as a beneficial and necessary stepping-stone to maturity. "The paradox," Winnicott notes, "is that what is good and bad in the infant's environment is not in fact a projection of the mother's power, but in spite of this it is necessary, if the individual infant is to develop healthily, that everything shall seem to him to be a projection" (Winnicott 586).

Thus the great threat haunting Morrison's "children" of all ages is the specter of orphanhood, an irremediable separation from the mother's nurturance. Pilate and Macon Dead, Guitar Bains *(Song of Solomon)*, Cholly Breedlove *(The Bluest Eye)*, Jadine and Son *(Tar Baby)*—all, like Sethe, have endured childhoods alone without parents. Jadine laments that only in the presence of her lover, Son, does she feel herself "unorphaned" (209); Son's own loss is assuaged only by the surrogate mothers of his home in Eloe and his tenacious memory of a legion of "fat black ladies in white dresses minding the pie table in the basement of the church" (119). In the same novel, Margaret's history of child abuse can be traced to her own mother's emotional abandonment. Pecola, too, is emotionally if not literally orphaned *(The Bluest Eye)*: seduced by the movie ideals of white America, the ironically named Pauline Breedlove finds only ugliness in her daughter's face and transfers her affections to her employers' blue-eyed child. In *Sula*, Hannah Peace's shattering admission that she loves but "just don't like" her daughter ends Sula's childhood, forcing an awareness of separation, isolation, and mortality that quickly is actualized by Hannah's death. Without firm assurance of maternal love, Morrison's grown children repeatedly confront life as alienated and restless figures.

Yet even a firmly realized bonding carries tensions and threats. In *Beloved*, as sometimes in life, the ecstatic moment of union between mother and child degenerates quickly into a nightmare. The source of the disruption appears to lie within the "perfect" harmony of the mother-infant bond itself. In her groundbreaking study, "Love for the Mother and Mother Love" (1939), Alice Balint characterizes the love that the pre-oedipal child feels for the mother as "naive egoism": "It is in fact an *archaic, egoistic* way of loving, originally directed exclusively to the mother; its main characteristic is the complete lack of reality sense in regard to the interests of the love-object" (95). The mother not only feeds, protects, and stimulates her baby; she also, psychologically, serves as the sole focus for the interior landscape, and all of the baby's desires, needs, and emotions cascade onto that single, subjectively conceived object of attention. As Freud notes in "Female Sexuality," such infantile love is boundless and insatiable: "Childish love knows no bounds, it demands exclusive possession, is satisfied with nothing less than all. But it has a second characteristic: it has, besides, no real aim; it is incapable of complete satisfaction and this is the principal reason why it is doomed to end in disappointment and to give place to a hostile attitude" (286). Here infantile love's dark undercurrent, which runs rampant at the end of the novel, reveals its shadowy presence. Alice Balint reminds us all that even healthy adults often find themselves unable to limit their demands upon their own mothers or to recognize completely the separation of egos and interests (97).

Morrison's women frequently recoil from the overwhelming demands that such childish dependence levies upon their resources, a retreat that Morrison bravely explores yet does not sanction. Several of Morrison's mothers discover the "threat" too late. Margaret, the abusive mother of *Tar Baby*, experienced sheer terror in the presence of her baby's "needfulness." Herself barely out of childhood when she became wife and mother, Margaret "was outraged by that infant needfulness. There were times when she absolutely had to limit its *being there;* stop its implicit and explicit demand for her best and constant self. She could not describe her loathing of its prodigious appetite for security—the criminal arrogance of an infant's conviction that while he slept, someone is there; and when he wakes, someone is there; that when he is hungry, food will somehow magically be provided" (236). Similarly, Eva Peace interprets her grown son Plum's drug addiction as an invasive attempt to return to her womb and, as a defense, incinerates him in his bed. Morrison's antitraditional younger women reject maternity entirely as a threat to autonomy: "I don't want to make somebody else. I want to make myself," proclaims Sula (*Sula* 92). Jadine's nightmares are crowded with women who thrust their breasts at her "like weapons," chastising her for rejecting the traditional female role. These "night women" embody the oppression that Jadine perceives in maternity: "The night women were not merely against her (and her alone—not him), not merely looking superior over their sagging breasts and folded stomachs, they seemed somehow in agreement with each other about her, and were all out to get her, tie her, bind her. Grab the person she had worked hard to become and choke it off with their soft loose tits" (*Tar Baby* 262). Though Jadine responds with delight to the beauty of the tarry swamp, Nature's primordial birthing place, she nonetheless recoils in terror from its suffocating embrace, a literal death that to her signifies the erasure of independence in traditional feminine nurturance.

In *Beloved,* Morrison graphically extends this threat into a rapacious struggle to the death for possession and self-possession. Cannibalistic imagery permeates the daughter's language as the beloved child begins to consume her mother's energies. With this transformation emerge emotional tremors equally recognizable to parents and children: deep-seated anxieties about mutual dependence, fear of losing autonomy, and mistrust of union.

Traumas of Memory

The psychological intricacies of Sethe's maternal bonds also point beyond the narrative fiction to overarching social and historical issues. The ambivalences of the familial drama simultaneously become the tool by which Morrison explores the broader situation of African Americans in the era immediately following the Civil War. As Morrison stated to

Memory and Mother Love

Christina Davis, "the discovery and affirmation of the truth about the black experience in the United States" is "the *only* preoccupation of Black American writers" ("Interview" 142). *Beloved* reworks the traditional slave narrative from a female perspective. Like Harriet Jacobs's (pseudonym Linda Brent) *Incidents in the Life of a Slave Girl*, Sethe's voyage toward freedom is complicated by the love for her children that precludes individual escape. Yet, as I hope to demonstrate, at the same time that the issues of motherhood provide a female variant of (general) slave history, they also illuminate the relationship of all of the novel's characters, both male and female, to their pain-fraught inner worlds of memory.

In an interview with Rosemarie Lester, Morrison herself insisted that she writes "without gender focus": "It happens that what provokes my imagination as a writer has to do with the culture of black people. I regard the whole world as my canvas and I write out of that sensibility of what I find provocative *and* the sensibility of being a woman. But I don't write women's literature as such. I think it would confine me. I am valuable as a writer because I am a woman, because women, it seems to me, have some special knowledge about certain things. [It comes from] the ways in which they view the world, and from women's imagination" ("Interview" 54). The intensity and depth of Morrison's understanding of mother-child bonds very clearly reflect her "special knowledge" of maternal sensibility, joy, and terror. With this knowledge, she explores the psychology of maternity both for its own value and as a vehicle by which she, as a black woman, can comprehend the legacy of slavery. Several years after manumission has become a legal reality, psychological wounds still obstruct the emergence of Sethe, Paul D, and Denver into true freedom. In the presence of the baby daughter whom she sacrificed in order to save, Sethe retastes and "rememories" the traumas of both motherhood and slave heritage. The slain daughter who returns to her family simultaneously suggests the haunting memories of a past that, like the beloved dead child, must be recognized, embraced, and openly mourned but finally laid to rest before the living can understand the present or proceed with the future.

In this first volume of a projected trilogy about African American experience, Morrison works through the voice and consciousness of former slaves recently freed in the upheavals of the Civil War. Writing through the sensibilities of people who lacked means to record permanently their own thoughts, Morrison nonetheless pursues the emotional complexity of their inner experience rather than the documented historical events in which they are embedded. Even more remarkably, Morrison focuses on the meaning of personal history of characters for whom all memory is anguish. Sethe, like Paul D, ultimately must "rememory" a past so dark and brutal that her mind has feverishly suppressed its incursions.

Sethe's story is based on the true case of Margaret Garner, an escaped slave who slit her baby's throat rather than see her recaptured into slavery (Lerner 60–63). Out of the death of Sethe's daughter, a reluctantly remembered event some sixteen years before the novel's narrative present, springs Morrison's broadest focus—the emotional destruction inflicted by the entire slave experience. The daughter's spirit persists as a "haint"—a ghost whose spiteful presence ceaselessly disrupts Sethe's present life. Pots of beans overturn, the dog is thrown into convulsions, shadowy figures appear. Both of Sethe's sons have fled and the remaining daughter, Denver, withdraws from the tension and community rejection of the family into emotional isolation and a one-sided complicity with the spirit.

In an analogous manner, memories continually intrude into Sethe's consciousness. Overwhelmed by sorrow, remorse, and a need to justify her act to the dead child itself, Sethe cannot confront memories of either her past at "Sweet Home" or of the unnamed baby: "she worked hard to remember as close to nothing as was safe. Unfortunately her brain was devious" (6). Both "visitors" from the past refuse to be forgotten, yet, in their coming, simply serve to reawaken sorrow. All her memories are either of pain inflicted by slave life or, more terribly perhaps, of lovely, cherished things tainted and blemished. "Boys hanging from the most beautiful sycamores in the world. It shamed her—remembering the wonderful soughing trees rather than the boys. Try as she might to make it otherwise, the sycamores beat out the children every time and she could not forgive her memory for that" (6). Sethe's unwilling recollections play an adversarial role. When they force their way into consciousness, her "devious" mind looks at them in horrified fascination and is rewarded with anguish. Consequently, whatever scant beauty or joy she felt in the old life must be thrust away because of the attendant pain. Things once loved cannot be cherished because their memory conceals and betrays the vicious reality that lies beneath their existence. Whole parts of her past self are suppressed. Halle, her own mother, her lost children, the beautiful trees of Sweet Home—such memories can only be admitted with shame, horror, and reluctance when they thrust their way into consciousness. Because the baby's life ended in a vivid splash of red blood, all colors that might serve as visual reminders are banished from the

Memory and Mother Love

small gray house. Every lovely thing remembered is a source of searing pain.

Sethe describes "rememory" and her fear of its power to Denver: "If a house burns down, it's gone, but the place—the picture of it—stays, and not just in my rememory, but out there, in the world. . . . The picture is still there and what's more, if you go there—you who never was there—if you go there and stand in the place where it was, it will happen again; it will be there for you, waiting for you. So, Denver, you can't never go there. Never" (36). The past lingers like a terrible trap to enmesh the unwary who attempt to revisit it. Since "nothing ever dies" totally, painful memories are avoided, skirted, shut away. All Sethe's energy for life turns on "keeping the past at bay" (42). She is unsuccessful, however, in barricading herself against the memories that continue to fascinate her with their horror, for "her brain was not interested in the future. Loaded with the past and hungry for more, it left her no room to imagine, let alone plan for, the next day" (70).

Paul D, who shared slavery at Sweet Home with Sethe and her lost husband, has also learned to "shut down a generous portion of his head" (41). After watching his friends destroyed and feeling himself bestialized by the slave experience, Paul D learned to defend himself against memories and emotions. Although this repression softens in Sethe's company, as she in his presence is tempted to "trust and rememory" (99), both Paul D and Sethe pull away from the intimate moment of shared memory to "the day's serious work of beating back the past" (73). Neither can open fully to emotional release: "Saying more might push them both to a place they couldn't get back from. He would keep the rest where it belonged: in that tobacco tin buried in his chest where a red heart used to be. Its lid rusted shut. He would not pry it loose now in front of this sweet sturdy woman, for if she got a whiff of the contents it would shame him" (72–73). In contrast, recapturing the vibrancy of the lost "red heart" of life was the source of joyful release in the ministry of Baby Suggs, Sethe's inspired mother-in-law. Her Call encouraged and supported her hearers to "lay it all down," to shatter the emotional burdens of past experience, to embrace the onslaught of feeling, unlocking and releasing both agony and longing in a wild dance of true liberation. Her message was "love your heart" (89). The debilitating price of repressing memory and emotion is evident in Paul's image of the rusty tin box that has replaced his own natural red heart. Thinking back to the prison camp where he learned to "love small," Paul comments: "to get to a place where you could love anything you chose—not to need permission for desire—well now, *that* was freedom" (162). Emotional freedom is the prerequisite for true emancipation. And such freedom in the present requires that the heart, like the physical self, be freed from the shackles of the past.

Paul D's supportive presence temporarily drives the ghost from the house. With his arrival, a palpable fragment of her past reemerges and Sethe first finds a promise of cathartic memory: "Maybe this one time she could stop dead still in the middle of a cooking meal—not even leave the stove—and feel the hurt her back ought to. Trust things and remember things because the last of the Sweet Home men was there to catch her if she sank?" (18). Within an hour of his coming, Sethe finds herself weeping over the stove in Paul D's sympathetic embrace, unburdening herself of the past. "Can't nothing heal without pain" was Amy Denver's wise maxim (78). Memory's pain helps to heal life's old wounds. For Paul D, too, the release that comes from sharing experience causes the "closed portion of his head" to open "like a greased lock" (41). For a brief, happy moment Sethe sees their shadows holding hands as she walks home from a carnival with Paul D and Denver, and she envisions a genuine future together as a family.

The baby's spirit has other needs, however. Blocked by Paul D's presence from the mother whom she desperately needs to love as well as to punish, the ghost returns as Beloved, an apparently homeless young woman who takes up residence with Sethe. Though unrecognized, Beloved wins back her mother's love, allies Denver even more closely with her, and systematically drives Paul D from the house. Since Sethe's own greatest hunger is for her lost daughter, her preoccupation with Beloved prevents the significance of Paul's absence from fully registering. She needs to release her thwarted maternal love as she once needed to give milk to her nursing daughter. Beloved feels the even more overpowering need of a psychological infant for her mother's presence, love, and smile.

With the reunion of mother and daughter, Sethe and Beloved emotionally reenter the past by recreating their intimate mother-child bond. Locked in the past herself, Beloved demands to be told stories about the old life, Sweet Home, and her mother's crystal earrings that she played with as a baby. She finds extreme pleasure only in personal memory because there *she* exists, just as Denver only wants to hear that part of her mother's escape story that centers on her own birth. And as Sethe begins to tell those stories, she finds "an unexpected pleasure" in the endeavor and soon discovers herself "wanting to, liking it" (58). Memories no longer intrude like guerrilla adversaries, for the past has been openly recognized, recaptured, and embraced. After the reunion, an exhilarating harmony fills the house and their lives. From this ecstatic moment arises the rhapsodic trio with which we began; in the reconstructed past, mother and daughters proclaim their mutuality, their absorption in each other, and the identity of their interests.

The Consuming Passion

The primary material manifestation of emotional exchange in *Beloved* is mother's milk, which is cherished, offered, stolen, and remembered as a tangible emblem of nurturant love. For Sethe, the milk her own fieldhand mother was forbidden to give her rankles in memory as the oldest of her wounds. When she herself fled slavery, nine months pregnant, the milk streaming from her nursing breasts provided the impetus to persevere, reminding her always that she had to get that milk to her baby. Here, as in Morrison's other novels, the disruption of the nursing function signals problems in the cultural as well as in the maternal realms. Peter Erickson describes the displacement in *Tar Baby* of Therese's ever-copious "magic breasts" by Enfamil, just as the "sacred properties" of maternity are threatened in the same novel by Jadine's sterile independence and as traditional black culture crumbles before white industrial greed. Ruth Foster prolongs grotesquely the nursing relationship with her son in a desperate attempt to forge for herself an identity against the "Dead" heritage of her husband's commercial assimilationism *(Song of Solomon)*. For Sethe, the memory of the milk violently wrested from her breasts by the mossy-toothed nephew of Schoolmaster continually recalls the brutal degradations foisted upon female slaves and her own inability to provide her children freely with all that the milk embodied: nurturance, care, and life itself. Sethe hungers to proffer those qualities still; she experiences a harmonious moment at dinner with Paul D and both girls as verification of her ability to provide "milk for all" (100), as she earlier had nourished both newborn Denver and the crawling daughter. And at the moment when Sethe recognizes Beloved's true identity, she and her daughters are sharing cups of warm milk around their fire.

Beloved's return to reclaim the physical and emotional nurturance from which she was prematurely weaned at first seems to be a positive event. Sethe and both daughters experience giddy bliss, rapturous tranquility, and an intimate sense of communion with each other as they whirl on the ice and snuggle in swaddling quilts with their cups of warm milk. For the first time in their tortured lives, moments of harmony and happiness seem possible. Christina Davis considers the moment of shared milk and swaddled warmth "the symbolic peak of the interaction among the three women and their search for identity: from this moment on, they will move toward a redefinition which implies a positive individuality" (155). From the perspective of psychological development, maturing into a truly "positive individuality" is the normal and desirable result of such mother-child intimacy as the three women recapture in this extraordinarily seductive moment. Yet only Denver moves decisively toward any sort of individuation. Beloved is locked by death into a fixed mind-set, and Sethe's future remains as ambiguous as the question mark of her last words in the book. Instead, Morrison explores the dangers of retreat into the past by examining the destructiveness of prolonged mutual dependence of mother and child. Intimate union becomes an incipient struggle for domination.

Morrison has previously explored "thick love," or obsessive maternity, which complements the destructive potential of infantile demand. The same maternal warmth, "thick and dark as Alaga syrup," which enshrouds the narrator of *The Bluest Eye,* can grow beyond control to emerge with destructive force. When Nel Wright attempts to compensate for her husband's desertion by clutching her children more tightly, her love for them metastasizes into "something so thick and monstrous she was afraid to show it lest it break loose and smother them with its heavy paw. A cumbersome bear-love that, given any rein, would suck their breath away in its crying need for honey" (*Sula* 138). Sethe's love, too, crushes both herself and her "baby" beneath the weight of maternal desire. She is not merely a passive victim of an insatiable ghost child, but is herself obsessed with reclaiming their severed mutuality. Her uterine waters break at the very moment that Beloved appears, signaling a second birth and renewed mother-infant relationship with this adult-bodied baby. "Maternal love is the almost perfect counterpart for the love for the mother" (Balint 101). Even in an ordinary family, mother and child exist as complementary nodes of a single biological unit (Winnicott 588). Because her *uncommon* experience of motherhood was deformed by slavery, Sethe now binds herself over to "normal" maternal activities with self-annihilating fervor. She lavishes all imaginable care, effort, and willing service on her returned child. Sewing bright dresses, embellishing the house with flowers, planting tasty rarities in the vegetable garden, playing games, and endlessly braiding Beloved's hair—Sethe attempts to provide whatever will delight her daughter, to the exclusion of securing for her family the necessities of life and basic sustenance. The family begins to starve when Sethe loses her job because of these maternal obsessions.

In the process of recreating Beloved's aborted infancy, Sethe obliterates the present and the possibility of future development. Her daughter's return ironically convinces Sethe that she no longer needs painful memories: "Think about all I ain't got to remember no more. Do like Baby said: Think on it then lay it down—for good. Paul D convinced me there was a world out there and that I could live in it. Should have known better. *Did* know better. Whatever is going on outside my door ain't for me. The world is in this room. This here's all there is and all there needs to be" (182–83). Sethe inverts Baby Suggs's intention. Baby Suggs, the visionary of the heart's call, counseled "laying down" the past as a precondition for engaging with the emotional range of the present. Sethe is able to abandon memories here because her past, embodied in Beloved, has forcibly reentered the present. Yet *past* it remains, and Sethe resigns herself ecstatically to the world of the dead child locked within her own room.

For Beloved herself, the binding grip of memory is inescapable. Her psychological development arrested forever at death, she can no more outgrow her dependence on Sethe's smile than she can alter the past. Indeed, the past that she occupies transcends her own short personal biography. Though this ghost child is miraculously endowed by Morrison with an individual voice and consciousness, Beloved also is enmeshed in the general history of her ancestors. In the lyric passage with which we began, Beloved not only speaks from her specific fictional perspective of a dead daughter longing for renewed union with her mother; at the same time, she images herself as an African captive on a slave ship. Her dream-memory of death merges with a racial nightmare of "the middle passage." The dark waters from which Beloved has returned are simultaneously the seas that buoy up the slave ship and into which the dead Africans are tossed. Since Sethe's mother endured the passage, the line of mothers and daughters returns full circle as Beloved's experience melds into that of her own grandmother. This is the ultimate nightmare of memory: one child's particular death cleaves open a wound so deep that it reaches back to the moment of enslavement. Like the spirit realm across the bridge that envelops Morrison's world of the living, a complexly woven fabric of history enshrouds each separate new hurt and injustice.[2]

"The woman with my face" figures prominently in both aspects of the vision. As always, the child both identifies herself with the mother and mimetically repeats her actions. The infant mind of Beloved/the captive perceives her own death as the mother's death and envisions the loss or desertion of "her woman" as the woman's body being dumped into the sea with other dead captives on ship. "She goes in the water   with my face" (212). Yet it is Beloved, of course, who reemerges from the water and out of the spirit realm of death. Yearning for the mother-figure is balanced on the slave ship by the presence of a dead man lying across the speaker's face, whom the captive child loves although he obstructs her view of the woman. If this image bears significance for Beloved's personal history, the dead man may be a dim recollection of her lost father Halle or, possibly, may recall Beloved's sexual union with Paul D, who also bars her from Sethe. In either case, a triangular "family romance" surfaces; the adult male is both wooed and resented by the child because he is a barrier to the mother.

Beloved returns with a ferocious hunger. On the slave ship that transports her to death, "I do not eat" (210). The sea, into which the dead Africans are tossed and from which Beloved herself reemerges (certainly an image of death itself), is the color of the moldy bread given the captives to eat, and that bread, in turn, is "sea colored." Beloved is "too hungry to eat it" (211). After Beloved's reunion with Sethe, Morrison's language emphasizes the use of milk and food as instruments of cannibalistic struggle between mother and child as well as means for sustenance. In her hallucinatory imagery, Beloved envisions realizing "the join" with Sethe through mutual oral consumption: "I want to join   she whispers to me   she whispers   I reach for her chewing and swallowing   she touches me   she knows I want to join   she chews and swallows me   I am gone   now I am her face" (213). Swallowing or being swallowed by the mother is Beloved's fantasized image for total unity. When she gazes at her mother, "Sethe was licked, tasted, eaten by Beloved's eyes" (57). The sadistic quality of such insatiable orality quickly becomes evident: as Sethe does give herself over to Beloved's demands, her own body and energies shrivel to a mere specter while Beloved grows fatter day by day. Because the ghost has returned with the body, powers, and faculties of a young adult, she is able to satisfy her voracious demands

Memory and Mother Love

upon the mother more completely than any ordinary child can hope to do. The infant literally devours its mother's substance.[3]

The hunger that haunts the novel's conclusion is both physical and metaphoric. Yearning for completion through another person is as impossible to satisfy as the concurrent desire to which Sethe binds herself over—to find a full life within the past. In either case, total submersion constitutes self-annihilation. After the rapturous interlude of harmony and warm milk around the fire, Sethe and her child embrace in a deadly struggle, "starving but locked in a love that wore everybody out" (243). Though pent-up love overwhelms Sethe, she is unable to justify her act to Beloved (and to herself) as she yearns to do. Numerous psychological torments emerge here, as Sethe unleashes her general guilt about the past and confusion over her chosen course of action, "trying to persuade Beloved, the one and only person she felt she had to convince, that what she had done was right because it came from true love" (251). She expends all her energy without appeasing Beloved, who reacts with fury to any imagined or recollected lapses of love and attention. As Sethe realizes in a lucid moment, "Unless carefree, motherlove was a killer" (132). Although the novel exquisitely evokes the fervent and sacrificial devotion of maternity, no sentimentality clouds Morrison's cautionary note. The moment of recognition and reunion with the dead child, the destroyed fragment of a past self, is rapturous and satisfying. Yet it must remain a stepping-stone and not the ground of existence. Both mother-infant bonding and rememory are essential for human survival, yet either, if unrestrained, devours the agents.

Maturity, Individuation, and Community

Morrison seems to offer the same route to liberation from the constricting vortices of both mother-infant merger and rememoried pain, a route that lies in the common strategies for individuation seized upon by maturing children. Maturation is synonymous with "the infant's change from being merged with the mother to being separate from her, or to relating to her as separate and 'not me'" (Winnicott 589). Nel Wright, accordingly, is able to envision her own autonomy only at the moment of detachment from her mother. When Helene inappropriately smiles at the white conductor who humiliates her, Nel's image of her domineering mother dissolves into "custard," ending her trusting dependence. Her subsequent flash of recognition signals the dawn of maturity: "I'm me. I'm not their daughter. I'm not Nel. I'm me. Me" (*Sula* 28). Similarly, Sethe's runaway sons, Howard and Buglar, marked their emergence into maturity by physically separating themselves from their mother. Denver, who has the most complex relationship with their mother, moves into the most satisfying future life by establishing new bonds within her community.[4] For Beloved, however, frozen in emotional time, such growth is impossible.

Morrison's novels repeatedly parallel dysfunctional maternal and community bonds. Medallion's hostility to Sula's free and self-sufficient behavior completes the pattern of alienation inaugurated by her mother's detachment. Bereft of parental love, the "orphaned" children confront with equal pain the decaying of the cultural community. Pilate, singular in her defiance of loss, not only birthed herself from her dead mother's body but, in addition, alone preserves and transmits the narrative history of her ancestors *(Song of Solomon)*. Few of Morrison's other characters, however, can duplicate Pilate's transcendence of isolation. Pecola *(The Bluest Eye)* is scarred like Sethe by the dissolution of the maternal bond, yet her corollary loss is of any warm support system such as that which sustained Cholly through his own mother's abandonment. Pecola's inability to make contact with either her distant and critical mother or Aunt Jimmie's rural feminine community renders her defenseless against the literal and figurative rapes that destroy her. Failed marigold seeds and the hostile earth that kills them end *The Bluest Eye* with a metaphor for the nurturance irretrievably lost in the inhospitable chill of North Lorain, Ohio. In *Tar Baby*, Jadine not only rejects her own maternal possibilities and her duties as a daughter but simultaneously forsakes her African American cultural roots. Before leaving the Caribbean for Paris and her white suitor, she replicates the judgment of her European art training: "Picasso *is* better than an Itumba mask. The fact that he was intrigued by them is proof of *his* genius, not the mask-makers'" (74). But to grow beyond the isolation and anguish of orphanhood, Morrison suggests, such cultural and community bonds must be reestablished.

As anticipated in Morrison's earlier novels, the community also emerges as the proper successor to excessive mother-child identification.[5] These two relationships properly complement rather than contest each other. Milkman's return to Shalimar and reconnection to his mythic heritage triggers his mature consciousness of love and gratitude toward his mother and Pilate, the two women who gave him life although "he had never so much as made either of them a cup of tea"

Memory and Mother Love

(*Song of Solomon* 331). So, too, integration into the Cincinnati community enables Denver to return to Sethe with meaningful aid.

Because the house on Bluestone Road is shunned by neighbors and therefore isolated, Denver's early dependence on her mother continues until Paul D arrives. Denver's first venture out of the yard at age seven to Lady Jones's parlor schoolroom taught her the joys of learning adult skills and enjoying a peer group. Yet when one of the children initiated Denver into her own family secrets, her response was to retreat permanently into the safe womb of the house and into herself. At the same time, her "monstrous and unmanageable dreams about Sethe" began: she, like her brothers, dreads that "dark thing" in her mother that might emerge again and claim her as its next victim. In Denver's section of the lyric trio, she recalls her fantasy that Sethe "cut my head off every night. Howard and Buglar told me she would and she did" (206). "I spent all of my outside self loving Ma'am so she wouldn't kill me" (207). This ambivalence captures the emotions of a child who is ready but unable to break away from the mother. Since a submerged ego is a "dead" ego, one without an autonomous identity, Denver's anxiety about her own nonexistence is projected onto her mother as a murderous impulse.

In her loneliness, Denver created a fantasy alliance with the ghost sister, Sethe's "other" victim. Yet with Beloved's return, the mutual intensity of Sethe and Beloved's interest in each other weaves a wall that separates Denver from both her ambivalently loved mother and her sister-surrogate. She must find another focus for affection, a new strategy for life. At the same time, Denver realizes that her mother, not Beloved, is being destroyed by their intense submersion of identities. She watches Sethe dwindle away as Beloved grows plump and viciously demanding.

When Denver finally leaves her own yard for the first time in years, she feels that she is stepping off the "edge." She stumbles away in absolute, uninformed terror about the unknown world, the whites who live "out there," and the threat of all experiences and feelings that lurk beyond the safe house, the mother's embrace, and her own inward focus. She finds, however, immediate support and a new life of contentment independent of both mother and sister. Denver rediscovers what is perhaps the most successful strategy for adult development: she replaces the solitary maternal bond with a larger community of adults and opens herself to an empathetic network of fellows. First with food offerings and friendly support and finally by banding together in an ancient wordless song to drive out the insatiable ghost, the women of the community "inaugurated her life in the world as a woman" (248). In a conflation of goals from slave narratives and domestic romance, Denver gains a paying job, an interested male friend, and reading skills. Paul D, also driven out of the house by Beloved's power, similarly finds himself newly integrated into the community. Both Denver and Paul D learn to function independently within a group, no longer emotionally dependent on a single person but open to a web of relationships and thus able to feel whole and function freely. Ready to receive support from the community, they are also ready to contribute to it.

Morrison once wistfully envisioned an artist's private and public aspects coexisting in a balanced state of harmony. She compared her ideal to the shouts of worshipers in a black church, where individual emotions are aired publicly within a supportive community: "It is a very personal grief and a personal statement done among people you trust. Done within the context of the community, therefore safe. And while the shouter is performing some rite that is extremely subjective, the other people are performing as a community in protecting that person" ("Rootedness" 339). In the outskirts of Cincinnati, Baby Suggs's Call made possible just such a connectedness. In her presence men, women, and children laughed, danced, wept, and sang out their deepest private yearnings within the fabric of community support that she created. Both Denver and Paul discover the comfort and enhanced strength of existence provided by that fabric.

The women of the Cincinnati outskirts are also able, as a group, to unite their power and reclaim a member fallen from fellowship. Though alienated from Sethe since her baby's death, the community responds decisively to her personal need. Mobilized by Janey and Ella, the thirty women arrive armed only with their voices to exorcise a demon. At Ella's shout, the women "took a step back to the beginning" where "there were no words": "For Sethe it was as though the Clearing had come to her with all its heat and simmering leaves, where the voices of women searched for the right combination, the key, the code, the sound that broke the back of words. Building voice upon voice until they found it, and when they did it was a wave of sound wide enough to sound deep water and knock the pods off chestnut trees. It broke over Sethe and she trembled like the baptized in its wash" (261). In the next moment, Bodwin arrives, Sethe mistakes him for Schoolmaster and attempts to kill him, Denver wrestles her mother to the ground, and Beloved disappears. In the background of these nearly instantaneous events sounds the ancient moan of the thirty women, their song and presence the catalyst for action. As a community they have enabled Denver to mature and Paul

Memory and Mother Love

to regain his strength; now the community wrestles with Beloved for her mother's attentions.

The acute anxiety that for many young children attends the mother's presence and absence apparently contains a threat far more apocalyptic than adults can imagine. Without that maternal presence, psychoanalysts report, the child actually fears that its self and identity might physically disintegrate (Winnicott 589). Just such a threat hovered over Beloved earlier, when her mother brought Paul D back into her bed. As Paul anticipated fathering a new baby, which would dislodge the other daughters from their mother's sole affection, Beloved saw one of her teeth effortlessly dislodge from her mouth and felt despair: "This is it. Next would be her arm, her hand, a toe. Pieces of her would drop maybe one at a time, maybe all at once. Or on one of those mornings before Denver woke and after Sethe left she would fly apart" (133). And indeed Beloved finally does evaporate at the climax of the novel. Unlike a normal child, Beloved cannot mature into a healthy member of the community; her particular demands upon the mother cannot coexist with other relationships of support, nor, unchecked, could she permit Sethe to maintain extramaternal bonds. When her mother's focus is momentarily diverted by the exorcising wail of the women, Beloved vanishes into air.

Like the community, Sethe and Paul's incipient relationship also promised mutual support before it shattered under the force of Beloved's presence. Paul D borrows an image for their friendship from Sixo's description of his woman: "She is a friend of my mind. She gather me, man. The pieces I am, she gather them and give them back to me in all the right order" (272). Like the submersion of child in mother, a mature adult relationship holds together the pieces of a person. But whereas a child depends totally on the mother to fuse the pieces into a wholeness and viability that they otherwise would not possess, Sixo and Paul begin from an acceptance of the piecemeal nature of identity. The pieces of the self, like the fragments of the past that haunt us, are varied and contentious. But they do cohere. Not the existence of identity but its right order is fragile. The novel's conclusion affirms the regenerative power of two nurturant adult relationships: a heterosexual union and the support of the black community.

Sethe's final words ambiguously point to the possibility of her own self reemerging from the maternal abyss. "Me? Me?" she asks in response to Paul D's assertion that she herself, not the dead child, is her "own best thing" that she needs to nourish and feed. She names her self apart from

Beloved, yet in a question form. The novel can be read either as reasserting Sethe's "me" or questioning its existence. Queried by Christina Davis about the equally open-ended conclusions of *Tar Baby* and *Song of Solomon*, Morrison connected her choice to the African American oral tradition: "You don't end a story in the oral tradition—you can have the little message at the end, your little moral, but the ambiguity is deliberate because it doesn't end, it's an ongoing thing and the reader or the listener is in it and you have to THINK" ("Interview" 149).

Coda

"It was not a story to pass on," insists the novel's coda. Despite the "footprints" that come and go, the histories of the sixty million African Americans to whom Morrison dedicates the book have been forgotten "like an unpleasant dream." Morrison reinscribes the footprints and renames the nameless forgotten ones "Beloved." To comprehend that past, Morrison invokes the complex range of maternal emotion. This most deeply seated of human feelings must have been violently stretched, tested, and deformed in the lives that preceded our own. At the same time, mother love serves as a metaphor for memory of the past. The alternatives of pre-oedipal suffocation and reciprocal adult relations also suggest the possibilities for reconnecting with the past: resistance, total preoccupation and submergence, or a tenacious awareness that carries remembrance into the present as an essential component of an emancipated future. *Beloved* reclaims a previously unwritten portion of black history, a task that Morrison insists to Christina Davis is "paramount in its importance": "You have to stake it out and identify those who have preceded you—resummoning them, acknowledging them is just one step in that process of reclamation—so that they are always there as the *confirmation* and the affirmation of the life that I personally have not lived but is the life of that organism to which I belong which is black people in this country" ("Interview" 142–43). Morrison enables us to glimpse the tremblings and uncertainties with which the first generation after the Civil War must have embarked on life as a freed people, bearing their legacy of scarred memory. At the same time, the historical dimension continues to impinge on life in the present. As in a healthy maternal bonding, each person must be able to recognize, name, and embrace that lost part of history without becoming terminally submerged in its anguish and injustice. Acknowledging both loving identification with "the child" and anxiety about engulfment, Morrison offers us a route into the future.

Notes

1. For an overview of the psychoanalytic literature about mother-infant relationships, see Chodorow 57–91.

2. Morrison considers the African American tradition of connection to a benevolent spirit world and one's ancestors in "Rootedness" (343). In *Beloved* the dead, unappeased by life, are not the concerned helpers that Morrison describes but instead, like the dead man on the captive girl's face, suffocate the living.

3. Freud cites the recurrent charge that the mother gave too little milk, for too short a time, as maturing daughters' perennial rationalization for turning away from their mothers. Freud considers early weaning in Western society as a cause of such pervasive anger, then demurs: "But I am not sure whether, if one analyzed children who had been suckled as long as those of primitive races, one would not encounter the same complaint. So great is the greed of the childish libido!" (Freud 289).

4. Winnicott points out that when a prolonged merging of maternal-infant identities prohibits development, a child has only two choices—permanent regression in merger with or total rejection of the mother (592). Nancy Chodorow, in her study of gender differences in development, concludes that boys are more easily able to experience themselves as separate from their mothers than are girls (164–70). Her theory accords with the strategies of Sethe's four children. While Howard and Buglar achieve separation through physical rejection, Beloved never outgrows identification, and Denver moves into empathetic connection.

5. Numerous articles emphasize the crucial role of community (particularly a community of women) in Morrison's earlier novels: see Christian, Denard, Harris, and O'Shaughnessy. Morrison herself comments that the recurring presence of a chorus in her novels captures the community's viewpoint ("Rootedness" 341).

Works Cited

Balint, Alice. "Love for the Mother and Mother Love." *Primary Love and Psychoanalytic Technique*. Ed. Michael Balint. London: Tavistock, 1965. 91–108.

Chodorow, Nancy. *The Reproduction of Mothering: Psychoanalysis and the Sociology of Gender*. Berkeley: U of California P, 1978.

Christian, Barbara. "Community and Nature: The Novels of Toni Morrison." *Journal of Ethnic Studies* 7.4 (1980): 65–78.

Davis, Christina. "*Beloved:* A Question of Identity." *Présence Africaine* ns 145 (1988): 151–56.
Denard, Carolyn. "The Convergence of Feminism and Ethnicity in the Fiction of Toni Morrison." McKay 171–79.
Erickson, Peter B. "Images of Nurturance in Toni Morrison's *Tar Baby.*" *College Language Association Journal* 28 (1984): 11–32.
Freud, Sigmund. "Female Sexuality." *International Journal of Psycho-Analysis* 13 (1932): 281–97.
Harris, Trudier. "Reconnecting Fragments: Afro-American Folk Tradition in *The Bluest Eye.*" McKay 68–76.
Lerner, Gerda. "The Case of Margaret Garner." *Black Women in White America.* New York: Random, 1972. 60–63.
McKay, Nellie, ed. *Critical Essays on Toni Morrison.* Boston: G. K. Hall, 1988.
Morrison, Toni. *Beloved.* New York: Knopf, 1987.
―――. *The Bluest Eye.* New York: Holt, 1970.
―――. "Interview with Toni Morrison." With Christina Davis. *Présence Africaine* ns 145 (1988): 141–50.
―――. "An Interview with Toni Morrison, Hessian Radio Network, Frankfurt, West Germany." With Rosemarie K. Lester. 47–54.
―――. "Rootedness: The Ancestor as Foundation." *Black Women Writers (1950–1980): A Critical Evaluation.* Ed. Mari Evans. Garden City, NY: Anchor/Doubleday, 1984. 339–45.
―――. *Song of Solomon.* New York: Knopf, 1977.
―――. *Sula.* New York: Knopf, 1973.
―――. *Tar Baby.* New York: Knopf, 1981.
O'Shaughnessy, Kathleen. " 'Life life life life': The Community as Chorus in *Song of Solomon.*" McKay 125–35.
Winnicott, D. W. "The Theory of the Parent-Infant Relationship." *International Journal of Psycho-Analysis* 41 (1960): 585–95.

Maxine Hong Kingston's Fake Books

DEBRA SHOSTAK

> "That's it, my present to you," said Wittman. "Got no money. Got no home. Got story."
> —Maxine Hong Kingston, *Tripmaster Monkey: His Fake Book*

Maxine Hong Kingston has noted that she relishes the discrepancies that emerge when her brothers and sisters share with her their memories of events from their family's history: "sometimes there's disagreement, like when one brother said 'That wasn't opium the men were smoking,' and my other brother said 'Oh yes, it was. That *was* opium.' And I like that difference in seeing because it could have been either way; one remembered it one way and one the other. That gives me two stories for one event" (Interview 14). Clearly, her interest lies less in history per se than in events as they are remembered; that is, the past provides pleasure and meaning not insofar as it is reconstructed authoritatively (as if such reconstruction were possible), but rather to the degree that memories provide a record of human participation in recreating the past. That accounts of the past are multiple and contradictory is a testament to human invention instead of a failure of record keeping.

Kingston reminds us that "history" includes the variable possibilities of memory, and each of her books is an attempt to weave an understanding of the historical experience of being Chinese-American. Scraps of memory—Kingston's own memories, as well as those of her family—provide the warp, while story, lore, and fantasy supply the weft. *The Woman Warrior* (1977), *China Men* (1980), and *Tripmaster Monkey: His Fake Book* (1989) all complicate our understanding of what constitutes memory, how memory can document the past, and how the past itself is plural. Kingston's narratives accomplish this feat by their metafictional self-references; she foregrounds the act of storytelling as the means by which culture is remembered and transmitted. She is by no means alone in her assault on positivist assumptions about historiography. In exploring how humans use narrative to make sense of the past, for example, the historian Louis O. Mink works to unseat the "commonsense" distinction between history and fiction (129). Hayden White presses the point further, arguing that historical narratives are "verbal fictions, the contents of which are as much invented as found and the forms of which have more in common with their counterparts in literature than they have with those in the sciences" (42); he insists, however, that the formal character of historical narratives "in no way detracts from the status as knowledge that we ascribe to historiography" (61). The point here is that narrative, whatever its purposes and materials, by definition both creates—rather than reflects—story and draws on formal conventions. It provides a way of knowing the real world, building knowledge according to the familiar patterns of story. Like other approaches to knowledge, narrative finds a primary source in memory. Memory can serve as a kind of narrating subject, making coherent wholes out of meaningless fragments, and White's conclusions are key in explaining how the selective and inventive functions of memory construct knowledge by reconstructing versions of the past.

The powers of memory are inextricable from those of the imagination in their workings and effects. Both are inventive, both work from pieces of material reality, and both strive for coherence. As Mary Warnock has observed, "in recalling something, we are employing imagination; ... in imagining something, exploring it imaginatively, we use memory" (76). Memory's ability to engender knowledge is particularly significant in the development of a multiethnic historical record. For self or community to be identified as multiethnic, it must derive from at least two places, locales that are either literally (spatially) or figuratively (culturally) distinct, and often at great distance from one another. The self or group then resides at significant remove from at least one of the home places, real or symbolic. Because identity originates in one's knowledge of personal and group history—that is, in accounts of events involving known actors in particularized places—the multiethnic person defines him- or herself in part by what he or she is absent from. In general, memory is *about* absence. It concerns itself with the pastness of time past and with filling gaps in the known continuum of experience. The imaginative capacity of memory to recover and reinvent images and ideas of absent places bridges the locales, supplying a crucial sense of self.[1] Where knowledge of the past may be obscured by geographical, temporal, and social conditions, as in the historical understandings of a people dispossessed of a sense of place, memory most poignantly takes on the fundamental character described by Natalie Zemon Davis and Randolph Starn:

Maxine Hong Kingston's Fake Books

it is "a substitute, surrogate, or consolation for something that is missing," an "index of loss" (3, 4). As Kingston shows in each of her books, memory becomes an obvious source for the past both when the past remains undocumented in conventional ways and when the events of the past have been played out thousands of miles distant from those who would recover and retell them. Such has been the historiographical predicament of what Kingston terms the "brief and dying culture" of Chinese America (*Tripmaster* 6). This culture lasted approximately a century, from the waves of Chinese immigration during the 1850s and 1860s to the evidence of assimilation over the last few decades, found by Ronald Takaki among such clues as the " 'Yappies'—'young Asian professionals'—[who] drive BMWs, wear designer clothes, and congregate at continental restaurants" (79, 4). Especially for Chinese-Americans like Kingston, living at the latter end of the "dying" culture's century, the vacuum of historical identity created by immigration and assimilation can be, at least in part, filled by the imaginative exercise of memory.

Significantly, Kingston envisions memory not only as the product of individual consciousness, but also as a communal phenomenon, most noticeable in the oral tradition of storytelling, in which stories recount the lives and events, real or apocryphal, that support a culture's understanding of itself.[2] Public texts, either orally transmitted or fixed in written documents, in what Dominick LaCapra calls "textualized remainders" (128), serve as the material of both private and cultural memory. Kingston gives access to these textualized remainders—which may be myths, legends, histories, films, novels, poems, or plays—by quoting them directly, by alluding to them, and by retelling them. Kingston's writings draw attention to the very documents that might be used in writing history, the texts of a culture, and at once both undermine and validate their authority as documentary evidence. The nature of the evidence is responsible for this effect: because many of the "documents" have been transmitted orally rather than written, they are plural and, frequently, contradictory.

The plurality of the historical record, conceived in this manner, might seem at first glance to limit its value as historical knowledge. Not only are the textualized remainders in large part verbal fictions, but they also almost by definition compete among themselves for authoritative status. Kingston, however, has the tradition of Chinese letters behind her implied critique of positivist historiography. The classic novels of Chinese dynastic history (compiled between the fourteenth and the eighteenth centuries, and upon several of which Kingston draws heavily in *Tripmaster Monkey*) were culled from the elaborate and lengthy plots of storytellers, who were known to tell a single story over the course of months or a year during many storytelling sessions at the local teahouse (Hsia 9). A novelist—the literate compiler of oral materials—might have a wealth of versions, variations, and embellishments at the disposal of his fictive imagination. At the same time, the novels were based on historical events, and the storytellers whose stories the novelists whittled into shape had always, according to C. T. Hsia, "honored the convention of treating fiction as fact" (16). Like the storytellers and their audiences, writers and readers drew no distinction between the fictive and the "real" to limit the authenticity of the novelistic accounts as historical, and this is borne out in the dynastic novels' reception, since they were generally "written and read as popular history" (16). Within the culture to which the stories were addressed, then, their authority as sources of historical knowledge was not in question, and this despite both their accommodation to the novelist's aesthetic and imaginative play and their inclusion of fantastic and supernatural episodes.

In a sense, Kingston, her sources, and I are all collapsing one of the important distinctions between oral and written culture—that between the fluidity and diversity of oral transmissions and the fixity of the written word, which appears to carry the weight of authority in its very stasis. The classic Chinese novels that stabilized the dynastic stories obliterated or elided the differences among those stories, seeming to offer to their readership the "facts" of the past. Likewise, Kingston's fashioning of fragmented memories and textualized remainders gives the illusion of the whole cloth of experience, but when she exposes the source of historical knowledge as narration—as the *process* of narrating and comprehending narrative—she makes the oral/written distinction, as well as its implied difference in authority, consistently evasive.[3] If history is known through stories, what does it matter whether the stories are told or read? In any event, whatever illusion of definitiveness Kingston's recorded narration maintains in her readership is soon punctured, since even where the sources are written documents, the memories they constitute made comparatively static, their meanings are nonetheless transformed by their recitation in a culture—and, often, a language—alien to their place of origin.

Transformation, of course, is an essential principle of oral culture. Each storyteller puts his or her personal stamp on the story, and each telling is different. Memory and invention are the supreme authorities, and no version carries greater truth value than another. In fact, as Barbara Herrnstein Smith has argued, narrative versions remind us that

> For any particular narrative, there is no single *basically* basic story subsisting beneath it but, rather, an unlimited number of other narratives that can be *constructed in response* to it or *perceived as related* to it. . . .
> . . . For any given narrative, there are always *multiple* basic stories that can be constructed in response to it because basic-ness is always arrived at by the exercise of some set of operations, in accord with some set of principles, that reflect some set of interests, all of which are, by nature, variable and thus multiple. (217, Smith's emphasis)

That there is no "basic" story suggests that those who participate in a culture are free to reinvent stories in accord with their—and their culture's—principles and interests, without losing power or truth value as the stories are transformed.

This is notably useful in a multiethnic setting, like that of Kingston's Chinese-American culture, where the source materials are widely disparate in language and custom; their revision allows for an emerging body of "texts," both oral and written, that is truly multicultural. In other words, Kingston's use of both Chinese and American cultural references, in quotations, allusions, and embedded legends, begins the work of documenting a unique Chinese-American culture. These public texts, re-imagined in terms of Chinese-American experience, both emerge from the memories of that culture and its members and become its common memory. Were Kingston not to reinvent her source materials, her narratives would be marred by an either/or fallacy—each textualized remainder would be either Chinese (in translation), or American (in English),[4] but not convincingly integrated so as to provide historical identity to Chinese-American experience. Recreation, rather than simple repetition or translation, is essential. As Joanne Frye notes, in exploring Kingston's use of legends in *The Woman Warrior*, "The stories . . . become interpretive strategies for her own lived experience as a female and are never severed from that experience. Each story . . . interacts profoundly with the foundation narrative of her own immediate experience: the autobiography of fact, of daily lived reality" (298). In like manner, the public texts Kingston incorporates to tell her culture's story are no longer discrete or independent; they, too, become enmeshed with the daily and more broadly historical lives of Chinese-Americans.

Kingston recognizes how liberating narrative can be, both for the storyteller and for the culture about whom (and/or to whom) the story is told, because one can shape the products of memory—and so their meaning—through selection, elaboration, and context. She put the issue succinctly, from another direction: "Somehow I think there's something wrong with oral histories. People are treating them like *sacred* material when what they are is *raw* material" ("This is the Story" 6, Kingston's emphasis). The process Kingston advocates revises memory itself, and transformation keeps meanings vital in cultures, which are always themselves evolving. As she remarked in a 1987 address, "Mythology dies if you don't change it" ("Moving Images"). In a sense, what her work suggests is a way to recapture in writing the fluidity of oral transmission, which she sees as functioning actively in the world. Kingston told Arturo Islas that the oral tradition "has the impact of command, of directly influencing action. . . . Writing is static. The story will remain as printed for the next two hundred years and it's not going to change. That really bothers me, because what would be wonderful would be for the words to change on the page every time, but they can't. The way I tried to solve this problem was to keep ambiguity in the writing all the time" (Interview 18). Memory for Kingston is both bearer and transformer of culture, and it is precisely at the point of ambiguity, where it seems possible that the words are changing on the page to reflect contradictory memories, that transformation begins. The transformation is of conventionally Chinese or Western cultural material into specifically Chinese-American material, in order to construct a Chinese-American past.

It is important to consider precisely what material Kingston chooses for her sources, because she links popular and "high" cultures in her attempt to devise a multiethnic past. Included among the public texts she quotes or alludes to are Chinese legends and ballads, which emerge from a long tradition of oral transmission and which bridge the gap in paradoxical ways. While several of the Chinese legends she draws on are classic codifications of popular oral stories, the form in which they are available to Kingston—as novels—may be seen as a reaction against the oral tradition (Hsia 11).[5] Despite their attempts to give the seal of authority to selected narrative versions, however, the novels were at first disdained for their vernacular style by the contemporaneous scholarly elite trained to esteem poetry, philosophy, essays, and commentaries on the classics of the Chou dynasty (ca. 1027–256 B.C.) and to despise colloquial stories (Scott 18). Nevertheless, as Arthur Waley has observed, the novels "were read by everybody who could read, although nobody probably would admit having read them. And schoolboys were severely punished for having read and enjoyed them" (Wu 3). These novels became so widely known that, as Kingston reports in *Tripmaster Monkey,* they were performed as plays among Chinese immigrants in nineteenth-century America. That is, the novelistic form that endeavored to make the historical record literate never fully succeeded in wresting the material from the hands of public performers and storytellers, and this parallel tradition of letters and oral recitation is part of what seems to fascinate Kingston about her Chinese cultural legacy. The idea of narrative to which Kingston first drew attention in the "talk-stories" of *The Woman Warrior* precisely captures this parallel. As a child she heard legends and familial stories, which her book fixes and attempts to understand, by remembering (and re-membering) them and making them coherent within an interpretive scheme. At the same time, she recaptures the very changeability of their nature as oral artifacts, presenting her uncertainty about their details as well as their uneasy relationship to historical "fact."

In addition to retelling the talk-stories about China, Kingston massively incorporates Western materials that likewise emerge from both popular and educated culture. This is particularly true in *Tripmaster Monkey*. In Kingston's last book and only novel, one finds the most extravagant array of quotations, allusions, and embedded stories—in fact, one might argue that the whole point of the novel is to weave a Chinese-American fabric out of snippets of apparently unrelated cultural memories.[6] In the novel, Robert Service's poetry rubs shoulders with excerpts from Whitman and Rilke; the meditations of the protagonist shift from *Hamlet* to *West Side Story*. Clearly, for Kingston, the effort to understand a multiethnic historical identity makes any cultural influences fair game, but there is another explanation as well, most visible in *Tripmaster Monkey*, but applying convincingly to both *China Men* and *The Woman Warrior*. The clue can be found in a guiding metaphor of the novel, mentioned only in *Tripmaster Monkey*'s subtitle: *His Fake Book*.

The fake book is the text used by pop and jazz musicians to jog the memory; it contains simple melodies and chordal accompaniments for standard tunes and is used as the basis for improvisation. The idea of a fake book is Kingston's translation not just of the language but of the cultural artifact of *hua-pen*, the prompt books used by professional Chinese storytellers in the serial recitals of their epics (Scott 17; Ma and Lau xxii).[7] *Hua-pen* would typically include the major episodes of a traditional story, but storytellers were known for adding new episodes in their recitations (Scott 68). The contents of the prompt books would have been available to the compilers of the dynastic novels, who, like the professional storytellers, would edit, elaborate, and add to the major episodes. The improvisational nature of both telling and writing down the classic stories is clear, and it is this characteristic that Kingston translates into the idiom of American popular culture when she refers to the "fake book." In a sense, each of her books can be seen as a fake book, gathering both central and peripheral texts—the melodies and accompaniments, as it were—from Chinese, American, and Chinese-American culture, from her past as well as her family's, to inspire the creative memory. In remembering, narrating, and recreating these sources, Kingston works like a musician in performance. She avails herself of any useful materials at hand, incorporating figures from both elite and common culture. She improvises upon familiar tunes and rhythms to make them new—and to make them express her understanding of herself and her multiethnic culture.

That understanding seems to change across the three narratives, in part because Kingston grapples in different ways with the meaning of having a hyphenated cultural identity. The first book, *The Woman Warrior*, seems both to question and celebrate the hyphen, to place emphasis equally on either side of it. Kingston plumbs the memories of her childhood in the United States, including the talk-stories she heard and the fantasies she entertained, but it is a childhood haunted by China, by a place that is other to her own experience except as it is narrated to her. In this sense, she is trying to construct, through her own narration of remembered stories, half of what she feels as a plural identity. But she later begins to repudiate the doubleness suggested by the hyphen, partly as a response to the misreadings of her first book ("Cultural Mis-readings" 60). In *China Men*, she demonstrates the historical shift from one singular identity (the Chinese father in the first main chapter) to another singular identity (the American brother in the final main chapter), a shift that indicates that her family's experience has passed through hyphenated identity but has attempted to leave it behind. She writes: "I want to discern what it is that makes people go West and turn into Americans. I want to compare China, a country I made up, with what country is really out there" (*China Men* 87). Making distinctions between her cultures of origin remains important; she endeavors to observe and classify the particulars of cultural identity conceived in geographical terms. *Tripmaster Monkey* defiantly reasserts the shift in the preceding book, emphasizing the result of the process of cultural transformation through assimilation.[8] But Kingston is careful to define assimilation neither as appropriation nor annihilation; the assimilation process changes the local—American—culture in contact with the Chinese as much as the Chinese culture is changed in contact with the American. She satirizes hyphenation and pleads for a reorientation of cultural identity: "We need to take the hyphen out—'Chinese American.' 'American,' the noun, and 'Chinese,' the adjective" (327).

Because of her developing notion of cultural identity, and despite the notable fierceness of *The Woman Warrior*, Kingston's project in that book is in some ways less insistent, more qualified and uncertain, than it is in *Tripmaster Monkey*. While the autobiographical inquiry of *The Woman Warrior* is directed largely toward exploring the meaning of being Chinese-American (the hyphen still intact), the means of the inquiry is for Kingston to recover the Chinese past from which she feels excluded. Her motivation is to "try to understand what things in [her] are Chinese," and to do this, she needs to distinguish "What is Chinese tradition and what is the movies" (*Warrior* 5–6)—that is, Western representations of Chinese culture. What she knows of this past she learns only through her mother's habit of "talking-story," by nature unreliable, as she accuses her mother toward the end of the book: "You lie with stories. You won't tell me a story and then say, 'This is a true story,' or, 'This is just a story.' . . . I can't tell what's real and what you make up" (202). The irony is that Kingston's relationship to her mother resembles the reader's relationship to Kingston's narrator; the narrator also flouts the distinction between reality and fantasy, fiction and nonfiction, in her efforts to rethink her culturally assigned role.[9] What she has learned from her mother about storytelling is, of course, what enables her to create a version of Chinese-American cultural history by revising and multiplying the stories she remembers, at the risk of contradiction—and, perhaps, *because* of contradiction.

Three prominent examples of Kingston's method of storytelling in *The Woman Warrior* are instructive. In the first, which draws on a cautionary tale her mother tells about Kingston's aunt, the "No Name Woman" of the opening chapter, Kingston makes visible her process of revising raw material to suit her interests. She transforms her mother's memory into several wildly divergent stories; once she reaches a final interpretation, it becomes her own memory of her aunt. Where Kingston's mother has told her only the "facts" of her aunt's illegitimate pregnancy, punishment by the villagers, and death in the family well, Kingston tries to imagine her aunt's secret life, obscured by the "facts" that have been arranged to warn Kingston about the necessity of obedience, chastity, and devotion to the family. In her effort to make her aunt's life touch her own, Kingston conjures her variously as a victim (7), a wild woman

(8), a martyr (11), and, finally, a spite suicide (16), the configuration that seems most satisfying to her sense of justice.

The development of this narration serves as a model for the way Kingston later improvises on public texts. The most striking example appears in the story of the woman warrior, Fa Mu Lan, based on an anonymous ballad from northern China in the sixth century (Waley 113). In the original ballad, Fa Mu Lan epitomizes filial piety, humility, and loyalty to her community: she serves in the emperor's army in place of her father, fights as a skilled soldier to defeat the enemy, and returns to her village to resume her domestic duties. The "facts" of Kingston's version are the same, but the thrust and details of the story—its meaning—are vastly different, in keeping with the defining questions of Kingston's narrative. She herself commented that the "White Tigers" chapter in which the story appears "is not a Chinese myth but one transformed by America, a sort of kung fu movie parody" ("Cultural Mis-readings" 57). Like the 1970s TV show *Kung Fu,* Kingston's version of Fa Mu Lan subverts Chinese values and customs even as it introduces them to her Western audience—most obviously, in incorporating a focus on individual attainment and independence. Here, the girl spends many years in training, isolated from her family, in order to be the savior of her people; she learns superhuman powers of self-control; she leads vast armies into battle, rather than simply following as a foot soldier; and she secretly has a family, in defiance of the assumption that the heroic and the domestic cannot mix. In addition, Kingston freely interpolates details from another well-known Chinese figure, Yue Fei, a patriot on whose back was carved a mandate for revenge (*China Men* 53). In adopting the male experience to testify to her woman warrior's power and devotion, she is clearly untroubled by any need to maintain the integrity of the central text of Fa Mu Lan. Throughout, she allows the meanings of her added material to exist in seemingly harmonious contradiction to the meaning of the original ballad. Most important, she appropriates the revenge fantasy of Fa Mu Lan for herself, transforming the community's legend into a first-person account. The narration records, as it were, Kingston's memory of her own past, even as it comes to stand for her understanding of her position as a Chinese-American who is not so much *between* two worlds is *in* both of them.

That peculiar cultural positioning is represented concretely in the final example of a reimagined public text included in Kingston's autobiographical narrative. The story of the second-century poetess, Ts'ai Yen, who was abducted by the Southern Hsiung-nu (the Huns) and made the commander's wife, is well known in China, especially from her cycle of poems, *Hu chia shih pa p'ai* (Eighteen songs of a barbarian reed pipe), and from subsequent cycles by Liu Shang and Wang An-shih.[10] Ts'ai Yen stands for the exile, the unwilling immigrant, who must learn to survive in the midst of a culture—and, importantly, a language—not her own. In Kingston's sources, Ts'ai Yen grieves; she seems a desolate victim of her captors, passive, yearning, and even self-pitying. The nomad landscape seems harsh, barren, and unforgiving, and she barely speaks of the people among whom she is living. As David Leiwei Li has observed, this aggrieved tone is missing from Kingston's account of the tale (510–11). In its place is power and even exhilaration: Ts'ai Yen fights like a warrior woman, "cut[ting] down anyone in her path during the madness of close combat" (*Woman Warrior* 208), and she communicates through song with the people whose language she cannot speak. This is a significant improvisation on Kingston's part. In Liu Shang's sixth poem, Ts'ai Yen laments that "All day and all year I keep my mouth closed. / 'Yes' and 'no' and accepting and giving things away all depend on finger gestures; / For expressing our feelings, speech has become less useful than the hand" (*Eighteen Songs* [32]). Kingston picks up on the captive's linguistic isolation, but she alters the experience to speak to her own history. In *The Woman Warrior*, Ts'ai Yen's sons, who speak no Chinese, laugh at her and cruelly imitate her "with senseless singsong words" (208), suggesting the cultural distance between first- and second-generation Chinese-Americans, like Kingston and her parents, who seem often to fail to understand one another. The Ts'ai Yen of the poetic cycles never seems to connect with her captors and is no more at peace when she returns to the Han people than when she was in captivity; the eighteenth and final verse of *Hu chia shih pa p'ai* concludes on a despairing note: "Just as the sky and the earth are separated from each other, my sons are in the west while I am in the east. / Poor me, my unhappiness can fill the whole sky. / Although the universe is large, it is probably not big enough to hold my sorrow" (*Hu chia* [20]). Kingston turns the tale toward a hopeful cultural resolution, however, when the words of Ts'ai Yen's song communicate her feelings across the language barrier to the barbarians, and when, upon narrating her return to the Han lands, Kingston asserts that her song "translated well" (209). In other words, Ts'ai Yen comes to stand for the poet who, like Kingston, reshapes her memories of otherness into a meaningful narrative that can be taken as historical truth in her home culture.[11]

Kingston's second book, *China Men*, takes up similar questions in a different way. She becomes a bit player in the history of the men in her family, told across several generations. This family "history," compiled of memories recited to her and events she has witnessed or researched, and fleshed out by the fictive imagination into a full account, represents for Kingston the larger history of Chinese immigration and acculturation to the United States. As in *The Woman Warrior*, to recapture this past she makes recourse to public texts from both Western and Chinese cultural history. Juxtaposed in interchapters to the family's story, these texts gain new resonances that bear specifically on Chinese-American experiences of immigration and acculturation.[12]

A case in point is the legend of Tang Ao, which serves as a prologue to the book. Tang Ao, journeying to find the Gold Mountain—the Chinese metaphor for North America—is captured instead in the Land of Women. There he is feminized, his ears pierced, his feet bound, his face plucked, powdered, and painted (*China Men* 3-4). Kingston's source for the tale is *Flowers in the Mirror (Chin hua yuan)*, written in the early nineteenth century by Li Ju-chen. Li's novel is a satiric, very funny, and often fantastic story of the journey of Tang Ao, a scholar of the lowest rank, who seeks, through charitable acts, to "become an immortal by 'cultivating Tao' " (Tai-yi Lin 5, 7). Like Swift's Gulliver, Tang Ao and the family members who accompany him find themselves in all manner of places whose mores allow Li to comment upon contemporary Chinese society. One such place is the Land of Women to which Kingston alludes. But there are significant differences between the source and its reinvention in *China Men*. In Li's novel, it is Tang Ao's brother-in-law, Merchant Lin, who suffers the pain and humiliation of the traditional Chinese woman, and not Tang Ao himself, who manages to rescue Lin through a ruse. Perhaps Kingston alters this for the sake of economy, but a more compelling effect of her conflation of characters—her reinvention of the remembered tale—is to change its tone. Whereas Li's division of the story into the two characters makes for slapstick romance, in which Tang Ao by dumb luck and some cleverness can compensate for the foolish gullibility of his brother-in-law, Kingston's version emphasizes the isolation, pain, and humiliation of the captive man. When Li writes about the customs of the Land of Women, where gender roles are wholly reversed, he does so in order to expose comically what he sees as the absurd cruelty of conventional Chinese practices relating to femininity. Kingston uses the details of Li's story—especially those concerned with the feminizing of Merchant Lin—and adds some of her own, such as the threat to sew Tang Ao's mouth shut (4), to very different purpose. The conventional

Maxine Hong Kingston's Fake Books

icons of Chinese femininity—silencing, crippling, grooming—stand for Kingston less as a critique of Chinese conceptions of womanhood (although that is implied) and more as metaphors for the experience of Chinese males emigrating to America, where they were often effectively emasculated by Caucasian-American culture. Like his fellow workers, for instance, Kingston's great grandfather was prohibited from speaking by the overseer of the Hawaiian sugar plantation on which he labored (*China Men* 99–100, 102). The story of Tang Ao, remembered and transformed, becomes a way of rendering symbolically the analogous experience of the Chinese male in America.

Later, Kingston summarizes the epic elegy *Li Sao* (Lament on Encountering Sorrow) by Ch'u Yuan, China's earliest known poet (256), as a way to create a context of interpretation for what follows—the story of Kingston's brother who was sent to Vietnam. Ch'u Yuan is exiled because he advises his king against war; he wanders many years and finally drowns himself in despair because "he could not find one uncorrupted human being" (258). Kingston's allusion to the *Li Sao* makes sense only in ironic juxtaposition to her brother's experience. A pacifist like Ch'u Yuan, the brother is first exiled from the Chinese-American culture of his birth when he enlists in the Navy in order to avoid being drafted into another branch of the services. During basic training, he loses his appetite (286), signifying his will to live, as he learns how to participate in military activity, the symbol, to him, of human corruptibility. The irony that he is being trained as an American to kill people who are in profound ways like himself does not escape Kingston, but rather becomes an emblem of confused cultural identity. Disillusioned when he finally reaches Hong Kong, her brother finds that his life makes no more sense than it did before—that is, unlike the expectations in his "childish dream" (294), being in China does not clarify for him either his Americanness or his Chineseness. He returns from the war quietly despairing that "the things people did seemed to have no value" (304). The notion of corruptibility suggested by Ch'u Yuan's story comes for Kingston to represent the problem of the multicultural identity, which by definition implies a "corruption" of the cultural identities that stand to either side of the hyphen. Kingston documents the resulting experience of exile from each culture.

In another vein, Kingston transforms a public text in the reverse direction—from Western culture back toward Chinese culture. She represents an interchapter, "The Adventures of Lo Bun Sun," as a summary of "a book from China about a sailor named Lo Bun Sun." As the story develops, however, it becomes increasingly clear that "Lo Bun Sun" is a parody of the way Anglo-Americans mock the English pronunciation of Chinese-American immigrants ("l's" for "r's," and so forth), and it also suggests self-parody; at the same time, Kingston satirizes the Anglicizing of Chinese culture. Lo Bun Sun is Robinson, as in Robinson Crusoe, and it is Defoe's novel that Kingston summarizes, translated into Chinese terms. Like the legend of Tang Ao, as well as the material of several other interchapters and interpolated stories—"The Ghostmate," for example, or "The Wild Man of the Green Swamp"—the story of Lo Bun Sun metaphorically documents the history of Chinese-American cultural exile, where the immigrants experienced their transition to American culture as castaways who must use their resources to survive in a hostile environment. Kingston's memory of this as "a book from China" (225), expressed ambiguously (is this a book that happened to come in Chinese translation, or one that originated in China?), nevertheless suggests the way a transformed version may be taken for memory—that is, can testify to the past.[13]

Numerous other examples of reimagined textualized remainders appear in both of Kingston's earlier books, but I would like to explore the novel *Tripmaster Monkey: His Fake Book* in greater depth because it provides such a wildly playful range of examples in which oral and written stories are transformed into cultural memory. In this book, too, Kingston makes most explicit the way in which she sees memory at work in the process of transformation, providing a sense of historical identity to the dispossessed. The process is epitomized when the protagonist, Wittman Ah Sing, and his new wife, Taña, visit the rooms of his grandmother, PoPo. There they see a "memory village" (191), a tiny but detailed model of a Chinese village, complete with houses, pigs, a well, fields, and thirty-three lichee trees (192). The memory village is a relic of immigration; new immigrants would study it so that when they had to tell U.S. immigration officials about their place of origin, the stories of all the immigrants would agree. The point, as Wittman notes, is that the village as it appears in the model never existed: "It is not a model *of* anything, do you understand? It's a memory village" (192, Kingston's emphasis). That is, the memory village is a fabrication, a story created and retold for purposes of self-protection, in order to give the immigrants the appearance of an authoritative historical identity. The irony, as Kingston suggests, is that the immigrants came to believe the stories they told, incorporating them into their memories and understandings of themselves, so that

Wittman is able to tell Taña that PoPo fetched water from this well and that twenty of the lichee trees belonged to his great-great-uncle (192). The fictive narrative has been transformed into historical truth.

But there is no bitterness to Kingston's irony here; rather, she meets the transformative power of memory with awe and affection. The principle of transformation, in fact, is crucial to Kingston's conception of Wittman. Wittman often appears in the guise of the titular Monkey, a beloved figure from the sixteenth-century epic novel by Wu Ch'eng-en, *The Journey to the West (Hsi yu chi)*.[14] Monkey is the King of the Monkeys, who possesses magical powers and is spiritually advanced; he protects a seventh-century monk, known as Tripitaka, who is journeying to India in order to bring Buddhist sutras back to China. The novel is a comic allegory about the Buddhist notion of *maya* (illusion) and human attachment to the world of the senses (Hsia 148), and Monkey is the character most savvy about human fallibility. A trickster and shape-shifter, Monkey is known for his seventy-two transformations (Wu 241), and Kingston translates this capacity into Wittman's ingenuity when he repeatedly reinvents himself and the artifacts of his culture.

Wittman Ah Sing is a self-proclaimed bardic singer. He declares that he "want[s] so bad to be the first bad-jazz China Man bluesman of America" (*Tripmaster* 27), and his fake book seems to include the whole range of Western and Chinese culture. At quick count, there are more than two hundred references in the novel to icons of Eastern and Western culture, especially modern American culture, both elite and popular. Poets, playwrights, and novelists find transhistorical and transcultural mention alongside actors, actresses, musicians, and political figures; Mao Tse Tung and Marilyn Monroe appear together on one page (198), James Boswell and Tonto on another (120). *Tripmaster Monkey* alludes to dozens of novels, plays, films, even TV shows, many of which had virtual cult followings in the late sixties and early seventies, the time in which the novel is set. Kingston quotes freely from other public texts, especially poems; poems of Walt Whitman, for example, make appearances both in chapter titles (e.g., "Trippers and Askers," which derives from the fourth section of "Song of Myself") and in excerpts.

Walt Whitman, in fact, provides a clue to Kingston's method here. Wittman Ah Sing was named by his father after the American poet: the "Ah Sing" echoes Whitman's mission to celebrate his country and himself; and the misspelled "Wittman" represents both the connection to and distance from American culture of this character whom, Kingston has implied, she sees as a new Everyman ("The Coming Book" 184). That is, Wittman stands for the transformation of American culture in contact with Chinese-American culture. He is an American Everyman, not only a Chinese-American Everyman. His significance to Kingston may in part explain her choice of setting for the novel: the San Francisco Bay area in the 1960s. Kingston creates in her reference to this time and place an additional level of historiographic inquiry, since she reimagines in multiethnic terms—thereby claiming for multiethnic experience—a part of the past that has become iconic for a certain generation of Americans. She alters our memories of the center of the counterculture at the same time that she makes use of some of the counterculture's most storied features. In public memory, of course, the sixties were a time of revolution, a time of altering consciousness in social and personal spheres through "mind-expanding" drugs and political action. The aim of the counterculture was both to rewrite history and reinvent the future, in part by incorporating the fabulous into the everyday. Kingston's Wittman becomes a representative of this movement, participating in the drug culture at Lance Kamiyama's party and creating an improbable community in the improbably short time it takes him to stage his epic drama. The result of his activities is to revise our memories of the countercultural movement so that it is no longer Caucasian or even black and white, but has a distinctively multiethnic cast. Wittman's barrage of allusions and quotations is the raw material of cultural memory that he needs to create his epic vision of Chinese-American historical experience. His vision is, ultimately, of the unhyphenated *American* experience that Kingston wishes to offer as our common history when she has Wittman revise the title of Wu's novel: "There is no East here. West is meeting West. . . . This is The Journey *In* the West" (308, Kingston's emphasis). Wittman translates both Chinese and Western texts into his own culture; his ambition is to be the "reader of the tribe" (247), and he aspires for someone to "dig his allusions" (13). Like Monkey, he incarnates the principle of transformation, playing complicated riffs on old stories for the sake of his culture's knowledge of itself.

Wittman is a raging, exuberant talker and storyteller whom even the narrator cannot seem to shut up (282). As a storyteller, he is metaphorically the novel's "tripmaster," the person who talks others through their drug trips, enriching their hallucinations and keeping them from harm, and his reading is part of what qualifies him for the role. When the narrator remarks, "It must be that people who read go on more macrocosmic and microcosmic trips" (88), she suggests that it is one's contact with public texts that gives one the power to imagine even without artificial stimulation and the grounding to make the trip safe for everyone. Wittman's function as tripmaster is most obvious in the novel's several set-pieces, in which Kingston transforms her sources—the classic Chinese novels—in order to create the epic Chinese-American theater that is Wittman's dream. Each retelling becomes a mixture of Chinese and Western motifs. For example, in Wittman's version of the fourteenth-century compilation *The Romance of the Three Kingdoms (San-kuo-chih yen-i)*, probably by Lo Kuan-chung,[15] he describes a palace that "is defended against the elephant army by knights on black stallions, *Trigger* palominos, and stout Mongolian ponies" (170, emphasis added). The Roy Rogers allusion both startles with its incongruity and tames for the reader embedded in American culture the potential exoticism of the translated story. Later, when Wittman acts out a scene from the novel *The Water Verge (Shui hu chuan)*,[16] a story of 108 Chinese outlaws, he turns it into a combination of Southwestern tall tale, with references to Three-Finger Jack and Sacramento (260–61), and Marx Brothers' slapstick routine: he steals the Groucho Marx sight-gag, saying "Walk this way" and then following with "a banana-peel run, slip-sliding around the room" (258). In each case Wittman's memory of the tale is informed by his contact with American popular culture, and what he illuminates in his narration are the unexpected resemblances between disparate cultural materials—resemblances and sympathies that make the blending of elements into a Chinese-American cultural memory seem possible.

Kingston's most extensive reinvention of a source appears as Wittman begins to stage his epic play, running across several nights. In narrating Wittman's play, Kingston at times quotes verbatim from *The Romance of the Three Kingdoms,* and she condenses much of the climactic part of its plot, but in addition to conflating and reordering the episodes, she narrates some subtle but telling variations and embellishments. Whereas Lo Kuan-chung's novel emphasizes the nobility of one of its heroes, Gwan Goong,[17] Kingston chooses to underscore his supernatural reappearances after his death and his "powers over illusions" (177). In Chinese mythology, Gwan Goong is the god of war and literature (Scott 37), and as such, he has presided over each of Kingston's books—riding to battle before her self-projection in the "White Tigers" fantasy of *The Woman Warrior* (38) and represented in a picture in her family's dining room in *China Men* (126). In *Tripmaster Monkey,* Gwan Goong serves as the model for Wittman's dramatic role and his muse, as he becomes the director and master of ceremonies for the cultural improvisation of his theatrical epic. *The Romance of the Three Kingdoms*, set in the second and third centuries, concerns a hundred years of political strife and war over the Chinese empire. As such, its story metaphorically represents for Wittman—and Kingston—the ethnic "battleground" of America and the hundred years of struggle over the turf of cultural identity.

A few examples of Wittman's Monkey-like narrative transformations of his source should suffice. In Kingston's source, when Gwan has been captured by Sun Ch'uan and is about to be put to death, his response to Sun's offer that he surrender in order to save his life is heroically contemptuous; he calls Sun "My blue-eyed boy! My red-whiskered rodent!" (Lo 240). The rest of the short scene concerns politics and military strategy: Sun, respecting Gwan, wants to encourage him to defect, but his officers counsel execution (240–42). Kingston quotes Gwan's line but elaborates the scene to another effect. Wittman narrates that Sun Ch'uan offers "brotherhood, familyhood, a marriage for your daughter with my son." When Gwan scorns the offer, Sun calls him a "barbarian" for continuing the war (*Tripmaster* 275). Kingston has translated the exchange so that it signifies an offer of assimilation, not political power; Gwan Goong's refusal of the symbolic marriage represents for Kingston a larger refusal to assimilate according to the terms set by the dominant culture. In this sense, she represents both a historical observation about Chinese resistance to assimilation into American culture and an ideological point about the reasons for this resistance. Later, she interpolates an episode in which Gwan's line—"My blue-eyed boy. My red-whiskered rodent" (284)—is repeated. Here, Gwan is an apparition haunting Sun, and the line is what alerts us (and Sun) to the identity of the alien voice emerging from the body of one of Sun's men. When Gwan's visage takes shape across the man's face, "His eyebrows and the creases beside his mouth are vertical black lines; his eyes and face are blood red—War incorporated" (284). Kingston, then, stresses the god Gwan's reign over warfare, reinventing Gwan's presence as the spirit of vengeance in order to bespeak anger against the dominant power; this anger foreshadows that which Wittman expresses at length in the novel's concluding chapter, when he recites a list of stereotypes and a partial history of discrimination against Chinese-Americans. A similar transformation of the remembered text appears near the end of this passage. In the source, Liu Pei, one of Gwan Goong's two sworn brothers, is ill, and the ghosts of Gwan and Chang Fei, the third brother, appear to him. Gwan tells him that "the time is not far off when we shall be reunited" (Lo 277), which Liu interprets as foretelling his death. Kingston retains the line as "The time is not far off when we shall be together again," but in her version, Liu

Maxine Hong Kingston's Fake Books

Pei responds that "We will the three of us all go home" and the narrator—who may be either Wittman or Kingston's narrative voice—apostrophizes, "O home-returning powers, where might home be? How to find it and dwell there?" (284). Clearly, she is reinterpreting the story as one of cultural exile.

Kingston reinvents not just the plots, but also the conventions of her source materials. The Chinese stories that originated in prompt books were notable for their use of the vernacular (Ma and Lau xxii); Kingston's diction, which attempts to capture the richness of the American idiom, emerges from a range of linguistic styles and class origins, here flippant, hip, or snappy, there elevated. A randomly chosen example, from Wittman's farewell to his job, juxtaposes the line "A green razzberry to you, World" to Melville's famous lines, "Ah Bartleby. Ah Humanity" (65). Likewise, Kingston avails herself of some of the formal characteristics and motifs of her sources. Her use of self-reflexive linking devices between chapters imitates the conventions of a novel like *Flowers in the Mirror*, whose chapters generally end with the formulation, "If the reader would like to know . . . please read/turn to the next chapter" (e.g., Lin 23, 31, 35, and so forth). The convention is a throwback to the oral tradition, in which storytellers would encourage their audience to reappear for the next night's narration. In early chapters, Kingston copies the sources directly, concluding the second chapter, for example, this way: "*Our* monkey man will live—he parties, he plays—though unemployed. To see how he does it, go on to the next chapter" (65). But by the end of the novel, she is altering the tag-like form in accordance with its cultural context. Chapter 7 ends with the lines, "To entertain and educate the solitaries that make up a community, the play will be a combination revue-lecture. You're invited" (288). Here she takes on the confiding tone of the carnival barker, and the casualness is appropriate to a twentieth-century American audience raised on television commercials. Too, the excess and busy-ness of *Tripmaster Monkey*, which has elicited adverse—or at least weary—responses among some reviewers,[18] resembles the rhythms of traditional Chinese stories; C. T. Hsia, for example, has described the "interminable campaigns" and "fuss and bustle" of *The Water Verge* (85). But here as well Kingston translates her sources into the terms of her subject matter, because the extravagance of her imagination in the narrative is in keeping with the fuss and bustle of the culture about which she writes—the time of Day-glo colors, acid rock, happenings, and "free love." In each case, Kingston transforms source narratives and narrative conventions to erase the boundaries implied by her two cultural traditions, so as to create an indivisibly multicultural narrative.

Clearly, then, the form of her narrative is dictated by Kingston's need to represent the experience of ethnic hyphenation in such a way that she can affirm it as *American* experience. The difficulties of such affirmation are suggested when Wittman insists "We allthesame Americans" (282); his locution simultaneously makes an important claim to cultural identity and undermines it by showing the symptomatic linguistic alienation of some Chinese-Americans. Because of these complex relations to "American" identity, the marriage that Kingston has Gwan Goong refuse becomes a potent symbol for her. Wittman marries white Taña, not Chinese-American Nanci Lee; going one better on the "integrated marriage" (150) of his friend Lance, Wittman learns to make the marriage work by looking beyond the chaos of domestic life toward the satisfactions that can come from unromantic union. This is precisely the pragmatism Kingston finds necessary within multicultural relations. The conjugal metaphor is at play in numerous ways in the novel, ranging from linguistic to sexual unions. The very title of the novel weds the Chinese Monkey to the American hippie tripmaster. Wittman's last defiant act at his sales job is to set up a Barbie doll to be "raped" by a mechanical monkey (64-65); here, the union metaphor is inverted, as Kingston, inspired by both her protean prototype and her recreated image of Gwan Goong, takes vengeance against the exploitation of Chinese-American culture by American consumer culture—that is, against the kind of stereotyping that causes whites to associate Chinese-Americans with Buddha-shaped bottles of Jade East cologne (27). The marriage metaphor is, however, righted again when Wittman and Taña make love for the first time and share a hallucination, a kind of waking dream that they narrate together (157-58). Significantly, the proof of their cultural union, of their shared consciousness, is their common story.

Kingston's understanding of storytelling as an act in which teller and hearer participate mutually explains why multicultural references proliferate in the novel. Wittman's chosen venue, the theater, is representative of the way Kingston envisions narrating as a unifying social act. Wittman has a dual recognition that "The ethnos is degenerating" (255) and the "theater has died" (141)—meaning the century of Chinese-American theater, whose many acting companies performed the Chinese classics. Desiring to bring it back as "deep-roots American theater" (141), Wittman determines, in the spirit of the old Judy Garland/Mickey Rooney movies, to put on a play. The play, which garners a wide and enthusiastic audience, climaxes the novel and develops as an extravagant pastiche of cultural references. In addition to rehearsing central events from *The Romance of the Three Kingdoms,* it includes a minstrel show starring the Siamese twins Chang and Eng, whose physical joining satirizes the problem of hyphenated identity; it recapitulates the history of Chinese-American immigrants in the guise of a John Wayne western; and its finale is a fireworks display that causes actors and audience to mingle, "breaking rules of reality-and-illusion" (303). This concluding scene proves that the play has served one radical function of the theater, to unify a community ritually. And it has unified the community of the novel by evolving a common set of memories, drawn from other, fragmented cultural materials, to interpret the community's experience.

Kingston underscores the need for community in a number of ways, each centered on the possibilities of storytelling. Her narrator, for example, often makes herself visible as both observer and participant in the narrated action, and the result is that the boundaries between narrator and object of narration become vague. When she describes the local scene at Grant Avenue, she writes that "they/we call it Du Pont Gai" (26). Later, a question of Wittman's suggests that he is "remembering when *we* were kids and poor" (101, emphasis added). The narrator's use of the first-person plural is only the most obvious example of the way Kingston undermines "us/them" thinking, otherwise implicit in the conventional third-person narration that seems to dominate the novel. By breaking the convention, Kingston works toward a reimagining of the narrative situation in communal terms that hark back to her oral sources. What she attempts in devising her narrative voice is to accomplish the union signified when, in the parable of cultural exile Lance tells as his life story, he repeats the redemptive line "Our stories are your stories" (125).

The infiltration of the narrative voice into the community constructed in the narrative—a process imitated by Wittman himself as he narrates his stories and play excerpts—suggests one of the more interesting effects of Kingston's conception of storytelling in this novel. That effect, which happens to accord with some postmodern notions of subjectivity, is that the unitary, essentialist self disappears into the web of discourses about the self. Thomas Docherty has described postmodern subjectivity in apt terms for understanding Kingston's narration: "the speaking subject is never a single individual; in discourse, the subject is constituted discontinuously at every discrete moment not only by what it says, but also by the languages or discourses and silence which surround it: this is as much as to say that the subject can never be the singular 'I'—if subjectivity exists at all, it can only do so in the form of communal subjectivity, 'we' " (269).[19] When Wittman acknowledges that he has been "inventing selves" (19) through talking, he admits to a kind of fluid subjectivity, a dissolution of the self in narrative. Fittingly, of course, this view of subjectivity resembles in its flexibility the variations of the oral tradition. As we have seen in considering narrative versions, no single representation of the self—no single story about it—can stand as the authoritative version. It is in this sense that another possible meaning of the novel's subtitle comes into play: in a postmodern disclaimer of the book's authority, Kingston can dismiss it as a *fake* book, like the "fake" selves or stories she and her protagonist spin out.

The novel refuses to rest at this interpretation, however. Rather, it engages in the double or contradictory movement that Linda Hutcheon identifies as characteristic of postmodern fiction. The fake book (or self) nevertheless has presence, a being in time. Hutcheon writes: "postmodernism establishes, differentiates, and then disperses stable narrative voices (and bodies) that use memory to try to make sense of the past. It both installs and then subverts traditional concepts of subjectivity" (118). That is, *Tripmaster Monkey* asserts the selfhood of its central figure—and Wittman is wont to assert himself vociferously—by narrating the history of that self, at the same time that his very narration, by its plurality of stories, makes such an assertion impossible.

But even this explanation is insufficient to account for the trajectory of the novel. Kingston's significant departure is to show the dissolution of self in the narrative act for other, more social purposes. When Wittman is "inventing selves," he is inventing them not just for himself, but for the audience to whom (and for whom) he speaks. His "we" is both the self as many selves and the self as continuous with its social environment. His audience assembles by the accidents of time and place to form his community; as the narrator reports in summarizing Wittman's philosophy of life: "Do the right thing by whoever crosses your path. Those coincidental people are your people" (223). Whereas Wittman resists the assumption of a ready-made and externally defined community of Chinese-Americans ("I am not going to the prom with the only Chinese girl in the class" [59]), he welcomes the multiethnic community that forms around his storytelling. Yet even though he retains his noisy individuality, Wittman still is dispersed as a presence across the community created by his narrative, so that he frequently becomes indistinguishable from the novel's narrative voice. When, for example, Wittman is dismayed by a screening of *West Side Story*, a two-line paragraph appears, reading, "Where are you, Bugs Bunny? We need you, Mr. Wabbit in Wed" (72). Is this Wittman's comment, or the narrator's? In this manner, Kingston suggests the possibility of a transpersonal or communal self. It is a self created by the narrative process. Such a self, conceived inextricably as part of a larger social body, has its own past, but it also participates directly in—and can recite—the past of the group. It speaks, then, a multivocal discourse that, not surprisingly, is reminiscent of folk culture, of the oral mode of storytelling that is so much a part of Kingston's conception of narrative. The self can be figured as the speaker of the tale and the bearer of memory, but they are a tale and memory that belong first and foremost to the community.

What Kingston has done is analogous to what her character Charley does earlier in the novel: he recites the plot of a film, *The Saragossa Manuscript,* in such a way that "he got [his audience] to be inhabiting the same movie" (103). Even though Wittman is unable thereafter to locate the film, to prove that it existed as something other than Charley's fantasy or his own hallucination, he recognizes the power of Charley's retelling to create memory: "Some of those who heard the movie told at the fireside will think they'd seen it. All of them will remember a promise of something good among cannonballs and skulls" (103–4). The apparently unrecoverable *Saragossa Manuscript* epitomizes the importance of the oral tradition; its visual reality lost to history, it becomes a purely verbal text, existing only in memory and its retellings. Kingston teases us with the very title of the film, which suggests a written and provisional text (a manuscript) rather than a visual text—and thereby points to another way to make the words seem "to change on the page every time."

Like the actual film of *The Saragossa Manuscript,* which Vincent Canby described as a "spirited and often completely incomprehensible mélange of tall story, miller's tale, surreal dream and philosophical double-talk" (Canby 247), and which Kingston summarizes as a film about stories within stories as a way of telling history, *Tripmaster Monkey* is a lavish, wildly assembled novel about the making of cultural memory. The richness of reference in this book, as in the earlier ones, suggests the almost limitless possibilities of Monkey's seventy-two transformations. The array of tunes in Kingston's fake books appears large enough to fill a library—it encompasses the whole range of texts from Chinese and Western culture. Indeed, Kingston seems to point in each multifoliate text to a very particular understanding of memory: to remember is to translate and to translate is to improvise. Such translation is how we know ourselves as cultural beings.

Notes

1. See Kingston's comment that memory is "insignificant, except when it haunts you and when it is a foundation for the rest of the personality" ("Eccentric Memories" 178).

Mary Warnock has written wisely about the relationship between memory and personal identity. She argues that "any truly recalling memory must . . . contain the idea of self. Whether through images or through direct knowledge, to count as a memory a cognitive experience, or thought, must contain the conviction that I myself was the person involved in the remembered scene. The image, if there is one, must be labelled not only 'this belongs to the past' but also 'it belongs to *my* past' " (58–59). In this sense, identity is dependent upon memory. The notion can be extended to include memories of those who are connected to one—one's family or cultural group—so that their involvement in a remembered scene, when narrated to one, also belongs to one's past.

2. Linda Ching Sledge makes an important point in regard to Kingston's particular version of cultural transmission when she notes that Kingston relies on the Chinese tradition of "talk-story" *(gong gu tsai)* throughout her books: "Talk-story is by my definition a conservative, communal folk art by and for the common people. . . . Because it served to redefine an embattled immigrant culture by providing its members immediate, ceremonial access to ancient lore, talk-story retained the structures of Chinese oral wisdom (parables, proverbs, formulaic description, heroic biography, casuistical dialogue) long after other old-country traditions had died" (143). In general, Sledge's recognition that Kingston has a "notion of the ethnic literary artist as one in a long line of performers shaping a recalcitrant history into talk-story form" (146) provides a significant precedent for arguing that memory and narration can construct a story of the past that bears truth value for its culture.

3. Kingston expresses her deconstruction of this distinction—and especially of the hierarchical value normally assigned to literate culture—when she tells Linda Ching Sledge, "The way I see it, there has been continuous talk-story for over 4,000 years and it spans China and America. Once in a long while during these millenia, somebody writes things down; writing 'freezes' things for a bit, like a rock, but the talk-story goes on around and from this rock" (Kingston to Sledge, 23 July 1981, qtd. in Sledge 147).

4. Although, obviously, Kingston is writing in English, the linguistic pair Chinese/English is not imbalanced or misleading in the same way that I am suggesting untransformed texts might be. This is because English *is* the language of Chinese America—that is, of those people who see themselves as Chinese-Americans rather than as Chinese living in the United States. (In this sense, clearly, there are many "Chinese Americas.") Not only is English the language available to Kingston, but it is also the only language that can faithfully render Chinese-American experience.

5. Hsia argues that, while the professional storytellers tended to interpret history and legend "in accordance with the concept of moral retribution . . . reward[ing] the virtuous and punish[ing] the wicked," the compilers of the historical

novels were "inclined to follow the official historians and to share their Confucian view of history as a cyclic alternative between order and disorder, as a record of the careers of great men engaged in a perpetual struggle against the periodically rampant forces of anarchy and sensuality" (11).

6. Like the previous two texts, *Tripmaster Monkey* is not easily classifiable by genre, in large part because of its incorporation of other materials. Patricia Lin argues that "any attempts at reading Kingston require a revision on the part of the reader's assumptions about literary genres, authorial voice, and the question of veracity—particularly as her works pertain to 'truthful' or 'accurate' representations of Chinese Americans" (333) and that the "failure to recognize *Tripmaster Monkey* as something both more and less than a novel deprives the work of a place among the representative voices of the postmodern era" (334). Lin makes the point about genre in order to argue for the book's postmodernity. Because, however, the book is structured around the actions of fully invented characters—who, unlike those in *The Woman Warrior* and *China Men* are suggested to be projections neither of Kingston herself nor of her family—and because the point of the novel is largely to underscore the way that fictive narrative creates meaningful cultural history, I will refer to the book as a novel.

7. Ma and Lau point out that, while the scholar Lu Hsun interpreted *hua-pen* as prompt books, specialists no longer accept that interpretation, seeing the term *hua-pen* simply as another term for "story" (xxii). Nevertheless, the idea of the prompt book lies firmly within the information about Chinese cultural history available to Kingston and, given her use of public texts, seems an apt analogy.

8. In important ways, Kingston conceives of this shift linguistically: "when I wrote *The Woman Warrior* and *China Men* . . . I was trying to find an American language that would translate the speech of the people who are living their lives with the Chinese language. They carry on their adventures and their emotional life and everything in Chinese. I had to find a way to translate all that into a graceful American language. Which is my language. But . . . I ha[dn't] had a chance to play with this language that I speak, this modern American language—which I love. . . . So I was trying to write a book with American rhythms. This is what *Tripmaster Monkey* is" ("*MELUS* Interview" 71).

9. For an excellent discussion of Kingston's refusal to distinguish "fact" from "fiction," see Frye 294–95.

10. Liu Shang wrote his cycle in the eighth century (these poems are translated in *Eighteen Songs of a Nomad Flute*), and Wang An-shih composed yet another cycle in the eleventh century (*Eighteen Songs* [1]). Kingston may be drawing on any or all of the cycles. Significantly, while Ts'ai Yen's and Liu Shang's cycles differ in a number of details, the tone and meaning of the narratives comprising the two cycles remain the same: Ts'ai Yen mourns bitterly over her abduction and distance from her home, she despairs, and yet when the Han messenger arrives twelve years later to ransom her and bring her back to China, she feels great pain to leave behind the two sons she bore to the Hsiung-nu chief.

I wish to thank Vivien Chan for her invaluable help in translating Ts'ai Yen's *Hu chia shih pa p'ai* for me. The translation cited is hers.

11. For a parallel argument about Kingston's use of this legend in developing a sense of female identity, see Joanne Frye, who writes that Kingston "claim[s]

for herself the power of Ts'ai Yen, the power of language both to shape and to convey reality: the power of narrative to bridge cultural barriers and to reinfuse the female identity with the strength of an affirmed selfhood" (300).

12. Kingston has discussed the different ways she incorporates the mythic texts into the structure of her first two books as a response to the differences between men's and women's experiences in the United States: "In *The Woman Warrior*, when the girls and women draw on mythology for their strengths, the myth becomes part of the women's lives and the structure of the stories. In the men's stories . . . they are separate narratives. . . . [T]hose men went to a place where they didn't know whether their mythology was giving them any strength or not. They were getting very broken off from their background. . . . So, the myth story and the present story become separated" ("Eccentric Memories" 179–80).

13. Kingston's ambiguous language nicely reflects her own uncertain knowledge: "I didn't know until I got to school that *Robinson Crusoe* was an English novel. Because it had gone into Chinese as spoken story. So my parents spoke the story *Robinson Crusoe*. . . . I got to school, and I thought, oh, so this is what this stuff is" ("*MELUS* Interview" 70). Her text reproduces for the reader the epistemological confusion concerning origins inherent in the multiethnic experience.

14. Thirty of the one hundred original chapters of *Hsi yu chi* have been translated by Arthur Waley under the title *Monkey*.

15. About half of the original 120 chapters are translated by Moss Roberts in *Three Kingdoms* (1976), and Roberts has recently published a more complete translation: *Three Kingdoms: A Historical Novel* (Berkeley: U of California P-Foreign Language, 1993).

16. *Shui hu*, compiled in the fourteenth century, is attributed variously to Lo Kuan-chung, to Shih Nai-an, or to them jointly (Hsia 77). J. H. Jackson translated the novel under the title *Water Margin,* attributing it solely to Shih Nai-an.

17. I adopt Kingston's transliteration of the Chinese name for the god as it appears in *Tripmaster Monkey*. She has changed this from book to book: in *The Woman Warrior*, the figure appears as Kuan Kung and in *China Men* as Guan Goong. Roberts translates his name as Kuan Yu *(Three Kingdoms)*, the historical personage from whom the god derives. Elsewhere, I adopt the transliteration of Chinese names as they appear in the various translations I have consulted, even though they may be inconsistent with one another.

18. See, for example, Le Anne Schreiber's comment that "too often [Wittman] is just a windbag" (9); Nicci Gerrard's assertion that "Chinatown speech and its stereotypes collide and allusions accelerate until *Tripmaster Monkey* loses the downward drag of plot" (28); or the remark of Anne Tyler, who is otherwise favorable: "at other times the effect is exhausting—much as if that 23-year-old had taken up residence in our living room, staying way too long . . . and wearing us out with his exuberance" (46).

19. See Malini Johar Schueller's argument that ethnicity is linguistically constructed—that is, a matter of discursivity (73–74). Schueller is attempting to gainsay essentialist definitions of ethnicity, and her argument about the relations between cultural discourse and identity provides important theoretical support for thinking about Wittman's—and Kingston's—capacity to create cultural memory out of textualized remainders.

Works Cited

Canby, Vincent. Rev. of *The Saragossa Manuscript*. *New York Times Film Reviews, 1971–1972*. New York: New York Times and Arno, 1973. 247.

Davis, Natalie Zemon, and Randolph Starn. Introduction. *Memory and Counter-Memory*. Special issue of *Representations* 26 (Spring 1989): 1–6.

Docherty, Thomas. *Reading (Absent) Character: Towards a Theory of Characterization in Fiction*. Oxford: Clarendon, 1983.

Eighteen Songs of a Nomad Flute: The Story of Lady Wen-chi. Intro. and trans. Robert A. Rorex and Wen Fong. New York: Metropolitan Museum of Art, 1974. N. pag.

Frye, Joanne S. "*The Woman Warrior:* Claiming Narrative Power, Recreating Female Selfhood." *Faith of a (Woman) Writer*. Ed. Alice Kessler-Harris and William McBrien. New York: Greenwood, 1988. 293–301.

Gerrard, Nicci. "Wittman Ah Sing." Rev. of *Tripmaster Monkey*, by Maxine Hong Kingston. *New Statesman and Society* 2 (25 Aug. 1989): 28.

Hsia, C. T. *The Classic Chinese Novel: A Critical Introduction*. New York: Columbia UP, 1968.

Hu chia shih pa p'ai. Ed. Nanjing Museum. N.p.: Shanghai People's Art [1961]. N. pag.

Hutcheon, Linda. *A Poetics of Postmodernism: History, Theory, Fiction*. New York: Routledge, 1988.

Kingston, Maxine Hong. *China Men*. New York: Knopf, 1980.

———. "The Coming Book." *The Writer on Her Work*. Ed. Janet Sternburg. New York: Norton, 1980. 181–85.

———. "Cultural Mis-readings by American Reviewers." *Asian and Western Writers in Dialogue: New Cultural Identities*. Ed. Guy Amirthanayagan. London: Macmillan, 1982. 55–65.

———. "Eccentric Memories: A Conversation with Maxine Hong Kingston." With Paula Rabinowitz. *Michigan Quarterly Review* 26.1 (Winter 1987): 177–87.

———. Interview. *Women Writers of the West Coast: Speaking of Their Lives and Careers*. Ed. Marilyn Yalom. Interview by Arturo Islas. Santa Barbara: Capra, 1983. 11–19.

———. "A *MELUS* Interview: Maxine Hong Kingston." With Marilyn Chin. *MELUS* 16.4 (Winter 1989–90): 57–74.

———. "Moving Images: From Shao-lin to Woman Warrior." Keynote address. U of Wisconsin, Madison. 2 Apr. 1987.

———. "This Is the Story I Heard: A Conversation with Maxine Hong Kingston and Earll Kingston." With Phyllis Hoge Thompson. *Biography* 6.1 (Winter 1983): 1–12.

———. *Tripmaster Monkey: His Fake Book*. New York: Knopf, 1989.

———. *The Woman Warrior: Memoirs of a Girlhood among Ghosts*. New York: Knopf, 1977.

LaCapra, Dominick. *History and Criticism*. Ithaca: Cornell UP, 1985.

Li, David Leiwei. "The Naming of a Chinese American 'I': Cross-Cultural Significations in *The Woman Warrior*." *Criticism* 30.4 (Fall 1988): 497–515.

Lin, Patricia. "Clashing Constructs of Reality: Reading Maxine Hong Kingston's *Tripmaster Monkey: His Fake Book* as Indigenous Ethnography." *Reading the Literatures of Asian America*. Ed. Shirley Geok-lin Lim and Amy Ling. Philadelphia: Temple UP, 1992. 333–48.

Lin, Tai-yi, trans. and ed. *Flowers in the Mirror*. By Li Ju-chen. Berkeley: U of California P, 1965.

Lo Kuan-chung. *Three Kingdoms*. Trans. and ed. Moss Roberts. New York: Pantheon, 1976.

Ma, Y. W., and Joseph S. M. Lau. *Traditional Chinese Stories: Themes and Variations*. New York: Columbia UP, 1978.

Mink, Louis O. "Narrative Form as a Cognitive Instrument." *The Writing of History: Literary Form and Historical Understanding*. Ed. Robert H. Canary and Henry Kozicki. Madison: U of Wisconsin P, 1978. 129–49.

Schreiber, Le Anne. "The Big, Big Show of Wittman Ah Sing." Rev. of *Tripmaster Monkey*, by Maxine Hong Kingston. *New York Times Book Review* 23 Apr. 1989: 9.

Schueller, Malini Johar. "Theorizing Ethnicity and Subjectivity: Maxine Hong Kingston's *Tripmaster Monkey* and Amy Tan's *The Joy Luck Club*." *Genders* 15 (Winter 1992): 72–85.

Scott, Dorothea Hayward. *Chinese Popular Literature and the Child*. Chicago: American Library Association, 1980.

Shih, Nai-an. *Water Margin*. 2 vols. Trans. J. H. Jackson. Hong Kong: Commercial, 1976.

Sledge, Linda Ching. "Oral Tradition in Kingston's *China Men*." *Redefining American Literary History*. Ed. A. LaVonne Brown Ruoff and Jerry W. Ward, Jr. New York: MLA, 1990. 142–54.

Smith, Barbara Herrnstein. "Narrative Versions, Narrative Theories." *On Narrative*. Ed. W. J. T. Mitchell. Chicago: U of Chicago P, 1981. 209–32.

Takaki, Ronald. *Strangers from a Different Shore: A History of Asian Americans*. Boston: Little Brown, 1989.

Tyler, Anne. "Manic Monologue." Rev. of *Tripmaster Monkey*, by Maxine Hong Kingston. *New Republic* 200 (17 Apr. 1989): 44–46.

Waley, Arthur, trans. *Chinese Poems*. London: Allen, 1946.

Warnock, Mary. *Memory*. London: Faber, 1987.

White, Hayden. "The Historical Text as Literary Artifact." *The Writing of History: Literary Form and Historical Understanding*. Ed. Robert H. Canary and Henry Kozicki. Madison: U of Wisconsin P, 1978. 41–62.

Wu Ch'eng-en. *Monkey*. Trans. and ed. Arthur Waley. New York: John Day, 1943.

Memory and the Ethnic Self:
Reading Amy Tan's *The Joy Luck Club*

BEN XU

The Chinese-American milieu in a San Francisco neighborhood furnishes the main contingent of characters in Amy Tan's *The Joy Luck Club*. What the four families in that book, the Woos, Jongs, Hsus, and St. Clairs, have in common is mother-daughter relations. The mothers are all first-generation immigrants from mainland China, speaking very little English and remaining cultural aliens in their new world. The daughters are all born and educated in America, some even married to "foreigners." Within the microcultural structure of family, the only means available for mothers to ensure ethnic continuity is to recollect the past and to tell tales of what is remembered. Lamenting the failing marriage of Lena, her daughter, and Lena's unfamiliarity with the "Chinese ways of thinking," Ying-ying St. Clair voices the anxiety and helplessness shared by all the mothers in the book: "All her life, I have watched her as though from another shore. And now I must tell her everything about my past. It is the only way to penetrate her skin and pull her to where she can be saved" (274).[1]

In her mother's eyes, because Lena, without a memory of the past, allows herself to be borne by the bustle of life, she doesn't know who she is and cannot hold herself together. It may be true that through her mother's memory, Lena will learn to share a belief in certain rules, roles, behaviors, and values that provide, within the family and the overseas Chinese community, a functional ethos and a medium of communication. But will she, even if she unexpectedly finds herself confronted by a hurt that has a special connection with her mother's past, have access to her mother's deeply buried anxiety, psychic need, specific mental habits, and life-world perception? Can she really share her mother's unrepeatable life experience? Can she ever learn how to overstep her own existential limits through her mother's story? What if she has to take cognizance of a barrier in her present existence that will eternally be a barrier between her and her mother? These questions can be asked not only about Lena, but also about all the other daughters in *The Joy Luck Club*. In this essay I will take a close look at the conflict between the two generations of the book and the existential unrepeatability that separates them; and through examining the complexity of the operations of memory, I will also explore how the recollection and narration of the past are related to a present sense of ethnic identity.

"Memory" is an intellectually seductive concept, capable of drawing on a diverse literature, from the cognitive concerns of speculative philosophy on the one hand to experimental psychological probes of the processing-storage-retrieval function of mind.[2] Yet because the intellectual roots are so diffuse and the connotations quite varied, I should clarify the two basic assumptions that I make when I use this term in my discussion of the ethnic identity in *The Joy Luck Club:* first, a premise of the narrative construction of memory, and second, an emphasis on its social-psychological mechanism.

Most of the philosophical thinkings of memory lapse almost inadvertently into the idiom of the static picture by conceiving of memory as a particular content of the mind, as an image, a presentation, an impression, and so on.[3] However, it is not just that we have images, pictures, and views of ourselves in memory, but that we also have stories and narratives to tell about the past that both shape and convey our sense of self. Our sense of what has happened to us is entailed not in actual happenings but in *meaningful* happenings, and the meanings of our past experience, as I will explore and defend in my reading of *The Joy Luck Club,* are constructs produced in much the same way as narrative is produced. Identity, as well as the implicated self-definition and self-narrative, almost certainly will be activated from memory. Recent social-psychological studies have shown that self-images bring forth a host of intricately related self-knowledge and self-identity, whose information, values, and related beliefs are socially situated as well as psychologically useful.[4] Such understanding of the social-psychological mechanism of memory narrative is also implied in recent studies of narrative. Hayden White suggests that, in the narrative of individual life as well as in the narrative of history, the meaning of a given set of events, which he recognizes as taking the form of recurring tropical enfigurations, is not the same as the story they consist of (111). Using as a guideline his differentiation of two kinds of narrative meanings without committing to his tropological explanation of them, we may, in memory narrative, distinguish its *life-story* from the *existential perception* it entails. If the life-story

Memory and the Ethnic Self

is marked by a seeming actuality, the existential perception is what transforms the casual daily events into a functioning mentality or an existential concern that is not self-evident.

This bifurcate view of memory narrative permits us to consider a specific life-story as imagery of existential themes or problems about which the story is told, and the existential perception as a comprehensive context in which meaningful questions can be asked about the factual events of that life-story (what, how, and especially why). A functioning mentality, such as the survival mentality, which characterizes all the mother characters in *The Joy Luck Club,* hardly enters into view with factual occurrences. It manifests itself only in the distribution of existential themes of the memory narrative. Memory narrative does not represent a perfect equivalent of the events it purports to describe. It goes beyond the actuality of events to the determination of their coherency as an existential situation, and this general picture of life in turn assigns exemplary values to the events that are awakened in memory by a functioning mentality.[5]

This awakening of memory by a person's present mentality is illustrated by Ying-ying St. Clair's story of her childhood. When Ying-ying was four years old, she became separated from her parents on a Moon Festival trip to a scenic lake, and while watching a performance of Moon Lady, she made a wish that she could not remember for many decades. It was only after her first broken marriage, a second one to a kind but alien Irishman, and many "years washing away my pain, the same way carvings on stone are worn down by water," when she was "moving every year closer to the end of my life," that she remembered that on that night, as a child of four, she "wished to be found" (64, 83).

Of the four mother characters in *The Joy Luck Club,* Ying-ying had the happiest childhood. Her family was very wealthy and took good care of her. Her getting lost from her family on a festival trip was no more than a small accident with no harmful consequences. However, this insignificant incident in her early childhood is remembered as an emblem of her unfortunate life. This is the memory of a survivor of bad times, who has lost her capacity to remember a different life even though she did once experience it. The memory itself has become a psychic defense, which helps to justify her social disengagement, her fatalistic perception of the world as a system of total control, and her fascination with extreme situations and with the possibility of applying their lessons to everyday life.

Ying-ying's survival mentality is typical of all the women characters who belong to the Joy Luck Club. All the Club Aunties have experienced two kinds of extreme situations: one is famine, war, forced marriage, and broken family in China, and the other is cultural alienation, disintegration of old family structure, and conflict between mother and daughter in America. In order to survive the drastic changes in their lives, these women need to maintain a psychological continuity, a coherent picture of life-world, and a continuity of self. Such a need requires the assuring structure of memory narrative: life-story narrative, with the genre's nominal continuity of aims and intentions, hopes and fears. Memory is for them a socializing, ego-forming expression of anxieties, hopes, and survival instinct.

Indeed, the Joy Luck Club itself, with a magnificent mah jong table at its center, is an expression and embodiment of that survival mentality and its strategies of psychic defense. Suyuan Woo, mother of the book's first narrator, started the first Joy Luck Club in wartime Kweilin as a refugee running away from the triumphantly advancing Japanese troops. In times of trouble, everyday life became an exercise in survival, both physical and mental. If "hero" means someone who takes decisive action during a time of crisis, then for Suyuan Woo, whose life was in crisis, survival itself became a decisive action—a heroic action, albeit a pathetic and disenchanted one. In order to hang on to living, the club members in Kweilin tried to "feast," "celebrate [their] good fortune, and play with seriousness and think of nothing else but adding to [their] happiness through winning" (11). As Suyuan herself explains: "It's not that we had no heart or eyes for pain. We were all afraid. We all had our miseries. But to despair was to wish back for something already lost. Or to prolong what was already unbearable" (11–12).

Suyuan starts the second Joy Luck Club in San Francisco in 1949. This time she is a refugee fleeing from the triumphant Communists in China. This second club is both a memory of the first club and a renewed means of survival. For those new club members newly immigrated to America, "who had unspeakable tragedies they had left behind in China and hopes they couldn't begin to express in their fragile English," the happy moments of playing mah jong are the only times they can "hope to be lucky"—"That hope was our only joy" (6, 12).

If the mah jong club reflects and is part of the Club Aunties' survival endeavor, it is not just a commonsense survival, which describes the difficulty of making ends meet, or alludes to the fear of poverty. It expresses the perception that they are all survivors in the sense that they have lived through dark times and have emerged in the new world. It indicates the urgency to hold one's life together in the face of mounting pressures, which are seen in the dire light reflected from their memories of specific events that victimized them in earlier times. Understanding is made necessary when one encounters the unfamiliar, the unknown, the uncanny. The process of understanding ordinarily begins with the displacement of the thing unknown toward something that is known, apprehended, and familiar. The process of understanding thus begins with an experiential shift. The domain of the unknown is shifted, by renewing the old strategy of survival, toward a domain or field presumably already mastered. All the stories included in the first section of the book are about mother-narrators' experiences of victimization. These old memories help shift the narrators, especially in an unfamiliar environment, to a growing belief that people are all victimized in one way or another by events beyond their control.

However, memories are not one-way tracks, as some early philosophers would like to suggest.[6] If the past casts a shadow on the present through memory, the present also preimposes on the past by means of memory. It is worth noting that John Perry, a philosopher who has written widely on the relationship between memory and personal identity, believes that "A sufficient and necessary condition of my having participated in a past event is that I am able to remember it" (69). The one-way-track memory is what Nietzsche calls the "inability to forget," a symptom of a sick person who has given in to past failures and discomforts, making the present unbearable and the future hopeless. What we find with the Joy Luck Club mothers is what Nietzsche calls "memory of the will," an active memory that is sustained by the will to survive (Nietzsche "Second Essay"). Suyuan has told her refugee story in so many varied ways that her daughter does not know how to relate them to reality and can only take them as "a Chinese fairy tale" (12). These stories, in the form of memory, test Suyuan's ability to forget. These stories are her symptomatic records of a traumatized soul making a desperate effort to push back the memory of the tragic loss of a husband and two baby daughters during the war. The real memory was suppressed but did not go away; and Suyuan, as her second husband feels intuitively, "was killed by her own thoughts," which she could not even articulate to her husband and daughter (5).

Not only does Suyuan's early experience of extreme situations result in a defensive contraction of self, but it also transforms her relationship with her daughter into one of survival: a fear that she will lose her connection with her daughter and that her experiences, thoughts, beliefs, and desires will have no future successors. The daughter may look like the mother or even identify with her; and yet, the two are still worlds apart from each other. John Perry makes a very important differentiation between "identification" and "identity," pointing out, "Identity is not a necessary condition of identification. I can identify with the participant in events I did not do, and would not do, even if they were to be done" (76). Georges Rey, in his study of the existential unrepeatability of personal experience and identity, emphasizes the impossibility of passing on identity through the narrative of memory:

> There are ... an alarmingly diverse number of ways in which one person might come to share the seeming memories of another: vivid stories, hallucinations.... All my and my grandfather's hopes to the contrary, he does not survive as me, no matter how much I seem to recollect (and even take as my own) the experiences of his life from having heard of them at his knees. This is partly because we were both alive when I heard and identified with them; and, for all our not inconsiderable mutual concern, none of it was (strictly) personal. I didn't thereafter enjoy any privileged access to his feelings and thoughts. (Rey 41)

Memory is not just a narrative, even though it does have to take a narrative form; it is more importantly an experiential relation between the past and the present, projecting a future as well. It is the difference of experiential networks between Suyuan Woo and her daughter that accounts for the daughter's resistance to the mother's nagging about hard work and persistence, as well as for her confusion about the mother's constant sense of crisis.

Hard work and persistence are with the mother—and most "diligent" Chinese immigrants—less self-sufficient virtues than means and conditions of survival. These qualities are desirable to her just because she learned from her previous experiences that they are attributes of a "winner" in life, and she is going to treat them only as such. It is only on the usefulness of these qualities that she will base her self-approval for exercising them. Even though she knows pretty well that her daughter will never get a Ph.D., she keeps telling her friends and neighbors that Jing-mei Woo is working on it. This is less a lie or wishful thinking than an expression of her survival instinct: what the mother seeks from her friends and neighbors is not the kind of approval that applauds her daughter's personal qualities, but the conviction for herself that her daughter possesses the attributes of a survivor. It is too easy to advance

Memory and the Ethnic Self

diligence, frugality, or whatever as the Chinese ethnic qualities. What is wrong in such a view is an essentialist interpretation of these qualities as *inherent* "Chinese" attributes and a blindness to their special relations with a particular kind of ethnic memory.

The disposition for many first-generation Chinese immigrants in America to see life as a constant test of survival, to the extent that it almost becomes ethnic symbolism, is a complex mentality. It is deeply rooted in China's past of hardship and numerous famines and wars. The word in Chinese that denotes "making a living in the world" is *qiusheng* (seeking survival) or *mousheng* (managing survival). The Chinese classics are full of wisdom on how to survive, whether it be Taoist escapism, Confucian doctrine of the mean, or legalist political trickery. The lack of religion and of a systematic belief in an afterlife in Chinese culture indicates the preoccupation with the urgency of surviving in the present world. The simultaneous contempt for business (and "the rich")[7] and love of money (in the form of thriftiness) support the view of money not as a measure of success but as a means of survival.

However, survival mentality in China has never become a symbol of nationality and ethnicity. It is part of the living conditions that have remained intact with little change throughout centuries; but it has never been mobilized and turned into what Werner Sollors, in his *The Invention of Ethnicity,* calls "kinship symbolism." Only when a Chinese person is uprooted from his own culture and transplanted into an alien one does he become aware of the fluidity, proteanness, and insecurity of his self. It is not until then that he feels the need to define himself by a reference group, or even deliberately manages a certain image or presentation of self using the symbolism of survival. "Ethnicity," as Sollors aptly observes, "is not so much an ancient and deep-seated force surviving from the historical past.... It marks an acquired ... sense of belonging that replaces visible, concrete communities whose kinship symbolism ethnicity may yet mobilize in order to appear more natural" (xiv). The newly acquired ethnic awareness of being Chinese in America and the sense of urgency about the individual's and the group's preservation and survival register the waning of the old sense of a durable public world, reassuring in its definiteness, continuity, and long-tested survival strategies.

Once the imagery of confinement, insecurity, alienation, and extreme situations takes hold of the imagination of an ethnic group, the temptation to extend this imagery to lesser forms of stress and hardship and to reinterpret every kind of adversity or difference in the light of survival proves almost irresistible. Things as trifling as the Chinese way of playing mah jong, which, according to the mothers in *The Joy Luck Club*, is different from and far superior to the Jewish mah-jongg, is jealously guarded as a matter of immense significance. The excessive concern with being "genuinely Chinese" announces the abandonment of efforts to adapt to a mixed and heterogeneous society in favor of mere ethnic survival.

Even at the mah jong table people have to face the agony of how to survive. "We used to pay mah jong," explains Auntie An-mei to Jingmei, "winner take all. But the same people were always winning, the same people always losing." This is what life has always been: there has to be someone who is a loser and a victim. But the San Francisco Joy Luck Club Aunties reformulate their mah jong game so that it becomes, symbolically at least, a game with no losers: "We got smart. Now we can all win and lose equally. We can have stock market luck. And we can play mah jong for fun, just for a few dollars, winner take all. Losers take home leftovers!" (18).

The change in the mah-jongg game may appear insignificant. But it reflects the Club Aunties' view of the loser as a victim who fails to survive and their belief that one should make every effort to defend oneself against the bruising experience of being a loser, even at a mah jong table. Such a view can alter the way competition and rivalry are experienced. Competition, whether it be in a chess game, in a piano performance, or for a college degree, now centers not so much on the desire to excel as on the struggle to avoid a crushing defeat. A willingness to risk everything in the pursuit of victory gives way to a cautious hoarding of the reserves necessary to sustain life over the long haul. For Lindo Jong, her daughter's chess championship is not merely proof of her talent. It is more essentially her attribute of being "lucky" and being a winner. Worldly success has always carried with it a certain poignancy, an awareness that "you can't take it with you"; but among the Chinese, glory is more fleeting than ever, and those who win a game worry incessantly about losing it.

Lindo Jong gives her daughter Waverly her own talisman of luck—"a small tablet of red jade which held the sun's fire," (98) in order to add to the latter's "invisible strength." Her daughter's chess battle becomes her own battle. But the worry and concern of her subtle survivalism is not appreciated by her daughter, who accuses her mother of using her to show off and trying to take all the credit. Lindo Jong's "all American made" daughter has a hard time understanding why her mother believes that "luck" and "tricks" are more valuable and more important than

Memory and the Ethnic Self

"skill" and "smartness." "You don't have to be so smart to win chess," Lindo Jong tells her daughter, "It is just tricks" (187).

Waverly Jong feels immobilized by her mother's "sneak attack" (191) and at first completely misses the disenchanted heroic style that underlies the "sneakiness" of her mother's attack. What she fails to see is that her mother's "sneakiness" is meant to prepare her for dealing with the unpredictable future, in which she will constantly find herself faced with unstructured situations and the need to survive on her own. In contrast to the American strategies of survival that Waverly has been introduced to (such as upward mobility, security in legal protection, and active individual choice), Lindo Jong's survivalist strategy of "sneakiness" or "trickiness" is miserably nonheroic and shamefully "Chinese." Waverly fears and despises her mother and resists her mother's teaching. Puzzled by her daughter's reaction, Lindo Jong confesses: "I couldn't teach her about the Chinese character. How to obey parents and listen to your mother's mind. How not to show your own thoughts, to put your feelings behind your face so you can take advantage of hidden opportunities. Why easy things are not worth pursuing. How to know your own worth and polish it, never flashing it around like a cheap ring. Why Chinese thinking is best" (289).

The wearing of a mask is to Lindo Jong an heroic act—an act necessary for the survival of poor immigrants like herself, who feels "it's hard to keep your Chinese face in America" (294). Wearing a mask means the ability to suppress one's true feelings and emotions—even to deceive—in order to be allowed to live. She is not unaware of the debt that the mask wearer has to pay to human guile; but in her understanding there is no rage that rips the heart, no passion of combat that stresses the heroic deeds of ethnic rebellion. With many Chinese-Americans like Lindo Jong, survivalism has led to a cynical devaluation of heroism and to a resignation that is tinged with a bitter sense of humor.

When they first arrived in America, Lindo Jong and An-mei Hsu worked in a fortune cookie factory, making Chinese sayings of fortune for American consumption. Lindo Jong was wondering what all this nonsense of Chinese fortunes was about. An-mei explained to her:

> "American people think Chinese people write these sayings."
> "But we never say such things!" [Lindo Jong] said. "These things don't make sense. These are not fortunes, they are bad instructions."
> "No, miss," [An-mei] said, laughing, "it is our bad fortune to be here making these and somebody else's bad fortune to pay to get them." (299–300)

Lindo Jong knows that the Chinese wearing of the mask, just like those Chinese fortunes, can convince many Americans that they know and understand Chinese people. She also has an unusual insight into the risk that the mask wearer can become psychologically dependent upon the mask, even when the mask is not needed. Continued wearing of the mask makes it difficult for the wearer of the mask to be her real self. Maskedness has almost become the ethnic symbolism for Chinese-Americans like Lindo Jong, who thinks like a person of "two faces," being neither American nor Chinese (304).

In a self-consciously two-faced person like Lindo Jong we find a detached, bemused, ironic observer, who is almost fascinated by the fact that she has not a self that she can claim as "me." The sense of being an observer of one's own situation and that all things are not happening to "me" helps to protect "me" against pain and also to control expressions of outrage or rebellion.[8] Survivors have to learn to see themselves not as free subjects, but rather as the victims of circumstances, be they the current situation or predetermined fate or disposition.

Chinese Taoist culture helps to maintain this kind of victim mentality because it reinforces a passive if not fatalist attitude toward life. The influence of Taoism, in its popularized form, is obvious in the way *ying-yang-wu-hsing* is used by the mothers in *The Joy Luck Club* to explain why the life of the unlucky people is what it is. In this popularized form of Taoism, human life is a constant struggle for a precarious balance between *ying* and *yang,* affected even by the placing of your bedroom mirror or the location of your condominium apartment. *Wu-hsing* (the five elements: water, fire, wood, metal, and earth), which were conceived by the Taoist masters as five fundamental phases of any process in space-time, become the mystical ingredients that determine every person's character flaw according to one's birth hour: "Too much fire and you had a bad temper. . . . Too much water and you flowed in too many directions" (19).

Rose Hsu Jordan, like her mother, An-mei, has too little wood, and as a consequence, she bends to other people's ideas. Her marriage with Ted breaks down because he is annoyed by her lack of decision. Measured by the *wu-hsing* system, none of us has all the five character elements perfectly balanced, and therefore every one of us is by nature flawed. This view of human imperfection may appear like the Greek view of tragic flaw. But the Chinese view of character flaw has no interest in any unyielding defiance to fate. The wily Chinese wisdom and belief that heroes do not survive inform the disenchantment with conventional codes of defiance and heroism. While the Greek tragic heroes face their inevitable destruction with dignity and grace, the believers in *wu-hsing* want to survive by amending the flaw through nonheroic small acts such as taking special names—the "rose" in Rose Hsu Jordan's name, for example, is supposed to add wood to her character.

Both Rose Hsu Jordan and her mother regard themselves as victims of circumstances, but, belonging to two different generations, they resort to different strategies in order to alleviate their fear of disaster. An-mei Hsu copes with everyday mishaps by preparing for the worst and by keeping faith in hope. Her faith in God, which she held for many years before her youngest boy was drowned, was less a religious belief for which she was ready to sacrifice herself than a survival strategy of keeping herself in hope. Although An-mei keeps telling her daughter to make her choice, or even to indulge in a fantasy revenge for the wrongs suffered by women, she is prepared to accept the worst thing that can happen to a woman: the fate of being a woman, "to desire nothing, to swallow other people's misery, to eat my own bitterness" (241).

An-mei's faith in God, or, after the death of her boy, in hope, is to her American-made daughter only a fatalist's self-created illusion. "[My mother] said it was faith that kept all these good things coming our way," Rose Hsu Jordan tells us with her tongue in cheek, "only I thought she said 'fate,' because she couldn't pronounce that 'th' sound in 'faith.' " Rose has to be tempered by her own suffering before she will discover that "maybe it was fate all along, that faith was just an illusion that somehow you're in control" (128).

Instead of relying completely on her mother's advice, Rose, devastated by her broken marriage, goes to her psychiatrist. Psychiatry for Rose, the young Chinese-American, has played the role of modern successor to religion. In psychiatry, the religious relief for souls has given way to "mental hygiene" and the search for salvation to the search for peace of mind. Rose tells her psychiatrist about her fantasy revenge against Ted and feels like having "raced to the top of a big turning point in my life, a new me after just two weeks of psychotherapy." She expects an illuminating response from her psychiatrist. However, just as her mother was forsaken by God, Rose is let down by her mundane savior: "my psychiatrist just looked bored" (211). It is only after her frustrating experience with her psychiatrist that Rose feels an accidental connection of a shared fate between herself and her mother. The mother and daughter are covictims of a common threatening force over which they have no control. It is when Rose, in her dream, sees her mother planting trees and bushes in the planter boxes, adding wood to both of them, that she lets us get a close view of a mother-daughter relation that is defined neither by blood tie nor by material service, a relation that is neither Chinese nor American, but Chinese-American.

This mother-daughter relationship with a unique ethnic character is what we discern not only in the Hsu family, but also in the families of Woos, Jongs, and St. Clairs. The family tie between the mother and daughter in each of these Chinese-American families is no longer what determines the Chinese daughter's obligation or the Chinese mother's authority. Family features shared by mother and daughter in those Chinese-American families are not something to be proud of, but rather something that causes embarrassment on one side or the other, and often on both sides. However, neither does this mother-daughter relationship rest, as is common in the American family, on material service. The cross-generation relationship rests on a special service the mother renders to the daughter: the mother prepares the daughter for the extreme situations of life, gives her psychic protection whenever possible, and introduces her to resources she needs to survive on her own. The mother does all this not in the capacity of a self-righteous mother, but as a covictim who has managed to survive. The traditional role of a Chinese mother has been greatly curtailed in America. If formerly she represented an automatic authority, now she is unsure of herself, defensive, hesitant to impose her own standards on the young. With the mother's role changed, the daughter no longer identifies with her mother or internalizes her authority in the same way as in China, if indeed she recognizes her authority at all.

The loosened family tie and shaky continuity between the two generations represented in *The Joy Luck Club* account for the particular narrative form in which their life acts and events are told. These stories share no apparently recognizable pattern or fully integrated narrative structure. The character relations are suggested but never sufficiently interwoven or acted out as a coherent drama. Our attention is constantly called to the characteristics of fiction that are missing from the book. It is neither a novel nor a group of short stories. It consists of isolated acts and events, which remain scattered and disbanded. It has neither a major plot around which to drape the separate stories, nor a unitary exciting climax that guides the book to a final outcome.

Yet all these customary ingredients have a place in *The Joy Luck Club*. The successions of events are fully timed and narrators of these events are carefully grouped in terms of theme as well as generation distribution (mothers and daughters). The book's sixteen stories are grouped into four sections: the two outer sections are stories by three mother-narrators and Jing-mei Woo, who takes the place of her recently deceased mother; and the two inner sections are stories by four daughter-narrators. The stories in the first two sections are followed by successive dénouements in the next two sections, leading to a series of revelations. All the energies set in motion in the first story of the book, which is told by the book's "framework" narrator, come to fruitful release in the book's last story, told by the same narrator, Jing-mei Woo.

Just as the mah jong table is a link between the past and present for the Club Aunties, Jing-mei Woo, taking her mother's seat at the table, becomes the frame narrator linking the two generations of American-Chinese, who are separated by age and cultural gaps and yet bound together by family ties and a continuity of ethnic heritage. It is Jing-mei Woo who tells the book's two frame stories, the first and the last. These two frame stories, ending with a family reunion in China, suggest strongly a journey of maturity, ethnic awakening, and return-to-home, not just for Jing-mei Woo, but metaphorically for all the daughters in the book. This experience is like a revelation—a sudden unveiling of the authentic meaning of being "Chinese." The ecstatic character of this experience is well expressed by Jing-mei Woo: "The minute our train leaves the Hong Kong border and enters Shenzhen, China, I feel different. I can feel the skin on my forehead tingling, my blood rushing through a new course. My mother was right. I am becoming Chinese" (306).

At this moment, she seems to come to a sudden realization that to be "Chinese" is a lofty realm of being that transcends all the experiential attributes she once associated with being a Chinese, when she was unable to understand why her mother said that a person born Chinese cannot help but feel and think Chinese:

> And when she said this, I saw myself transforming like a werewolf, a mutant tag of DNA suddenly triggered, replicating itself insidiously into a syndrome, a cluster of telltale Chinese behaviors, all those things my mother did to embarrass me—haggling with store owners, pecking her mouth with a toothpick in public, being color-blind to the fact that lemon yellow and pale pink are not good combinations for winter clothes.
>
> But today I realize I've never really known what it means to be Chinese. I am thirty-six years old. My mother is dead and I am on a train, carrying with me her dreams of coming home. I am going to China. (306–7)

The book has, for other daughters, other moments of revelation like this one experienced by Jing-mei Woo, though they are of a more subtle nature and of less intensity. It is at these moments of revelation, often after their own sufferings in life, that the daughters come to realize the value of and reason for their mothers' survival mentality and the disenchanted heroism of mask and endurance and begin to hear the rich and multiple meanings in their mothers' stories instead of mere dead echoes of past acts and events. They become less resistant to identifying with their mothers and more receptive to the humble wisdom of the previous generations. The change from resistance to acquiescence signifies simultaneously the growth of a mature self and the ethnicization of experience.

The need to ethnicize their experience and to establish an identity is more real and more perplexing to the daughters than to the mothers, who, after all, are intimate with and secure in their Chinese cultural identity in an experiential sense, in a way their American-born daughters can never be. The daughters, unlike their mothers, are American not by choice, but by birth. Neither the Chinese nor the American culture is equipped to define them except in rather superficial terms. They can identify themselves for sure neither as Chinese nor American. Even when they feel their identity of "Americanness" is an estrangement from their mothers' past, there is no means of recovering the Chinese innocence, of returning to a state that their experiential existence has never allowed them. They are Chinese-Americans whose Chineseness is more meaningful in their relationship to white Americans than in their relationship to the Chinese culture they know little about. The return to their ethnic identity on the part of the daughters is represented in *The Joy Luck Club* as realizable on a level where a real split between the existential self and the ethnic self is alluded to by a narrative rivalry between "tale of the past" and "tale of the present." Not only are the contrast and discontinuity between the two types of tales metaphorical of the split of self, but also their organizing narrator, Jing-mei, is symbolic of the split self of the daughters' generation.

The ethnicization of experience does not automatically mean an ethnic identity. The ethnicized and mature self acquiesces to the ethnic affiliation that fixes its patterns and meanings, but at the very point of acquiescence, it registers discomfort with such constraints. Indeed, the strange blending of acquiescence and resistance accounts for the fact that the return to the motherland in *The Joy Luck Club* is temporary and disillusioning, no more than a "visit." Such a visit is at once an assertion of "going home" and a painful realization of "going home as a stranger."

Therefore, the significance of the book's frame device of return-to-home and its satisfaction of the reader's formal expectations should not disarm our critical query as to whether the ethnic self really represents a

Memory and the Ethnic Self

higher form of self or self-awareness. The book's frame device suggests the split between the true but unrecognized self and the false outer being whose sense of self and identity is determined by the need to adjust to the demands of a fundamentally alien society. Such a dualist view of self offers the reassuring but problematic concept of ethnic reality as that which is familiar and recuperated and which, in the homeland, loyally awaits our return even though we turn from it. It assumes that the "inner" or "true" self is occupied in maintaining its identity by being transcendent, unembodied, and thus never to be discovered until the moment of epiphany. This cozy view of return to the authentic self suggests not only a split between the existential self and the ethnic self, but also a fixed hierarchy of them, with the changing and trapped existential self at the bottom and the essential and free ethnic identity at the top. However, this hierarchy is unstable: the ethnic self, just like the existential self, is neither free nor self-sufficient, and therefore never an authentic or genuine self. Our ethnic experience, no less than our existential experience, depends on the mediation of others. We become aware of our ethnicity only when we are placed in juxtaposition with others, and when the priority of our other identities, such as individual, class, gender, and religious, give place to that of ethnicity. Like other kinds of identities, ethnic identity is not a fixed nature or an autonomous, unified, self-generating quality. It is a self-awareness based on differentiation and contextualization. The self is not a given, but a creation; there is no transcendent self, ethnic or whatever else. Ethnic awareness is not a mysteriously inherited quality; it is a measurable facet of our existence, whose conditions and correlates are the only context in which we can understand how we reconstitute feelings and inner knowledge of our own ethnic being.

Notes

1. Amy Tan, *The Joy Luck Club* (New York: Ivy, 1989). Quotations are cited parenthetically in the text.
2. Philosophers dealing with memory are typically concerned with its representative function, as capable of bringing to our mind images (St. Augustine and others), presentation (Aristotle), impressions (Aristotle and others), ideas (Locke and Hume), and the immediate or present objects in memory (A. D. Woozley and others). See, for example, Aristotle, "On Memory and Reminiscence," *The Basic Works of Aristotle*, ed. R. McKeon (New York: Random House, 1941); Augustine, *Confessions* 10. 8–19; John Locke, *An Essay Concerning Human Understanding*, 2

vols., ed. A. C. Fraser (Oxford, 1894) bk. 2, chap. 10; David Hume, *A Treatise of Human Nature*, ed. L. A. Selby-Bigge (Oxford, 1888) bk. 1, pt. 1, sec. 3; pt. 3 , sec. 5; A. D. Woozley, *Theory of Knowledge* (London: Hutchinson's University Library, 1949), 2–3. The psychological study of memory owes a substantial debt to Hermann Ebbinghaus, who singlehandedly moved memory from the domain of the speculative philosopher to the province of the experimental scientist. In the two-volume *Practical Aspects of Memory: Current Research and Issues* (Chichester, Eng.: Wiley, 1988), M. M. Gruneberg, P. E. Morris, and R. N. Sykes put together a whole variety of approaches and methods that are used today in experimental psychological studies of memory, such as eyewitnessing, autobiographical memory, maintenance of knowledge, and so forth.

3. Aristotle, St. Augustine, John Locke, David Hume, etc. (see note 2).

4. See for example H. Markus, "Self-Schemata and Processing Information about the Self," *Journal of Personality and Social Psychology* 35 (1977): 63–78; S. T. Fiske and S. E. Taylor, *Social Cognition* (Reading, MA: Addison-Wesley, 1984); B. R. Schlenker, "Self-Identification: Toward an Integration of the Private and Public Self," *Public Self and Private Self*, ed. R. F. Baumeister (New York: Springer-Verlag, 1986), 21–62.

5. John Perry refers to this cognitive hermeneutic circle of memory, and the reciprocal reality between a person who remembers and the things that he remembers. He writes, "That my present apparent memory of a past event stands at the end of a causal chain of a certain kind leading from that event is not something I can directly perceive, but something believed because it fits into the simplest theory of the world as a whole which is available to me" (69).

6. This view was most representatively voiced by the nineteenth-century British philosopher Sir William Hamilton, who regarded memory as one of the undeniable conditions of consciousness. See, for instance, "Lecture XI," *Lectures on Metaphysics and Logic*, ed. H. L. Mansel and John Weitch (Edinburgh: W. Blackwood and Sons, 1859–1860), 205. Identity is explained as constituting in the assurance that our thinking ego, notwithstanding the ceaseless changes of state, is essentially the same thing. What such a view fails to see is that in remembering, a person not only records what has happened to him but also strives toward a restitution of his own ego—a construction of a continuous, integrated sense of his real existence in relation to time, nature and society, cause and effect.

7. The Chinese proverb *weifu buren* suggests the incompatibility between "being rich" and "being benevolent."

8. In today's mainland China, the wearing of a political mask is still practiced as a gesture of self-preservation and, hopefully, of potential resistance.

Works Cited

Nietzsche, Friedrich. *The Genealogy of Morals*. Trans. Francis Golffing. New York: Anchor, 1956.

Perry, John. "The Importance of Being Identical." Rorty. 67–90.

Rey, Georges. "Survival." Rorty. 41–66.

Rorty, Amélie Oksenberg, ed. *The Identities of Persons*. Berkeley: U of California P, 1976.

Sollors, Werner, ed. *The Invention of Ethnicity*. New York: Oxford UP, 1989.

White, Hayden. *Tropics of Discourse: Essays in Cultural Criticism*. Baltimore: Johns Hopkins UP, 1978.

Traveling Light:

Immigration and Invisible Suitcases

in M. G. Vassanji's *The Gunny Sack*

ROSEMARY MARANGOLY GEORGE

Following Barbara Harlow's practice of naming literary genres by political and ideological contents rather than by formal attributes, it could be argued that the contemporary literary writing in which the politics and experience of location or rather of "dislocation" are the central narratives be called the "immigrant genre."[1] Distinct from other postcolonial literary writing and even from the literature of exile, it is also closely related to the two. For the immigrant genre, like the social phenomenon from which it takes its name, is born of a history of global colonialism and is therefore an undeniable part of postcolonialism and of decolonizing discourses. And, like the distance that exile imposes on a writing subject, writers of the immigrant genre also view the present in terms of its distance from the past and future. This genre, I will argue, is characterized by a disregard for national schemes and by a narrative tendency toward repetitions and echoes—a feature that is often displayed through plots that cover several generations. Most importantly, the immigrant genre is marked by a curiously detached reading of the experience of "homelessness" that is compensated for by an excessive use of the metaphor of luggage, both spiritual and material.

I argue for a distinct genre because such a move lessens to some degree the burdens and constraints that contemporary criticism has placed on the category known as "postcolonial literature."[2] In the West today, the literature that is recognized as postcolonial is that produced by authors with a "Third World" affiliation. It is read as being chiefly concerned with issues of nationalism and/or national allegory as well as with articulating a critique of colonialism. Though written in English or French, it is expected to *and does* constantly "translate" itself by dexterously and continuously explaining the local allusions, practices, and cultures that

Traveling Light

are incorporated into the narrative. Thus, although usually located in the non-West, this fiction's ultimate literary destination is taken to be the Western metropoles.

It can be said that in the postcolonial era, all locations, all writers, all subjects are postcolonial, in that the history of colonialism is shared by the globe albeit with different impacts on different locations and peoples.[3] Yet, while colonization is part of the historical (and even current) *baggage* of all nations involved, the onus of what is called "postcolonial discourse" is borne by writers and academic practitioners whose personal histories include birth, childhood, and possibly an early education in one of the former colonies, but whose work is published and received by Western publishing houses and academic (as well as other) readers. Much of this writing qualifies for the category of the "immigrant genre."

For readers in the West, as well as for readers in the once-colonized parts of the world, there is as much familiar landscape as there is foreignness in this genre. Given that immigrant fictions are often concerned with the experience of immigration to Western nations and are written in global languages, these fictions seem to straddle the geographic world. As a result this literature travels well. It is therefore not surprising that when we in the West talk of postcolonial fiction our reference is usually *specifically* to the immigrant genre. Similarly, the recent focus on internationalism or cosmopolitanism as exhibited in literature is read on the body of texts generated by the processes of immigration, migration, and exile.[4]

In the last four decades, numerous novels have taken the issues of immigration as their central narratives. For example, *Bye-Bye Blackbird* by Anita Desai (1970); *Wife* by Bharati Mukherjee (1975); *Second Class Citizen*, Buchi Emecheta (1974); *Shame*, Salman Rushdie (1983); and *Meatless Days*, Sara Suleri (1989). As early as 1956 Samuel Selvon published *The Lonely Londoners*, a novel on West Indian immigrants in England. In 1976, A. Sivanandan, editor of *Race and Class*, drew attention to the literary and economic connections that mandated reading the practice of immigration as well as the discourses it produced as *directly* linked to the history of imperialism. More recently, in "DissemiNation: Time, Narrative, and the Margins of the Modern Nation," Homi Bhabha puts forth a theoretically nuanced reading of the writing that inscribes the nation from its margins.

Assessing the work of immigrant writers in Canada, Jürgen Hesse argues that the "cultural burdens" that these writers carry "will be of little or no value to them" as writers. Their cultural knapsack, he writes, "is less of a movable asset; it becomes a hindrance within the bewildering cultural landscape which they are entering" (87). Immigrant novels themselves suggest that traveling light or arriving with luggage can both be serviceable ways of entering the new location. The question might rather be how to distingush the heavy luggage from the light. Over and over again in the literature of immigration there are scenes that catalogue the spiritual, material, and even linguistic luggage that immigrants carry over. Rushdie's novel *Shame* explores the nature of that luggage.

> When individuals come unstuck from their native land, they are called migrants. When nations do the same thing (Bangladesh), the act is called secession. What is the best thing about migrant peoples and seceded nations? I think it is their hopefulness. Look into the eyes of such folk in old photographs. Hope blazes undimmed through fading sepia tints. And what's the worst thing? It is the emptiness of one's luggage. I'm speaking of invisible suitcases, not the physical, perhaps cardboard, variety containing a few meaning-drained mementos: we have come unstuck from more than land. We have floated upwards from history, from memory, from Time. (71)

Some fictional immigrants, like Annie John, the seventeen-year-old protagonist of Jamaica Kincaid's novel, determinedly leave their native lands without baggage.[5] *Annie John* is an Antiguan *Bildungsroman* that ends with Annie's immigration to England. On the morning of her departure from Antigua for England, where she will train as a nurse, Annie resolves never to return and never to remember:

> The things I never wanted to see or hear or do again now made up at least three weeks' worth of grocery lists. I placed a mark against obeah women, jewelry, and white underwear. (135)

Annie John's anger stems from feeling betrayed by an ambitious and adoring mother who wants the best that a colonial education can offer her daughter. This "best," as I argue later, necessarily includes separation, distance, and finally leaving Antigua.

Exile, though very different from immigration, is the other instance in which one carries the baggage of the past—in one form or another—along wherever one wanders. In *After the Last Sky*, an evocative narrative on the lives of present-day Palestinians, Edward Said writes of the ways in which Palestinians living in exile handle such luggage:

> These intimate mementos of a past irrevocably lost circulate among us, like the genealogies and fables of a wandering singer of tales. Photographs, dresses, objects severed from their original locale, the rituals of speech and custom: much reproduced, enlarged, thematized, embroidered, and passed

> around, they are strands in the webs of affiliations we Palestinians use to tie ourselves to our identity and to each other.
>
> Sometimes these objects, heavy with memory—albums, rosary beads, shawls, little boxes—seem to me like encumbrances. We carry them about, hang them up on every new set of walls we shelter in, reflect lovingly on them. Then we do not notice the bitterness, but it continues and grows nonetheless. Nor do we acknowledge the frozen immobility of our attitudes. In the end the past owns us. (14)

The vicious, debilitating injustice of exile that coats the narrative here is missing in the immigrant novel. The immigrant genre is often marked by a detached and unsentimental treatment of the experience of "homelessness"—which has (as in the cast of *Annie John*) often been read as apolitical.

That sentiment accompanying the absence of home—homesickness—can cut two ways: it can be a yearning for the authentic home (situated in the past or in the future) or it can be the recognition of the inauthenticity of all homes. In the context of the immigrant novel it is the latter that usually prevails. For instance, *The Lonely Londoners* begins one cold winter afternoon at Waterloo station, where Moses, an immigrant from Trinidad, waits to pick up a new immigrant from Jamaica. When Henry Oliver saunters off the train "as if he in an exhibition hall on a pleasant summer evening," Moses is shocked to see that he is wearing a light summer suit. Having ascertained that Oliver is not sick, Moses proceeds to ask him about his luggage:

> "Where your luggage?"
> "What luggage? I ain't have any. I figure is no sense to load up myself with a set of things. When I start work I will buy some things."
>
> Now Moses is a veteran, who living in this country for a long time, and he meet all sorts of people and do all sorts of things, but he never thought the day would come when a fellar would land up from the sunny tropics on a powerful winter evening wearing a tropical suit and saying that he ain't have no luggage. (18)

The tone adopted by immigrating subjects in novels like *The Lonely Londoners* or *Bye-Bye Blackbird* is one of cocky defiance, fear, awe, nervousness, and always an underlying excitement. "Floating upwards," to use Rushdie's term, the immigrant reconstructs a series of oxymorons: new histories, new memories, new time, new belongings. Ultimately then, it is from the cardboard boxes with their "few meaning-drained mementos" that invisible luggage is created, and repeatedly recreated, as an empowering bag of tricks that tells the textured tale of who the immigrant is and where he or she belongs.

The Gunny Sack, a novel by M. G. Vassanji, an East African writer of Indian origin, fabricates an elaborate reading of wandering that spans whole continents and an entire century. In this essay, I base my formulation of the immigrant genre primarily on this novel,[6] which was published in 1989 in the Heinemann African Writers Series. While it is not representative of all novels of immigration, and while the motivations of its immigrant characters cannot be mapped onto every immigrating subject in and out of fiction, it serves as a useful text through which to read "this immigrant business," as Rushdie calls it in *Shame* (89).

The Gunny Sack offers a historical narrative of cross-continental immigration from India to East Africa to North America over the course of four generations of the Govindji family. It narrates the lives and fortunes of the various members of this family of traders and shopkeepers on the East African coast: from the arrival of the patriarch Dhanji Govindji in Zanzibar in 1885 to his great-grandson Salim Juma's departure to the United States in the mid-1970s. The opening event, set in the 1970s in an unnamed city in North America, is the funeral of Ji Bai, who was the daughter-in-law of Dhanji Govindji. After the funeral, the primary narrator of this text, Salim Juma (also called Kala), Ji Bai's grand-nephew, inherits the gunny sack that she carried with her through the last years of her life.

This gunnysack, the prototype of the humble traveler's suitcase, is filled with a lifetime of mementos secreted away by Ji Bai; these objects activate the narratives that make up the novel. The opening paragraph demonstrates the uncontainable slippage between what Rushdie calls the "invisible" and "cardboard variety" of luggage:

> Memory, Ji Bai would say, is this old sack here, this poor dear that nobody has any use for any more. Stroking the sagging brown shape with affection she would drag it closer, to sit at her feet like a favorite child. In would plunge her hand through the gaping hole of a mouth, and she would rummage inside. Now you feel this thing here, you fondle that one, you bring out this naughty little nut and everything else in it rearranges itself. Out would come from the dusty depths some knick-knack of yesteryear: a bead necklace shorn of its polish; a rolled-up photograph; a cowrie shell; a brass incense holder; a Swahili cap so softened by age that it folded neatly into a small square; a broken rosary tied up crudely to save the remaining beads; a blood stained muslin shirt; a little book. There were three books in that old gunny that never left her bedside.... (3)

The gunny sack brings a familial history of wandering into the present of the fourth-generation characters. Its contents bring to the basement

Traveling Light

apartment in the Western metropolis memories of a wandering life as "trading immigrants," a life that had a corresponding identity *prior* to the limited "marginal" sense of self that immigration is said to impose on the contemporary immigrant (52).

When Kala first opens it, a ball of cotton lint floats out of Ji Bai's gunny sack, and with this lint, the sack, a "Shehrazade postponing her eventual demise spins out yarns, telling tales that have no beginning or end, keeping me awake night after night, imprisoned in this basement to which I thought I had escaped" (5). Kala here refers to the sack as a "Shehrazade postponing her eventual demise." What does the rather offhand mention here of her "eventual demise" indicate? And how does the basement in the Western metropole serve as an *escape* that would paradoxically be compromised, if the gunny sack of memories were let loose in it?

In coming to terms with the gunny sack and its shifting status as albatross or sustenance, Vassanji's novel engages with several of the issues central both to the literature and to the theorizing of the discourse of immigration. It does this, first, by the narrative use of repetition and echoes to construct meaning from the time- and space-frames of the immigrant; second, by the thematics of multiple generations; and third, by displaying immigration as a challenge to national projects.

Repetition

On reading *The Gunny Sack*, we may ask as Bhabha does in *Nation and Narration*, "But what kind of 'present' is this if it is a consistent process of surmounting the ghostly time of repetition?" (295). The narrative present in this novel, which is mainly available in the first and last chapters, is set in an unnamed Western metropole. The events that gain the significance and recognition that we habitually assign to "plot" and "story-line" are those that are relevant to this narrative frame.

At the end of the first chapter, the narrator writes: "Sona and Kala: Our nicknames. Gold and black. The colours of Africa" (12). Here, "Africa" is the continent, the nation, that is ambiguously left behind. There is nostalgia for it. The word activates memory and stories, but even as it pervades the present, *it is the past*.[7] Yet nowhere in these novels do we see a "present" that is unmarked by the past. No place is significant except insofar as it is like or unlike other places. A spectacular example of this phenomenon of immigrant novels is found in Desai's *Bye-Bye Blackbird* when Dev, the young immigrant protagonist who has just arrived in London from India, first walks down High Street:

> His mood of carelessness, so easy and so fluid, of familiarity and ease, changed quickly out on the High Street where he was a stranger again and all was strange to him. Yet not—he paused and faltered, bumping into a passerby or two—so strange after all. Somehow recognizable too, faintly, surrealistically, for strolling lopsidedly down the High Street, it seemed to him he was strolling down the Mall of a Himalayan hill station, the Mall of Simla or Mussoorie or Darjeeling or any one of the little towns that the heat-maddened, homesick British colonists had created in the incongruous Himalayas, created in the shape and memory of little English country towns and little English suburbia, left oceans behind.... Now, recognizing in the High Street those echoes of the Indian hill station Malls, he realized that the holiday retreats of his childhood had not been the originals he had taken them to be but copies.... Too dazed to retain any haughty poise, he exclaimed, "But this is the Mall!" (12–13)

In this context, for the colonial subject Dev to enter the world of the colonizer is to have his past instantly compromised or otherwise radically altered, for he *now* sees the frame of reference that guided the architecture of his past world. A nice reversal of this incident is offered in the opening passage of *First Light,* a novel by Leena Dhingra, where the "frame of reference" that guides an eleven-year-old new immigrant through London streets is her memory of the Monopoly game board.

> Eleven years old and walking down Piccadilly on my own, I felt safe. It was my first time in London, but I feel quite safe. "I'm in Piccadilly now so I can't go to jail because the lowest the double dice can turn is two!"(1)[8]

No journey in *The Gunny Sack* is recorded except in terms of its difference from or similarity to earlier journeys. No event, no relationship, the list is endless ... with the result that the narrative cannot describe Ji Bai's funeral in the opening scene except in terms of other funerals that it is not. As a result, the entire narrative in this first chapter is split by bracketed asides that bring in the past, and other asides that should be in brackets. The ostensibly bracketed asides, such as

> A sob stifled, a wail choked (practised wailers some of these), the coffin was closed. (4)

train us to recognize the unbracketed but potentially bracket-able asides that bring past and future into the syntax of the present:

> I could see the body shrink under icy pressure, the skin dry and peel off and fly away like a kite, the skeleton rattle and fold and rearrange itself to form a

neat square heap like the firewood that was once sold outside her store in Dar. (4–5)

In this sentence, as elsewhere, one could claim that it is the present that is bracketed or even erased out of the narrative—except for the "neat square heap" that echoes the Swahili cap "so softened by age that it folded neatly into a small square" in the gunny sack. The present thus serves primarily as a frame that the narrative throws around a multilayered "recollection" of the event being described.[9]

The distraction and/or comfort offered by these memories of other times and places make the immigrant more multifaceted a figure than does the equation that delivers a subject who is marginal and who therefore yearns for assimilation into the mainstream. I would like to suggest that it is the search for a location where one can feel at home, in spite of the obvious foreignness of the space, that propels the discourse engendered by the experience of immigration. While the desire for assimilation into the mainstream is popularly read as the trademark of the immigrant experience, this "feeling at home" may or may not require assimilation. At the same time, the process of making oneself at home is a project that may not be completed even by several successive generations.

Generations of Wanderers

Vassanji's use of the multigenerational saga is a crucial manifestation of the immigrant narrative's continuous project of straddling several times, spaces, and languages. As the narrative maps the lives and travels of several generations, it also marks the changing political map of the world in which these generations live. Hence, one can compare Dhanji's travels in search of his son, unrestricted by passports and visas, with the second, third, and fourth generation's travels, which are marked by secrecy, forged passports, and immigration interviews. Of course, lest we indulge in nostalgia for the ease with which Dhanji crossed lands, we are told that he did so with money stolen from the funds entrusted with him for safekeeping by his sect. And, as the narrative suggests, the consequences of this theft can (and do) erupt on the surface of the present.

The "Shamsi" sect to which Dhanji Govindji's family belongs, though invented by Vassanji, is similar to existing religious organizations. The sect has a worldwide network that serves as a support system for wanderers or immigrants who need to be made at home in an unfamiliar place.[10]

285

Thus there are *Mukhis* or religious heads, wherever Shamsis live, "in London, in Singapore, in Toronto":

> You could land in Singapore and call up the local mukhi. "Mukhi Saheb," you say, "I am new here and I need a little help." "Where are you staying?" the mukhi would ask. He doesn't let you finish. "No, no, no, that simply won't do. Aréy, listen to me, you come here first, then we'll see."
> Which is exactly what young Dhanji Govindji did. (10)

And nearly two hundred pages and nearly a hundred years later in the story, when Kala is sent to a remote camp as part of his National Service duties, he does what his great-grandfather had done before him: he inquires about the local *mukhi*.

We might be tempted to see in the existence of this semireligious sect a form of community that provides the benefits of both family and nation, but Vassanji once again refuses us such a resting place. The Shamsi community is beset with its own deceptions: first, the stealing of community funds by Dhanji, and second, his violent death, allegedly at the hands of sect members. In Kala's case, there is the attempt by an Indian family of fake Shamsis to seduce Kala into marrying their daughter by showering him with hospitality when he is far from his home.

The Gunny Sack continually chronicles the ways in which immigrants articulate a sense of home amid homelessness by building on familial and communal ties, ties that intrude on the individual's sense of independence and self-interest in ways that only "family" is allowed to do. Indeed, the very limits of "family" can be problematic. During the British crackdown on the Mau Mau movement, Juma refuses to risk his family's safety in order to hide the son of Mary, the Kikuyu woman who had been like a surrogate mother to him. The narrator, Kala, who is Juma's son, remembers this incident from his childhood as "one more bad memory" that "the gunny would like to throw out."

> "The police would have found him anyway," said my father. We never saw Mary again. Perhaps she too was taken away, to be screened, detained even. Was she a Mau Mau sympathizer? What did we know of her—a friend from another world who came periodically and then once at night in an hour of need—whose memory we now carry branded forever in our conscience.... (78)

The terms in which this "bad memory" is recalled are marked by syntactical ambivalence and incompleteness: Mary is, after all, from "another world" and yet, there is the guilt of having failed her in her hour of need. In a moment of crisis, the shelter offered by "home" and "family" becomes exclusive.

Traveling Light

Again, what determines "family" is not always evident. Huseni, for instance, is stepson in his father Dhanji Govindji's house because he is born of Dhanji's union with Bibi Taratibu, the African slave woman. But, ousted by Dhanji's marriage to Fatima, the narrator tells us, "Gentle Bibi Taratibu, *of course*, had to go. She moved to a house *at the further end* of the village, *bordering* the forest" (13, emphasis added). She is pushed to the margins, and, as the novel tells us repeatedly in its descriptions of the geographical layout of several colonial urban and rural settlements, the location of Bibi Taratibu's house at the border of the forest throws her back into the African section of the village. Replaced by the legally and racially legitimate wife Fatima, Taratibu is no longer "family." Thus the immigrant community constructs its own marginal places and persons.

Perhaps it is coresidence rather than blood that determines family. Thus Kulsum's sister's children, Mehroon and Yasmin, as well as her brother's three daughters, Shamin, Shiraz, and Salma, live with her at various times as cared-for and caring members of her family. And yet, Juma, who lived as a child and young man with his aunt's family, was made painfully aware of his status as an inferior outsider. Clearly, for Juma and for his father, Huseni, before him, it is their "mixed" blood, the result of the union between Indian male and African female, that serves to mark them as different. In the next generation, Salim Juma, who inherits his father's dark skin, is nicknamed "Kala"—the word for "black" in several North Indian languages—and he is the person in his generation who falls in love with an African.

But the desires of different generations of immigrants differ, and it is this that makes the interaction between generations such a vital feature of the immigrant novel and experience.[11] Would the story be different if the Dhanji Govindjis had stayed with the Bibi Taratibus and if together they had had Africa's children? Early in the novel Vassanji's narrator considers this alternate history that did not take place:

> Tell me, Shehrbanoo, would the world be different if that trend had continued, if there had been more Husenis, if these chocolate Husenis with curly hair had grown up unhindered, playing barefoot in kanzus and kofias, clutching Arabic readers.... (11)

What is wistfully contemplated here is a knitting together of different racial communities through marriage and procreation.

In the opening address at the "Nationalisms and Sexualities" conference held at Harvard University in the summer of 1989, Benedict Anderson examined the proximity of politics and sexuality in nationalist novels. Working primarily with Indonesian nationalist novels, Anderson claimed that "love" in nationalist novels leaps across politically unbridgeable chasms, such as intercaste, interclass, and interrace marriages and sexual unions. Though such "impossible loves" are doomed to fail, according to Anderson their presence in the nationalist novel serves to eroticize the nation by making its narrative one of love and passion.[12]

Accordingly, here, in *The Gunny Sack,* we have Dhanji and Taratibu and later Amina, the young African woman, and Kala: two unions that leap over political and social chasms, but which do not succeed in bringing together different communities. Taratibu represents the old Africa of slavery and (female) exploitation; Amina is used as an eroticized symbol of young Africa. The danger of one union revealing itself as double of the other is always present—for Amina and Kala, as much as for the reader. Hence there is, despite the evident regret, very little surprise worked into the narration of the failure of these relationships. The narrator does not quite succeed in convincing the reader, in the passage quoted above or in other passages, that his love for Amina is any different from the sexually exploitative relationship Dhanji had with Taratibu. The pattern of repetition is so forcefully suggested that neither the characters nor the reader can shake it off. Kala is subject to the same myths as the rest of his community, so when it comes to loving and living with an African woman he cannot imagine doing so other than in ways that would violate the pattern of relationships that have his community's sanction. Thus history repeats itself and Kala, like the men and women in earlier generations, follows the well-trodden path of allowing a racially legitimate wife to be chosen for him.

Challenging National Projects

In "DissemiNation," Bhabha argues that today the modern nation is written at its margins by those who occupy those spaces. According to Bhabha, a great number of persons occupy the margins: "the colonized," "women," as well as "the migrant" and the "immigrant." Moreover, the difference between those at the margins and the mainstream citizen *itself* refuses the harmony imposed by those who suggest that nations are born of peoples sharing an imagined community. For Bhabha's intention is, in part, to force a rethinking of Anderson's *Imagined Communities,* which argues that nations come into being when diverse people imagine a sense of shared community.[13] According to Bhabha's corrective, those at the margins of modern nations "disturb the ideological manoeuvres through which 'imagined communities' are given essentialist identities" (300). The discourse produced at the margins, then, serves as a "supplement" to "the dominant discourse" and as such "antagonizes the implicit power to generalize, to produce the sociological solidarity" (306). Immigrants and other wanderers are, according to Bhabha, "themselves the marks of a shifting boundary" of the modern nation (315). And this shifting boundary writes a doubleness, splitting, or ambivalence into the narratives produced at the margins. Ultimately, Bhabha claims that it is "through this process of splitting that the conceptual ambivalence of modern society becomes the site of *writing the nation*" (297).

Yet one could argue just as well that the "nation" is precisely that which is *not* inscribed by the writing produced at the margins. Perhaps the location sought in these instances ought not to be read in terms of national subjectivity and/or national space. Immigration, one could argue, *unwrites* nation and national projects because it flagrantly displays a rejection of one national space for another more desirable location, albeit with some luggage carried over.

We could alternatively examine this issue by attempting to assign a national allegiance to Vassanji's novel. While the book is published in Heinemann's African Writers Series, it could just as easily be part of the "ethnic" literature of Canada, which is where Vassanji lives, writes, and works as a teacher. His text would, then, fall into the category of "South Asian Canadian Literature," the title of an article written by Vassanji and published in an Indian literary journal.[14] Vassanji himself is the editor and founder of the *Toronto South Asian Review*. The acknowledgments for his novel include mention of "assistance" from the Ontario Arts Council and Multiculturalism Directorate. And India could, of course, stretch the limits of her literary field and claim Vassanji as one of her own far-flung writers.

Vassanji's text at its boundaries—the beginning and the end—disturbs the national calculations of the Western nation (Massachusetts or Canada), and all through the text the saga of this family disturbs the imperial calculations of first the Germans, then the British, and later of independent Tanzania's Ujamaa socialist project. For Bhabha, when the supplements are taken into account, "the language of national collectiveness and cohesiveness is [what is] now at stake" (304). And what the living at the edge, in basements or at the margins, calls for is a doubleness (variously present as repetitions, as a sense of déjà vu) in the discourse that such experience engenders. Yet, Bhabha's theory of "DissemiNation" or of "double writing" from the margins is "not simply," he claims, "a theoretical exercise in the internal contradictions of the modern liberal nation" (299). Rather,

> The postcolonial space is now "supplementary" to the metropolitan centre; it stands in a subaltern, adjunct relation that doesn't aggrandise the presence of the west but redraws its frontiers in the menacing, antagonistic boundary of cultural difference that never quite adds up, always less than one nation and double.
> From this splitting of time and narrative emerges a strange, empowering knowledge for the migrant that is at once schizoid and subversive. (318–19)

Here Bhabha seems to equate the postcolonial with the migrant and the migrant with the subaltern. In "Woman in Difference," Gayatri Spivak argues, like Bhabha, that the modern nation is (ready or not) being written over by those at the margins. Commenting on a short story by Mahasweta Devi entitled "Doulati, the Bountiful," Spivak draws attention to those left out of the "relay race between Empire and Nation, between imperialism and independence" (107). Here, the reference is to the specific Indian aboriginal communities about which Mahasweta writes. These aboriginals, or *Adivasis* as they are called in India, occupy in Spivak's words the "space that cannot share in the energy of this reversal [from colony to independent nation]" (106). Spivak uses the conclusion to Mahasweta's story to further her argument with great impact. Doulati, an *adivasi* woman sold into prostitution, is found on the morning of independence day to be lying dead on a clay map of India drawn by a patriotic schoolmaster in the school yard for the day's celebrations. The presence of her putrid and diseased body on the map makes it physically impossible to stage any kind of flag-day ceremony. Spivak comments: "The space *displaced* from the Empire-Nation negotiation now comes to inhabit and appropriate the national map, and makes the agenda of nationalism impossible" (127–28). Spivak correctly describes this space as "the habitat of the subproletariat or the subaltern." And Mahasweta's stories amply demonstrate how these communities are erased out of national calculations.

However, the immigrant who often opts out of national projects such as liberation-day euphoria is *not* always subaltern. Especially not the immigrant who speaks her story through collections of luggage—spiritual, material, linguistic, written, or oral. The Indian communities in Africa, while they are on the margins and supplementary to the modern nations imagined there, are not automatically or necessarily subaltern. Entering the African continent as traders from as early as the sixteenth century, and later brought in by British imperialists to build the railway that was to link all of British Africa, the Indians have often occupied a privileged position vis-à-vis Africans in Africa. A similar position was occupied by the Greek and the Lebanese communities in West Africa. Outside Africa, the Syrian community in Antigua provides another example of a minority group that has established itself in a position of privilege. The local antagonism against these communities was and is also quite similar. In *A Small Place*, Kincaid's strongly worded assessment of Antigua today, the Syrian community is introduced in the course of a description of a palatial house:

> The people who live in this house are a merchant family who came to Antigua from the Middle East less than twenty years ago. When this family first came to Antigua, they sold dry goods door to door from suitcases they carried on their backs. Now they own a lot of Antigua; they regularly lend money to the government, they build enormous (for Antigua), ugly (for Antigua), concrete buildings in Antigua's capital, St. John's, which the government then rents for huge sums of money; a member of their family is the Antiguan Ambassador to Syria; Antiguans hate them. Not far from this mansion is another mansion, the home of a drug smuggler. . . . (11)

The antagonism in the above passage cannot be smoothed over. Antigua is too small a place with too few resources to allow one Syrian family, albeit a powerful one, to set up home here. As in *The Gunny Sack*, the links between trade and colonial (and neocolonial) exploitation are too close to be ignored by the indigenous population or at least by parts of it.

As *The Gunny Sack* and other documents demonstrate, under colonialism (British and German), the Indians were used as a buffer class and race that further distanced the Europeans from the Africans. It was a buffer status that was adopted and adapted by the Indians as they strove to maintain their identity as outsiders. Consider this "theory of creation" that is attributed to Kulsum, the narrator's mother, a pivotal figure in the text:

> When God was well and ready after all his exertions finally to create mankind, he sat himself beside a red-hot oven with a plate of dough. From this he fashioned three identical dolls. He put the first doll into the oven to finish it, but, alas, brought it out too soon: it came out white and undone. In this way was born the white race. With this lesson learnt, the almighty put the second doll into the oven, but this time he kept it in for too long. It came out burnt and black. Thus the black race. Finally the One and Only put the last doll inside the oven, and brought it out at just the right time. It came out golden brown, the Asian, simply perfect. (73)

The passage brings to light an important aspect of "immigritude." This myth-making that Kulsum passes on to her children suggests that those at the margins may read their marginality as a positive, even superior stance from which to experience the modern nation.[15] While this may be an instance of the "strange empowering knowledge" that Bhabha attributes to the immigrant, there may be absolutely no desire on the part of immigrants to write themselves into a national discourse *except* as aliens.[16]

The problems arising from this immigrant stance of maintaining distance from the mainstream come to a head when the center refuses to include the (alien) margin as a part of the whole and decides to evict it. As amply illustrated by the fate of the Indians expelled empty-handed in 1972 from Idi Amin's Uganda, the "adjunct" or, following Bhabha, "supplementary" position occupied by these Indian communities in East Africa was and is indeed precarious. But a community that has sat on the fence (or rather that has a history of literally being the fence that divided colonizer from the colonized) is endangered when a unifying national discourse, as in a postindependence era, requires it to pick allegiances. The immigrants in Vassanji's text have always already renounced such allegiances. Writing on the implications (for the Indian communities) of the British and German conflict as it extended to their respective colonies in East Africa during the World War I period, Vassanji states:

> Among the trading immigrant peoples, loyalty to a land or a government, always loudly professed, is a trait one can normally look for in vain. Governments may come and go, but the immigrants' only concern is the security of their families, their trade and savings. Deviants to the code come to be regarded and dismissed as not altogether sound of mind. Of the ten storeowning families in Rukanga, seven were Indian; six packed up and were ready to leave by dawn. Again, the gunnies stuffed with one-rupee notes, the jewelry tied around their waists; once more the promises of returning. . . . (52)

This passage challenges Bhabha's assertion that it is the "nation" that is written or rewritten at these marginal sites. For the immigrant characters in this novel, having left one national space, leaving another and yet another are given facts of the wandering life.[17] Bhabha writes:

> The scraps, patches and rags of daily life must be repeatedly turned into the signs of a national culture, while the very act of the narrative performance interpellates a growing circle of national subjects. (297)

Traveling Light

This argument holds only for immigrants who actively desire for themselves an integration into a national culture as national subjects. In *The Gunny Sack*, the "scraps, patches and rags of daily life" are "repeatedly turned into the signs of" *a family history—that is of little value to most family members*. It is what the immigrant *may choose* as a compensation for the lack of other filiations, rather than as a microcosmic or allegorical version of the nation.

Vassanji's text repeatedly displays the nitty-gritty details of living at the margins of a constantly changing center. Over the century that the novel covers there are several changes of power at the centers of the colonial and then national spaces in East Africa. The repercussions on the margins are different in each instance, and the immigrant has to make sure that she or he is not too deeply implicated in any political allegiance if he or she is to survive the new order. The narrative displays the political flexibility that is necessary for the immigrant's survival. Toward the end of the World War I, sensing that a German defeat is imminent, the Indian community in this novel prepares to leave German Rukanga in East Africa:

> Once more the promises of returning, the hiring of men to watch over what was left behind.... The mukhi stayed; and so did Ghulam's brother Abdulla, who had learnt German in Bibi Wasi's classroom in Matamu and became Germany's lifelong friend.
> The road to Dar es Salaam was uneventful. They stayed close to the railway line and after some time saw a train. They also saw motor vehicles and troops moving west and hailed. "Biritish, Zindabad! Rani Victoria, Zindabad!" (52–53)

The decision to stay or leave is a pragmatic one and "loyalties" change over the course of a paragraph. This passage suggests that in this context the politics of the profession, rather than those of national affiliation or disaffiliation, rule the day. Here, a livelihood made from trading between borders requires that one have a foothold on either side of the fence. Hence, the move from being subjects of Deutsch Ost Afrika to being British subjects is marked through shouts of "long live Queen Victoria," a comic hailing because she is long dead, but politically astute because she is a metonym for the British empire. This declares to those in the trains and motor vehicles (the entering British troops) that the Indians are already compliant with the new order. There is apparently no need for forced conversions here.

Scenes of "leave-taking" mark the boundaries of these texts in ways that display the ease with which fictional narrative defies the confines that (national) border controls try to impose on immigrants. Suleri's autobiographical novel *Meatless Days* begins with the following passage:

> Leaving Pakistan was, of course, tantamount to giving up the company of women. I can tell this only to someone like Anita, in all faith that she will understand, as we go perambulating through the grimness of New Haven and feed on the pleasures of our conversational way. Dale who lives in Boston, would also understand. She will one day write a book about the stern and secretive life of breast feeding and is partial to fantasies that culminate in an abundance of resolution. And Fawzi, with a grimace of recognition, knows because she knows the impulse to forget. (1)

In the very first paragraph, then, this novel lays bare the marks of the immigrant genre: the easy movement between past, present, and future, and between Pakistan, New Haven, and Boston, as well as the juxtaposition of recognition and the impulse to forget. As is typical of this genre, the narrative does not "leave" Pakistan. And yet the novel is set going by this act of leave-taking.

The frequency of scenes of leave-taking in the novels on immigration poses a question: is the postcolonial globe no more than places one tries desperately to leave and places one tries desperately to get entry into? In Kincaid's novel, Annie John thinks of herself as she walks to the boat jetty that will take her away from Antigua to England:

> My mother and my father—I was leaving them forever. My home on an island—I was leaving it forever. What to make of everything? I felt a familiar hollow space inside. I felt I was being held down against my will. I felt I was burning up from head to toe. I felt that someone was tearing me up into little pieces and soon I would be able to see all the little pieces as they floated out into nothing in the deep blue sea. (144)

Try as she might, Annie cannot gather together a self identity that is more substantial than "a familiar hollow space inside." Attempting to suture together her past and future, she feels herself torn into little pieces. All she can muster together is a name:

> "My name is Annie John." These were the first words that came into my mind as I woke up on the morning of the last day I spent in Antigua, and they stayed up there, lined up one behind the other, marching up and down, for I don't know how long. (130)

Following the trajectory of a successful colonial education means leaving Antigua. For the "best" colonial education nurtures in the colonial subject a rejection of the home country as a necessary step in a "proper" education. This rejection is fueled by Annie's school lessons in literature,

Traveling Light

geography, history, and economics, which teach that England is the ultimate destination. Hence, those who learn their lessons best are those who immigrate to the mother country. Annie John has already left Antigua before she takes the ship out.

For Sona in *The Gunny Sack,* leaving Tanzania occasions an understanding of himself as a colonial subject, one of Britannia's step-children. This mirror is held up to him at the London airport where he stops en route to the United States. In his first letter from London, he describes waiting in line to get immigration clearance at the airport:

> And how does Britannia treat her offspring who come from all over the world to pay their respects? At the Airport, lines, long lines: coloured, white, coloured, white. . . . A coincidence? Hardly. First class and second class British subjects. You look at the others in your line, and you wonder, Am I one of these? Why do they look so strange . . . and dark? You ask yourself, Why do these Indian women always travel with bedding, for God's sake? You want to move away from them and then you check yourself. It could be your mother. You smile. (236)

He reports his conversation with the women in his line, "Kidhar se atey ho? Amritsar. Aap? Tanzania" ("Where are you coming from? or Where are you from? Amritsar? And You? Tanzania"). While the Hindi word *kidhar* translates most accurately as "where" or "whether," the sentence that would best convey the sense of "where do you belong" would use the word *kaha* instead. Yet *kidhar* is appropriate here because it better suggests the temporary nature of "belonging" and "leaving" that becomes quite everyday in the context of immigration. What is equally significant is that neither of the two says "India" or "I'm Indian" in reply to the queries although that is the basis of striking up this conversation and confidently conducting it in Hindi. Does this recognition convey the existence of a flexible identity of "Indian" that survives transportation? In this case, the ability to exchange a few sentences in a common language makes one's country of origin a mere circumstance.

For the immigrant in this novel, identity is linked to a specific location (here India) only hypothetically. There is no urgent desire to return to the place on the map called India. Elsewhere, as in Said's *After the Last Sky,* Palestinian identity without a Palestine is marked with the anguish of homelessness that is absent in Sona's letter. Said writes:

> No Palestinian census exists. There is no line that can be drawn from one Palestinian to another that does not seem to interfere with the political designs of one or another state. While all of us live among "normal" people, people with complete lives, they seem to us hopelessly out of reach, with

their countries, their familial continuity, their societies intact. How does a Palestinian father tell his son and daughter that Lebanon (Egypt, Syria, Jordan, New York) is where we are, but not where we are *from?* (23)

The centrality of "nationhood" and the importance of "state designs" in the context of exile are defused in the immigrant novel. The urgency with which Said's narrative awaits a viable Palestine is in sharp contrast to the exuberance with which Sona looks forward to the move to the United States. On his way to Harvard, Sona has done better for himself than other offspring of Britannia, including the suspicious immigration official who interrogates him at the airport in London. He writes in his letter of this interrogation session:

"You've completed school."
"Yes, that's why I'm going to university."
"You don't want a job in London, for instance?"
"Why would I want a job here when I've got a scholarship to study in America?"
"This scholarship. They just gave it to you?"
(Is he jealous?)
"Yes."
"Anyone can apply?" (Not you, if you're so dense.)
Finally, after several hours, he let me through. (237)

Like his traveling ancestors, Sona is able and willing to move to the most desirable location available to him, in this case, Harvard University, Cambridge, Massachusetts.

The final section of the novel deals with the coming of age of the fourth generation, that of Kala and Sona. Set in the 1960s and early 1970s, the political events in this section revolve around Tanzanian independence.[18] The novel examines the impact of Julius Nyerere's Ujamaa socialist project, and the status of Indians in this newly defined national "family."[19] What this section demonstrates is that while immigrants disturb the easy interpellation of national subjects by a hegemonic national discourse, the very formulation of national projects such as Ujamaa challenges, disturbs, and threatens the immigrants' project of "being immigrants," of remaining marginal, on the fence.

Consider the silence in the Indian section of Dar es Salaam during the independence-day celebration. In a passage that begins with "Independence was painless," a phrase that is repeatedly used, Vassanji reveals the pain that exists for the Indian—the pain of not knowing whether in Tanzania one is the enemy:

> Independence was painless. A Man's colour is no sin in Tanganyika, said Nyerere.... Tanganyika is not Congo, where nuns were raped and hundreds murdered and shops looted.... (156)

It is not clear if the "wide, stocky pipes left in the center of the road" for the purpose of supporting street decorations on independence day will be used as anti-Indian riot weapons as is rumored to have happened elsewhere in newly independent Africa.[20] But the Indian community decides to play it safe; they stay indoors.

> Independence was painless. Prince Philip came to give the country away, but in Kichwele we stayed home and followed the events in the newspapers and on the radio. And on independence day, at midnight, zero hour, while the decorated street below was empty of man or motor vehicle, sitting silent, neglected, like a bride not picked up on the fateful day: upstairs, sitting quietly around the ancient Phillips oracle, we saw in our mind's eye the lights turn off at the National stadium, the Union Jack quietly come down and the lights turn on again to reveal the new green and black and gold national flag flying; we heard the thunderous applause in our sitting room, carried by radio waves, and again, we all swore, far away at the National stadium, carried this time by the wind. (156–57)

This scene is familiar to readers of postcolonial African fiction: the joyous celebration at the changing of flags that marks independence, a new national beginning.[21] Yet this time around, the fictional apparatus speaks from the margin of this national event. It is as with a wedding where the best seats are taken by family members. The narrator cannot give a firsthand account because he does not have a firsthand experience of this crucial moment in Tanzanian national history. Hence, in one of the key instances in which a people imagine themselves as a nation, the immigrant keeps a safe distance. Prince Philip comes to play "father-of-the-bride" and "give the country away." But the Indian part of town is "like a bride not picked up on the fateful day." And yet, this scene, more than any other in the novel, makes this an African, or more specifically, a Tanzanian (even nationalist) novel.[22]

What grants membership into "Families"? Who are the outsiders? *The Gunny Sack* explores the different constructions of "family," "home," "community," and "nation" as ideological and physical structures that engender the self. Nevertheless, one is also compelled to note how every assertion of "belonging" is systematically undercut by the narrative.

To the question "where is the immigrant at home?" this novel adds the question "what is *not* a foreign place for immigrants?" In the following passage, in the exchange between Aziz and Kala, when the former hands over Ji Bai's gunny sack to the latter, the use of "here" and "there" may confuse the reader, but the referents are apparently clear to the speakers themselves:

> "Come, come.... what if she had died there? Would you have posted it?"
> "But she died here...."
> She had said that she would travel, and Aziz accompanied her, first to India and then here. Wherever she went the gunny went with her. Did she know she would die in this foreign place, then? (5)

Here, Vassanji suggests that one *can* be at home in foreign places. For some immigrants, home is traveling with gunny sacks, always postponing Shehreazade's "eventual demise." For others like Aziz's family, feeling at home requires the burning, the forgetting of the gunny sack and of memory. In keeping with the novel's repetitive narrative style, the issue is reframed in another context when Kala goes on his National Service camp trip and is urged by his relatives to take along a big black trunk filled with Indian snacks and other "essentials" for surviving life in the camp. Once he gets there, Kala is punished by his supervisors for bringing along excess baggage; his punishment is to run up and down a hill with his trunk on his head. A few weeks after this grueling experience, Kala writes in a letter to a friend:

> We Indians have barged into Africa with our big black trunk, and every time it comes in our way. *Do we need it?* I should have come with a small bag, a rucksack. Instead I came with ladoos, jelebis, chevdo. Toilet paper. A woolen suit. And I carried it on my head like a fool. (204, emphasis added)

"Do we need it?" Does the immigrant need the "invisible luggage"? At the end of this novel, Kala attempts to liberate himself from the "baggage of paraphernalia" that is his past (268). Releasing the gunny sack's narratives is a first step toward this "disposition of the past" (268). Kala yearns to "embrace the banal present," but such banality comes only at the cost of great violence. The last image we have of the gunny sack is as follows: "She lies on the floor, crumpled, her throat cut, guts spilled, blood on the floor" (268). For Annie John there is no compensation for the lack of "Home," and the anger and frustration of this novel seeps into Kincaid's 1990 "sequel" *Lucy*. At the end of *Lucy*, however, the young woman protagonist begins to come to terms with her "homelessness" through the act of writing. Like Kala in *The Gunny Sack*, Lucy writes in order to be reconciled with her past and thus to lighten her immigrant luggage.

Traveling Light

Belonging in any one place requires a judicious balancing of remembrance and forgetting. Writing on the discourses that inscribe the modern nation, Bhabha states: "it is this forgetting—a minus in the origin—that constitutes the *beginning* of the nation's narrative" (310). He goes on to add:

> It is through this syntax of forgetting—or being obliged to forget—that the problematic identification of a national people becomes visible. (310)

To this *The Gunny Sack* responds: which "nation"? India? East Africa? Tanzania? Britain? the United States? Canada? And which "national people"? Here, there are only generations of wanderers.

Notes

1. See "The theoretical-historical context" in *Resistance Literature* by Harlow, which builds on the theory put forward in 1981 by the Kenyan writer Ngũgĩ (38), which divided literature into that of oppression and that of the struggle for liberation, thus challenging the conventional (Western) practices of distinguishing between literary texts on the basis of form. Also noteworthy is "What Is a Minor Literature?" by Deleuze and Guattari. Using Kafka and Joyce as their prime examples, Deleuze and Guattari define Minor Literature as that which displays the following three characteristics: the deterritorialization of language, the connection of the individual to a political immediacy, and the collective assemblage of enunciation. They add: "We might well say that minor no longer designates specific literatures but the revolutionary conditions for every literature within the heart of what is called great (or established) literature" (18). Deleuze and Guattari argue that their concern is with "the more objective concept" rather than with questions that ask: "What is a marginal literature?" or "What is a popular literature?" or "What is a proletarian literature?" See Rosaldo's refusal of this theory (which he sees as Eurocentric) in "Politics."

2. What happens to the category of "postcolonial literature" after this subcategory of immigrant literature is carved out of it? I would like to suggest that rather than shrinking, the category of "postcolonial literature" would *expand* to include all twentieth-century literature produced from any location that is informed by the dynamics of colonialism. Under this rubric, all literary texts that unsentimentally examine the seductive pleasures of "feeling at home" in homes, genders, specific races or classes, or in communities and nations, could be read as "immigrant" fictions. Such an extensive examination of contemporary fiction is beyond the scope of this paper.

3. In " 'Commonwealth Literature' Does Not Exist," Rushdie argues against the straitjacket imposed on writers across the globe by the term and by the literary preoccupations that are seen as requisite to this fiction. I would like to suggest that by expanding the parameters of the "postcolonial" one ensures that no single formulation, however elastic, can cover this vast artistic terrain.

4. See, for example, *Salman Rushdie* by Brennan. Brennan coins the term "Third-World Cosmopolitan" in an attempt to categorize and contextualize the works of writers like Rushdie, Derek Walcott, Isabel Allende, Gabriel Garcia Marquez, Bharati Mukherjee, etc.

5. *Lucy* by Kincaid "continues" and updates this narrative in the U.S. though with different characters.

6. My intention is not so much to attempt a taxonomy of immigrant fictions as, enabled by the arguments formulated in the novels, to intervene in the ongoing theoretical discussions on postcolonial literature and literary theory.

7. "China," in Tan's *Joy Luck Club*, operates similarly for the generation of "mothers" in that novel.

8. Note that "Piccadilly" is right next to "Jail" on the English Monopoly board.

9. This pattern of repetition continues through the novel: the ball of kapok glides out and sails away like Ji Bai's skin, like a kite, like Sheru's yarns, like Dhanji Govindji's travels, like Yasmin's going to England to train as a nurse, like Begum going off to England with Mr. Harris the physics teacher, like Sona going to Cambridge, Massachusetts, like Kala who follows him there. . . . The list is endless.

10. In *Immigrant Success Story*, Arthur and Usha Helweg note that in the early decades of this century, thousands of Indians left India and traveled by sea and land to Africa, Europe, and North and South America with "hostel *gurudwaras* providing refuge and support along the way" (54). In a footnote, the Helwegs add that "Sikh communities which held to the custom of offering in their *Gurudwaras*, food and lodging to needy travelers, were scattered throughout the British Empire. Migrants often took refuge in the Sikh *Gurudwaras*."

11. For instance, the affiliations of first-generation Japanese-American writers and readers are very different from those of the second-generation, English-speaking *nisei* or third-generation *sansei* writers. Similarly, for the contemporary Palestinian, the personal experience of exile is recounted in terms of whether one is *jil filastin* (those who have known and lived in Palestine before its partition) and *jil al-nakba* (those born after 1948). Memory and desire operate differently for different generations. In *Mississippi Masala*, Nair's recent film on Indian immigrants in the U.S., the confrontation between the young heroine and her father on the issues of love and race are typical of this generational difference.

12. Anderson's address was entitled "Holy Perversions." Also on the panel was Sommer, who made similar connections between erotics and politics. See, as well, Hubel, who examines the metaphoric marriage between Britain and India, which was commonly used in the narratives written by colonial writers. Imperialism is thus represented as a marriage between the masculine Britain and the coy, mysterious India. Anderson's most recent book, *Language and Power*, reads selected Indonesian cultural texts in terms of this dynamic of power and passion.

13. See especially 15–16. Anderson's text emphasizes the many ideological apparatuses that work toward mobilizing this sense of the nation as an imagined unity.

14. The *Literary Criterion* is published by the Department of English, Bangalore University, in Bangalore, Karnataka State, India.

Traveling Light

15. Hesse makes a somewhat similar point. His reference is, however, to the cultural superiority complex of Canadian immigrants who came from Europe. He states: "To be part of multi-ethnic and multicultural affairs in Europe can well breed a feeling of cultural superiority when compared to the straitlaced, unidirectional and repetitive examples of much of North American cultural products.... Sure some of us immigrant writers feel superior to this banal culture" (98–99). While we are familiar with this assessment of Canada and the United States as no more than faint and/or fake echoes of Europe, there is another point being made here. Hesse argues that the immigrant, in this case from Europe, is culturally superior "as [a] result of having had intimate knowledge of several cultures simultaneously" (89).

16. When Bhabha theorizes about "wandering migrants" he focuses on the "foreignness of languages," on "loss," on "voids," "death," "opacities," and "untranslatable silences" (315–19). Enabled by Berger's work on Turkish immigrants in Germany, Bhabha sets out to examine "the desolate silences of the wandering peoples ... that 'oral void' that emerges when the Turk abandons the metaphor of a *heimlich* national culture: for the Turkish immigrant the final return is mythic ..." (316). Later in this section of his argument, Bhabha notes that "this silent Other of gesture and failed speech becomes what Freud calls that 'haphazard member of the herd'" (316). Given the Turkish worker's unfamiliarity with the German language, Bhabha concludes that: "The object of loss is written across the bodies of the people, as it repeats in the silence that speaks the foreignness of language" (315). The view from *within* the Turkish immigrant community as available in oral and written texts may be quite different. Bhabha himself somewhat alters his view of "desolate silences" when he includes Rushdie's theorizing on the immigrant experience in *Satanic Verses* into his reading of migranthood (317–19). Like Rushdie, Vassanji's narrative speaks *from* the position of the immigrant rather than *of* those at the margins.

17. Although the texts I read challenge Bhabha's assertions, clearly wandering is not always painless. Nair's *Mississippi Masala* further complicates the distinctions between exile and immigration that this paper attempts to enunciate. Set in the late 1980s in Mississippi, Nair's film narrates the story of an Indian immigrant family that had been evicted from Uganda in the early 1970s. Different members of this family view their predicament differently. The father, played by Roshan Seth, suffers the anguish of exile. Uganda was and is his homeland. His wife (Sharmila Tagore) and daughter (Sarita Choudhury) view this event in their past and their much more circumscribed present condition of "homelessness" (the family rents two rooms in a relative's motel) with greater equanimity. The film follows two parallel plots: the daughter's romance with an African American (Denzel Washington) and the father's slow rejection of the "pleasures" of absolute identification of himself with a place on the map. At the end of the film the father returns to Uganda for a short visit and finds that his growing detachment to the idea of national belonging makes an immigrant of him. He discovers that he will be happy to live wherever his family resides. Meanwhile, back in Mississippi, the young lovers set off to wander the world together. Their first stop will be Jamaica and from there they will go to Africa, to India....

18. Briefly, Tanganyika was a German colony till after World War I, when the

League of Nations put the area under British administration. After World War II, it was declared a United Nations Trust Territory, again under British administration with the understanding that the British would work toward eventual independence for Tanganyika. Julius Nyerere led this independence movement. He entered politics in the early 1950s, and in 1954 pulled several factions together to form the Tanganyika African National Union. He was elected first prime minister and then president of Tanganyika and later of independent Tanzania. Popularly known as Mwalimu (teacher), Nyerere set up a sophisticated, nonviolent socialist program for Tanzania both before and after independence.

19. *Ujamaa* translated from Swahili would roughly mean "family" or "familyhood" and the word suggests the social responsibility that being part of a family entails. This was the ideology that was to be carried out in various community and self-help projects around the nation. Nyerere's socialist project also included a two-year compulsory work program for university students, called National Service, under which scheme students were sent to work on road construction, irrigation, and other rural development projects that would challenge their elitism as members of an educated class. This and other reforms were to ensure that the notion of the national family for which members (including the elite) took up their responsibility was to be put into material practice. See Davidson for a wider understanding of Tanzanian politics in the context of postcolonial Africa.

20. Fellows writes that in Tanzania, Kenya, and Uganda, there were by independence a total of four hundred thousand Indians among the thirty million Africans in the three countries. The Indian population controlled about four-fifths of the commerce in these countries, from the big trading houses to the small *dukas*. In Tanzania, one of the poorer African nations, at the end of the year of independence (1961) there was no dramatic positive change in the national income or the personal wealth of individuals as had been expected. A drop in world prices of sisal fiber (used in the manufacture of rope and packaging material, such as gunny sacks) and a drop in world coffee prices led to worker layoffs, diminishing profits, and increased resentment against whites and Indians. State-sanctioned confiscations of white farms and Indian businesses were frequently enacted by youth groups. Deportation of Indians was on the rise, especially of those who had not given up their Indian or British passports. Violence and looting were commonplace as Africans attempted to get control of their own economies.

21. See Lazarus for an account of the significance of these ceremonies of independence in the popular understanding of national history, especially as re-presented in African literature. In drawing attention to the ceremony itself, Lazarus's intention is to stress that ". . . unless we grasp the huge significance that the (re)attainment of nationhood carried for African intellectuals in these years of decolonization, it is almost impossible for us to understand the subsequent trajectory of African literature. We cannot make sense of the problematic of postcolonialism in this literature unless we read it as relating, very concretely and immediately to the headiness of initial expectations of independence" (3).

22. Correspondingly, there is not even a passing reference to the Indian struggle for independence nor to the handing over of power in the context of the Indian subcontinent.

Works Cited

Anderson, Benedict R. O'G. "Holy Perversions." Keynote Panel 1. Nationalisms and Sexualities Conference. Harvard University, Cambridge, MA, 16 June 1989.

———. *Imagined Communities: Reflections on the Origin and Spread of Nationalism.* London: Verso, 1983.

———. *Language and Power: Exploring Political Cultures in Indonesia.* Ithaca: Cornell UP, 1990.

Berger, John. *A Seventh Man: Migrant Workers in Europe.* Harmondsworth: Penguin, 1975.

Bhabha, Homi K. "DissemiNation: Time, Narrative, and the Margins of the Modern Nation." *Nation and Narration.* Ed. Bhabha. London: Routledge, 1990. 291–332.

Brennan, Timothy. *Salman Rushdie and the Third World: Myths of the Nation.* New York: St. Martins, 1989.

Davidson, Basil. *Which Way Africa? The Search for a New Society.* London: Penguin, 1967.

Deleuze, Gilles, and Félix Guattari. "What Is a Minor Literature?" *Kafka: Toward a Minor Literature.* Trans. Dana Polan. Intro. Réda Bensmaïa. Minneapolis: U of Minnesota P, 1986. 16–27.

Desai, Anita. *Bye-Bye Blackbird.* Delhi: Hind, 1970.

Dingra, Leena. *First Light.* New Delhi: Rupa, 1991.

Emecheta, Buchi. *Second Class Citizen.* 1974. New York: Braziller, 1975.

Fellows, Lawrence. *East Africa.* London: Macmillan, 1972.

Harlow, Barbara. *Resistance Literature.* New York: Methuen, 1987.

Helweg, Arthur W., and Usha M. Helweg. *An Immigrant Success Story: East Indians in America.* Philadelphia: U of Pennsylvania P, 1990.

Hesse, Jürgen Joachim. "Speaking with Voices of Change: Immigrant Writers and Canadian Literature." *Journal of Ethnic Studies* 19.1 (1991): 87–100.

Hubel, Theresa. " 'The Bride of His Country': Love, Marriage, and the Imperialist Paradox in the Indian Fiction of Sara Jeanette Duncan and Rudyard Kipling." *Ariel: A Review of International English Literature* 21.1 (1990): 3–19.

Kincaid, Jamaica. *Annie John.* New York: Penguin, 1986.

———. *Lucy.* New York. Penguin, 1990.

———. *A Small Place.* Markham, ON: Penguin, 1987.

Lazarus, Neil. "Great Expectations and the Mourning After: Decolonization and African Intellectuals." *Resistance and Postcolonial African Fiction.* New Haven: Yale UP, 1990. 1–26.

Mahasweta, Devi. "Doulati, the Bountiful." Unpublished ms.

Mukherjee, Bharati. *Wife.* Markham, ON: Penguin, 1975.

Nair, Mira. dir. *Mississippi Masala.* Goldwyn, 1992.

Ngũgĩ wa Thiong'o. *Writers in Politics: Essays.* London: Heinemann, 1981.

Rosaldo, Renato. "Politics, Patriarchs, and Laughter." *Cultural Critique* 6 (1987): 65–86.

Rushdie, Salman. " 'Commonwealth Literature' Does Not Exist." *Imaginary*

Homelands: Essays and Criticism 1981–1991. New York: Granta, 1991. 61–73.

———. *The Satanic Verses.* New York: Viking, 1989.

———. *Shame.* New York: Knopf, 1983.

Said, Edward. *After the Last Sky: Palestinian Lives.* New York: Pantheon, 1986.

Selvon, Samuel. *The Lonely Londoners.* London: Longman Caribbean Writers, 1956.

Sivanandan, A. "Race, Class and the State: The Black Experience in Britain." *Race and Class* 17 (1976): 347–68.

Sommer, Doris. "Love and Country in Latin America: An Allegorical Speculation." *Cultural Critique* 16 (1990): 109–28.

Spivak, Gayatri Chakravorty. "Woman in Difference: Mahasweta Devi's 'Doulati, the Bountiful.' " *Cultural Critique* 14 (1989–90): 105–28.

Suleri, Sara. *Meatless Days.* Chicago: U of Chicago P, 1989.

Tan, Amy. *The Joy Luck Club.* New York: Putnam, 1989.

Vassanji, M. G. *The Gunny Sack.* London: Heinemann, 1989.

———. "South Asian Canadian Literature." *Literary Criterion* 19.3–4 (1984): 61–71.

Rediscovering Nineteenth-Century Mexican-American Autobiography

GENARO M. PADILLA

Mexican-American autobiographical narrative came into formation when Mexicans were colonized by the United States, when, as David Weber writes, they were "quickly conquered, subjected to an alien political system in an alien culture" (140). The rupture of everyday life experienced by some seventy-five thousand people who inhabited the far northern provinces of Mexico in 1846 opened a terrain of discursive necessity in which fear and resentment found language in speeches and official documents warning fellow citizens to accommodate themselves to the new regime or at least to remain quiet lest they be hurt or killed outright (Chávez, chap. 3); in personal correspondence where anger and confusion were voiced to intimates;[1] in poetry, *corridos* (ballads), and *chistes* (jokes) which made *los americanos* the subject of ironic humor, linguistic derogation, social villainy; and in Spanish-language newspaper editorials and essays that argued for justice and equality for Mexican-Americans in the new regime.[2] Autobiographical desire also arose as part of this discursive necessity: memory—shocked into reconstructing the past of another socionational life set squarely against experience in "an alien political system in an alien culture"—gave rise to an autobiographical formation in which the desire for historical presence was marked in everything from the episodic *Personal Memoirs* of John N. Seguín (1858) to the historiographic multivolume "Recuerdos históricos y personales tocante a la alta California" (Historical and Personal Recollection Regarding Alta California, 1875) of Mariano G. Vallejo in northern California; from the autobiographies of two cousins in Texas, José Policarpio Rodriguez and Santiago Tafolla, both of whom fought for the Confederacy, to the "Memorias" of Rafael Chacón, whose narrative describes both the American military invasion and his later service in the Union army; from the brief personal narratives of California women such as Eulalia Pérez's "Una vieja y sus recuerdos" (The Memories of an Old Lady, 1877) and Apolinaria Lorenzana's "Memorias de la Beata" (Memories of the Pious

Woman, 1878), to the fully sustained autobiography of Cleofas Jaramillo, *Romance of a Little Village Girl* (1955). Unfortunately, these autobiographical narratives remain generally unpublished and unread. Vallejo's "Recuerdos históricos y personales," like Lorenzana's "Memorias de la Beata" and scores of other California narratives, remains in manuscript within the vast holdings of the Bancroft Library at the University of California at Berkeley; and, even though published, both Rodriguez's *The Old Guide* (ca. 1900) and Jaramillo's *Romance of a Little Village Girl* have been out of print for decades and are nearly impossible to find. Scores of autobiographical narratives from throughout the West and Southwest therefore remain silent.

Discovering, identifying, reading, and categorizing autobiographical narrative is a major undertaking, especially when such work has little and often no precedent. Recent scholarship in Mexican-American literary history, carried out almost exclusively by Chicano scholars, is recovering what will amount to a huge inventory of literary material which must, and shall, overturn the ethnocentric assumption that Mexican-American culture has a meager literary tradition. Without such a collective and critical undertaking, one would think that there had been no autobiographical voice within a culture that has had a vital literary tradition for hundreds of years. Yet only recently has even contemporary autobiography begun to receive serious attention as a distinct genre (Padilla, Márquez, Saldívar 1985). In 1988 *The Americas Review* published a special issue on *U.S. Hispanic Autobiography* in which essays on Oscar Zeta Acosta, Ernesto Galarza, Richard Rodriguez, Gary Soto, and Anthony Quinn and personal narratives of nineteenth-century Mexican California women appear with essays posing theoretical questions about autobiographical ideology, cultural subjectivity in autobiographical narrative, and the autobiographics of recent verse chronicles. In his *Chicano Narrative: The Dialectics of Difference,* Ramón Saldívar has written saliently on "the rhetoric of autobiographical discourse . . . [and] the ideologies that surround" Richard Rodriguez's *Hunger of Memory: The Education of Richard Rodriguez* (1982) and Ernesto Galarza's *Barrio Boy: The Story of a Boy's Acculturation* (1971). In fact, the socio-ideological problematics of autobiographical self-fashioning in contemporary Chicano writing, imbricated as it is with questions about Chicano literary production as a major articulation of resistance to American social and cultural hegemony, appears in nearly all of the current thinking on Chicano autobiography as a genre in which individual experience and collective historical identity are inextricably bound. However, almost all of the scholarship

Nineteenth-Century Mexican-American Autobiography

has focused on issues operating in contemporary Chicano autobiography, as though autobiographical consciousness and narrative production—with all of the problems of identitarian inconsistency, ideological contradiction, rhetorical maneuvering—had developed only in the last two or three decades. This fixation on the contemporary period has had the effect, in my estimation, of reaffirming the perception that Chicano literature is a recent phenomenon. More problematically for our own work, it has largely ignored prior personal narrative formations in which ideological complications—historical repression as well as contestatory articulation—comprise the originary preoccupation with autobiographical expression in Mexican-American culture.

The intention of my work here, therefore, is to show that the formation of autobiographical consciousness—with all of the ideological and rhetorical stresses it now evinces—originated in prior narrative concern about marking individual and collective experience. Encouraged by the archival recovery and the critical reexamination of early African American and Native American literary production, I wish to help win back a Mexican-American literary tradition that has been, not lost, but ignored and suppressed. Like that work undertaken by black scholars in reconstructing the African American literary heritage,[3] my work aims not only to resuscitate dormant autobiographical material, but to refigure the complex system of cultural coding, aesthetic desire, oppositional purpose, which since 1848 has produced autobiographical discourse within a dangerous social space. Likewise, my thinking has been influenced by the rigorous and provocative critical attention Native American autobiography is receiving from innovative scholars like Arnold Krupat, who reads the complex power relations at work in "bicultural composite composition" of Native American autobiography as a contestatory "textual equivalent of the frontier" (33), and Hertha Wong, who reads Native American "pictography as autobiography." Rather than regarding Native American autobiography as the textual equivalent of the museum in which the noble but vanished Indian is represented as a cultural relic, Krupat argues that it is in the textual "presentation of an Indian voice not as vanished and silent, but as still living and able to be heard that the oppositional potential of Indian autobiography resides" (34). Krupat's assiduous reconstruction of the social, historical, and ideological conditions under which Native American autobiography was (and is) produced provides an exemplary model of analysis, one which has forced us to rethink the naive expectations for cultural representation that have too often been brought to the reading of ethnic autobiography. And although she agrees that most Native American autobiography is the product of narrative collaborations with white anthropologists and historians, Hertha Wong has rather audaciously challenged the common assumption that Native Americans did not engage in "autobiographical activity" before contact with Europeans. Wong's revisionist work argues that "long before ethnographers came along, Native Americans were telling, performing, and painting their personal histories. One potential preliterate model of autobiography, at least among Plains Indian males, is the pictographic personal narrative. The symbolic language of pictographs allowed preliterate Plains Indians to "read" about each other from painted robes, tipis, and shields (295). Reading scores of self-representing pictographic narratives, Wong details the rich tradition of storytelling in which self and communal identity share the same comfortable space of tribal life. Her project reminds us that the forms of "autobiographical activity" are various, that the very category of the "self" is in many cultures bound up with the idea of community, and, most importantly, that autobiographical consciousness itself is culturally divergent, complex, and variable in its articulation.

While there are obviously vast differences among post-1848 Mexican-American personal narrative, the formation of African American autobiography as it evolved from the slave narrative, and the recording of Native American autobiography, there are significant similarities in the extracultural representational function inscribed in each for registering opposition to racial and ethnocentric assumptions. Perhaps the most compelling socioliterary associations among the three traditions is what Henry Louis Gates, Jr., in describing the collective function of slave narrative practice, refers to as "a communal utterance, a collective tale, rather than merely an individual's autobiography." Given the physical and spiritual demoralizations to which African Americans as a group had been subjected by slavery, individual autobiographers understood that the "character, integrity, intelligence, manners and morals" of the entire community was staked on "published evidence provided by one of their number" (x). For Native Americans, as Krupat points out, while the nineteenth-century collaborative production of Native American autobiographies generally served as "an acknowledgment of Indian defeat," the Indian prisoner whose life story was recorded opened space for narrating the expansionist brutality visited not only upon the speaker but upon all of his people. The Native American speaker, often a tribal leader, recognized the collective function of the autobiographical occasion and,

Nineteenth-Century Mexican-American Autobiography

rather than focusing only upon himself, articulated identity within the context of a culture that was being systematically destroyed. Likewise, after 1848, Mexican-Americans were conscious of the historical consequences of such "communal utterance." As Mariano Vallejo wrote to his son, his "Recuerdos históricos y personales" (1875) would oppose negative representations of Mexican Californians pervasive in both pre-and post-1848: "I shall not stop moistening my pen in the blood of our unfounded detractors . . . you know I am not vindictive but I am and was born hispano. To contradict those who slander is not vengeance, it is to regain a loss" (Emparán 86). Vallejo's "Recuerdos históricos y personales" tends toward a strategy of historiographic refutation against "our unfounded detractors" rather than focusing on his own rather remarkable personal and public accomplishments.

The heavy burden of collective representation, however, created a problem for Mexican-American autobiography as it had for slave narrative. As William Andrews points out, nineteenth-century Whites produced and read slave narrative "more to get a first hand look at the institution of slavery than to become acquainted with an individual slave" (5). Indeed, as John Blassingame, Thomas Couser, Robert Stepto, and Houston Baker have all shown, the struggle for narrative autonomy by African Americans was waged against scores of white abolitionist editors, amanuenses, and publishers who not only sponsored slave narratives but, through the complex authenticating apparatus which framed the narrative, "addressed white readers over the invisible bodies of black narrators" (Couser 120). I would likewise argue that, after 1848, Anglo-Americans in general were not interested in encouraging the production of, much less in reading, personal narrative which would acquaint them with the perceptions and feelings of Mexicans who had presumably just been granted all the rights of American citizenship. Whereas slave narratives were indeed published and often widely distributed to promote the abolitionist cause, Mexican-American personal narratives—for example, the more than one hundred personal narratives of nineteenth-century Mexican Californians—were meant to function only as supplemental material for American historians and were, therefore, quite intentionally not published. Hence, scores, perhaps hundreds, of Mexican-American personal narratives remain in small state and regional historical society libraries and university special collections, as well as in major archival repositories like the Huntington and Bancroft libraries. Only when we undertake the difficult work of recovering our autobiographical literature from such archival incarceration will the "collective utterance" of our autobiographical tradition disclose its origins, evolution, and cultural significance. Only by activating Houston Baker's "anthropology of art" (xv–xvii) for Mexican-American autobiography can we, as William Andrews advises, begin to reconstruct the "full context in which a genre originated, evolved and took on cultural significance" (4). Like Baker, I believe that "an imaginative reconstruction of a cultural context is mandatory" (xvii) if we are to understand the complex, interrelated codes which constitute the "cultural sign" of autobiographical narrative which emerges from social trauma, dislocation, and suppression.

2

The contradictory positions Mexican-Americans have occupied in American society since the United States-Mexican War of 1846–48 develop as narrative obsession in much autobiographical expression throughout the nineteenth and much of the twentieth century. The earliest post-American narratives record, in their different forms and in different registers, the effects of the military takeover on the Mexican community in general and on individuals specifically. And although I agree that class divisions, regional differences and gender distinctions must be carefully calculated into our understanding of how people responded variously to the American annexation, I believe that the life histories of Mexican-American women and men tend, as a group, to express a wide sense of individual and communal disjuncture. Whether embittered, confounded, acquiescent, resistant, self-denying or assertively defiant, the personal narratives I have read display a set of responses that mediate the nascent national and existential realities imposed upon the daily lives of Mexican(-American)s by a regime that mouthed a rhetoric of democratic ideals but practiced unrelenting hostility in its relations with them. This historical situation has for over a century sustained a rhetorical site upon which Chicano literary production has had as one of its generative principles the reconciliation of vexing contradictions. In autobiographical literature, we see again and again a narrative ground (often a battleground) upon which an individual is contending with social, cultural, and ideological forces that simultaneously so disrupt identity as to unfix it, yet, paradoxically, in disrupting identity establish identity as a destabilized condition.

Since autobiographic narrative produced after 1848 was marked by a

Nineteenth-Century Mexican-American Autobiography

need to meditate upon the upheaval that traumatized the entire spectrum of Mexican-American life, the narrative retrieval of the past may be seen as the direct product of sociocultural stress, often of outright dread of impending personal harm, of a sense that the world was coming to an end—which in many respects it was. The post-1848 personal narratives, as a group, exhibit an obsessive nostalgic tendency to recreate "los dias pasados" (the days of yore) as a means of divesting the second half of the nineteenth century of its absurdity. However idealized the pre-American cultural community may appear in these narratives, the autobiographical reconstitution of life before the occupation was less a self-deluding compensation or naive wish-fulfillment fantasy than what I consider a strategic narrative activity—conscious of its general social implications—for restoring order, sanity, social purpose in the face of political, social, and economic dispossession. Dispossession often articulated itself in an autobiographical sigh of deep sadness and longing for another sociocultural life, but there is always a barely suppressed rage running within the same narrative. Throughout the Southwest, nostalgia mixed with anger functioned to mediate the manifold social forces which infringed upon the spirit of those people who resided in the vast territory that became the Western United States in 1848, but which geo-spiritually became a kind of floating island upon which Mexican(-American)s were left to work out their historic destiny.

But, of course, our history begins well before 1848. So does our literary culture. So does autobiographical impulse. Before drawing the line at 1848, I wish to suggest that more work on indigenous and Spanish colonial autobiographical articulation which prefigures later formations must be undertaken by succeeding scholars who, I hope, will extend the terrain of autobiographical scholarship beyond my work here.

On the indigenous side of the Chicano cultural heritage one might argue, as many scholars indeed have, that the pre-Columbian literature of Mexico comprises a cherished part of the Chicano's literary estate.[4] Suggestive of the kind of "anthropology of art" open to further development, therefore, I encourage further study of "autobiographical activity" that may be measureable in indigenous Mexican literature. As a project in and of itself, I invite succeeding scholars to engage in an "anthropology of art" which will rigorously document the autobiographical activity of pre-Columbian Mexico, as well as succeeding autobiographical writing, and then calculate the influence of an indigenous autobiographical poetics on the contemporary Chicano literary production. On the European side of the *mestizo* cultural face, one can indeed trace a continuous

Spanish colonial discourse of conquest, exploration, and settlement between 1492 and the beginning of the nineteenth century which charts the formation of a new subjectivity in the Americas. Alvar Núñez Cabeza de Vaca's *Relación* (1542), one may say, represents the first autobiographical account of life in the New World, which together with Pedro Castañeda's narrative *Relación de la jornada a Cíbola* (Report on the Expedition to Cíbola, 1582) of Francisco Vásquez de Coronado's expedition of 1540–42, Juan de Oñate's *Proclamación* (1598), Fray Alonso de Benavides's *Memoria* (1630), Fray Eusebio Kino's *Favores Celestiales* (Celestial Favors), and scores of other military and missionary *relaciones, diarios, memorias,* and *viajes* (travels) constitute an enormous field of narrative that may be considered in part autobiographical. After all, American literary historians have identified British travel narratives, journals, diaries, histories as the first literary productions of the nation; likewise, autobiography scholars have been quick to identify William Bradford's *Of Plymouth Plantation,* John Winthrop's *Journal,* Mary Rowlandson's *Captivity Narrative,* Samuel Sewall's *Diary,* and numerous other histories and personal narratives as part of the nation's autobiographic tradition. Both the Spanish and the British narratives, as well as the full range of the indigenous literary production of the Americas, all constitute the beginnings of American literature since they produce a textual domain shaped by the experience of the Americas.

The project to recover the pre-Columbian, indigenous, and Spanish colonial literary tradition must commence, but I would like to suggest, along with literary historians Luis Leal and Raymund Paredes, that such prior traditions be considered not as separate, but separately from that literary production that followed the United States-Mexican War of 1846–48.[5] Like Leal and Paredes, therefore, I wish to argue that a Mexican-American literary formation begins with the American violence that ripped the Mexican map in Tejas in 1836, and then completely blanched the geography of northern Mexico in 1846–48. For it is the literature written after the invasion by the United States which begins to name us as a people living upon a distinct, startling, and confounding plane of history. As Juan Bruce-Novoa argued in an influential essay, the space between the social signifiers—Mexican-American—opened at this historical juncture: "we are the space (not the hyphen) between the two . . . the intercultural possibilities of that space. We continually expand the space, pushing the two influences out and apart as we claim more area for our reality."[6]

Nineteenth-Century Mexican-American Autobiography

As Raymund Paredes points out in a significant essay, "The Evolution of Chicano Literature":

> The great divide in Chicano history is the year 1848 when the Treaty of Guadalupe Hidalgo ended twenty-one months of warfare between Mexico and the United States. . . . Although a distinctive Mexican-American literary sensibility was not to emerge for several generations, the signing of the [Treaty], more than any other event, required southwestern Mexicans to reassess their relationships to the old country and the United States. (36)

Among the many modes of reassessment, an autobiographic narrative formation opened at this break, a narrative formation that emerged from rupture itself, from the necessity of restoring and sustaining the past in everyday life while reconstituting life within the rupture, transforming rupture into the expanding, and expansive, space of intercultural possibility. A Mexican-American literary formation which would "expand the space" and "claim more area for our reality" arose from that traumatic historical moment when the United States violently appropriated northern Mexico in the midnineteenth century (see McWilliams, Acuña, Pitt). The war itself and the rapid Americanization of the West set off a social, political, economic, linguistic, and cultural shock wave which generated a rhetorical situation in which Mexicans inscribed themselves upon history as a warrant against oblivion. The violent transformation of a well-established society forced a systemic shift in the modes of cultural self-recognition which would eventually develop into a cultural production steeped in resistance to American society, even as people accommodated themselves to sociopolitical reality. After 1848 a crushed social economy led to radical transformation in the cultural epistemology: the disorientation of defeat and the profound rupture in everyday life produced a situation in which subordination constituted a new grid of subjectivity. In other words, even though most people retained the daily self-identificatory practices of language, social customs, and communal relations, the rupture produced a situation in which Mexican people were forced to adapt to an alien social economy while increasingly struggling to remember themselves with a culture and a history of their own.

3

Among the earliest autobiographic narratives in the Southwest are José Antonio Menchaca's "Reminiscences" (ca. 1850) and Juan Seguín's *Personal Memoirs* (1858), both of which are ambivalent and often bitter defenses of complicity in the Anglo-Texas rebellion of 1836. Seguín's brief personal narrative, for example, is an anguished attempt to come to terms with a string of events that, within the space of a few years, saw him transformed from a member of the landed Tejano elite who fought for Texas' independence from Mexico (because, as he says, he believed in American democratic ideals) to an outcast who suffered political and economic dispossession. Ironically, Seguín was forced to retreat to Mexico when his life was threatened by Americans and then, absurd as it may sound, he fought on the side of the Mexican army when it recaptured San Antonio, where he had just served as American mayor. Seguín's *Personal Memoirs* is in many of its details the prefigurative narrative of the forms of personal and cultural schizophrenia witnessed in succeeding Mexican-American autobiographical narratives.

In Texas alone there are other narratives that exhibit the transformation of the cultural subject discovered in the Seguín memoirs. Santiago Tafolla's unpublished "Nearing the End of the Trail" (ca. 1890) is the life history of a man who ran away from home when he was twelve, spent his youth traveling in the eastern United States with an Anglo benefactor, settled in Texas, and then fought on the side of the South during the Civil War, only to be forced to desert when he and fellow Mexicano Confederate troopers learned they were about to be lynched by white soldiers because they were "greasers." José Policarpio Rodríguez's narrative *"The Old Guide": His Life in His Own Words* (1897) describes his life as a "Surveyor, Scout, Indian Fighter, [and] Ranchman" and ends as a conversion narrative much in the Augustinian tradition. As it turns, out, Tafolla and Rodríguez were cousins who both became Protestant ministers late in life and who remember each other in their respective narratives. Another duo who met on and off the pages of their memoirs were Jesse Pérez, Texas lawman, and Catarino E. Garza, journalist, union organizer, and revolutionary. Garza's "La lógica de mis hechos" (The Reasoning of My Activities) is a 280-page handwritten manuscript that describes the social conditions of Mexican-Americans in South Texas and St. Louis, Missouri, between 1877 and 1889, and details his own efforts to help establish the *sociedades mutualistas* (mutual aid societies) before he returned to Mexico to participate in the Revolution of 1910. And Jesse Pérez, strangely enough, was a member of the Texas Rangers in the 1890s when that group was terrorizing the Mexican-American communities of South Texas. In the early 1920s, Pérez struggled with a typewriter to compose his "Memoirs," part of which recounts those occasions when he chased Garza along the border as Garza and other revolutionaries ran guns from Texas into Mexico. However, unlike other Rangers, Pérez never saw his "Memoirs" published, perhaps because the very notion of a Mexican Texas Ranger was a contradiction in terms.

In New Mexico, Padre Antonio José Martínez wrote and published his autobiographical brief, "Relación de méritos" (Report on Merits), on his own (and the first) printing press in New Mexico in 1838. Martínez's "Relación de méritos" describes his birth in Taos, New Mexico, in 1793, his boyhood in a land-owning family, his marriage to María de la Luz Martín, who bore him a daughter but soon thereafter died, leaving him a young widower who decided to become a priest at twenty-four. Not only did Martínez become a priest, he became the politically influential and widely revered prelate who was excommunicated from the Church in 1861 by Archbishop Jean-Baptiste Lamy because he resisted the liturgical Americanization in New Mexico which denigrated the Mexican clergy and robbed the people of locally established religious practices. Citing the library of doctrinal texts which constituted his intellectual personality, the "Relación de méritos" describes Martínez's socio-intellectual formation and the theological knowledge which would eventually put him at doctrinal odds with a bishop who had been sent to New Mexico with the express purpose of Americanizing the Mexican Catholic populace. Although Padre Martínez was a member of the constitutional convention and the territorial legislature, when he defended the religious cultural practices of his people he was vilified by Lamy and his assistant, Reverend Joseph Machebeuf, and driven ignominiously from his pulpit in Taos. In 1927, Willa Cather's *Death Comes for the Archbishop* perpetuated and perhaps forever hardened the image of Padre Martínez as a brutal, self-aggrandizing, and ugly man who dictated the lives of his Mexican parishioners and stood in the way of American progress. Although recent biographical scholarship is restoring Padre Martínez's historical and cultural significance, his own extant writings, scores of letters and essays, as well as "Relación," have yet to be collected and published.

In addition to Padre Martínez's, there are also other journals and narratives by New Mexican political and military figures that require further examination. In 1833, five years before Martínez published the "Relación de méritos," Rafael Chacón was born outside of Santa Fe to a family with deep roots in Nuevo Mexico and who, like most other Nuevomexicanos, lost their homelands after the American conquest. Chacón was a thirteen-year-old cadet in the Mexican militia when the Americans invaded New Mexico; after 1848 he mustered in as a soldier in the American army, fighting in the only Civil War engagement in New Mexico territory and campaigning against the Navajo and Apache. After his retirement from the military in the 1860s, he struggled to build a home for his family under difficult economic and social conditions. Chacón, who wrote his "Memorias" between 1906 and 1912, remembers the terror instilled by the invading Americans as well as his service in the American army where he and his fellow Nuevomexicanos were treated disrespectfully. However, what I found most appealing about Chacón's "Memorias" are not the military exploits Jacqueline Meketa, his translator and editor, finds remarkable, but rather the sense of cultural and familial devotion which motivates the composition of a personal document he hopes will textually sustain the family name in a time of social uncertainty.

After the turn of the century, there are a group of New Mexicans whose lives spanned the last quarter of the nineteenth century and whose autobiographies chart the transformation of the social and political life of the territory. Miguel Antonio Otero, Jr. (1859–1944), the son of a prominent Santa Fe *político*, went to school in St. Louis and went on to become territorial governor of New Mexico from 1897 to 1903. Although not produced until the 1930s, Miguel Antonio Otero's autobiographical trilogy charts his experience from 1859, when he was born in St. Louis, Missouri, to his years as territorial governor of New Mexico at the turn of the century. *My Life on the Frontier, 1864–1882* (1935) provides a fascinating account of Otero's boyhood on the Missouri and New Mexico frontier, where he met such legends as Wild Bill Hickock, Buffalo Bill Cody, and Billy the Kid. *My Life on the Frontier, 1882–1897* (1939) relates his experiences as a young man rising to affluence and political power in New Mexico and ends with notice of his appointment as territorial governor by President McKinley. Otero's *My Nine Years as Governor of the Territory of New Mexico, 1897–1905* (1940) records in detail his years in office as the first Hispanic governor of the state since the American conquest, his futile attempts to gain statehood for New Mexico, his help in organizing Theodore Roosevelt's Rough Riders (among them many Nuevomexicanos whose loyalty to the United States was still in question), and his rise to national prominence during the late territorial period in New Mexico.

From the 1920s through about 1950, a group of women in New Mexico wrote books in which cultural traditions, family and community customs, and social history are combined with personal narrative. Their versions of personal life history and culture are mostly a form of narrative pageantry in which the Spanish colonial past is imagined as a vital element of New Mexican Hispanic identity with, like many of the men's, little reference to Indian and Mexican heritage. Nina Otero Warren's *Old Spain in Our Southwest* (1936); Cleofas Jaramillo's *The Genuine New Mexico Tasty Recipes: Old and Quaint Formulas for the Preparation of Seventy-Five Delicious Spanish Dishes* (1939); *Sombras del Pasado/Shadows of the Past* (1941) and *Romance of a Little Village Girl* (1955); Aurora Lucero White-Lea's *Literary Folklore of the Hispanic Southwest* (1953), and Fabiola Cabeza de Baca's *The Good Life: New Mexico Traditions and Food* (1949) and *We Fed Them Cactus* (1954) are all books that may generally be characterized as a hybrid of personal narrative, folkloristic transcription, recipe book, and family, community, and general sociocultural history. Cultural traditions and daily customs are not only transcribed but given personal, familial, and historical context in *Old Spain in Our Southwest, Sombras del Pasado/Shadows of the Past,* and *The Good Life*. Recipes for traditional foods are contextualized by personal and familial *recueredos* (memoirs) to such a degree that culinary and cultural knowledge are inextricably bound. And, as Tey Diana Rebolledo points out, such knowledge tends to be topographically distinct and gendered: "Recipes are integrated with accounts of folk life, as if the female sense of rootedness and place is passed down through the distinctive foods nature offers" (102). The personal reminiscences of *We Fed Them Cactus* and *Romance of a Little Village Girl* are likewise tied to such traditional narrative practices as relating *cuentos* (folktales), *romances* (narrative ballads), religious drama like the *pastorelas* (pastoral plays), and *recuerdos* (memoirs) in which the personal life is matrixed within a family genealogy of *tías* and *tíos* (uncles and aunts) *abuelas y abuelitos* (grandparents), *primas hermanas* (first cousins), *padrinos* (godparents) and *compadres* (coparents and close family friends). In fact, community, family, and personal history are usually so integrated that, while cookbooks such as Jaramillo's *The Genuine New Mexico Tasty Recipes* and Cabeza de Baca's *The Good Life* are ethnographic texts, they are also what Anne Goldman calls "culinary autobiographies." Goldman describes such narrative as a complex form of cultural and self representation: "reproducing a recipe, like retelling a story, may be at once cultural practice *and* autobiographical assertion. If it provides an apt metaphor for the reproduction of culture from generation to generation, the act of passing down recipes from mother to daughter works as well to figure a familial space within which self-articulation can begin to take place." Intergenerational exchange of cultural knowledge thus constitutes a form of cultural subjectivity rooted in an enduring sense of place, in a sense not only of rootedness but ownership of cultural terrain.

These narratives, however, tend to read the past nostalgically, evoking a harmonious and happy cultural domain while occluding the social fragmentations of the present. Indeed one discovers a tendency to dismiss this body of writing for what Raymund Paredes rightly refers to as its "hacienda mentality." Yet, I also agree with Tey Diana Rebolledo, who reframes our thinking about such narrative production by reminding us that during this period (1930s to 1950s) most "women had no education and even those who did had little leisure to write. Nor were they encouraged to write; they were confined to fairly rigid gender roles, carefully watched and cared for. It is a wonder they wrote at all" (99). More recently, Rebolledo has gone a step further to argue that this group of women were neither "naive" nor "innocent" in their writing, that in fact they established a set of "narrative strategies of resistance" that are "constantly subverting the 'official' text" of Anglo-American writing about Nuevomexicanos, which offered little more than a romanticized representation of a people whose "quaint" customs and culture were ostensibly disappearing in the modern Anglo world. Rebolledo agrees with my contention elsewhere that this group of women writers constructs a sentimental and nostalgic view of the past which is a form of embryonic resistance, yet convincingly argues that women's strategies of resistance were not merely " 'sparks' of dissent" but complex and powerful narrative articulations of self and culture that consciously operate to subvert Anglo-American hegemony (1990: 135).[7]

In California the largest single group of personal narratives was collected in the 1870s by Hubert Howe Bancroft, book dealer, document collector, and professional historian, who solicited scores of oral dictations from the *Californios,* as the California Mexicans called themselves. These narratives undergird his massive *History of California* published in seven volumes between 1884 and 1889, as well as *Pastoral California* (1888),[8] an often ethnocentric and romanticized history of pre-American California society. As Bancroft himself wrote of the project in *Literary Industries* (1890), he and his field assistants collected some "two hundred volumes of original narrative from memory by as many early Californians, native and pioneers, written by themselves or taken down from their lips . . . , the vivid narratives of their experiences" (282). Most are personal narratives collected as oral dictations by Bancroft's field researchers Enrique Cerruti and Thomas Savage, who during a period of some six years traveled a wide circuit from San Francisco to San Diego transcribing the lives of the *Californios*.⁹ There are, from my count, over one hundred Californio personal narratives of lengths varying from ten pages to a fair number that are hundreds of pages long. I must confess not only my sense of wonder, but my sense of resurrective power at discovering scores of disembodied voices, textualized lives stored away in Bancroft's manuscript storehouse of California lives during the 1870s: María Inocente Avila, "Costas de California" (Things about California); Juan Bernal, "Memoria de un Californio;" Josefa Carillo de Fitch, "Narración de una Californiana;" Rafael González, "Experiencias de un soldado" (Experiences of a Soldier); Apolinaria Lorenzana, "Memorias de la beata;" José del Cármen Lugo, "Vida de un ranchero" (A Rancher's Life); Eulalia Pérez, "Una vieja y sus recuerdos;" Pío Pico, "Narración histórica;" Vicente Sánchez, "Cartas de un Angelino" (Letters of an Angelino); Felipa Osuña de Marrón, "Recuerdos del pasado" (Memories of the Past); Pablo Véjar, "Recuerdos de un viejo" (An Old Man's Recollections) (Mss. Bancroft Library). These and scores of other personal narratives still await the kind of exhaustive recovery, editing, translation, and publication which will rescue them from archival obscurity.

This Californio manuscript collection constitutes a major narrative formation, solicited by Bancroft but composed in collaboration or alone by individuals who wished to relate the history of their community in their own language and from their own cultural perspective in a manner that, as it turned out, often contested popular and historiographic representations of Mexican Californians, which by the 1870s were highly derogatory at worst or condescending at best. Mariano G. Vallejo, Juan Alvarado, Juan Bandini, Pío Pico, and Antonio María Osío were some of the men of power and influence in pre-American California who composed sustained collaborative narratives in which the "self" figures prominently in the social transformation that was displacing them even as they wrote. Mariano Vallejo's "Recuerdos históricos y personales tocante a la alta California" (1875) occupies some five volumes of nearly one thousand pages of historical and personal impressions of California society before and after the American occupation.

Vallejo's "Recuerdos" confirms Georges Gusdorf's proposition that "memoirs are always . . . a revenge on history" (36). For Vallejo, the "Recuerdos" was a form of discursive revenge upon negative representations of Mexicans undergoing construction during his own lifetime, as well as a form of prior "revenge" upon the negative history he had reason to believe would be written about his people after him. I have no doubt that Vallejo collaborated on the "Recuerdos" to gratify his own ego; after all, he claimed that Bancroft's projected *History of California* could not be written without the name Vallejo at its center. Vallejo was indeed among that class identified by Gusdorf as "the minister of state, the politician, the military man [who] write in order to celebrate their deeds (always more or less misunderstood), providing a sort of posthumous propaganda for posterity that otherwise is in danger of forgetting them or of failing to esteem them properly" (Gusdorf 36). Nevertheless, Vallejo also recognized the stakes involved for all of his people when he wrote the "Recuerdos" and encouraged other Californios to relate their narratives; in a letter to a friend, he wrote that unless they did so they would "disappear, ignored by the whole world." Vallejo's work indeed operates as "a sort of posthumous propaganda for posterity," except that, as a keen response to the historiography of his own moment, the "Recuerdos" was preemptive narrative intended not so much to forestall as to master-script Bancroft's history. Rather than strictly self-aggrandizing, therefore, his writing and document gathering constituted a forceful act of opposition to contemporary as well as future historiographic erasure. As he wrote to his son, Platón, when he was nearly finished with the huge five-volume undertaking, "the history will come out and it will be as you've heard me say many times, the truth impartially written so it can serve posterity as a guide."

The Bancroft collection also contains about fifteen narratives by women that describe events before and during the Americanization of the territory from a gendered perspective which both criticizes patriarchal constraint in Mexican society and yet refutes common assumptions that Mexican women were not bothered by the conquest. Indeed, one of the reasons there are not more narratives is that many women were so angry with the Americans that they simply refused to collaborate in giving their personal narratives; as Leonard Pitt writes in his classic study *The Decline of the Californios*: "The widows of the Carrillo brothers stiffly refused any recollections, and Señora José Castro bristled at the merest suggestion that she should contribute information to clear her husband's clouded reputation" (281). And although Rosalía Vallejo de Leese did speak, she was so incensed that she speaks through clenched teeth about the American conquest; "those hated men inspired me with such a large dose of hate against their race," she recalls, "that though twenty eight years have elapsed since that time, I have not forgotten the insults heaped upon me, and not being desirous of coming in contact with them I have abstained from learning their language" (1876, Ms. Bancroft Library). Notwithstanding their ambivalence, other women like María

Nineteenth-Century Mexican-American Autobiography

Inocente Avila, Catarina Avila de Ríos, Apolinaria Lorenzana, María Angustias de la Guerra, and my favorite, Eulalia Pérez, a woman said to be 139 years old when her life story was recorded, are among some dozen women who offer revealing views on gender relations in Californio society and disclose their own strategies of self-empowerment.

As Sidonie Smith argues in *The Poetics of Women's Autobiography*, "since the ideology of gender makes of woman's life script a nonstory, a silent space, a gap in patriarchal culture, the ideal woman is self-effacing rather than self-promoting, and her 'natural' story shapes itself not around the public, heroic life but around the fluid, circumstantial, contingent responsiveness to others that according to patriarchal ideology, characterizes the life of woman.... From that point of view, woman has no 'autobiographical self' in the same sense that man does. From that point of view, she has no 'public' story to tell" (50). However, as Smith suggests, women have long resisted such voicelessness and have likewise reconstructed themselves as figures possessed of a will to power in the world. Rather than subordinate themselves to domestic memory, that is, to a version of the "women's sphere," which would make of their "life script a nonstory, a silent space, a gap in patriarchal culture," Mexican-American women—speaking their lives to Bancroft—invariably voiced resistance to the patriarchal domination which characterized social relations in Mexican California and figured themselves as working actively in the social world they inhabited along with—not at the side of—men. At the behest of Bancroft's assistants, Eulalia Pérez's and Apolinaria Lorenzana's personal narratives may begin with descriptions about their domestic work in early California missions, but voice quickly opens toward recollection of their tough-minded independence and will toward self-sufficiency in a male-dominated society. From Angustias de la Guerra, Bancroft's interlocutor Thomas Savage wished to solicit information on "government matters" and political events because of her affiliations with powerful public men—her father, her brothers, and her first husband. What one witnesses in the women's narratives, however, is that women like de la Guerra remember themselves as agents in political events rather than as domestically passive witnesses to men's activities in the public realm. In fact, de la Guerra figures herself and other women as sociopolitically perspicuous and courageous, whereas the political patriarchs of the country were, she charges, more often than not blind to the threat of American encroachment, enfeebled by political corruption, and embarrassingly cowardly when "it came time to defend the country."

As with nearly all nineteenth- and early twentieth-century autobiographic narratives by Mexican-Americans, the archaeological recovery of the Californio narratives requires lifting these life histories from their lower-case status, chipping away the Bancroft text which encases them, brushing the dust off their covers, and by publishing and reading them, restoring their voices. Felipe Fierro, Vallejo's contemporary and the editor of the San Francisco newspaper *La Voz del Nuevo Mundo* (The Voice of the New World), recognized the gravity of recording life histories when he pleaded with his readers to participate in the Bancroft project, not for Bancroft's benefit but in anticipation of the day their stories would be given a public life of their own. Fierro's editorial comments to the Californios in *La Voz* on 7 March 1876 echoed in other parts of the West: "De ese modo llegará el día en que los sucesos, lo mismo que los servicios de los buenos ciudadanos sean dados a la luz de una manera digna de ellos" [In such manner the day will arrive when the events, as well as the contributions, of these good citizens will be given public light in a manner deserving of them].

4

Among the issues that come into question when thinking about the Californio personal narratives is the *auto*biographical integrity of the narratives. The degree to which these dictated narratives direct, distort, or otherwise decentralize the autobiographical subject is, I believe, an important issue. I argue that, whereas for Bancroft the collection of these personal narratives was foundational research for his *History of California* project, for the narrators themselves it was the critical and perhaps only occasion for recreating the life of the self, together with the world inhabited by that self. Yet, precisely because some of the narratives to which I refer were neither self-composed nor meant, strictly, to function as autobiography, claiming autobiographical status for certain texts once again raises the proprietary issue of genre, which must be clarified. To echo one of the questions Arnold Krupat asks about Native American autobiography: "to what extent is it responsible to treat works presented as contributions to history and ethnography as works of literature?" (31–32). Such an issue is of immediate concern for anyone intent upon explaining the sociocultural, ideological, and discursive conditions that underlie the formation of autobiographical consciousness in Mexican-American society. The dilemma confronted by Krupat, H. David Brumble, and other scholars of Native American autobiography who have had to consider the autobiographical fashioning of native people by Anglo-American amanuenses, whether historians, anthropologists, poets, or journalists serves as both warning and instruction for my work. As Krupat saliently points out: "Indian autobiographies are collaborative efforts, jointly produced by some White—who translates, transcribes, compiles, edits, interprets, polishes, and ultimately determines the form of the text in writing—and by an Indian who is its subject and whose life becomes the content of the 'autobiography' whose title may bear his name" (30).

One can no longer naively read collaboratively produced narrative without thinking about editorial construction with all of its customary manipulations, performative stagings, transcriptional excisions, translations (not to mention mistranslations), additions, and refashionings. Certainly, the problematics of Hubert Bancroft's collection of scores of California personal narratives from oral dictations with all of the editorial mechanics of formulaic questioning (masked in most narratives but noticeable when comparing statement clusters on certain crucial historical events), the selecting out of many informants whose memories were considered faulty, and the hurried pace of collection mentioned in the prefatory statements of the field collectors and evinced by numerous transcriptional truncations require recognition and analysis of the power differential inscribed within the very formation of autobiographical articulation. Although we must of course recognize and assess the interpolations of editorial construction, we must also recognize that, as Krupat suggests, bicultural collaboration is a site of contention for authority over narrative self-representation (at the ground level of speech), as well as the site of socially symbolic contestations over the Mexican-American's political, cultural, and social status in the United States. The disclosure of individual experience and the overlay of individual personality upon the description of external sociopolitical events mark the Californio narratives with distinct autobiographic authority, just as the signature of the "I" identifies authorial status in various autobiographical enunciations, markings, and representations throughout the narratives. Autobiographical authority, I would therefore argue, needs not be thought of as issuing only from the hand which scribes personal experience, but rather from what I believe is a deep human desire to shape and control narrative, to modulate its articulation by that small stubbornness of voice that insists on its own story and that reconstructs the past in a register which claims ownership of the past, especially when ownership of the present is endangered.

Central to this reclaiming of the past was the narrative habit of remembering oneself within a community of the past. It is no surprise, therefore, to see that many of the nineteenth- and early twentieth-century narratives which comprise the beginnings of Chicano autobiography construct a culturally matrixed subjectivity in which the "I" is subsumed within a narrative of regional or cultural history. This displacement of a self-absorbed "I"-centered narrative by narrative in which the cultural "We" is reconstituted may be regarded as a filial act. The historicizing "I" indeed sustains itself by narratively restoring the cultural ecology in which it lives: the history of the cultural community constitutes the history of the "I" or, to put it another way, the "I" is but an empty cipher, a floating signifier without content until it is grounded by a collective identitarian utterance, by an act of cultural recuperation of the kind Cleofas Jaramillo refers to as describing a "current invisible to the stranger and understood only by their inhabitants" or, as in the case of Mariano Vallejo, reading himself into the Spanish colonial and Mexican social and political history of California. Indeed, such narratives reside outside the formal boundaries scholars have traditionally reserved for a singularly self-disclosing text, "a retrospective prose narrative produced by a real person concerning his own existence, focusing on his individual life, in particular on the development of his personality."[10] However, as more and more autobiography scholars, especially feminist and third-world practitioners, are arguing, traditional genre constraints have been exclusionary and must be renegotiated, wedged open to alternate forms of self-representation—historiography, cultural ethnography, folkloristic narratives—which do not focus exclusively upon the development of individual personality so much as upon the formation, and transformation, of the individual within a community transformation. Hence, narratives that some scholars would consider more properly within the domain of social history or cultural ethnography, but which I believe a culturally historicized and contextually reaccentuated reading will discover to be a kind of communitarian autobiography, must not be categorically dismissed as nonautobiographical. This is not to argue that Mexican-American autobiographical expression is devoid of ego (Mariano Vallejo telling Bancroft's scribe, "I will not be hurried or dictated to. It is my history and not yours I propose to tell."), but rather that in the years after 1848 the entire community underwent such a global assault that even powerfully self-assertive individuals like Vallejo were put in a position of reading their own lives against the ruins of their social world. Therefore we must read for autobiographical content within a complex narrative matrix in which the individuals who composed or related their communal histories were simultaneously composing the history of the self and its shaping, twisting, reconfiguring response to social transformation in a voice (voices, really) which appropriated the exogenous historiographic and ethnographic discourses through which they were licensed to speak.

Mariano Vallejo, like Juan Seguín before and Cleofas Jaramillo after, knew that claiming ownership of the past (however that past was fashioned) must fill a space emptied of presence by American social domination and its adjunct, a historiography of the American conquest which discursively decimated Mexican people. Fully cognizant that they must write their own history or, as he wrote to Anastacio Carrillo, "disappear, ignored of the whole world" (Pitt 278), Vallejo wrote 900 pages of personal memoirs in the 1860s only to have the manuscript burn in a fire which destroyed his home in 1867. Then, while he was traveling throughout California in the 1870s, writing his own memoirs once again and encouraging men and women of his generation to dictate their personal narratives as well as to archive their papers, Vallejo beseeched people to remember and restore the past against misrepresentation and betrayal. As Leonard Pitt writes, because they "perceived themselves not merely as the victims of annexation or assimilation, but of deliberate betrayal and bone-crushing repression" Mexican Californians like Vallejo emphasized "injustice, violence and broken promises in their memoirs" (Pitt 278, 283). Indeed nostalgia appeared in their memoirs, but memory was politicized by loss and anger. Rather than uncritical celebration of an idyllic and unobtainable past, therefore, nostalgia may be seen to function as ideological opposition to having one's world destroyed. The autobiographical formation in Mexican-American culture may indeed figure the past as utopian, but this is because post-1848 life was a nightmare; so, if the social economy of pre-American life was fashioned as coherent and sane, it was because the present of the American regime was culturally incoherent and socially insane. Nostalgia for an earlier world emerges from grief for a world lost, which, because it tends to suffuse the past with a glow of the ideal and idyllic, masks the anger underlying dislocation that produces nostalgia in the first place. In other words, nostalgia is a realization that there are future stakes involved in the reconstruction(s) of the past. To remember is not only the act of not forgetting but an act of not being forgotten, just as remembering the past as utopian cultural terrain reveals the very condition of cultural dislocation which makes a necessity of such retrospective communitarian idealization. Figured as a studied response to displacement and erasure, a narrative of nostalgia may be read as a consciously produced strategy of opposition rather than an unmediated and noncritical reflex to displacement. Anger, therefore, finds its outlet in this controlled strategy of revisiting the past as idyllic—at least in comparison to the ruins and hostility of the post-1848 present.

Unless we wish to think of our *antepasados* (forebears) as either blind or stupid, therefore, I believe we must recontextualize our reading of their narrative production in order to understand their social and discursive situations. We must recognize that colonized Mexicans were often speaking out of both sides of their mouths with visionary social purpose. What may at first appear as ideologically subordinate speech actually constitutes multiaddressed utterance in which pragmatic appeasement reads at one surface of language while anger and opposition read at other, and often upon the same, surfaces. Such strategic utterance, I maintain, constitutes a form of rhetorical camouflage which first appropriates a public "voice" for an individual from an otherwise "silenced" group and then turns that voice to duplicitous purpose. Discursive duplicity functions to communicate different stories to different audiences, with an implicit understanding that one's own people will, to invoke Fierro's comment, someday read them "de una manera digna de ellos" (in a manner deserving of them). We must read early literary discourse, and autobiography specifically, in a manner that restores the difficult conditions under which they were produced and through which they must speak to us—that future audience to which Fierro referred and for which Vallejo hoped. The narrative reconstitution of an idealized prior world may indeed be tainted by utopian imagination, but both the original trauma of displacement (American conquest of 1846–48) and an unrelenting assault upon the cultural habitat established a form of autobiographical consciousness in which Seguín, for example, understood that his posterity's future was staked in establishing a version of the past, a historical text, which had to stand against erasure at worst, or negative historical representation at best. Post-1848 Mexican-American autobiographical narrative projects a future condition, therefore, in which a Chicano reader in the late twentieth century reads personal narrative "de una manera digna de ellos." That is, as an expression of our collective historical desire to sustain presence in the face of a still unrelenting assault upon our history, culture, and literary production.

Nineteenth-Century Mexican-American Autobiography

Notes

1. Leonard Pitt records one such example of correspondence between brothers Antonio María and Pablo de la Guerra, member of an affluent and politically influential California family: "As he set out for the 'new world' of the north [northern California], Antonio vowed to his brother to 'write something of my compañeros that will entertain you.' He did so in a series of lively letters which illuminate the Californio's sense of alienation outside his home precincts" (*The Decline of the Californios* 141–47).

2. Pitt, for example, devotes an entire chapter to the work of Francisco P. Ramirez, who edited and published *El Clamor Publico*, a Los Angeles newspaper which, in addition to carrying general news about Latin America, argued forcefully on behalf of Mexican Americans (184, 181–89).

3. See John Blassingame, *Slave Testimony: Two Centuries of Letters, Speeches, Interviews, and Autobiographies*; Gilbert Osofsky, ed., *Puttin' on Ole Massa: The Slave Narratives of Henry Bibb, William Wells Brown, and Solomon Northrup*; Arna Bontemps, ed. *Great Slave Narratives*; Robert Stepto, *From Behind the Veil: A Study of Afro-American Narrative*; Joanne Braxton, *Black Women Writing Autobiography: A Tradition within a Tradition*.

4. There have been scores of essays by Chicano scholars which seek to recover the connections to pre-Columbian literature and culture. For the most complete collection of essays on appropriation of pre-Columbian myth, metaphor, and culture see *Aztlan: Essays on the Chicano Homeland* (Albuquerque: Academia/El Norte Publications, 1989), Rudolfo A. Anaya and Francisco Lomelí, eds.

5. As Leal says, "We shall consider works, especially dating before 1821, written by the inhabitants of this region with a Spanish background, to belong to an early stage of Chicano literature" ("Mexican American Literature: A Historical Perspective" 22).

6. Here I accept Bruce-Novoa's recent "compromise" in "The Space of Chicano Literature Update: 1978," of his original proposition that the space signified "the intercultural *nothingness*."

7. Rebolledo's essay, "Narrative Strategies of Resistance in Hispana Writing," provides a provocative and thoughtful exchange with views I had expressed in a 1987 conference paper published as "Imprisoned Narrative? Or Lies, Secrets and Silence in New Mexico Women's Autobiography."

8. *History of California*, vols. 1–7, and *Pastoral California*, like all of Bancroft's historical work, were published by his own San Francisco publishing house, the History Company.

9. Both Cerruti and Savage left manuscript reports of their ethnographic expeditions that contain valuable insight into their collection methods.

10. Lejeune, "The Autobiographical Contract," additionally insists that such forms as the memoir, diary, and autobiographical poem do not properly satisfy the "conditions" of autobiography. There is, of course, a rather large body of critical literature that has moved well beyond a rigid definition of autobiography as a singularly self-disclosing text that reads something like St. Augustine's or

Rousseau's *Confessions*. To follow Francis R. Hart, "Notes for an Anatomy of Modern Autobiography," autobiography proper is no longer restricted to the construction of "a personal history that seeks to communicate or express the essential nature, the truth, of the self."

Works Cited

Acuña, Rodolfo. *Occupied America: A History of Chicanos*. 2d ed. New York: Harper, 1981.
Amador, José María. "Memorias sobre la historia de California," ms. Bancroft Library, U of California, Berkeley.
Andrews, William. *To Tell a Free Story: The First Century of Afro-American Autobiography, 1760–1865*. Chicago: U of Chicago P, 1988.
Augustias de la Guerra, María. "Ocurrencias en California," 1878, ms. Bancroft Library, U of California, Berkeley.
Augustus, Jennings Napoleon. *A Texas Ranger*. Dallas: Turner, 1930.
Ávila, María Inocente. "Cosas de California," ms. Bancroft Library, U of California, Berkeley.
Baker, Houston. *The Journey Back: Issues in Black Literature and Criticism*. Chicago: U of Chicago P, 1980.
Bancroft, Hubert Howe. *History of California*. 7 vols. San Francisco: History Company, 1884–1889.
———. *Literary Industries*. San Francisco: History Company, 1890.
———. *Pastoral California*. San Francisco: History Company, 1888.
Bernal, Juan. "Memoria de un Californio," ms. Bancroft Library, U of California, Berkeley.
Blassingame, John. *Slave Testimony: Two Centuries of Letters, Speeches, Interviews, and Autobiographies*. Baton Rouge: Louisiana State UP, 1977.
Bontemps, Arna, ed. *Great Slave Narratives*. Boston: Beacon, 1948.
Bruce-Novoa, Juan. *RetroSpace: Collected Essays on Chicano Literature, Theory, and History*. Houston: Arte Público, 1990.
Cabeza de Baca, Fabiola. *The Good Life: New Mexico Traditions and Food*. Santa Fe, 1949. Santa Fe: Museum of New Mexico, 1982.
———. *We Fed Them Cactus*. Albuquerque: U of New Mexico P, 1954.
Carillo de Fitch, Josefa. "Narración de una Californiana," ms. Bancroft Library, U of California, Berkeley.
Cather, Willa. *Death Comes for the Archbishop*. New York: Knopf, 1927.
Cerruti, Enrique. "Ramblings in California," ms. Bancroft Library, U of California, Berkeley.
Chacón, Rafael. "Memorias." 1912. (Chaps. 1–3) U of Colorado Library, Boulder.
Chávez, John R. *The Lost Land: The Chicano Image of the Southwest*. Albuquerque: U of New Mexico P, 1984.
Columbus, Christopher. *The Journal*. Trans. Cecil Jane. New York: Potter, 1960.
Couser, Thomas G. *Altered Egos: Authority in American Autobiography*. Oxford: Oxford UP, 1989.

Nineteenth-Century Mexican-American Autobiography

Douglass, Claude L. *The Gentlemen in the White Hats: Dramatic Episodes in the History of the Texas Rangers*. Dallas: Turner, 1934.
Emparán, Madie Brown. *The Vallejos of California*. San Francisco: U of San Francisco, 1968.
Fierro, Felipe. Editorial. *La Voz del Nuevo Mundo* [San Francisco] 7 Mar. 1876.
Garza, Catarino E. "La lógica de mis hechos," 1877–1889, ms. Benson Latin American Collection, Mexican American Archives, U of Texas, Austin.
Gates, Henry Louis, Jr. "Introduction." *The Classic Slave Narratives*. New York: New American, 1987.
Gillet, James B. *Six Years with the Texas Rangers, 1875–81*. New Haven: Yale UP, 1925.
Goldman, Anne. " 'I yam what I yam': Cooking, Culture and Colonialism." *De/Colonizing the Subject: Politics and Gender in Women's Autobiographical Practice*. Ed. Sidonie Smith and Julia Watson. Minneapolis: U of Minnesota P, 1992. 169–95.
González, Rafael. "Experiencias de un soldado," ms. Bancroft Library, U of California, Berkeley.
Gusdorf, Georges. "Conditions and Limits of Autobiography." Rpt. in *Autobiography: Essays Theoretical and Critical*. Ed. James Olney. Princeton: Princeton UP, 1980. 28–48.
Hart, Francis R. "Notes for an Anatomy of Modern Autobiography." *New Literary History* 1 (1969–70): 485–512.
Jaramillo, Cleofas. *Cuentos del Hogar*. El Campo, Texas: Citizen, 1939.
———. *The Genuine New Mexico Tasty Recipes: Old and Quaint Formulas for the Preparation of Seventy-Five Delicious Spanish Dishes*. 1939. Santa Fe: Seton Village, 1942.
———. *Romance of a Little Village Girl*. San Antonio: Naylor, 1955.
———. *Sombras del Pasado/Shadows of the Past*. Santa Fe: Ancient City, 1941.
Krupat, Arnold. *For Those Who Come After: A Study of Native American Autobiography*. Berkeley: U of California P, 1985.
Lea, Aurora (Lucero-White). *Literary Folklore of the Hispanic Southwest*. San Antonio: Naylor, 1953.
Leal, Luis. "Mexican American Literature: A Historical Perspective." *Revista Chicano-Riqueña* 1 (1973): 32–44. Rpt. *Modern Chicano Writers: A Collection of Critical Essays*. Ed. Joseph Sommer and Thomas Ybarra-Frausto. New York: Prentice, 1979. 18–30.
Lejeune, Phillippe. "The Autobiographical Contract." *French Literary Theory Today*. Ed. Tzvetan Todorov. New York: 1982.
———. *On Autobiography*. U of Minnesota P, 1989. 3–30.
Leon-Portilla, Miguel. *The Broken Spears: Aztec Accounts of the Conquest of Mexico*. Boston: Beacon, 1961.
———. *Los Antiguos Mexicanos através de sus Crónicas y Cantares*. Mexico City: Fondo de Cultura Economica, 1961.
———. *Pre-Columbian Literatures of Mexico*. Norman: U of Oklahoma P, 1969.
Lorenzana, Apolinaria. "Memorias de la beata," 1878, ms. Bancroft Library, U of California, Berkeley.
Martínez, Padre Antonio Jose. "Relación de méritos," 1838, ms. New Mexico State Records Library.

McWilliams, Carey. *North from Mexico: The Spanish-Speaking People of the United States.* Philadelphia: Lippincott, 1948. rpt. New York: Greenwood, 1968.

Meketa, Jacqueline Dorgan. *Legacy of Honor: The Life of Rafael Chacón, A Nineteenth-Century New Mexican.* Albuquerque: U of New Mexico P, 1986.

Menchaca, José Antonio. "Reminiscences," ca. 1850, ms., ts. Barker Texas History Center, U of Texas, Austin.

Osuña de Marrón, Felipa. "Recuerdos del pasado," ms. Bancroft Library, U of California, Berkeley.

Otero, Miguel Antonio, Jr. *My Life on the Frontier, 1864-1882.* New York: Pioneers, 1935.

———. *My Life on the Frontier, 1882-1897.* Albuquerque: U of New Mexico P, 1939.

———. *My Nine Years as Governor of the Territory of New Mexico, 1897-1905.* Albuquerque: U of New Mexico P, 1940.

Padilla, Genaro M. "Imprisoned Narrative? Or Lies, Secrets and Silence in New Mexico Women's Autobiography." *Criticism in the Borderlands: Studies in Chicano Literature, Culture, and Ideology.* Ed. Hector Calderon and José David Saldívar. Durham, NC: Duke UP, 1991. 43-61.

———. "Self as Cultural Metaphor in Acosta's *The Autobiography of a Brown Buffalo.*" *Journal of General Education* 35 (1984): 242-58.

———. " 'Yo sola aprendí': Mexican Women's Personal Narratives from Nineteenth-Century California." *Revealing Lives: Autobiography, Biography, and Gender.* Ed. Susan Groag Bell and Marilyn Yalom. New York: State UP of New York, 1990.

Paredes, Raymund. "The Evolution of Chicano Literature." *Three American Literatures.* Ed. Houston A. Baker, Jr. New York, 1982. 33-79.

Pérez, Eulalia. "Una vieja y sus recuerdos," 1877, ms. Bancroft Library, U of California, Berkeley.

Pérez, Jesse. "Memoirs," ts. Barker Texas History Center, U of Texas, Austin.

Pico, Pío. "Narración historica," ms. Bancroft Library, U of California, Berkeley.

Pitt, Leonard. *The Decline of the Californios: A Social History of the Spanish-Speaking Californios, 1846-1890.* Berkeley: U of California P, 1971.

Rebolledo, Tey Diana. "Narrative Strategies of Resistance in Hispana Writing." *The Journal of Narrative Technique* 20 (Spring 1990): 2:134-46.

———. "Tradition and Mythology: Signatures of Landscape in Chicana Literature." *The Desert Is No Lady: Southwest Landscapes in Women's Writing and Art.* Ed. Vera Norwood and Janice Monk. New Haven: Yale UP, 1987. 96-124.

Rodríguez, José Policarpio. *"The Old Guide": His Life in His Own Words.* Dallas: Methodist Episcopal Church, ca. 1897.

Saldívar, Ramón. *Chicano Narrative: The Dialectics of Difference.* Madison: U of Wisconsin P, 1990.

———. "Ideologies of the Self: Chicano Autobiography." *Diacritics* (Fall 1985): 25-34.

Sánchez, Vicente. "Cartas de un Angelino," ms. Bancroft Library, U of California, Berkeley.

Savage, Thomas. "Report on Labors on Archives and Procuring Material for the

History of California," 1874, ms. Bancroft Library, U of California, Berkeley.

Seguín, John N. *Personal Memoirs: From the Year 1834 to the Retreat of General Woll from the City of San Antonio, 1842.* San Antonio: Ledger Book and Job Office, 1858.

———. Personal Memoirs, 1858, ts. Barker Texas History Center, U of Texas, Austin.

Smith, Sidonie. *A Poetics of Women's Autobiography: Marginality and the Fictions of Self-Representation.* Bloomington: Indiana UP, 1987.

Stepto, Robert. *From Behind the Veil: A Study of Afro-American Narrative.* Urbana: U of Illinois P, 1979.

Tafolla, Santiago. "Nearing the End of the Trail," ca. 1890, ms. Benson Latin American Collection, Mexican American Archives, U of Texas, Austin.

Vallejo, Mariano Guadalupe. "Historical and Personal Memoirs Relating to Alta California." Trans. Earl R. Hewitt, ts. Bancroft Library, UC Berkeley.

———. "Recuerdos históricos y personales tocante a la alta California." 5 vols. 1875, ms. Bancroft Library, U of California, Berkeley.

Vallejo, Salvador. "Notas historicas sobre California," ms. Bancroft Library, U of California, Berkeley.

Vallejo de Leese, Rosalía. "History of the 'Osos,' " 1876, ms. Bancroft Library, U of California, Berkeley.

Véjar, Pablo. "Recuerdos de un viejo," ms. Bancroft Library, U of California, Berkeley.

Vigil, José María. *Nezahualcoyotl, el rey poeta.* Mexico: Andrea, 1957.

Warren, Nina Otero. *Old Spain in Our Southwest.* New York: Harcourt, 1936.

Weber, David J. *Foreigners in Their Native Land: Historical Roots of the Mexican Americans.* Albuquerque: New Mexico UP, 1973.

Wong, Hertha. "Pictography as Autobiography: Plains Indian Sketchbooks of the Late Nineteenth and Early Twentieth Centuries." *American Literary History* 1 (Summer 1989): 295–316.

Select Bibliography

This list supplements scores of items mentioned in the Introduction and listed in the Works Cited following each of the fourteen individual essays.

Anderson, Benedict. *Imagined Communities: Reflections on the Origin and Spread of Nationalism*. London: Verso, 1991.

Awkward, Michael. *Inspiriting Influences: Tradition, Revision, and Afro-American Women's Novels*. New York: Columbia UP, 1989.

Bennett, Gillian. "Narrative as Expository Discourse." *Journal of American Folklore* 99 (1986): 415–34.

Boelhower, William. *Through a Glass Darkly: Ethnic Semiosis in American Literature*. New York: Oxford UP, 1987.

Bruce-Novoa, Juan. *RetroSpace: Collected Essays on Chicano Literature, Theory, and History*. Houston: Arte Público, 1990.

Buenker, John D., and Lorman A. Ratner, eds. *Multiculturalism in the United States: A Comparative Guide to Acculturation and Ethnicity*. New York: Greenwood, 1992.

Burke, Peter. "History as Social Memory." *Memory: History, Culture and the Mind*. Ed. Thomas Butler. New York: Oxford UP, 1989.

Butler, Thomas, ed. *Memory: History, Culture and the Mind*. Oxford: Basil Blackwell, 1989.

Byerman, Keith. "Remembering History in Contemporary Black Literature and Criticism." *American Literary History* 3 (1991): 809–16.

Campbell, Jane. *Mythic Black Fiction: The Transformation of History*. Knoxville: U of Tennessee P, 1986.

Cheung, King-Kok. *Articulate Silences: Hisaye Yamamoto, Maxine Hong Kingston, Joy Kogawa*. Ithaca: Cornell UP, 1993.

Christian, Barbara. *Black Women Novelists: The Development of a Tradition, 1892–1976*. Westport, CT: Greenwood, 1980.

Clayton, Jay. "The Narrative Turn in Recent Minority Fiction." *American Literary History* 2 (1990): 375–93.

———. *The Pleasures of Babel: Contemporary American Literature and Theory*. New York: Oxford UP, 1993.

Collins, Patricia Hill. *Black Feminist Thought: Knowledge, Consciousness, and the Politics of Empowerment*. Boston: Unwin Hyman, 1990.

Connerton, Paul. *How Societies Remember*. Cambridge: Cambridge UP, 1989.

Dashefsky, Arnold. *Ethnic Identity in Society*. Chicago: Rand McNally, 1976.

Select Bibliography

Davis, Natalie Zemon, and Randolph Starn. "Memory and Counter-Memory." Special Issue of *Representations* 26 (Spring 1989).

Dearborn, Mary V. *Pocahontas's Daughters: Gender and Ethnicity in American Culture*. New York: Oxford UP, 1986.

Dixon, Melvin. *Ride Out the Wilderness: Geography and Identity in Afro-American Literature*. Urbana: U of Illinois P, 1987.

Erikson, Erik. *Life History and the Historical Moment*. New York: Norton, 1975.

Fischer, Michael M. J. "Ethnicity and the Post-Modern Arts of Memory." *Writing Culture: The Poetics and Politics of Ethnography*. Ed. James Clifford and George E. Marcus. Berkeley: U of California P, 1986.

Frisch, Michael H. "The Memory of History." *Presenting the Past: Essays on History and the Public*. Ed. Susan Porter Benson, Stephen Brier, and Roy Rosenzweig. Philadelphia: Temple UP, 1986.

Georges, Robert A. "Timeliness and Appropriateness in Personal Experience Narrating." *Western Folklore* 46 (1987): 115–20.

Greene, Gayle. *Changing the Story: Feminist Fiction and the Tradition*. Bloomington: Indiana UP, 1991.

Hall, Stuart. "Ethnicity: Identity and Difference." *Radical America* 23.4 (1991): 9–20.

Hamerow, Theodore S. "Disturbing Echoes of Old Arguments about Ethnic Experience." *The Chronicle of Higher Education* 4 (Aug. 1993): A36.

Harris, Middleton, comp. *The Black Book*. Ed. Toni Morrison. New York: Random, 1974.

Hendricks, William O. "Folklore and the Structural Analysis of Literary Texts." *Language and Style* 3 (1970): 83–121.

hooks, bell. *Yearning: Race, Gender, and Cultural Politics*. Boston: South End, 1990.

Horno-Delgado, Asuncion, Eliana Ortega, Nina M. Scott, and Nancy Saporta Sternbach, eds. *Breaking Boundaries: Latina Writings and Critical Readings*. Amherst: U of Massachusetts P, 1989.

Hutcheon, Linda. *A Poetics of Postmodernism: History, Theory, Fiction*. New York: Routledge, 1988.

Kammen, Michael. *Mystic Chords of Memory: The Transformation of Tradition in American Culture*. New York: Knopf, 1991.

Kelley, Mary. "The Politics of Memory in America." Rev. of *Mystic Chords of Memory: The Transformation of Tradition in American Culture*, by Michael Kammen. *Boston Globe* 24 Nov. 1991: A15.

Kim, Elaine. "Defining Asian American Realities through Literature." *The Nature and Context of Minority Discourse*. Ed. Abdul R. JanMohamed and David Lloyd. New York: Oxford UP, 1990. 146–70.

Kolodny, Annette. "The Integrity of Memory: Creating a New Literary History of the United States." *American Literature* 57 (1985): 291–307.

Krupat, Arnold. *The Voice in the Margin: Native American Literature and the Canon*. Berkeley: U of California P, 1989.

LaCapra, Dominick. *History and Criticism*. Ithaca: Cornell UP, 1985.

Lee, A. Robert. "Acts of Remembrance: America as Multicultural Past in Ralph Ellison, Nicholasa Mohr, James Welch and Monica Sone." *Multiculturalism and the Canon of American Culture*. Ed. Hans Bak. Amsterdam: U of Amsterdam P, 1993. 81–103.

Select Bibliography

Lipsitz, George. *Time Passages: Collective Memory and American Popular Culture.* Minneapolis: U of Minnesota P, 1990.

Lloyd, David. *Anomalous States: Irish Writing and the Postcolonial Moment.* Durham: Duke UP, 1993.

Marin, Peter. "Toward Something American." *Harper's* July 1988: 17–18.

McDaniel, George W. *Hearth & Home: Preserving a People's Culture.* Philadelphia: Temple UP, 1982.

McDowell, Deborah E., and Arnold Rampersad, ed. *Slavery and the Literary Imagination.* Baltimore: Johns Hopkins UP, 1989.

Minh-Ha, Trinh T. *Woman, Native, Other: Writing Postcoloniality and Feminism.* Bloomington: Indiana UP, 1989.

Morgan, Kathryn L. *Children of Strangers: The Stories of a Black Family.* Philadelphia: Temple UP, 1980.

Morrison, Toni. "Memory, Creation, and Writing." *Thought* Dec. 1984: 385–90.

———. *Playing in the Dark: Whiteness and the Literary Imagination.* Cambridge: Harvard UP, 1992.

———. "Rootedness: The Ancestor as Foundation." *Black Women Writers (1950–1980): A Critical Evaluation.* Ed. Mari Evans. Garden City, NY: Anchor-Doubleday, 1984. 339–45.

Ordonez, Elizabeth J. "Narrative Texts by Ethnic Women: Rereading the Past, Reshaping the Future." *MELUS* 9.3 (1982): 19–28.

Pratt, Mary Louise. " 'Yo Soy La Malinche': Chicana Writers and the Poetics of Ethnonationalism." *Callaloo* 16 (1993): 859–73.

Reilly, John M. "Criticism of Ethnic Literature: Seeing the Whole Story." *MELUS* 5.1 (1978): 2–13.

Rivero, Eliana S. "(Re)writing Sugarcane Memories: Cuban Americans and Literature." *The Americas Review* 18 (1990): 164–82.

Rodriguez, Joe. "The Chicano Novel and the North American Narrative of Survival." *Denver Quarterly* 16.3 (1981): 63–70.

Rogin, Michael. " 'Make My Day!': Spectacle as Amnesia in Imperial Politics." *Representations* 29 (1990): 99–123.

Rubin, Steven J. "Ethnic Autobiography: A Comparative Approach." *The Journal of Ethnic Studies* 9 (1981): 75–79.

Saldívar, José. *The Dialectics of Our America: Genealogy, Cultural Critique, and Literary History.* Durham: Duke UP, 1991.

Saldívar, Ramón. *Chicano Narrative: The Dialectics of Difference.* Madison: U of Wisconsin P, 1990.

San Juan, E., Jr. "Beyond Identity Politics: The Predicament of the Asian Writer in Late Capitalism." *American Literary History* 3 (1991): 542–65.

Seller, Maxine Schwartz, ed. *Immigrant Women.* Philadelphia: Temple UP, 1981.

———. *To Seek America: A History of Ethnic Life in the United States.* Englewood Cliffs, NJ: Prentice, 1977.

Spillers, Hortense J., ed. *Comparative American Identities: Race, Sex, and Nationality in the Modern Text.* New York: Routledge, 1991.

Steinberg, Stephen. *The Ethnic Myth: Race, Identity, and Class in America.* New York: Atheneum, 1981.

Thelen, David. *Memory and American History.* Bloomington: Indiana UP, 1990.

Select Bibliography

Thornton, Jerome E. "The Paradoxical Journey of the African American in African American Fiction." *New Literary History* 21 (1990): 733-45.

TuSmith, Bonnie. *All My Relatives: Community in Contemporary Ethnic American Literatures.* Ann Arbor: U of Michigan P, 1993.

Vizenor, Gerald, ed. *Narrative Chance: Postmodern Discourse on Native American Indian Literatures.* Albuquerque: U of New Mexico P, 1989.

Warnock, Mary. *Memory.* London: Faber, 1987.

Waters, Mary C. *Ethnic Options: Choosing Identities in America.* Berkeley: U of California P, 1990.

White, Hayden. "The Historical Text as Literary Artifact." *Clio* 3 (1974): 272-303.

Willis, Susan. *Specifying: Black Women Writing the American Experience.* Madison: U of Wisconsin P, 1987.

Wong, Sau-ling Cynthia. *Reading Asian American Literature: From Necessity to Extravagance.* Princeton: Princeton UP, 1993.

Yates, Frances Amelia. *The Art of Memory.* Chicago: U of Chicago P, 1966.

Editors and Contributors

Robert E. Hogan is Professor of English and Chair of the Department of English at Rhode Island College. He has published articles on Herman Melville, Edward Bellamy, and John Updike in journals such as *Studies in American Fiction* and *Ball State University Forum*.

Amritjit Singh, Professor of English at Rhode Island College, is currently at work on an intellectual biography of Richard Wright's final phase, for which he has received fellowships from ACLS, NEH, the Rockefeller Foundation, and the W. E. B. Du Bois Institute for Afro-American Research at Harvard University. Books written and edited by him include *The Novels of the Harlem Renaissance* (1976), *India: An Anthology of Contemporary Writing* (1983), *The Magic Circle of Henry James* (1989), and *The Harlem Renaissance: Revaluations* (1989).

Joseph T. Skerrett, Jr., Professor of English at the University of Massachusetts, Amherst, has written extensively on African American writers, including James Weldon Johnson, Richard Wright, Toni Morrison, and Paule Marshall for journals such as *Callaloo*, *American Quarterly*, and *Twentieth-Century Literature*. Skerrett is the editor of *MELUS*, the journal of the Society for the Study of Multi-Ethnic Literature of the United States.

Betty Bergland, Assistant Professor of History at the University of Wisconsin, River Falls, has published articles on autobiography and ethnicity in *American Quarterly*, *Ethnic Forum*, and *The Yearbook of English Studies* as well as in several edited volumes.

Gert Buelens, a postdoctoral researcher with the Belgian National Fund for Scientific Research, has compiled *Deferring a Dream: Literary Sub-versions of The American Columbiad* (1994) with Ernst Rudin and is currently working on Henry James. He has taught at the Universities of Ghent and Nijmegen and has published articles and reviews on Jewish-American fiction, cultural theory, and American poetry.

Editors and Contributors

Jules Chametzky is Professor Emeritus of English at the University of Massachusetts, Amherst. His writings include *Our Decentralized Literature: Cultural Mediations in Selected Jewish and Southern Writers* (1986) and the introduction to Abraham Cahan's *The Rise of David Levinsky* (1993).

Terry DeHay, Assistant Professor of English at Southern Oregon State College, has published essays on Latin American poetry and postcolonial literature. Her current research interests include postcolonial discourse and feminist critical theory.

Rosemary Marangoly George, Assistant Professor of English and Cultural Studies, Department of Literature, at the University of California, San Diego, has published in *differences, Novel, MELUS,* and *Cultural Critique*.

Sharon Jessee teaches English at the University of Wisconsin, La Crosse. In 1992–93, she held a full-time fellowship at the Center for Twentieth Century Studies at the University of Wisconsin, Milwaukee.

Wolfgang Karrer is Professor of American literature at the University of Osnabrück, Germany. His fields of research include literary theory, twentieth-century poetry and fiction, and African American and Chicano literature. He has published books on parody and African American fiction and reference works on literary history. His latest books include *Minority Literatures in North America* (1990) and *The African American Short Story* (1993), both collections of essays by various scholars.

William Keough, Professor of English at Fitchburg State College, is the author of *Punchlines: The Violence of American Humor* (1990) and a collection of poetry, *Any Such Greenness* (1992). His short story "Last Word on a Pink Dress" won the 1992 Waterstone's award for the best story on an Irish theme.

Barbara Offutt Mathieson teaches English and world literature at Southern Oregon State College, where she also coordinates the International Writers Series.

Sandra Molyneaux, a graduate of the Johns Hopkins University, is a doctoral candidate in the Department of English at the University of Maryland. She is currently completing work on ecclesiastical architecture as metaphor in late-nineteenth-century American literature.

Genaro Padilla teaches English at the University of California, Berkeley. He edited *The Short Stories of Fray Angelico Chavez* (1987) and is the author

Editors and Contributors

of *Chicano Autobiographies: An Anthology* (1989) and *My History, Not Yours: The Formation of Mexican American Autobiography* (1993).

Angelita Reyes, Associate Professor of English and Women's Studies at the University of Minnesota, has published articles in *America*, *The Black Scholar*, and *Research in African Literatures*. Her article on Paule Marshall and Toni Morrison appeared in the collection *Politics and the Muse: Studies in the Politics of Recent American Literature* (1989).

Debra Shostak, Associate Professor of English at the College of Wooster, has published essays on Philip Roth and John Irving as well as an interview with Tim O'Brien. She is at work on a book about Roth's experiments in narrative representation.

Ben Xu is Assistant Professor of English at Saint Mary's College of California and the author of *Situational Tensions of Critical Intellectuals: Thinking through Literary Politics with Edward W. Said and Frank Lentricchia* (1992).

Index

Aaron, Daniel, 11, 13
Acculturation, 23, 98, 151, 244. *See also* Assimilation
Achebe, Chinua, 10
Acosta, Oscar Zeta, 306
Acuña, Rodolfo, 313
Adams, Henry, *The Education of Henry Adams*, 47
Africa, 6, 33, 138, 141, 185, 189, 190, 191, 200, 290–91, 297
African-American criticism, 11–12
African-American literature, 4, 5, 9–11, 14, 15, 26–44, 128–44, 179–97, 198–211, 212–32, 278–304, 307; and feminism, 9
African-American Review, 14
Akhmatova, Anna, "Lethe-Neva," 179
Alarcón, Norma, 13
Allen, Paula Gunn, 12, 14, 18, 22, 136, 140–43; *The Woman Who Owned the Shadows*, 135–38, 142
Alvarado, Juan, 319
Amerasia, 15
Americanization, 49, 53, 55, 68, 75, 78, 104–6, 160, 313, 315, 320
The Americas Review, 15, 306
Anderson, Benedict, 287–89
Andrews, William, 309–10
Androcentrism, 60, 63
Angelou, Maya, 31
Anti-Semitism, 63–64, 66, 98–101, 104, 109–110, 153
Antigua, 280, 294, 295
Antin, Mary, 6, 100; *From Polotzk to Boston*, 54, 66; "House of the One Father," 109–10; *The Promised Land: The Autobiography of a Russian Immigrant*, 23, 44–88, 90–97, 101, 104–6; 109–10; *They Who Knock at Our Gates*, 54
Anzaldúa, Glorida, 38; *Borderlands*, 135
Asian-American literature, 4, 13, 26–44, 233–60, 261–77, 297
Asian-Canadian literature, 21, 278–305
Assimilation, 6, 18, 23, 24, 89, 90, 91, 100, 102, 151, 235, 240–41, 250, 285; myth of, 26. *See also* Acculturation
Autobiography, 23, 24, 46–88, 89–113, 120, 129, 131; African-American, 307, 308; Mexican-American, 305–331; Native-American, 307, 308, 322–23
Avila, María Inocente, 319, 321

Baker, Houston A., Jr., 4, 11, 12, 13, 15, 309, 310
Bakhtin, Mikhail, 50, 80
Baldwin, James, *Another Country*, 8
Balint, Alice, 222; "Love for the Mother and Mother Love," 215
Bancroft, Hubert Howe, 319, 321, 323, 324; *History of California*, 318, 320, 322
Bandini, Juan, 319
Baraka, Amiri, 10
Barthes, Roland, 59, 62
Barthold, Bonnie J., 200, 209
Bataille, Gretchen, 12
Beane, Wendell C., 191
Bellow, Saul, 8
Benjamin, Walter, 128
Benston, Kimberly W., 11
Berger, John, 43
Bergland, Betty, viii, 23
Bergson, Henri, 128
Bernal, Juan, 319
Bhabha, Homi, 279, 283, 288, 290, 292, 299

341

Index

Biro, Yvette, 133
Black American Literature Forum, 14
Black Arts movement, 10
Blasing, Mutlu K., 131
Blassingame, John, 309
Bloch, Ernest, 130
Bloom, Alan, 4
Bodnar, John, 51, 79, 80
Boelhower, William, viii, 12
Bok, Edward, *The Americanization of Edward Bok,* 47
Bone, Robert, 11
Bontemps, Arna, 10
The Book of Kells, 152
Boundaries, 38, 82, 183, 289, 324; of experience, 10; narrative, 34; narrator/object, 252; racial/ethnic, 10; temporal, 34
Boyce-Davies, Carole, 183, 184
Bradley, David, *The Chaneysville Incident,* 19
Breen, Christine, *O Come Ye Back to Ireland,* 162
Brooks, Peter, 204
Brooks, Van Wyck, *America's Coming of Age,* 20
Brown, Claude, *Manchild in the Promised Land,* 77
Brown, Sterling, 11
Brown, William Wells, *Clotel,* 9
Bruce-Novoa, Juan, 13, 312
Brudno, Ezra, 101; *The Fugitive,* 23, 98–100, 102, 104
Brumble, H. David, 322
Buelens, Gert, 23, 104
Burns, Veronica, 161
Bus, Heiner, 135
Busia, Abena, 185

Cabeza de Baca, Fabiola, 317
Cabeza de Vaca, Alvar Nuñez, 312
Cahan, Abraham, *The Rise of David Levinsky,* 102
Callaloo, 14
Canby, Vincent, 255
Candelaria, Cordelia, 13
Caribbean, 14, 185, 187
Caribbean-American literature, 179–97, 278–304

Carillo de Fitch, Josefa, 319
Carnegie, Andrew, 47, 80
Carnival: as counter-memory, 179–97; defined, 186; as symbol of order and chaos, 187. *See also* Bakhtin, Mikhail
Carrillo, Anastacio, 325
Carroll, James, 146
Casteñeda, Pedro, 312
Cather, Willa, *Death Comes for the Archbishop,* 315
Chacón, Rafael, 305, 315, 316
Chametzky, Jules, 21
Chapman, Abraham, 10
Chaucer, Geoffrey, 4
Chavez, John R., 305
Chavez, Linda, 4
Ch'eng-en, Wu, *The Journey to the West,* 247
Chesnutt, Charles W., 9, 22, 164–78; *The Conjure Woman,* 166–74; "The Conjurer's Revenge," 169–71; "The Goophered Grapevine," 167; "The Gray Wolf's Ha'nt," 171–73; "Hot-Foot Hannibal," 173; "Mars Jeems's Nightmare," 168, 170; "Po' Sandy," 168, 173; "Sis' Becky's Pickaninny," 171–72; "Superstitions and Folklore of the South," 166, 167, 173, 174
Chesnutt, Helen M., 164, 168
Cheung, King-Kok, 13
Chin, Frank, 10, 13
China, 6, 31–32, 35, 38
Chinese-American literature. *See* Asian-American literature
Christian, Barbara, 12, 28, 33, 35
Christensen, Paul, 135, 141
Cisneros, Sandra, 39, 43; *The House on Mango Street,* 21, 28, 38, 40, 42, 135
Class, 180, 320; and ethnicity, 13
Clayton, Jay, 18
Cliff, Michelle, 180, 184
Coleridge, Samuel Taylor, 128, 129
Collective authority, 30, 32, 37
Collective myths, 166, 167, 182–92
College Language Association, 3, 4
Colonialism, 181, 186, 187, 188–89, 192, 278, 279, 292, 294
Colter, Cyrus, *The Chocolate Soldier,* 19
Community, 225–31, 319; Toni Morrison on, 228

Index

Condé, Maryse, 180
Cooper, Anna Julia, "Voice from the South," 164
Count Basie, 131
Couser, Thomas G., viii, 309
Cruikshank, Julie, 16

Darling, Marsha Jean, 198, 200, 204
Davis, Angela, 77, 81, 82
Davis, Charles T., 10
Davis, Christina, 217, 222, 230
Davis, Natalie Zemon, 234, 235
Davis, Rebecca Harding, *Life in the Iron Mills*, 119
de Oñate, Juan, *Proclamación*, 312
Dearborn, Mary V., 12, 54
Deconstruction, 26, 38, 43, 183
DeHay, Terry, 21
Delany, Martin, 7
Derrida, Jacques, 183
Desai, Anita, *Bye-Bye Blackbird*, 279, 281, 283, 284
DeShazer, Mary, 28, 30
DeVeaux, Alexis, 185
Devi, Mahasweta, "Doulati, the Bountiful," 290
Dhingra, Leena, *First Light*, 284
di Pietro, Robert, 14
Diaspora, 185-86, 189, 190, 199
Diedrich, Maria, 135
Dittmar, Kurt, 92, 96
Docherty, Thomas, 253
Double consciousness, 7, 20, 32, 92, 109-10, 147, 240, 242, 269-70, 272, 274. *See also* Identity
Douglass, Frederick, 7
Drucker, Sally, 105, 106, 108
D'Souza, Dinesh, 4, 6
DuBois, W. E. B., 7

Eco, Umberto, 129
Eliade, Mircea, 191, 192, 194
Ellis Island, 50, 51
Ellison, Ralph, 82, 132; *Invisible Man*, 198, 208
Emecheta, Buchi, *Second Class Citizen*, 279
Emparán, Madie Brown, 309
England, 280, 294, 295

Erdrich, Louise, 18, 43; *The Beet Queen*, 35; *Love Medicine*, 35; *Tracks*, 21, 22, 28, 35, 37, 38, 42
Erickson, Peter, 221
Ethnic studies, 48, 49
Ethnicity, 45-88, 90, 180, 234, 267; attitudes toward, 6, 7, 193; denial/repression of, 5-6; diffused ethnicity, 7-8; meaning of, 274-75; and religion: African, 199-201, Catholicism, 145-63, Judaism, 8-9, 45-88, 89-113, 114-26
Ethnocentrism, 20
Ethnicity school, 12, 13
Evers, Larry, 16
Existentialism, 119, 261-62, 263, 275, 310

Fabre, Michel, 11
Faulkner, William, 131
Fauset, Jessie, *Comedy American Style*, 9
Feminism, 9, 10, 12, 15, 81, 82, 114, 118-19, 121, 135-36, 138, 180-81, 184, 324; and film theory, 56; and gynocentrism, 183, 184; herstory, 139, 181; and women's studies, 48. *See also* Gender
Ferguson, Sally Ann H., 167
Ferraro, Thomas J., 11, 12, 13
Fiedler, Leslie, 11, 13, 115
Fierro, Felipe, 322, 326
Fine, David, 98
Finney, Brian, 205
Fisher, Dexter, 14
Folklore, 48, 52
Forkner, Ben, 155
Foucault, Michel, 18, 19
Freud, Sigmund, 9, 17, 20, 143
Freudian psychology, 137, 222, 224-25; cathexis, 129, 132; conscious, 128; Oedipal complex, 117; preconscious, 128; pre-Oedipal bond, 212, 214, 215, 230; repression, 129; unconscious, 128
Frye, Joanne, 237
Fryer, Judith, 165

Galarza, Ernesto, *Barrio Boy: The Story of a Boy's Acculturation*, 306

Index

Gans, Hebert, 7, 13
Gartner, Carol Blicker, 109
Garvey, Marcus, 7
Garza, Catarino E., 314
Gates, Henry Louis, Jr., 12, 82, 183, 308
Gayle, Addison, 10
Gelfant, Blanche, 126
Gender, 25, 321; Toni Morrison on, 217. *See also* Feminism
George, Rosemary Marangoly, 21
Georgi-Findlay, Brigitte, 138
"Ghost values," 8, 145, 147, 160, 161, 162
Girgus, Sam, 92
Gloster, Hugh, 11
Gold, Michael, 123
Goldman, Anne, 317
González, Rafael, 319
Gordon, Mary, 147, 163; "Edna O'Brien," 161; *Final Payments*, 156–61; *The Other Side*, 158–62; "A Writer Goes Home," 158, 161
Gratacap, Louis Pope, *Benjamin, the Jew*, 101, 102
Gray, Richard, 131
Greeley, Andrew, 162
Griffin, William D., 151
Gusdorf, Georges, 319, 320
Gutman, Herbert G., 50

Hackett, Alice Payne, 91
Halbwachs, Maurice, 17
Hall, Stuart, 16, 17, 19
Hamer, Fannie Lou, 31
Handlin, Oscar, 91, 92, 95, 109
Harlem Renaissance, 9, 11, 20
Harlow, Barbara, 26, 27, 278
Harper, Frances, 31
The Heath Anthology of American Literature, 15
Hegemony, 25, 28, 29, 30, 34, 35, 38, 190, 306, 318
Henderson, Stephen, 10
Hicks, D. Emily, 130
Hill, Errol, 186, 187
Hillerman, Joseph, 8
Himes, Chester, *The Third Generation*, 9
Hine, Lewis, 50, 51

Hispanic-American literature. *See* Latino-American literature
Historiography, 233, 235, 305
History, vii, 36, 38, 42, 48, 91, 93, 114, 121, 139, 166, 183, 190, 233; authentic history, 26, 31; collective history, 26; and "communal utterance," 309–10; and culture, 31, 32, 241, 244; of ethnic American writing, 3–25; and fiction, 234, 236; historical narratives, 234; and identity 237, 246, 306, 308; and memory, 233–34; and Mexican-American autobiography, 305–31; Paule Marshall, on, 185; shared, 65; written, 37, 235
Hoekzema, Loren, 63, 78
Hogan, Linda, 18
Hollander, John, 16
Holloway, Carla, 209
hooks, bell, 80, 81
Horn, Gabriel, 129
Horno-Delgado, Asuncion, 39, 41, 42
Horvitz, Deborah, 205
Howe, Irving, 11, 13, 115
Hsia, C. T., 236, 238, 247, 251
Hudson, Theodore R., 11
Huggins, Nathan, 11, 20
Hurston, Zora Neale, 194; *Mules and Men*, 22; *Their Eyes Were Watching God*, 22, 181–83
Hutcheon, Linda, 254

Identity, vii, 8, 16–18, 20, 30, 33, 35, 36, 49, 82, 90, 193–94, 222, 229, 262, 266, 275, 295–96, 316–17; American identity, 20, 25, 89, 158; collective identity, 76, 130, 306; confronting, 32; cultural identity, 28, 30, 241, 245, 250, 252; and diffused ethnicity, 7–8; gendered identity, 54; and history, 237, 246, 306; hyphenated identity, 20, 25, 233–60, 271–72, 274; intercultural, 32; and memory, 17; of minority women, 28–29; oppositional identities, 31; personal identity, 21, 28; plural identity, 240; remembered, 33; repressed, 29; "re-visioning," 32, 44; socio-political, 34
Idowu, E. Bolaji, 201

Index

Ifkovic, Edward, 14
Immigration, 5, 6, 21, 25, 45–88, 89–113, 145–63, 235, 246, 282, 283; American perceptions of, 6, 91–92, 108; depictions of, 50–52, 54, 55–80; immigrant genre, 21, 278–304; immigrant memory, 22–23; immigration laws, 5–6; "immigritude," 292
Imperialism, 290, 291
Intertexuality, 12, 180
Ireland, 5, 147, 151, 155, 156, 159
Irish-American literature, 23–24, 145–63
Islas, Arturo, 238
Isolationism, 6, 20, 109

Jackson, Blyden, 11
Jacobs, Harriet, *Incidents in the Life of a Slave Girl*, 217
James, Henry, 153
Jameson, Fredric, 27, 43, 89
Jaramillo, Cleofas, 306, 317, 324, 325
Jemie, Onwuchekwa, 11
Jessee, Sharon, 22
Jewish-American literature, 8–9, 14–15, 23, 45–88, 87–113, 114–126
Johnson, Charles, *Middle Passage*, 10
Johnson, James Weldon, 9
Jones, Bessie W., 209
Jones, Gayl, 10
Jones, LeRoi. *See* Baraka, Amiri
Journal of Ethnic Studies, 14
Joyce, James, 121, 123; *Ulysses*, 155
Ju-chen, Li, *Flowers in the Mirror*, 244, 251

Karrer, Wolfgang, 24
Kazin, Alfred, 115
Kennedy, William, 147, 156, 163; *Billy Phelan's Greatest Game*, 153–54, 162; *Ironweed*, 154–55; *Legs*, 151–53; *Quinn's Book*, 155
Keogh, William, 24
Khrushchev, Nikita, 115
Kim, Elaine, 13, 14
Kincaid, Jamaica, 291; *Annie John*, 280–81, 294–95, 298; *Lucy*, 298; *The Small Place*, 291
King, Martin Luther, Jr., 7
King, Rodney, 81

Kingston, Maxine Hong, 19, 24; *China Men*, 233, 239–40, 242–45, 249; "The Coming Book," 247; "Cultural Mis-Readings by American Reviewers," 240, 242; Interview, 233, 238; "Moving Images: From Shao-lin to Woman Warrior," 238; *Tripmaster Monkey: His Fake Book*, 233–260; *The Woman Warrior*, 233, 237, 239–41, 243–44, 249
Kino, Eusebio, 312
Kitsch, 124, 146, 152
Knapp, Steven, 29
Kogawa, Joy, *Obasan*, vii
Krupat, Arnold, 307, 308, 322, 323
Kuan-chung, Lo, *The Romance of the Three Kingdoms*, 249, 253

LaCapra, Dominick, 235
Lamming, George, 10
Larsen, Nella, *Passing*, 9; *Quicksand*, 9
Latino-American literature, 4, 5, 12–13, 15, 305–336
Lau, Joseph S. M., 239, 251
Lauter, Paul, 14, 15
Lawrence, D. H., *Women in Love*, 138
Leal, Luis, 312
Lerner, Gerda, 218
Lester, Rosemarie, 217
Lewisohn, Ludwig, 8
Li, David Leiwei, 243
Lim, Shirley Geok-lin, 13
Lin, Patricia, 251
Lincoln, Kenneth, 12
Ling, Amy, 13
Lipsitz, George, 82, 181–83
Lessing, Don S., 121
Lo, Kuan-chung, 250
Lorenzana, Aponinaria, 305, 319, 321
Lyons, Bonnie, 115, 117
Lyotard, Jean François, 19

Ma, Y. W., 239, 251
MacCabe, Colin, 28
McCracken, Ellen, 39
Macdonell, Diane, 50
McWilliams, Carey, 313
Magic realism, 138, 139. *See also* Márquez, Gabriel Garcia
Mailer, Norman, "White Negro," 8

345

Malamud, Bernard, 8
Malcolm X, 7, 82
Marginality and marginalization, 26, 27, 38, 43, 100, 166, 190, 194, 288–90, 292–93, 296
Marin, Peter, 8, 145, 146
Márquez, Gabriel Garcia, 306
Marshall, Paule, 23; *Browngirl, Brownstones*, 29, 184–85; *The Chosen Place, The Timeless People*, 29, 179–95; *Praisesong for the Widow*, 179–95; "Shaping the World of My Art," 184
Martínez, Antonio Jose, 315
Marx, Karl, 17
Master narratives, 43, 180
Materassi, Mario, 120, 121
Mathieson, Barbara Offutt, 22, 205–6
Mbiti, John, 199, 200, 201, 206
Melting pot, 26, 82, 147
MELUS (The Society for the Study of Multi-Ethnic Literature in the United States), 4, 10, 14
Memory, vii–viii, 16–19, 21–25, 49, 114–27, 233–35, 262, 266; and absence, 234; collective memory, 17, 18, 22–23, 24, 26, 34, 137, 138, 141, 142, 143, 164–78, 180, 190, 191, 208; countermemory, vii, 78, 82–83, 181–82, 183, 184, 186, 187, 189, 191, 195; cultural memory, 22, 23, 25, 31, 37, 81–83, 235, 239, 246, 248, 255; "disremembered," 180, 203, 205–8; and dreams, 139–40; evasion of, 124; and forgetting/amnesia/repression, 5, 7,17, 21, 23, 79, 82, 92, 122, 125–26, 128–44, 149, 164, 199, 203, 209, 218–19, 290, 294, 299, 325–26; immigrant memory, 22–23, 150; Maxine Hong Kingston on, 233; memory narrative, 263, 266; non-remembrance, 89, 98; "non-synchronous memory," 130; personal memory, vii, 17, 23, 24, 130, 139, 162, 191, 194, 220–21; "re-membering," 31, 32, 33, 34, 35, 39, 42, 53, 108, 239; and reinvention, 233, 234; rememory, 180, 202, 205, 209, 217–19, 225
Mexican-American literature, 26–44, 305–36
Middle passage, 9, 180, 185, 204, 207, 223

Mills, C. Wright, 121
Minh-ha, Trinh T., 139
Mink, Louis O., 234
Modern Language Association, 3, 4, 14
Modernism, 120, 123
Molina, Felipe, 16
Molyneaux, Sandra L., 22
Momaday, N. Scott, 18; *House Made of Dawn*, 19, 198
Moody, Anne, *Coming of Age in Mississippi*, 77; *Growing Up in Mississippi*, 48
Moraga, Cherrie, 13
Morrison, Toni, 135, 181–86; *Beloved*, vii, 16, 19, 22, 179–80, 198–211, 212–32; *The Bluest Eye*, 9, 10, 180, 214–15, 222, 226; "Interview with Toni Morrison," 217, 230; "Rootedness: The Ancestor as Foundation," 228; "The Site of Memory," 179, 182; *Song of Solomon*, 19, 209, 214, 221, 226–27, 230; *Sula*, 215–16, 222, 225–26; *Tar Baby*, 180, 214–16, 221, 226, 230; "Unspeakable Things Unspoken: The Afro-American Presence in American Literature," 198, 203; as a woman writer, 217
Moynihan, Daniel Patrick, 162
Mukherjee, Bharati, 6; *Wife*, 279
Multiculturalism, 5, 8, 10–11, 14, 15, 25, 131, 142, 187, 234, 237
Murray, Albert, 135–37, 143; *Train Whistle Guitar*, 130–33, 141–42
Murray, David, 12
Myrdal, Gunnar, 13

Naipaul, V. S., 10
Native-American literature, 4, 12, 14–16, 26–44, 128–44, 307
Nativism, 6, 108, 147
Naylor, Gloria, 10, 180
Neal, Larry, 10
Negro American Literature Forum, 14
The New Masses, 116
Newman, Katharine D., 10
Ngũgĩ wa Thiong'o, 10, 303
Nietzsche, Friedrich, 265
Nunley, John, 191

346

Index

O'Connell, Shaun, 146, 151
O'Connor, Edwin, 161, 163; *All in the Family*, 147–51; *The Last Hurrah*, 148, 150–51, 162
Olsen, Tillie, 21, 115, 120, 123, 126; "One Out of Twelve: Writers Who Are Women in Our Century," 121; "Requa," 119; *Silences*, 114, 117–19, 121; *Tell Me a Riddle*, 114, 118–19, 122–25; *Yonnondio: From the Thirties*, 119
Oppression, 27, 41–42, 59, 77, 82, 153, 216; bell hooks on, 81
Orality and oral tradition, 7, 15, 16, 18, 21–22, 27, 31, 36, 37, 132, 134, 135, 136, 140, 143, 164–65, 171–73, 182, 198, 230, 235, 236–38, 239, 246, 251, 255, 323. *See also* Storytelling
Ortega, Eliana, 39, 40, 41, 42
Otero, Miguel Antonio, Jr., 316
"Otherness" (the Other), 13, 18, 32, 43, 51, 205, 227, 243
Otten, Terry, 209
Owens, Louis, 12
Ozick, Cynthia, 9

Padilla, Genaro, 24
Paredes, Raymund, 312, 313, 318
Patriarchy, 28, 40, 41, 43, 47, 59–61, 66, 82, 134, 321
Pearse, Andrew, 186
Pérez, Eulalia, 305, 319, 321
Perry, John, 265, 266
Personal narrative. *See* Autobiography
Pico, Pío, 319
Pitt, Leonard, 313, 320, 325
Pluralism, 10, 11, 90, 108
Polacheck, Hilda Satt, 46; *I Came a Stranger: The Story of a Hull House Girl*, 48, 76, 77
Postcolonialism, 10, 21, 179, 180, 183, 184, 185, 290, 294; and literature, 278–79, 297
Postmodernism, 18, 130, 181–83, 253–54
Proust, Marcel, 128

Quinn, Anthony, 306

Race, 6, 16, 25, 82, 100; and physical appearance, 9–10
Racism, 81, 153–54. *See also* Anti-Semitism, Ethnicity, Slavery, Xenophobia
Rampersad, Arnold, 11
Realism, 28, 101, 124
Rebolledo, Tey Diana, 317, 318
Rector, Monica, 186, 187
Redding, Saunders, 11
Reed, Ishmael, *The Last Days of Louisiana Red*, 19; *Mumbo Jumbo*, 19
Repression, 18, 122, 156, 325; colonial and neocolonial, 27; of history, 139. *See also* Memory
The Revista Chicano-Riqueña, 15
Rey, Georges, 266
Reyes, Angelita, viii, 23
Rich, Adrienne, 44; "When We Dead Awaken," 30
Rideout, Walter, 115
Riis, Jacob, 80; *How the Other Half Lives*, 47; *The Making of an American*, 47
Robertson, James Oliver, 135
Rodriguez, José Policarpio, 305, 306, 314
Rodriguez, Richard, 6; *Hunger of Memory: The Education of Richard Rodriguez*, 48, 306
Roosevelt, Theodore, 91, 105
Rosenfelt, Deborah, 118
Roth, Henry: *Call It Sleep*, 114–17, 119–22; "The Dun Dakotas," 121; *Mercy of a Rude Stream*, 116, 120; *Shifting Landscape: A Composite, 1925–1987*, 120; *A Star Shines over Mount Morris Park*, 116
Roth, Philip, 8
Ruoff, A. LaVonne Brown, viii, 12, 14
Rushdie, Salman, 281; *Shame*, 279, 280, 282

Said, Edward, 280, 281, 295, 296
Saldívar, José, 13
Saldívar, Ramón, 13, 306
Salpeter, Harry, 95
Saussure, Ferdinand, 17
Schiff, Jacob, 106
Schiller, Herbert, 143
Schwab, Rosalind, Ach, 103
Schwarz-Bart, Simone, 180

Index

Scott, Dorothea Hayward, 238, 239, 249
Scott, Nina M., 39, 41, 42
Seguín, John. *See* Seguín, Juan
Seguín, Juan, 325, 326; *Personal Memoirs*, 305, 313, 314
Sekula, Allan, 49, 51, 52, 53
Selvon, Samuel, *The Lonely Londoners*, 279, 281
Shannon, William, 146, 159
Shostak, Debra, 24
Silko, Leslie, 16, 18, 19, 138
Singh, Amritjit, 11
Sivanandan, A., 279
Skerrett, Joseph T., Jr., 209
Slavery, 9, 22, 23, 164–78, 198–211, 212–32; and slave narratives, 217, 228, 308, 309
Smith, Barbara Herrnstein, 237
Smith, Sidonie, 63, 321
Sollors, Werner, 11, 12, 13, 91, 98, 267
Soto, Gary, 306
Spillers, Hortense, 12
Spivak, Gayatri Chakravorty, 26, 290
Stalin, Josef, 115
Stalvey, Lois Mark, *The Education of a WASP*, 8
Starr, Randolph, 234, 235
Stein, Gertrude, *How to Write*, 128
Steinberg, Stephen, 13
Steiner, Edward, 103; *The Mediator: A Tale of the Old World and the New*, 100, 101
Stepto, Robert, 12, 13, 14, 309
Stern, Elizabeth, 23, 91, 98, 104; *I Am a Woman—and a Jew*, 107, 108; *My Mother and I*, 23, 104–8, 110
Sternbach, Nancy Saporta, 39, 40, 41, 42
Stieglitz, Alfred, 51
Stone, Albert E., 53
Storytelling, 18–19, 22, 27–36, 37, 166–67, 181, 183, 185, 235, 236, 241, 248; as healing, 209; Maxine Hong Kingston on, 238; and myth, 233–60. *See also* Orality
Straight, Susan, 8
Studies in American Indian Literature, 14–15
Studies in American Jewish Literature, 14
Subjectivity, 45–81, 89, 181, 253–54, 306, 324

Suleiman, Susan Rubin, 131
Suleri, Sara, *Meatless Days*, 279, 294

Tafolla, Santiago, 305; "Nearing the End of the Trail," 314
Takaki, Ronald, 235
Tan, Amy, 38, 43; *The Joy Luck Club*, 21, 28, 30–33, 35, 42, 261–77
Tate, Claudia, 31, 205
Tedlock, Dennis, 16
Thelen, David, 146, 147
Third World, 38, 278; countries, 27; voices, 27; women, 28; writers, 27
Thurman, Wallace, *The Blacker the Berry*, 9
Tobenkin, Elias, *Witte Arrives*, 23, 102–4
Todorov, Tzvetan, 203
Toronto South Asian Review, 289
Truth, Sojourner, 7, 31

Ulibarri, Sabine, 136–37, 143; "Hombre sin nombre," 135; "Juan P.," 135; "La fragua sin fuego," 135; *Mi abuela fumaba puros*, 135, 140; *Tierra Amarilla*, 133–35, 141–42
Umansky, Ellen M., 105, 106, 108
Usandizago, Aranzazu, 93

Vallejo, Mariano G., 305, 309, 319–20, 324–26
Vassanji, M. G., 8; *The Gunny Sack*, 21, 278–304
Vizenor, Gerald, 18; *The Heirs of Columbus*, 19
Vonnegut, Kurt, 7

Wagner, Jean, 11
Walden, Daniel, viii, 10
Waley, Arthur, 238, 242
Walker, Alice, 10, 38, 43, 143; *Meridian*, 35, 141; "In Search of Our Mothers' Gardens," 27; *The Temple of My Familiar*, 21, 28, 30–31, 33–35, 42, 138–42; *The Third Life of George Copeland*, 35
Walton, Eda Lou, 115
Ward, Jerry W., 14
Wardlaw, Ruth, 92
Warnock, Mary, 234
Warner-Vierya, Myriam, 180

Index

Washington, George, 68, 69, 78
Washington, Mary Helen, 184, 185
Weber, David, 305
Welch, James, 18; *Fools Crow*, 19; *Winter in the Blood*, 128
Wendell, Barrett, 91
West Africa, 22, 188, 198, 199–201, 203, 204; concepts of, 198–211
West Indies. *See* Caribbean
White, Hayden, 234, 262
Whitman, Walt, 247
Whitt, Lena M., 165, 167
Williams, Niall, 162
Williams, Raymond, 29, 30
Williams, Sherley Anne, *Dessa Rose*, 10
Winnicott, D. W., 214, 222, 225, 229
Wong, Hertha, 307, 308
Wong, Sau-ling Cynthia, 13
Wu, Ch'eng-en, 238, 247

Xenophobia, 6, 54, 109

Yellin, Jean Fagan, 11
Yezierska, Anzia, 8
Young, James O., 11
Yuan, Ch'u, *Lament on Encountering Sorrow*, 245

Zangwill, Israel, *The Melting Pot*, 98, 104